**SEVENTH**

# PUBLIC RELATIONS PRACTICES

## Managerial Case Studies and Problems

### Allen H. Center, Fellow PRSA

*Distinguished Resident Lecturer*
*San Diego State University*
*Retired Vice President, Public Relations, Motorola Inc.*

### Patrick Jackson, Fellow PRSA

*Editor, pr reporter*
*Senior Counsel, Jackson Jackson & Wagner*
*Former Adjunct Faculty, Boston University*

### Stacey Smith, APR, Fellow PRSA

*Senior Counsel and Partner, Jackson Jackson & Wagner*
*Former Adjunct Faculty, University of Antioch New England Graduate School,*
*University of New Hampshire*

### Frank R. Stansberry, APR, Fellow PRSA

*Instructor, Public Relations, University of Central Florida (Retired)*
*The Coca-Cola Company (Retired)*

**PHI Learning Private Limited**
New Delhi-110001
2011

This Indian Reprint—Rs. 325.00
(Original U.S. Edition—Rs. 6415.00)

**PUBLIC RELATIONS PRACTICES—Managerial Case Studies and Problems, 7th ed.**
by Allen H. Center, Patrick Jackson, Stacey Smith and Frank R. Stansberry

Original edition, entitled *Public Relations Practices—Managerial Case Studies and Problems, 7th ed.* by Allen H. Center, Patrick Jackson, Stacey Smith and Frank R. Stansberry, published by Pearson Education, Inc., publishing as Pearson Prentice Hall.

**ISBN-978-81-203-4212-5**

Indian edition published by PHI Learning Private Limited.

This edition is manufactured in India, and is authorized for sale in India, Pakistan, Sri Lanka, Bhutan, Bangladesh, Nepal and the Maldives only.

Published by Asoke K. Ghosh, PHI Learning Private Limited, M-97, Connaught Circus, New Delhi-110001 and Printed by Mudrak, 30-A, Patparganj, Delhi-110091.

To Allen Center and Patrick Jackson, two of the most gifted and insightful practitioners of our time. May your vision and commitment to the profession of public relations be reflected for years to come through the students, teachers and professionals you have educated and empowered.

# A Tribute to Center and Jackson

## Allen H. Center, APR, Fellow PRSA, Leader, Writer, Teacher, Inspiration

By Glen M. Broom, San Diego State University
In memory of my dear friend, co-author, and mentor

Allen H. Center took early retirement as vice president of Motorola in 1973 to write the first edition of *Public Relations Practices*, a management case study book for advanced public relations students. Patrick Jackson joined Allen as co-author beginning with the fourth edition, published in 1990.

Allen's public relations career began during World War II in the Southwest Pacific. For three years in Guadalcanal, New Guinea, and the Philippines, Corporal Center edited a daily newspaper for the 13th Air Force Fighter Command Headquarters.

After the war, Allen returned to his prewar employment with the American Chicle Company in New York, while he searched for a job in his newfound calling—public relations. His search led to the position as publications editor, then public relations director, at Parker Pen Company in Janesville, Wisconsin.

He left Parker Pen after seven years to join Motorola as public relations director in the Consumer Products Division to help introduce color television. Then, the large Chicago advertising agency—Leo Burnett—lured him from Motorola, making him vice president of public relations. While holding this position two years, he also served as the president of the Chicago chapter of the Public Relations Society of America (PRSA).

He returned to Motorola in 1961, serving as corporate vice president for public relations until 1973. After finishing the first edition of *Public Relations Practices*, Allen tried again to retire in 1976—this time to Rancho Bernardo, California. San Diego State University invited Allen to teach part time, where he became the first and only person to hold the title, "Distinguished Resident Lecturer." He taught there until 1987.

In 1981, he received the PRSA's highest national honor—the Gold Anvil—for his contributions to advancing our field. In 1986, he was the second person to be inducted into the Arthur W. Page Society's Hall of Fame. (Page's son John was the first and Scott Cutlip the third.) The San Diego PRSA chapter awarded Allen its Otto Bos Lifetime Achievement Award in 2001.

He served as president of the Foundation for Public Relations Research and Education, now the Institute for Public Relations, 1973–1974. In 1977, he established and, with matching funds from the Motorola Foundation, endowed that organization's Pathfinder Award, which annually recognizes scholarly research in public relations.

Allen and his wife Nancy also endowed the Allen H. Center Lectureship in Public Relations at San Diego State University.

In a lifetime of achievement, Allen Center was a true pathfinder who set the standards and aspirations for the emerging profession that he saw as his "calling." Until his death in November 2005 at age 93, he served as role model for generations of students and practitioners who shared his vision of the social value and nobility of purpose in building harmonious relationships.

## A Colleague Remembers Pat Jackson

Pat inspired and encouraged us to think outside the box. He served as a beacon in a sea of professionals. Pat Jackson provided vision.

At a 1984 Schranz Lectureship at Ball State University, Pat challenged students and attending professionals to "lift their eyes above process and to concentrate on behavioral outcomes." The lecture is as fresh today as it was then. When the lecture was handed out in a recent conference where Patrick was speaking, he said, "Mel, have I been speaking on this need that long?" Of course, he had, and he kept challenging professionals to think about behavioral outcomes and to apply behavioral knowledge to performance until his death.

So how do we pay tribute to a man who influenced a profession, influenced public relations education, influenced recognition of the importance of high ethical values, and who stood as a leader in the profession and education in every sense of the word?

The answer is simple.

It is the only answer we can have. We simply must not allow the torch that Pat carried as the result of his love and belief in the public relations profession to go out or to touch the ground. Pick it up. A thousand hands. Carry it forward. When we do so, we will adequately honor him and what he stood for in our profession. Pat built vision and that is what we must have.

We treasure his memory and the values for which he stood.

—*Melvin L. Sharpe, APR, Fellow PRSA,*
*Professor & Coordinator PR,*
*Department of Journalism,*
*Ball State University*
*Muncie, Indiana*

# Brief Contents

# Contents

# Preface

As case texts mature, more and more often individual cases take on the aura of classics. It becomes difficult to remove a case that so well defines a subject, classically illustrates the models and theories, or, in its success or failure, teaches so well.

In this edition, we have updated numerous cases to show the long-term impact of good, and sometimes bad, public relations practices. We have moved some classic cases into different chapters to further illustrate the wide-ranging effect actions can have on an organization's success.

We have added nine new cases that deal with extraordinary problems—Hurricane Katrina, the Catholic Church scandal, building employee participation, an enormous product recall. Some of these events are definitive of our era. Others are simply about organizations trying to succeed using the tools and techniques of our profession. Each will assist students in growing into practitioners, as well as helping those already in the business to better meet the challenges of a daily practice.

The practical purpose of this text remains the same. We seek, with case studies and problems, to help future practitioners develop agility in the principles and the application of effective two-way communications in a wide variety of situations likely to confront them and their employers.

- We retained several timeless cases that involved turning-point issues or broke new ground in the maturing of the public relations function. These are identified as classics.
- Several cases with evolving subjects were updated.
- Cases that have lost timely significance were dropped.

## HOW THE BOOK IS ORGANIZED

1. *The first two chapters* describe the purposes of public relations and the manner in which the function deals with problems and opportunities.
2. The bulk of the book contains *real-life case studies* in eight chapters organized according to primary publics such as employees and media or major problems such as public issues, crisis management, and standards or ethics.
3. Each chapter has a *definitive introduction* providing insights that come to life in the cases that follow. Introductions vary in size and substance, tailored to the assumed knowledge of students. Employee relations, for instance, reflects that most students have had work experience of some kind, whereas crisis management contains elements most students will not yet have encountered.
4. Each chapter closes with a *case problem* or two for class discussion closely related to the thrust of the chapter.

We believe that there is enough variety to permit selectivity by educators, fitting the size of the class and the structure of the course—and enough provocation for lively classroom participation.

## THE AUTHORS AND THEIR APPROACH

Patrick Jackson taught at several institutions, was senior counsel at the public relations firm Jackson Jackson & Wagner, and in 1986, received The Gold Anvil, the highest honor in public relations for "lifetime achievement and contribution to the profession." However, Jackson was best known as editor of the public relations newsletter *pr reporter*. He was a highly sought speaker and presenter of workshops, and a practitioner who instigated several new strategies. His thinking is reflected throughout the book. Every new case and updated chapter reflects his ideas and the models he left for those who follow—his legacy to the public relations profession. Definitive passages were amended and updated to reflect the changes in the nature and emphasis of the calling and the roles and responsibilities of practitioners. Allen Center originated the book and remains its guiding spirit.

Frank R. Stansberry, APR, retired in 2006 as an instructor of public relations at the University of Central Florida. His career spanned 46 years of print journalism, agency and corporate public relations and, finally, education. A member of the Public Relations Society of America since 1971, he served the Society and the profession at every level—local, district, and national. He was inducted into the PRSA College of Fellows in 1997.

Stacey Smith, APR, has been practicing public relations for 26 years and is Senior Counsel at Jackson Jackson & Wagner. She worked side by side with Patrick Jackson until his passing in 2001. She has taught at both the graduate and undergraduate levels. She is a frequent public speaker on the subject of behavioral public relations and is the editor of *The Best of Pat Jackson in pr reporter,* a compendium of Jackson's writings, theories, and models published over his quarter of a century as editor of that publication.

The authors purposely chose to use a narrative description and avoided a set format for presenting each case. The real world does not come neatly packaged. The many teachers who regularly share their experiences with the text tell us they want students to gain experience in picking out the problem situation, delineating an environmental scan, and having to decide whether the solutions chosen were wise or flawed. Outlining the cases according to a formula denies them this most important learning from case studies.

Putting together a text of real-life case *studies*, contrasted with a collection of successful case *histories*, requires objective cooperation by the organizations represented, particularly when the subject, the scenario, or the conclusion is not laudatory. We are grateful for the information and illustrations supplied. We hope the cooperation pays off and this text enables instruction to be better attuned to the pressing needs of employers and the profession.

And finally, we would like to stress the importance and necessity of combining all public relations actions with both personal and professional ethics in behavior. PRSA's Member Code of Ethics (see the following and Chapter 10 for further discussion) deals with this combination. As the Code purports: "The foundation of our value to our companies, clients and those we serve is their ability to rely on our ethical and morally acceptable behavior."

---

## THE PRSA CODE OF MEMBER ETHICS

The Code has three parts:

1. Its **Values** are designed to inspire and motivate each member every day to the highest levels of ethical practice. These Values include: advocacy, honesty, expertise, independence, loyalty, fairness.

2. Its **Code Provisions** are designed to help each member clearly understand the limits and specific performance required to be an ethical practitioner. The Provisions cover: free flow of information, disclosure of information, safeguarding confidences, conflicts of interest, enhancing the profession. Each Provision includes discussion of the core principle, its intent, and guidelines on what a member is to do and not do. These will be continuously expanded by precedent-setting cases and experience in applying the Code.

3. Its **Commitment** mechanism ensures that every member understands the obligations of membership and the expectation of ethical behavior. It is a pledge that each must sign.

---

# The Purposes of Public Relations

## PUBLIC RELATIONS IS AN APPLIED SCIENCE

However firm our grasp of the principles, the history, and the theories of any field, we must be able to apply them to actual cases. This statement is true for the entry-level recent graduate and for the seasoned professional. The proof of capability is in handling cases successfully for employers or clients.

- The bottom line of public relations practice is in the results that come from putting theories and principles to work—in a way that benefits the organization issuing the paycheck *and* the society of which that organization is a part.

For this reason, the case study method of learning about public relations is an essential part of a practitioner's education. Case studies accurately model situations that organizations, managers, and public relations practitioners routinely face.

Though this book came into being primarily for use in the classroom—and includes practical exercises in each chapter suitable for students—it is also the major collection of carefully analyzed case studies for the field. Students can feel confident that they are using these cases right alongside seasoned veterans.

## PUBLIC RELATIONS IS A RESPONSIBILITY OF MANAGEMENT

Although everyone in the organization affects the organization's relationships with various publics, establishing public relations policies, goals, and activities is a managerial function. Public relations staffers are part of management.

In approaching the cases and problems presented in this book, an understanding of the meaning of *management* is essential. Here is a basic definition:

- *Management is getting things done with people.*

This statement means that managers work with and through others to carry out their assignments. Their job is not to do the work themselves but to guide and assist others in doing it. But there is another implication here that is related directly to public relations:

- *Management must be able to get the cooperation of people both inside and outside the organization in order to achieve the organization's objectives.*

Thus, *public relations* managers must build capabilities in both the internal and external aspects of management. For this reason, they are usually selected as much for their managerial abilities in leading a staff and counseling others in the organization as for their public relations skills. The cases and problems in this book will help you practice both aspects.

• The term *public relations* is often confusing because it is frequently used inaccurately. Used correctly, *public relations* describes the *processes* of practice—the techniques, strategies, structures, and tactics of the field. As such, the term is analogous to *law, medicine, nursing,* and so on. Too often, *public relations* is also used to describe the *outcomes* of effective practice—so we hear of "good public relations." The proper term for the desired outcomes of public relations practice is public *relationships*. An organization with effective public relations will attain positive public relationships.

## THE FOCUS OF PUBLIC RELATIONS IS ON BEHAVIOR

When an organization invests resources in public relations, it expects that something will be different than before or than it would have been had the investment not been made. Examples of change might be:

• Improved purchases by, and relationships with, customers
• Better community relationships
• Active support on issues from opinion leaders
• Reduced tension with watchdog agencies
• Greater employee loyalty or productivity
• More confidence in the value of a company's stock
• For a nonprofit agency, increased donations

If all public relations does is maintain the status quo, it is being used ineffectually. In addition, if it changes only the way people feel or think about the organization—and vice-versa—it has not realized its full potential. Effective public relations elicits mutually favorable *behavior* from both the organization and its publics.

**Behavior May Be of Three Types**

| Getting people to *do* something | Getting them *not* to do something | Winning their consent to *let the organization* do something |
|---|---|---|

Looked at from another perspective, the type of change sought may be to:

1. *Motivate* new behavior,
2. *Reinforce* existing positive behavior, or
3. *Modify* negative behavior.

In studying the cases we present, ask yourself what is different about behaviors after the public relations activities have been carried out. If the answer is nothing, you must consider whether public relations has failed.

## ELEMENTS THAT MAKE UP THE FUNCTION

In general, public relations is what public relations *does* (which is true of every field). The employer or client, by formulating objectives, and practitioners, by accepting those objectives, define the function for that organization at that time. Historically, the function has evolved from *one-way information transfer,* to a *two-way concept* of sending messages and listening to feedback, to the present idea of an organization's *adjusting harmoniously* with the publics on which it depends.[1] Underpinning this perspective, however, are at least six activities that are basic and endemic to practice:

1. **Research.** The first step in any project is to gather intelligence, in order to understand the variables in the case. What are key publics' opinions and attitudes? Who are the opinion leaders that matter? Which groups or persons are concerned enough to act?
2. **Strategic planning.** The situation and the data need to be formed into a strategy. Where are we now? How did we get here? Where do we want to be? How do we get there?
3. **Counseling.** Fellow managers must understand the plan and agree it should be implemented. They may have a role in implementation and, at least, will need to explain it to their staffs.
4. **Internal education.** People in the organization need to be informed about the plan and their roles in it. Public relationships are not formed only by the executives or the public relations professionals, but far more by *everyone who interacts* with customers, employees, the community, stockholders, and all other publics.
5. **Communication/action.** The plan must be carried out. Messages or appeals are sent to the various publics involved: activities or actions are staged; feedback must be interpreted; and everyone must be kept informed as the project unfolds.
6. **Evaluation.** Another type of research—evaluation—charts effectiveness, or lack of it, and very likely will result in a new plan.

Chapter 2 reviews how this sequence is applied with a four-step model.

## PLANNING: MANAGEMENT BY OBJECTIVES

Effective organizations have a business plan made up of *long-range goals* for the future and *short-term objectives* attainable soon. The name commonly given to this type of plan is *management by objectives,* or *MBO.*[2]

Within the statement of goals and objectives, the role expected of public relations is usually stated in general terms. Public relations activities are tied to overall objectives, creating what is called the **management concept** or **public relations strategy**.

The public relations staff then draws up a set of specific departmental goals and objectives. The staff members devise programs or campaigns, hire any needed outside

---

[1]For thoughtful analysis of the evolving definition, see Scott M. Cutlip, Allen H. Center, and Glen M. Broom, *Effective Public Relations*, 8th ed. Upper Saddle River, NJ: Prentice Hall, 1999, Chapter 1.
[2]Courses in marketing and business methods are recommended for all students planning a career in public relations whether in profit or nonprofit enterprises. Readers who want a detailed understanding of management by objectives (MBO) should see Norman Nager and T. Harrell Allen, *Public Relations Management by Objectives*, Lanham, MD: University Press of America, September 1, 1991.

talent, plan budgets, establish timetables, implement activities and communications, and evaluate results—all tied to the organization's overall business plan. This working process is called the **functional concept**, or **public relations tactics**.

One key to success in planning—observable in several cases in this book—is to anticipate problems and opportunities. This proactive, or preventive, approach is preferable to the reactive, after-the-fact, approach because it lets you take the lead, rather than being forced to respond to others. Increasingly, this **issue anticipation** approach is becoming one of the major values public relations is expected to provide.

## WHAT COMES ACROSS IS VALUES

More than anything, what public relations activities communicate are the values and vision of the organization—for better or worse. These may be socially positive, acceptable values or questionable ones. But whatever the explicit message sent forth, with it goes an implicit message of whether the organization really cares about people, the community, and the future; or instead is self-centered and concerned only with its immediate profits or success—or possibly even antisocial.

The primary value public relations professionals promote inside organizations is the *open system*. An open system fosters the willingness to adjust and adapt to change, with management sensitive to all interactions in the environment. Such managers are available, listen well, and communicate forthrightly both within the organization and with external stakeholders.

In contrast is the *closed system* organization, where change is difficult. Managers cling to the status quo, and seek to change the environment that is unfavorable to the old ways. Usually they try to limit or tightly control the flow of information. In such organizations, public relations is often on the defensive, forced to put forth the view, "If only you knew us better, you'd agree with us."

Private enterprise, as a system, is often accused of being closed. Often it seems to insist its ways are inviolate. "Everything, everybody else, must change to our ways" is the value that sometimes comes across. Needless to say, this attitude limits effectiveness.

For public relations practitioners, the conflict between open and closed systems of management poses a major issue:

- Must an organization always go along with public opinion?
- When is it acceptable to advocate change in public opinion?

Many cases discussed here illuminate this conundrum.

## THE COMMON DENOMINATORS

In almost all programs or campaigns, seven common characteristics prevail:

1. Concern about social norms, group attitudes, and individual behavior
2. A strategy embodying specific objectives, selected audiences, careful timing, and cost controls
3. Actions that are consistent with the mission, vision, policies, standards, and personality of the organization represented
4. Emphasis on the use of **communications and participative activities to persuade**, rather than the use of coercion

5. Consideration of the ethical and legal implications and consequences
6. A method of assessing the outcome in terms of benefits and costs
7. Translation of this assessment into decisions for continuation, alteration, or termination of the program

## PROVEN MAXIMS THAT EVERY PRACTITIONER MUST KNOW

As the library of case studies and the experience of scholars and practitioners have grown, the practice has accumulated an inventory of maxims with a high degree of reliability. Many of them derive from timeworn adages applied to persuasion and the formation of public opinion. Here are some examples of these maxims.[3]

1. An appeal to audience **self-interest** is most likely to be effective.
2. A **source of information** regarded as trustworthy, expert, or authoritative is most likely to be believed.
3. **Personal, face-to-face contact** is the most effective means of communication.
4. **Understanding a subject** is the first requisite for a communicator wishing to explain the subject to others.
5. **A suggested action or appeal**, as part of a message or coupled to it, is more likely to be accepted than a message by itself.
6. **Participation in, or awareness of, the decision process** increases the likelihood of acceptance.
7. **Personality needs and drives as well as peer group identity** affect the acceptance of messages and positions on issues.
8. **Degree of clarity, simplicity, and symbolism** has a direct and measurable effect on message acceptance.
9. **Explicitly stated messages** and appeals tend to produce more behavior or opinion change than explanations of concepts or theories.
10. **Major issues and events** cause wide swings in public opinion for brief periods. The degree of lasting change tends to diminish with the passage of time.
11. **Self-imposed censorship by the audience** in not paying attention or not feeling involved can vary the degree of opinion or behavior change substantially.
12. **Subsequent events that reinforce the original stimulus** for opinion or behavior change will tend to increase the degree and durability of the change.
13. **Messages related to goals** are more readily acceptable than messages related to the steps and methods of attaining the goals.
14. **When a public is friendly in a controversial situation**, presenting only one side of the issue tends to be effective. If the audience is not friendly, or is likely to be receptive to both sides, presenting both sides tends to be more effective.
15. In controversy, **opposing views seeking major change of opinion** tend to strengthen the positions held. Similarly, a strong threat to those positions tends

---

[3]The "maxims" offered here are, for the most part, simple restatements of tenets advanced as "laws" of public opinion by Hadley Cantril, "barriers to communication" described by Walter Lippmann, Roper's "hypothesis," and Gallup's "regulators of the absorption rate of new ideas." Students can develop some of their own "maxims" or "precedential guidelines" by relating such concepts as the diffusion process, the concentric circle theory, and the two-step flow of information to situations with public relations overtones in their lives or in the news.

to be less effective than a mild threat. A reliable assumption is that **people tend to resist change**.

16. When there is little to choose from between opposing views, a determining factor tends to be **the argument heard last**.

17. In a confusing situation involving opposing messages, people tend to **believe what they want to and hope for**, rather than messages that strike discord.

18. **Sensitivity to public leadership** is heightened in times of crisis or controversy. At such times, people affirm or disapprove more forcefully and openly.

## GUIDELINES FROM BEHAVIORAL SCIENCE

Although there are few strict rules in psychology, sociology, or anthropology, following are four well-proven guidelines from these disciplines as they apply to public relations.

### FOUR RULES FROM THE BEHAVIORAL SCIENCES

1. **The rule of ABUSE from Sociology**

   • People who *perceive* they have been, or *might* be, abused by an organization, its policies, or actions cannot hear what it is trying to say to them until the abuse is eliminated or at least acknowledged.

2. **The rule of PARTICIPATION from Psychology**

   • People will fully support only those ideas or programs they perceive they have had a voice in creating.

3. **The rule of REWARDS from Psychology**

   • People will ultimately do only those things for which they feel rewarded.

4. **The rule of CHEERLEADING from Anthropology**

   • Every successful organization of any type has at its core someone or several persons we would today call cheerleaders, urging the members on to success.

## PROFESSIONALISM

Edward L. Bernays described a **profession** as "an art applied to a science in a manner that puts public interest ahead of personal gain."[4] The practice of public relations lays claim to professionalism on seven counts:

1. A codified body of knowledge[5] and a growing bank of theoretical literature, precedents, and case studies

2. Insight into human behavior and the formation and movement of public opinion

3. Skill in the use of communications tools, social science technology, and persuasion to affect opinions, attitudes, and behavior

4. Academic training including the Ph.D., offered in colleges throughout the world, and professional development available through a multiplicity of professional societies

[4]Bernays, Edward L. *The Latter Years: Public Relations Insights* 1956–1986. Rhinebeck. NY: H&M Publishers, 1986, p. 138.
[5]See *The Public Relations Body of Knowledge,* updated periodically by The Public Relations Society of America (PRSA) (available in computer disk and book form).

5. A formal code of ethics[6]
6. A service that is essential in contemporary society
7. Nobility of purpose in harmonizing private and public interests—thus enabling individual self-determination and democratic societies to function

   In the cases presented in this book, observe whether the practitioners involved are meeting these tests of professionalism—and whether application of or failure to observe these guidelines has an impact on their effectiveness.

Success
must be **CONFERRED** on us
by **OUTSIDERS** like
customers
opinion leaders
neighbors
elected officials
vendors
voters
prospective employees
coalitions
stakeholders
shareowners
Therefore, the bottom line for every organization is
to **BUILD RELATIONSHIPS**
that **EARN TRUST**
and **MOTIVATE SUPPORTIVE BEHAVIORS**

## REFERENCES AND ADDITIONAL READINGS

Awad, Joseph. *The Power of Public Relations.* New York: Praeger, 1985.

Baskin, Otis, Craig Aronoff, and Dan Lattimore. *Public Relations: The Profession and the Practice,* 4th ed. New York: McGraw-Hill Higher Education, 1996.

Bernays, Edward L. *Crystallizing Public Opinion.* New York: Liveright, 1961. The first book on the field when it appeared in 1923— and still a good overview. *Public Relations.* Norman, OK: University of Oklahoma Press, 1952. *Engineering of Consent.* Norman, OK: University of Oklahoma Press, 1955.

Budd, John, Jr. "When Less Is More: Public Relations' Paradox of Growth," *Public Relations Quarterly* 35 (Spring 1990): 5–11.

Burson, Harold. "Beyond PR: Redefining the Role of Public Relations." Presented to the 29th Annual Distinguished Lecture of the Institute for Public Relations Research and Education, Inc., the Union League Club, New York, October 2, 1990.

Cutlip, Scott, Allen Center, and Glen Broom. *Effective Public Relations,* 8th ed. Upper Saddle River, NJ: Prentice Hall, 1999. Chapters 1–4.

---

[6]See PRSA's *Member Code of Ethics,* Chapter 10, p. 365–366.

Grunig, James, et al. *Excellence in Public Relations and Communications Management*. Mahwah, NJ: Lawrence Erlbaum Associates, 1992.

Grunig, James, David Dozier, and Larissa Grunig. *Manager's Guide to Excellence in Public Relations and Communications Management*. Mahwah, NJ: Lawrence Erlbaum Associates, 1995.

Haynes, Colin. *A Guide to Successful Public Relations*. Glenview, IL: Scott-Foresman, 1989.

Hiebert, Ray Eldon. *Precision Public Relations*. New York: Addison-Wesley, 1988. Compendium of essays by public relations notables.

Jackson, Patrick. "Tomorrow's Public Relations." *Public Relations Journal* 41 (March 1985).

Lesly, Philip. *Lesly's Handbook of Public Relations and Communications*, 5th ed. Chicago, IL: NTC Business Books, 1998.

*pr reporter* Vol. 31 No. 38 (September 26, 1988). Deals editorially with acceptance yet insecurity of function, urges reenergizing through social compact and professionwide management awareness program.

*The Public Relations Body of Knowledge* compiled by The Public Relations Society of America (PRSA). This resource provides abstracts of articles, lectures, books, and book chapters relating to relevant areas of public relations. Available from PRSA, 33 Irving Place, New York, NY 10003.

Wilcox, Dennis, et al. *Public Relations Strategies and Tactics*, 6th ed. New York: Longman, 2000.

# How Public Relations Deals with Problems and Opportunities

## WHAT IS PUBLIC RELATIONS?

Here is a formal three-part definition of **public relations**:

1. Public relations is a condition common to every individual and organization in the human environment—whether or not they recognize or act upon the fact—that refers to their reputation and relationship with all other members of the environment.
2. Public relations is the systematized function that evaluates public attitudes and behaviors; harmonizes the goals, policies, and procedures of an individual or organization with the public interest; and executes a program of action to earn public understanding, acceptance, and supportive behavior.
3. Public relations is the full flowering of the democratic principle, in which every member of society is valued for himself or herself, and has both a right and a duty to express an opinion on public issues, and in which policies are made on the basis of free exchange of those opinions that result in public consent.

In other words:

- Public relations is something everyone has.
- Public relations fosters the improvement of public relationships through specific activities and policies.
- Public relations is the cornerstone of a democratic society.

## PROACTIVE AND REACTIVE APPROACHES

An organization or corporation is a group of people working together for a specific purpose. That purpose invariably involves gaining the confidence of other people who will buy the product or use the service, invest in the organization's stock (or donate funds to nonprofit entities), and support its positions on issues. In short, every organization exists in a societal or people-oriented environment, first and foremost. The late counselor Philip Lesly called this the *human climate*.

Because people form impressions and opinions of one another almost without thinking about it, every organization has a reputation, be it good or bad. Most likely, it will be good with some people and bad with others, depending on the perspective of those people and their particular interactions with the organization. As it does between persons, this reputation influences the ability of the organization to win friends, persuade others to do business with it, or be trusted in public matters.

- *The managerial challenge is whether something is consciously done to face the fact of reputation and relationships.*

When something is consciously done, the result is a public relations policy: recognition by management that positive relationships with key publics are essential to success. This management concept (see Chapter 1) is usually carried out by forming a public relations department and assigning it the responsibility for building and maintaining positive working relationships inside and outside the organization.

The approach the public relations department takes, however, is another challenge. Many companies—too many, some observers say—operate in a *reactive* mode. They wait for public criticism, emergencies, or bad publicity before they act. They are usually likened to firefighters who don't get going until there's a fire.

Because reputations are formed and re-formed in people's minds continuously, and because public issue debates are constantly taking shape, a more strategic approach is to be *proactive*. This approach is like fire prevention. It constantly looks for potential opportunities and problems. Proactive public relations practitioners will be ready to take advantage of opportunities when they arise and to prevent potential problems from flaring up.

## STRATEGY AND PLANNING MAKE THE DIFFERENCE

Given the unpredictable nature of our world, there will always be unexpected situations that require reactive responses. But, just as promotions come to those who have worked hard for it, successful reactive responses are made by those who are prepared. The best preparation involves:

1. Understanding your organization's or client's business, operations, culture, and goals thoroughly
2. Learning as much as possible about the publics on which it depends for success
3. Putting that understanding and knowledge together in a formal strategic plan

With preparation, reactive responses are most likely to fit into the overall pattern of the public relations effort. Trouble comes when they do not fit—when what is put forward in response to customer complaints now contradicts what the company has been saying in publicity, publications, or advertising. The company is not speaking with One Clear Voice, and this "double talk" raises questions of its accuracy and trustworthiness.

In analyzing the cases in this book, you will not know as much about the subjects or organizations as you would want to were you actually involved in the case. Nevertheless, it should be apparent in most cases whether the public relations response was based on a strategic plan or just a hunch or gut feeling. More than anything else, planning makes the difference between success and failure.

# PRELIMINARIES TO PLANNING

Many misunderstandings and poor public relationships occur because a legitimate inquiry is not promptly and properly answered by deed or word. Many others occur because responses are ill-timed, inaccurate, or altered by the interpretation given by a critic, or they are blown out of proportion by news media seeking sensational headlines.

Naturally, given a choice between spot reaction and time for a thoroughly considered response, public relations practitioners would opt for the latter. Sometimes there is no choice; microphones are being thrust in your face or a political figure is waiting impatiently in the reception area.

The substitute for a thoroughly considered response is a **strategic plan** that anticipates at least broad topics that are likely to arise. Specific problems that affect public opinion and relationships rarely exist in isolation. Each one is connected to larger matters of public concern. By considering these problems in a plan, in advance, one often can deal with a problem before it arises. Mastering the planning process is an essential and basic skill of public relations. Such plans must take place within the context of the goals and culture of the organization, of course.

# THE PUBLIC RELATIONS PROCESS

In devising a program or campaign, practitioners follow a series of logical steps that overlap so that they constitute a continuous **four-step process** (often called the RACE model—*R*esearch, *A*nalysis, *C*ommunication, *E*valuation):

1. **Research**, which often includes formal research, to define clearly the specific problem or opportunity
2. **Analysis and planning** to devise and package a strategy
3. **Action, relationship building, and communication** to implement the strategy
4. **Evaluation** to determine results and to decide what, if anything, to do next or to do differently

## Step 1: Research

Public relations problems do not often come neatly bound with all the facts, nuances, and history carefully laid out. More likely, information and facts dribble in, some of it not seen until a critical moment in the course of events. Perceptions of what is going on, what is being experienced by stakeholders, run the gauntlet. It is the **practitioner's responsibility** to gather the facts and perceptions in order to build a plan that is both reasonable and effective. This is done through informal and formal research with internal and external stakeholders. A practitioner must look through the lens of every involved stakeholder group to determine how they view the situation and what their understanding or perceptions are for their position or current behavior. This, in turn, will guide the theoretical strategies used in planning and programming.

## Step 2: Analysis and Planning

Planning involves prioritizing stakeholder publics for the situation at hand. Time and budget will always influence what can be accomplished, so a practitioner must prioritize which publics are most critical to the current problem or opportunity. Setting goals and objectives for each public will guide strategies as well as specific activities and messages that are then developed as part of an overall plan. Budgets and timelines are set and assignments are made.

Frequently, thorough research will reveal a problem or problems that must be addressed before the planned program can continue or succeed. Taking remedial action to fix the problem is a necessary step at this point.

Setting appropriate goals is not easy. Far too many practitioners fail to set any goals at all for their activities or use vague, general words such as "improve" to define their goals. To ensure that the goals are strong enough to withstand scrutiny, a savvy practitioner will use the SMARTS acronym when setting goals for the program:

S = Specific: Is the goal direct and to the point?
M = Measurable: Is the outcome measurable?
A = Attainable: Is it possible to achieve this goal?
R = Realistic: Is it likely this goal will be met?
T = Time locked: How much time do you have? How much do you need?
S = Sufficient: If the goal is met, will you be where you need to be?

## Step 3: Action, Relationship Building, and Communication

Implementation of the public relations plan as laid out in step 2 is then undertaken. It is important to review the plan and tweak it based on the continually changing situation and the progression of stakeholder perceptions and behaviors. It is equally important to remain focused on the overall goals and not be swayed or drawn away from them by distractions. Activities in this step will include many one-way and two-way communication tools. The diffusion process shows us that building awareness and sending out information only builds awareness and interest; therefore, it is important to build in and implement relationship-building tools that involve two-way communication.[1]

## Step 4: Evaluation

A good public relations plan incorporates evaluation tools to determine how successful the plan has been in achieving the goals set forth. This evaluation should take place at two levels, or tiers: monitoring and measuring. The plan will include evaluation markers along the way to monitor as well help guide the plan as it is implemented. A plan that is constantly tweaked based on specific research is much more effective then one tweaked on gut instinct or management whims. The final evaluation—measurement—weighs the results of the program against the stated goals.

---

[1]For an in-depth look at the diffusion process, see "Diffusion of Innovations" by Everett M. Rogers, The Free Press, NY (1962) or "Diffusion Process" on Wikipedia.

# WHAT GOOD MODELS AND THEORIES BRINGS TO THE TABLE

**A *theory* is the application of knowledge that has been verified and confirmed to consistently "work" in consistent situations**. In other words, *theory* comprises the principles and methods of public relations. Most introductory texts explain theoretical approaches and models as a way of getting to the practice of public relations.

There has always been some healthy friction between theory and practice. Public relations, as a practice, did not begin with theory. It began with leaders such as Ivy Lee working on "gut instinct," while others, such as Edward L. Bernays, tried to apply behavioral science methods to reach what he called "the merger of public and private interests."[2]

Public relations education today continues this dichotomy. Some programs are "too theoretical" to be useful, critics say. The response is that dissimilar programs do not use enough theory, relying instead on anecdotal evidence—war stories. In truth, most public relations programs try to balance theory with good practical examples—examples that prove a particular theoretical point.

Theory is useful and necessary for public relations education. Specifically:

- Theory validates good practice:
  1. Theory is not case specific, but can be generalized over a broad range of clients and issues.
  2. A theoretical background enables a practitioner to move easily between jobs, industries, and clients.
  3. Theory increases efficiency.
  4. The theoretical approach is cost-effective. Trial and error are expensive.
  5. The theoretical approach is time-effective. Trial and error are time-consuming.
- Good theory helps move the practice of public relations into a profession. Good theory begets a body of knowledge that then facilitates the exchange of information necessary for a profession to sustain itself.
- Good theory, coupled with good research, helps the practitioner to chart a wise course. Good research will enable the practitioner to define the status quo, explain the status quo, and predict what actions are necessary to extend or modify the status quo to create the behaviors needed to meet the program's goals.

As public relations continues to move "past communication to achieving behavioral outcomes," good theory will become the backbone of the new models.

# THE BEHAVIORAL PUBLIC RELATIONS MODEL

As first posited by Pat Jackson, behavior is the only outcome that truly counts. What stakeholder groups think or feel about an organization or product means very little unless they "behave" in such a way that makes a difference. This means motivating people to (1) do something, (2) not do something, or (3) let you do something. Jackson suggested that too many practitioners think of themselves as

---

[2]Conversation with E. L. Bernays, 1989, Lake Buena Vista, FL.

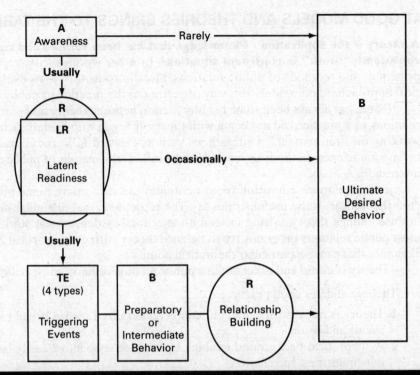

**FIGURE 2-1     Behavioral Public Relations Model**

communicators. They believe that their objective is to move information, facts, data, or feelings, evaluating success by clips, attendance, "reach," and similar measurements. To all of which knowledgeable employers or clients ask, "So what? What has changed because of this? Never mind what our publics are thinking; the question is what are they *doing?*"

The behavioral public relations model (see Figure 2-1) basically shifts the objective away from awareness as a goal to a behavioral response, and with it the focus on thinking, strategizing, and planning. Practitioners ask, "What behaviors am I trying to motivate?" rather than "What information am I trying to communicate?"

A behavioral strategic planning model can be useful:

1. What **behaviors** must be motivated, reinforced, or modified to achieve the plan's goals? Beginning every project by making a list of desired behaviors gives the practitioner a specific guide for what he or she is trying to accomplish. This is the most important step toward engendering those behaviors instead of thinking right away about messages, media, or activities.
2. Which stakeholder groups or segments must exhibit these behaviors or could prevent achievement of the goals by either withholding the behaviors or by overt opposition?
3. Because people often do not go straight to the ultimate desired behaviors, what intermediate behaviors might they have to be led through?

4. Because groups do not usually act spontaneously, who are the opinion leaders in these groups and what special behaviors must be sought from them to stimulate group behavior?

## Understanding the Behavioral Public Relations Model

The first step of the behavioral public relations model is **awareness**. A person cannot act on something that he or she is not aware of, so creating awareness is the natural first step in creating the desired behavior. This is one area in which mass media, as well as all other one-way media, are useful. Publicity via mass media is an excellent tool in creating initial awareness, as is paid advertising. However, according to the behavioral model awareness rarely, if ever, leads to behavior change or the ultimate desired behavior. What it does do is open a "file" in the mind of the stakeholder in which to store information and feelings about the subject. This process is called building *latent readiness.*

A person's propensity to develop a **latent desire to act** on the newly acquired awareness is the second step of the model. Latent readiness can be positive or negative, depending on the information and influences that build over time. If people (opinion leaders) the stakeholder respects add to the information positively or negatively, that will influence the direction in which the stakeholder *might* behave. Core values can also influence latent readiness.

Stakeholders might carry around this awareness and latent readiness to act for a long, long time before, if ever, doing something about the subject. What it takes to stimulate the behavior to happen is what Jackson calls the "triggering event."

A **triggering event** is an activity that motivates stakeholders to act on their latent readiness. It can be something that occurs naturally, such as a thunderstorm or the change of seasons. Election day is the triggering event for a politician running for office. The largest commercial triggering event each year is the holiday season. Noon is a triggering event for most consumers—lunchtime. Or it can be a manufactured triggering event—something that an organization can control and release to stimulate behavior—a sale at a store, a layoff of employees, an open house, or similar event.

Understanding triggering events is key to the behavioral public relations strategy. People are available to do, even ready to do, more than they actually do. Lack of time or money, other priorities, laziness, and a thousand other barriers inhibit them from undertaking the behavior spontaneously. Overcoming these barriers requires:

1. Constructing a triggering event that pushes the behavior into a priority position. For example, retailers hold sales to lure shoppers to buy goods they previously felt they could not afford or that were not a high priority.
2. Usurping naturally occurring triggering events in the lives of your stakeholders. For example, 40th birthdays start people thinking about their health.
3. Capitalizing on triggering events that randomly come along in the social environment. For example, "Sesame Street" tipped a revolution in early childhood education.
4. Fending off triggering events launched by competitors and opponents or occurring in the environment.

Appealing to people to go straight to the ultimate behavior is usually futile. Most people work through intermediate behaviors before proceeding to the ultimate behavior. The focus of public relations efforts should be on leading people to intermediate behaviors and concentrating appeals there. Asking right off for the ultimate behavior is usually ineffective.

If the intermediate activity puts the organization in direct contact with people—perhaps a celebration, meeting, or event—this is prime time to build face-to-face relationships with stakeholders. The combination of attracting them to an intermediate event and then building a relationship provides entrée for them to act the ultimate behavior. For example, hospitals hold educational seminars—building relationships between staff and attendees during the events—as a means of stimulating attendees to make the hospital their health-care center.

For most planned public relations programs, a natural triggering event does not occur. It is the skill of the practitioner to creatively find ways to trigger stakeholder behavior again and again, utilizing those small steps along the continuum as research to understand and be able to trigger the ultimate step at some point. Jackson said, "Public Relations is a process by which organizations establish positive relationships which lead to positive behavior." Therefore, *PR* could stand for "positive relationships" as well as "public relations."[3]

The goal or focus of modern public relations practice is positive behavior. This may be a positive behavior that is maintained, that is established for the first time, or that is converted from negative to positive. Regardless, positive action from the primary publics is the goal.

## A FIVE-STEP PUBLIC RELATIONS STRATEGY FOR THE TWENTY-FIRST CENTURY

A highly effective strategy for **planning and programming** emerges from the Behavioral Public Relations Model. This strategy is demonstrated in numerous cases throughout this book (ASA, Grassroots, Mercy, Dayton Hudson). It integrates the focus on behavior and relationship building with two-way communication methods and credible delivery mechanisms (opinion leaders and the organizational family). It relieves the practitioner of the constriction of feeling that the news media are the only way to communicate with the organization's stakeholders. It puts the practitioner back in control of the message and the relationships with the organization's publics. The key steps are to:

1. **Go direct:** Go around the critics and gatekeepers to get to the important people whose support is needed for the program's success.
2. **To key stakeholders:** Those who are interested can give supportive behaviors now or stop needed action through their opposition.
3. **Via opinion leaders:** Publics do not just spontaneously act; they are stimulated by the movers and shakers called *opinion leaders*.

[3]See "The Behavioral Public Relations Model" *pr reporter,* January 1, 1999.

**4. Using members of the organizational family:** Involve employees at all levels in customer relations activities, ambassador programs, and community relations outreach teams; put them in charge of building *local* relationships that earn *supportive* behaviors.

**5. On a local basis:** People operate within their local environments; all issues are local.

## THE CRITICAL IMPORTANCE OF RESEARCH

No public relations program should be undertaken without good research. Research gives the practitioner the in-depth understanding of what a stakeholder group is thinking and feeling and how stakeholders are currently behaving and why. Good research will describe, explain, and predict; thereby enhancing the practitioner's ability to create positive behavior. When problems do arise, they can usually be sorted into three distinct categories:

1. Ignorance
2. Apathy
3. Hostility

When *ignorance* is the problem, then education is usually the answer. When *apathy* is the problem, then motivation is the answer. These are the easy solutions. But when *hostility* is the problem, persuasion is the answer, and this is not easy to accomplish.

## THE PERSUASION MODEL

Persuading people to change their behavior is difficult for many reasons. Oftentimes, it is not worth the effort it would take to win the enemy over. Unless the success of a planned program of public relations is contingent on total buy-in, a better use of time and resources is to focus on the positive and uncommitted publics and not stir up the opposition (see the Phil Lesly model in Chapter 9).

The **persuasion model** is a successful model for persuading those who are hostile to an idea and who are required for the success of a program. First developed by San Diego practitioner Kerry Tucker, the model involves four steps:

1. Creating "dissatisfaction with the status quo"
2. Offering the program as a viable option to the status quo
3. Presenting benefits of adopting the new idea and consequences of rejecting it
4. Modeling the desired behavior[4]

The key, of course, is creating dissatisfaction with the status quo. In effect, the subject has to see and agree that the existing behavior (and the attitudes behind it) is wrong. This is why persuasion is so hard. Something called *self-persuasion* kicks in any time existing beliefs are challenged, and the normal reaction is to fight back to defend one's beliefs and behaviors.

---

[4]Tucker, Kerry, *PR Writing: An Issue-Driven Behavioral Approach,* 3rd ed., Prentice Hall (1997).

However, if a crack can be made in that wall of self-defense, then the second step is to quickly offer the new idea as a solution to the cognitive dissonance established by that crack. **Cognitive dissonance** was first explored by Leon Festinger in 1956 to understand how and why people resolve conflict in what they know, think, or believe.[5] His conclusion was that people would resolve conflict created by competing or even contradicting information by acquiring or inventing new thoughts or beliefs. Tucker relies on this conclusion in his persuasion theory.

The subject, upon hearing that past or existing behavior could be "wrong," will want to resolve this conflict. Tucker's theory posits that offering the desired behavior as a resolution at this point can lead the subject to adopt the new behavior.

Outlining the benefits of such adoption and the consequences of failing to do so simply reinforces the subject's decision and helps resolve doubts about changing his or her mind. In most cases, the benefits will be obvious and the consequences will be equal to, and opposite of, the benefits.

Finally, modeling the desired behavior presents a picture for the subject of the new world in which the new behavior is the norm. Such "modeling" enables the subject to mentally "fast forward" to a point in time when the positive results of this decision are obvious. It is a "better" world, because the subject is benefiting from the new behavior because the "benefits" have been truly beneficial.

The cases in Chapter 9, Public Issues, demonstrate how difficult it is, however, to move stakeholders from long-held beliefs. Often they move to strike out the conflicting information as "not believable or credible" in an effort to bring order to their own belief system.

## THE ROOTS OF BEHAVIOR

Jackson, Tucker, and others worked long and hard to understand behavior, knowing that one must understand how and why decisions are made before attempts to alter behavior can be successful. What this research revealed is pretty much common sense, but it is important to review it.

Behavior whether positive or negative, begins with the subject's personal history, which helps to shape the subject core values. *Core values* are those values that are not subject to much change, regardless of the circumstances. Former U.S. Senator Howard H. Baker, Jr. (R-TN) once defined core values as those values that "wouldn't change even if tempted by money, power or political advantage." That's a pretty good definition.

It is a person's **core values that drive attitudes that help to form opinions**. These attitudes and opinions are constantly challenged by new circumstances, experiences, and information. The wise person will examine attitudes and opinions regularly to see that they are still congruent with any new personal or societal changes that might have occurred.

Regardless, most people act on what they perceive to be in their best self-interest. The key word is "perceive," because in some instances people act in ways that are

---

[5]Festinger, Leon, *Theory of Cognitive Dissonance*, Stanford University Press (1959).

not really best for their long-term survival. (Smoking tobacco comes to mind. Some 20 percent of the American public still smokes, even after 50 years of medical evidence on its adverse impact on a person's health.)

So, what drives the positive behavior that is the goal of the public relations process? It might be well to look at what *doesn't* work. What doesn't work is simply providing information. As Tucker says, "no one is sitting out there waiting for your information."[6] Few people get up in the morning and look to mass media, for example, before getting dressed and going on with their lives. Thus, the one-way, asymmetrical communication models of the past—getting a story in the newspaper, for example— rarely created any positive behavior.

## THE TWO-WAY SYMMETRICAL COMMUNICATION MODEL

What does work is two-way, symmetrical communication. First introduced by Jim and Larissa Grunig at the University of Maryland, two-way symmetrical communication has its roots in first understanding the wants and needs of the subject and public and then shaping the organization's decisions and actions to meet that need.[7]

The concept is close to what Edward L. Bernays called the "merging of public and private interest." His idea was to use good research to determine which prosocial actions (as opposed to antisocial actions) would lead to the merger of public and private interests.

The Grunigs' theory has more to do with communication style. They considered and rejected both one-way asymmetrical communication and two-way asymmetrical communication because neither one emphasized the subject. According to the

---

### FOUR FRAMEWORKS OF PRACTICE

1. **Press agentry:** Propagandistic, seeks media attention; a one-way asymmetric model.

2. **Public information:** Disseminates accurate information but does not volunteer negative information or seek input; a one-way asymmetric model.

3. **Two-way asymmetrical:** Identifies those messages most likely to gain support of publics without having to change the behavior of the organization; thus it is manipulative. Change benefits the organization, but not necessarily the publics. The organization knows best and does not need the free marketplace of ideas.

4. **Two-way symmetrical:** Uses bargaining, negotiation, and conflict resolution strategies to effect change in the ideas, attitudes, and behaviors of both the organization and its publics for mutual benefit.

---

[6]Personal Interview with Kerry Tucker, 1992, PRSA Annual Conference.
[7]Grunig, James. F, and Larissa Schneider Gruing, "Toward a Theory of the Public Relations Behavior of Organizations: Review of a Program of Research," *Journal of Public Relations*, Vol. 1, No. 1–4 (1989), pp. 27–63.

Grunigs, communication must start with understanding the wants and needs of the subject public, something that asymmetrical communication fails to do.

## WHEN COMMUNICATION IS NOT ENOUGH

Oftentimes, communication alone does not get an organization where it needs to go. A final theory, **beyond communication**, involves altering the way *society* thinks and acts in order to achieve the level of change needed to satisfy an organization's goals. A case illustrating this model is presented in Chapter 8 (MADD Case). This concept involves using good communication strategy and tactics to make major societal changes.

The first step in societal change is to **affect mores**. *Mores* (pronounced "morays") are the informal rules by which we all agree to live. Although they are rarely written or formally adopted, they are very much a part of the way people live and work. Because of their informality, they are subject to change easily, which is a good thing. Flexibility is a desirable element in modern society.

How do mores work to shape behavior? Mores help to determine what society will or will not accept. Certain words are now permissible in public conversation, whereas a generation ago those same words would have been impolite. What is acceptable in the future will likely be different (for better or worse) than what is considered acceptable today.

Once mores have been in place long enough to become established policy, frequently **laws are enacted** to give them an official status. For example, whereas it was once impolite to smoke in an elevator, it is now against the law in most instances. Changing mores and creating new laws frequently help to move an organization's agenda well past what could be done through communication alone.

A final step in the process is the **engineered solution**. When persuasion, mores, and laws are ineffective, then a way to physically prevent the behavior might follow. An example is driving while under the influence of alcohol. There's no doubt that MADD has created a new, positive environment where mores say drunk driving is wrong, and the law agrees. Yet people continue to drive while impaired. An engineered solution might be a device built into a car's ignition system that requires a sober breath before a car can start. For smokers, such a solution might be a ceramic "cigarette" containing a small vial of nicotine. Puffing would release small doses of nicotine for the "smoker," while eliminating any second-hand danger or noxious odors for those around them.

Driven by new theory, modern public relations practice is prepared to "move beyond communication to behavior," as Pat Jackson preached for over 30 years. This "behavioral PR" puts public relations in a position to compete with other organizational departments in that its results can now be quantified and compared with previously established goals. Only when this happens can public relations hold its own in a corporate or organizational environment.

## 20 GREAT TRUTHS OF PUBLIC RELATIONS

1. The long-term security of the organization or product is far more important than short-term expediency.

2. Perception is reality, facts not withstanding.

3. Unfulfilled expectations create most PR problems.

4. Planning and preparation are invaluable. When disaster strikes, it's too late to prepare a crisis plan or build a legacy of trust.

5. The value of research is inestimable.
   a. Every planned PR program should start and end with research.
   b. Every PR plan should evolve from research.
   c. Research should be conducted at every step of the program.

6. PR needs to always play its position and let other departments—legal, operations, marketing, etc.—play theirs.

7. Communication must always follow performance.

8. PR frequently turns on timing. Knowing when to act is as important as knowing what to do.

9. If your client, product, or organization is challenged:
   a. Don't ignore the challenge.
   b. If the challenge is unfair, fight back as hard as you can.
   c. If the challenge has merit, fight for corrective actions.

10. The media–PR relationship will never be better than "professional." There are no favors for free lunches anymore.

11. Ad hoc pressure groups won't give up or go away. You have to deal with them directly or they will consume you in the media.

12. PR has to be involved from the beginning to have maximum impact.

13. Full and complete disclosure and communication is the best way to keep from getting greedy when entrusted with the public's money.

14. Doing the right thing is more important than doing the "thing" right. There is no such thing as "corporate" ethics. People are either ethical or they aren't, and these people determine the ethics of an organization.

15. If you have to say something, the truth is always best.

16. Appeals to other's self-interest are seldom unrewarded.

17. Involvement in the planning stages provides "ownership" and support.

18. If top management is not sold, the project will never succeed.

19. Absent trustworthy information, people assume the worst. Rumors thrive in the vacuum of no information.

20. Most negatives can become positives with a little creative effort and a lot of hard work.

*Source:* © Frank R. Stansberry, 1991.

# CHAPTER

## 3

# Employee Relations

The first public of any organization is its employees—the people who make it what it is. As management guru Peter Drucker reminds us, an organization is "a human community" that needs the contributions of everyone to function and be successful. Many times it appears that management does not recognize this fact. Sometimes managers act as if *they* are the organization and the others just an impediment. An interchange at the annual meeting of an auto company illuminates the truth of the matter. A shareholder asked the CEO why funds were being allocated to improve employee benefits instead of increasing dividends. "Because," he responded, "you and I don't know how to build cars, and they do!"

The situation is complicated by the fact that, in the overwhelming majority of business organizations today, managers and administrators are employees. They do not own the company, but merely manage it for the stockholders. Senior managers may own stock—but so may production workers, secretaries, and janitors. Executives can be hired and fired like everyone else. The true employer is the board of directors elected by the stockholders to oversee the business. In community hospitals, school districts, public interest organizations, government agencies, or membership associations, of course, there is no question of management ownership.

## A DANGEROUS ATTITUDE

It is easy, and perhaps all too common, to view employees as a cost in a line-item budget determining the price of a product or service. This attitude fosters the idea that the less an organization has to pay its employees, the lower the price of the product or service and, therefore, the more competitive the product or service can be in the marketplace.

This one-dimensional view of the labor force provided fertile soil for the tremendous growth of unions, which fought to have labor seen in a multidimensional view. Throughout the decades, unions forced their way into the smallest and largest companies. They won concessions on wages, safety, medical benefits, vacation, and retirement benefits, to mention just a few. Unions became as big as big business. Their influences are reflected in national and state laws as well as in volumes of judicial and regulatory decisions.

The 1980s, however, saw a tapering off of union influence. Union membership dropped; part of this drop is attributed to the significant population move from the unionized Northeast and Midwest to the Sunbelt, which has significantly fewer unions. The impact of foreign competition—foreign cars, for example—as well as the exporting of jobs to countries where labor is cheaper are two other trends that have an impact on the labor market.

Another major change in the employer–employee relationship is automation. The computer radically changes the role of the individual in many workplaces. The individual now competes with the robot for a place in the assembly line; in most instances the individual will lose the contest. If the computer and the robot take on most of the heavy work in the steel mill, most of the positions on the assembly line, and much of the information gathering and dissemination usually associated with general office work, what is left for the current and future individuals who would fill those jobs?

The trend is to a downsizing of the work force and to a service-oriented economy. This movement creates major reshuffling of jobs and people, with all the emotional stress attendant on such upheaval and readjustment. Layoffs and restructuring of organizations also weaken the loyalty of workers, which can affect morale and productivity. So can mergers and acquisitions.

Then there are legislative influences, such as NAFTA, the North American Free Trade Agreement, which allows organizations to move their production facilities around the continent, avoiding regulations and higher employee-benefit costs that impact pricing and profits.

Thomas Friedman, in his book *The World Is Flat: A Brief History of the Twenty-First Century,* writes at length about a variety of ways employees are being squeezed, including the two most prevalent: outsourcing and offshoring. Says Friedman, "No matter what your profession—doctor, lawyer, architect, accountant—if you are an American, you better be good at the touchy-feely service stuff, because anything that can be digitized can be outsourced to either the smartest or the cheapest producer or both."

During this significant time of transition, employer–employee relations change, but they are no less critical than in the past. Indeed, most people would argue that they are now more important than ever.

In a very real sense, frontline workers *are* the organization. They produce the product, provide the service, operate support systems, count the money, deal with customers, work with vendors—in short, the activities that make the organization function.

## BENEFITS OF EMPLOYEE PARTICIPATION

Because they are accountable to the board—the real and legal seat of power in most organizations—executives have responsibility as "the employer." Others needed to carry out the operations become "the employees." Yet if there is one significant trend in successful organizations worldwide, it is the melding of interests and heightened cooperation between management and employees. Recognition of several benefits from a united effort has brought this "workplace democracy" about:

1. As the founder of Honda Motors puts it, just as cars are gauged by horsepower, so organizations can be gauged by mindpower. If only the CEO thinks about

possible improvements, there is one mindpower. If only management, maybe 100–500 mindpower. But if everyone is encouraged to think about the company and his or her work in it, and then make suggestions, an organization can have 20,000 or more mindpower.

2. In a highly competitive economy, successful organizations are those that deliver customer delight. But customer delight depends on employee satisfaction; that is, dissatisfied employees are unlikely to delight customers, because their own irritations or feelings of abuse will get in the way. (The next time a retail clerk fails to give you delightful service, remember that he or she is probably the lowest paid, least valued, least trained worker in the store—and most likely part-time to boot. Yet the retail industry expects such employees to conduct *the* most important job, serving customers.) Success involves *everyone*—those who make the policies, those who design and produce the product or service, the sales personnel, janitors who keep the premises attractive, secretaries who answer the phone, and so on.

3. To build trusting relationships with customers, shareholders, communities, government, and other stakeholder publics, organizations need to speak with One Clear Voice. Management cannot say one thing in official pronouncements from the ivory tower and then have employees telling another story to the people with whom they interact. Achieving one voice requires shared values, which arise when employees are encouraged to participate in organizational decision making.

The benefits of mutually satisfactory employee–employer relations are significant. There are fewer work stoppages, less absenteeism, higher productivity, and fewer errors. Sometimes the benefits are symbolic, as when the employees of Delta Air Lines gave the airline an airplane during tough economic times. In a similar case, the 480 employees of Piggly Wiggly Carolina, a Charleston, South Carolina, grocery store and distributing business, conceived and organized the $40,000 "Rig for the Pig" campaign. Ninety-eight percent of the employees participated, voluntarily contributing two days' pay. In the end, they raised $7,000 more than was needed to buy the tractor-trailer truck they gave to the company.

## PUBLIC RELATIONS' ROLE

The public relations function, providing the communications channel between employers and employee groups, is important on both sides of the relationship. Practitioners are called on to participate more or less continuously in four phases of an employee's work experience:

- **The start.** For example, recruiting programs or help-wanted advertising, orientation sessions, tours, or kits of information.
- **On-the-job working conditions.** For example, employee publications, bulletin boards, feedback systems, training meetings, morale boosters, surveys of attitudes, complaint sessions, and teleconferencing.
- **Rewards and recognition.** For example, award programs, implementation of employee participation in civic affairs, staging of political science or economic

education events, old-timers' parties, open houses, wage increases or bonuses, promotions, annual reports to employees, and so on.
- **Work stoppage or termination.** For example, communications in a strike, layoff, or boycott problem, news about benefits for retires, a retiree publication. Projects to help laid-off employees relocate, or exit interviews.

In carrying out duties related to these four phases, the public relations people are usually teamed up with the human resources department in a large organization. In small organizations, all the duties related to employee relations and communication may be vested in one functionary, public relations or personnel.

No matter who is assigned the duties, the responsibility is as communicator, interpreter, and persuader for the employer. The duties include feedback of employee opinion and ideas as a guide to management. So public relations practices are the fulcrum of a two-way relationship-building and communication system, and therefore must earn the trust of the employees.

## RULES OF EFFECTIVE EMPLOYEE RELATIONS

Although a variety of tools are available to accomplish employee–employer communications, five basic principles prevail as guidelines for the practitioner:

1. **Employees must be told first.** Employees should be the first to be told information affecting them and their jobs; they should be told directly by the employer. The relationship is adversely affected when employees learn from outside sources about matters that affect them. If this happens, two-way trust is jeopardized. As a practical matter, external sources cannot do as complete a job of informing employees as the employer can. The grapevine is one of the worst possible sources in the eyes of employees, even though it ranks as high as No. 2 in actuality, according to a recent survey. News media as a source are just as bad.

2. **Tell the bad news along with the good.** All too often, organizations exploit internal news channels to report only "good" news, usually complimentary to the employer. That practice wears thin. The tools and the messages lose credibility. Motives become suspect. Employees look to other sources, such as unions and the grapevine, for a more balanced, objective perspective. Revealing good and bad news, openly and candidly, builds trust, common purpose, and productivity.

3. **Ensure timeliness.** Information important to employees has the same obsolescence as news of other kinds. Getting it out fast and accurately builds dialogue and trust. Delay opens the door to sources with half-truths, distortions, and bias unfavorable to the employer. Delay is the cause of most rumors, and, once started, rumors are difficult to dislodge. The employer's task is to be the first and most reliable source for employees. To do or be otherwise puts, and keeps, an employer on the defensive with those on whom the organization depends most for its success.

4. **Employees must be informed on subjects they consider important.** Years of studying employees' views of communication within their organizations reveal specific items they want to know about—often quite different from what

**TABLE 3-1 Subjects of Interest to Employees Change Little**

| Rank | Subject |
|------|---------|
| 1 | Organizational plans for the future |
| 2 | Job advancement opportunities |
| 3 | Job-related "how-to" information |
| 4 | Productivity improvement |
| 5 | Personnel policies and practices |
| 6 | How we're doing vs. the competition |
| 7 | How my job fits into the organization |
| 8 | How external events affect my job |
| 9 | How profits are used |
| 10 | Financial results |
| 11 | Advertising and promotional plans |
| 12 | Operations outside of my department or division |
| 13 | Organizational stand on current issues |
| 14 | Personnel changes and promotions |
| 15 | Organizational community involvement |
| 16 | Human interest stories about other employees |
| 17 | Personal news (birthdays, anniversaries, and so on) |

management thinks they want to know about (or *ought* to be told). The list has changed very little during the 30 years such research has been conducted. The chart in Table 3-1 summarizes biennial studies conducted in the 1980s (and updated in the 1990s) by the International Association of Business Communicators and Towers, Perrin, Forster & Crosby, a consulting firm specializing in internal relations (also known as the IABC-TPFC studies). Respondents were asked to rank subjects they want to read about on a scale of 1 to 10, with 1 being highest.

5. **Use the media that employees trust.** The IABC-TPFC studies also replicate others in telling the sources from which workers want to receive information. In order, they are:

   1. Immediate supervisor
   2. Small group meetings
   3. Top executives
   4. Large group meetings
   5. Employee handbook or other booklets
   6. Orientation program
   7. Regular local employee publication
   8. Bulletin boards
   9. Annual report to employees
   10. Regular general employee publication
   11. Upward communication programs

12. Audiovisual programs
13. Union
14. Mass media
15. Grapevine

Employees were asked in the above study which were their *actual* information sources, as opposed to this listing of *preferred* sources. Two were far out of line: *grapevine*, last on the preferred source list, was ranked second as an actual source; *bulletin boards*, number eight in preference, in actuality ranked third.

Participants in a 1999 communications study by IABC and Watson Wyatt cite e-mail as the most frequently used communications tool now (90 percent). But it is not a magic communications pill, according to the study. It received a low (55 percent) effectiveness rating. Clutter is a factor in its ineffectiveness. Employees receive a significant number of e-mails each day, both business and personal. An organization cannot be sure its employees are really taking the time to process and understand their electronic messages.

Using a focused communication strategy that combines a mix of methods and tools brings the most success, finds the study. This mix includes in-person meetings, printed newsletters, intranets, open-door policies, and e-mail.

- Key strategy is face-to-face interchanges, with managers and supervisors seen as communication links first and foremost—not only from the top down and the bottom up, but also laterally (between departments and work groups). Consequently, public relations departments often must coach and train supervisors and managers in interpersonal communication skills.

## FRONTLINE SUPERVISORS AS THE KEY COMMUNICATORS

The source employees most want to receive information from is their immediate or frontline supervisor—the most effective vehicle for communicating with employees, according to the previous list. Frontline supervisors are trusted and therefore more believable.

The communication process that passes information from top management down to employees through their immediate supervisors is sometimes called *cascading meetings*. It involves:

- Providing resources and training for frontline supervisors to relay information to their direct reports
- Giving supervisors advance notice and in-depth and meaningful information to share with employees
- Making subject matter experts available to immediately answer questions

This process helps relationship building within the management team. Supervisors get information in a timelier manner and feel more plugged into what's going on. And messages are delivered face-to-face to all employees in 24 hours using this process—which beats both the news media and the grapevine.

## TRUST IS ESSENTIAL

Trust directly impacts an organization's success and profits.[1] It contributes to job satisfaction, which leads to effectiveness, financial strength, competitiveness, and productivity. Trust must start with initiatives from the top.

If we look at organizations realistically, it is apparent that the most important people are those at the bottom—the frontliners. They make the product, deliver the service, sell the goods, and provide essential support mechanisms. In short, they more than anyone *are* the organization.

If, as shown in the diagram, you draw a line above the frontline supervisors (whether called team leaders, managers, or whatever), everyone above the line is overhead. The top of the pyramid is cost, not income generating. Those positions exist to support what the frontliners do.

Therefore, if management wants to earn trust, it must acknowledge this, and then formulate policies and processes that prove and continually symbolize it to the frontliners.

There are six components of trust:

1. **Openness.** Good news and bad must be shared with employees or they may suspect secrecy and conspiracy. Divulge plans in a timely fashion explaining the "whys."
2. **Shared values.** Management must share its vision with all employees and encourage employees to offer theirs.
3. **Consistency of words and actions.** Consistent treatment of all employees as well as consistency between management's words and actions are needed.
4. **Appreciation.** Management must show appreciation for employees' commitment to the organization.
5. **Feedback.** Employees' input must be solicited and considered, allowing them to speak out with impunity. Often, trouble stems from executives believing theirs is the only workable way.
6. **Autonomy.** Management must give employees respect, allowing them to work independently and monitor their own performance without breathing down their necks.

---

[1] According to a study by the International Association of Business Communicators, "Measuring Organizational Trust: A Diagnostic Survey & International Indicator." More information from 800-776-4222 or e-mail service_center@iabc.com.

# COMMUNICATING THROUGH TECHNOLOGY: PROS AND CONS

The convenience and speed of technology make it an alluring communication medium, but it needs to be used wisely. Once awareness has been created—preferably by face-to-face communication where possible—technology (e-mail, Internet, and intranet sites) is useful for reinforcing the message.

The advantages of technology include a quick way to give and get feedback, which shortens the communication cycle time, convenient information storage and retrieval, reduced communication costs, a flatter corporate hierarchy when an employee with an idea or concern can share it directly with an individual (from a senior manager to an immediate supervisor) without having the message reviewed and filtered by others, and the ability to collaborate with others. It allows people on different floors, different time zones, and different continents to have immediate access to working documents and data.

On the negative side it's impersonal and increases the risk of dehumanizing relationships; it's generally done quickly, even impulsively, and thus increases the likelihood for misunderstanding; it's a pull medium, which means the receiver must want it and seek it; information security is still a big concern for many; and often it is not *information mapped* (a visual layout that makes text easy to read and understand, reduces long paragraphic text to bite-sized chunks bulleted for easy scanning, and offers a source for more details).

The main impact of technology, as one PR firm CEO put it, is "speed without analysis, data without wise interpretation."[2]

---

### TRUSTWORTHINESS NOW MEANS HOLDING BACK NOTHING

Public relations counselor Bruce Harrison advises in dealing with key publics such as employees, it's not enough to just communicate honestly. Organizations are finding that in order to foster trust, they must be entirely open and show all evidence, a method called "transparent communication." Organizations need to let constituents know,

- Here's how we're making the decision. Here are the facts that led us to make this decision.

- Here are the options. Let's look at them together so you can help us make the decision.

- We believe we're being forthright and candid but you judge for yourself. Here are the data. What do you think?

Intranets are one way to implement this strategy with employees. Minutes of meetings, policies, plans and strategies, financial results, and other data are posted there for any interested employee.

This type of policy is the key for any organization to be considered trustworthy today.

*Source: pr reporter* Vol. 35 No. 36, September 21, 1992, p. 3.

---

[2]*pr reporter's* 30th Annual Survey of the Profession. Vol. 41 No. 38. September 28, 1998.

## REFERENCES AND ADDITIONAL READINGS

Bailey, John, and Richard Bevan. "Employee Communication." Chapter 12 in *Lesly's Handbook of Public Relations and Communications*. 5th ed. Chicago, IL: NTC Business Books, 1998.

Barr, Stephen. "Smile! You're on Corporate TV." *Communication World* 8 (September 1991): 28–31.

Beer, Michael, Russell Eisenstat, and Bert Spector. "Why Change Programs Don't Produce Change." *Harvard Business Review* (November/December 1990): 158–166.

Brody, E. W. *Communicating for Survival*. New York: Praeger, 1987.

Casarez, Nicole B. "Electronic Mail and Employee Relations: Why Privacy Must Be Considered." *Public Relations Quarterly* 37 (Summer 1992): 37–40.

Cutlip, Scott, Allen Center, and Glen Broom. "Media for Internal Publics." Chapter 9 in *Effective Public Relations*. 8th ed. Upper Saddle River, NJ: Prentice Hall, 1999.

Davids, Meryl. "Labor Shortage Woes: How Practitioners Are Helping Companies Cope." *Public Relations Journal* 44 (November 1988).

Drucker, Peter. "The Responsible Worker." Chapter 21 in *Management: Tasks, Responsibilities, Practices*. New York: Harper and Row, 1974.

Friedman, Thomas L. *The World Is Flat: A Brief History of the Twenty-First Century*. New York: Farrar, Straust Giroux, 2006, p. 15.

Herman, Roger, and Joyce Gioia. *How to Become an Employer of Choice*. Winchester, VA: Oakhill Press, 2000.

Holtz, Shel. *Public Relations on the Net*. New York: AMACOM, 1999.

Pfeffer, Jeffrey. *The Human Equation: Building Profits by Putting People First*. Boston. MA: Harvard Business School Press, January 1998.

*pr reporter Special Report: A Probing Look at Employee Relations Today: How to Shape World-Class Internal Relationships and Communications*. Exeter, NH: PR Publishing, 1998.

*pr reporter* Vol. 42 No. 29 (July 26, 1999). "'Are You Being Served?' Study Finds Employee Politeness Is Huge Determinant of Customer Loyalty, as PR Has Insisted."

*pr reporter* Vol. 42 No. 1 (January 4, 1999). "In an Era of Mistrust and Skepticism, Making Your Organization One People Can Trust Is the Ultimate Differentiator."

*pr reporter* Vol. 40 No. 15 (April 14, 1997). "The Psychology of Customer Delight: PR's Vital Role."

*pr reporter* Vol. 39 No. 34 (August 26, 1996). "Some Metrics on How Well Employee Participation Pays Off."

*pr reporter* Vol. 37 No. 21 (May 23, 1994). "Action Research Unites Staff and Management in Satisfying Customers."

*pr reporter* Vol. 36 No. 40 (October 11, 1993). "Communication, PR Ideas Drive Unique Re-Engineering Plan"—An outstanding case study that puts all the organizational trends together.

*pr reporter* Vol. 34 No. 49 (December 16, 1991). "PR's Role in Culture Change."

*pr reporter* Vol. 32 No. 34 (August 28, 1989). "Survey Finds Trust in Management Translates into Quality."

Skutski, Karl. "Conducting a Total Quality Communications Audit." *Public Relations Journal*, April 1992, 20–32.

Smith, Alvie. *Innovative Employee Communication: New Approaches to Improving Trust, Teamwork and Performance*. Upper Saddle River, NJ: Prentice Hall, 1991.

-------------------------------------C A S E S-------------------------------------

# Case 3-1   Investing in Employees Pays Off

Aaron Feuerstein, president of Malden Mills, celebrated his 70th birthday at a family party on the evening of December 11, 1995. At the same time, less than 30 miles away, his factory exploded into flames. By midnight, a company official summoned Feuerstein to the scene. At stake was the future of more than 3,000 employees and their families. What happened within the next 72 hours are the guts and the glory of this story.

Feuerstein and his management team needed effective crisis management and immediate communication to tap into the company's reservoir of employee goodwill. In a business environment of layoffs, mergers, and downsizing, it was assumed that a fire of this magnitude would bring an end to an era for Malden Mills. But that was not the Feuerstein way of doing business, nor had it been in the 90 years since his grandfather began the business in the mill town of Lawrence, Massachusetts.

## History of the Mill

Malden Mills is a family owned and operated mill situated on the riverbanks of Lawrence, Massachusetts. During the Industrial Revolution, the Merrimack River was home to many textile factories. Over the years, and as technology progressed, most of these mills were abandoned for areas with cheaper labor. Feuerstein, contrary to the trend of cutting labor costs to increase profits, moved into those empty mills. "It depends on your vision of business," was his comment.

## Feuerstein's Vision of Business: Employees Are Assets

Feuerstein is a devout Jew and his belief drives his decision making. A cornerstone of his thinking is a 2,000-year-old saying from the Jewish tradition: When everything is moral chaos, try your hardest to be a "mensch"— a man of highest principles. Malden Mills had no board of directors or shareholders. Feuerstein answered to his own belief system, and its wisdom was apparent:

- In 1980, Malden Mills declared Chapter 11 bankruptcy and laid off workers. Research and development was aggressively pushed—making an investment in brand equity. Out of this came the discovery of the lightweight, resilient, wool-like fabrics under the brand names Polarfleece® and Polartec®. This put Malden Mills back in business. Feuerstein *hired back every worker* he had let go after the bankruptcy.
- Feuerstein knows the correlation between loyal employees and loyal customers. Customer retention at Malden Mills Ran roughly 95 percent, which is world class.[1]
- Major retailers such as L.L. Bean, Eddie Bauer, Lands' End, Patagonia, and North Face carry the Malden Mills products not just as a picture in a catalog but with a history of the product and the company line itself.
- Malden Mills is a union shop and has long invested heavily in technology that eliminates jobs, but *has never had a strike.*

[1]Thomas Teal, "Not a Fool, Not a Saint," *Fortune*, November 11, 1996, Vol. 134 No. 9, pp. 201–203.

## Employment at the Mill Prior to December 1995

Armed with new upscale product lines, Malden Mills flourished. Aaron Feuerstein, at the helm, geared up for plant expansion. Employees were happy with their wage and benefit package. An average employee received about $3 per hour more than at similar plants—with full benefits.[2] Employees were given annual bonuses in addition to other benefits. From 1982 to 1995, revenues in constant dollars more than tripled while workforces barely doubled.[3]

## December 11, 1995—The Night of the Fire

Prior to the fire, the Malden Mills complex had nine functioning buildings. While the mills were poised to receive new and updated machinery, none of the current workforce was to be displaced. In a matter of hours, the fire leveled three of the nine buildings within the Malden Mills complex. A fourth was saved by the heroic efforts of employees and firefighters on the scene. No one was killed, however, 33 were injured. Some 1,800 of the 3,200 workers were temporarily displaced less than three weeks before Christmas.

## December 13, 1995—Less Than 48 Hours Later

In the local high school gymnasium, Feuerstein announced to his employees, and local and national media, that employee salaries and benefits, as well as holiday bonuses, would be paid. For 90 days the salaries of the displaced workers were paid; benefits continued for 6 months. He also assured them they would be called back to work. Plant reconstruction would begin immediately.

In repeated surveys, *the number 1 topic of interest to employees is organizational plans for the future.*[4] At Malden Mills, employees received this desired information. They knew where they stood and that they were a vital part of Feuerstein's decision to rebuild. He followed the four basic principles of employer–employee communications: (1) tell employees first, (2) tell the bad news along with the good, (3) ensure timeliness, and (4) inform employees on subjects they consider important.[5]

Media both lauded and mocked Feuerstein's decision. Was this man crazy? Or was he shrewd and calculating with a self-serving motive? In the days of massive and cold-hearted downsizing—AT&T had experienced 44,000 layoffs and IBM had over 100,000 layoffs—why didn't this 70-year-old man take the money and run? Feuerstein's comment: "What kind of an ethic is it that a CEO is prepared to hurt 3,000 people who are his employees and an entire city of many more thousands . . . in order for him to have a short-term gain? It's unthinkable."

## Corporate Conscience Brings Free Publicity

News of this event spread as quickly as the fire in the mills. Stories of his plans ran in many newspapers and magazines across the country. Feuerstein was invited to the 1996 Presidential State of the Union address. Post-fire publicity created an element of goodwill among consumers, increasing demand and building loyalty.

---

[2]Richard Jerome, "Holding the Line: After Fire Wrecked His Mill, Aaron Feuerstein Didn't Let His Workers Down," *People Weekly*, February 5, 1996, Vol. 45 No. 5.
[3]Teal, 201–203.
[4]See Chapter 3, page 26.
[5]See Chapter 3, page 25.

In 2001, aware of the goodwill generated by Feuerstein's actions, the Malden Mills story was presented in ads with Feuerstein as the spokesman surrounded by his employees.

## The Payoff

In the long run, Malden Mills' worldwide business grew 40 percent from pre-fire levels.[6] In less than two years, all but a handful of the original 1,800 displaced employees were back on the factory floor. "Customer and employee retention at Malden Mills runs roughly 95 percent."[7] The percentage of off-quality products went from 6 to 7 percent pre-fire to 2 percent post-fire.[8] Once the fourth plant, which wasn't completely destroyed in the fire, was up and running, Feuerstein walked among the employees. All present shared tears and thank yous. Employees promised to pay him back "tenfold." Before the fire, that plant produced 130,000 yards per week. After the fire, production increased to 200,000+ per week, clearly the result of employee goodwill. In the past decade, Malden Mills has grown 200 percent with sales over $300 million a year and customers in more than 50 countries.

Malden Mills is a symbol of heroics. As one practitioner recently said, "I feel good wearing my Polartec jacket knowing how that man treats his employees." That kind of **customer loyalty is earned**, not sold.

The goodwill Malden Mills banked from the fire continued to pay dividends in late 2001 when the company sought bankruptcy protection. The loss of customers after the fire (they had to sign contracts elsewhere in the interim) and three warm winters hurt sales. The company was $140 million dollars in debt. However, lenders did not seek to liquidate the company, which was an option available to creditors. The goodwill continued to pay off when in 2004 Malden Mills hired a new president and CEO to run its day-to-day operations. The U.S. Government continues to be a major customer for Malden Mills' Polartec® garments, supporting Malden Mills through Department of Defense research contracts on combat clothing. ∎

---

## QUESTIONS FOR DISCUSSION

1. Discuss the elements of an employee communications plan and how it impacted the decisions Feuerstein made.
2. What steps would have been taken had he decided not to rebuild the factory?
3. How would the closing of the mills have impacted the branding that occurred after the fire?
4. If you were the public relations director, what would you have suggested be done differently?
5. What would you recommend be done to ensure continued high levels of employee satisfaction?
6. How might this have been handled differently if it was a shareholder-owned organization? What would you recommend to management in that case to achieve similar outcomes?

---

[6]Julie K. Hall, "Malden Climbs Up from the Ashes," *Times Mirror Magazines, Inc.*, STN, Vol. 22, No. 2, p. 7.
[7]Teal, 201–203.
[8]Shelly Donald-Coolidge, " 'Corporate Decency' Prevails at Malden Mills," *The Christian Science Monitor*, March 28, 1996.

# Case 3-2   Southwest Airlines—Where Fun, LUV, and Profit Go Hand-in-Hand

Making customers happy is the number one priority at Southwest Airlines. Although this goal might not seem unusual in the highly competitive U.S. economy, the primary method of reaching it—through employee satisfaction—is innovative. By developing strong relationships with its employees, Southwest has pleased its customers and fueled its growth—from a three-destination, short-haul Texas airline to the fourth largest airline in the United States (in terms of passengers carried).

## A Turbulent Beginning

In 1966, Rollin King, a San Antonio entrepreneur who owned a small commuter service, and his banker, John Parker, noted how expensive and inconvenient it was to travel between Houston, Dallas, and San Antonio—areas that were in the midst of strong economic and population growth. King approached Herb Kelleher, then one of his San Antonio lawyers, with an idea, and the three men researched the feasibility of the proposal.

By early 1967, Kelleher filed papers to incorporate Air Southwest Co. King and Kelleher raised the initial capital and political support for the venture. Kelleher was prepared for political and legal battles with established Texan airlines, but he didn't realize the length to which they would have to go to get their planes in the air.

Established airlines, contending that the market was saturated, filed lawsuits to stop Southwest, and a restraining order was granted. Southwest appealed the case to the Supreme Court of Texas and was granted a reprieve, only to be slapped with another suit. Four years later, after many restraining orders, appeals, and court cases, Southwest was finally able to take off. Unfortunately, most of its capital was gone, spent fighting for the chance to exist.

## Time to Fly—With Limited Resources

By the time it was ready to fly, Southwest had just four planes and fewer than 70 employees. The new airline was forced to set outrageously low fares—unheard of in the industry—to attract customers. Feeling threatened, the competition matched Southwest's fares, forcing the new airline to reduce prices even more. At one point, Southwest management was unable to make payroll and was forced to decide whether to lay employees off or sell a plane.

It was a turning point for the company, setting a foundation for its future: Management chose to put employees first. In return for not laying off a single employee, Southwest asked employees to master the "10-minute turn" so the airline could keep the same flight schedule it had planned with four airplanes. A plane would arrive at an airport, deliver passengers, refuel, and prepare the plane for departure of another flight—in 10 minutes.

- The faster the turnaround, the lower the operating costs, the more flights that can be achieved in one day, the lower the fare.
- This means employees must be exceptionally motivated.

An article in *Chief Executive Magazine*[1] points to this event as the foundation

---

[1]*Chief Executive Magazine*, July 1, 1999.

of Southwest's success: "The tradition of Southwest employees, from pilots to ramp agents, pitching in to do what's necessary to help the company, was born."

## Discovering the Key to Success

From its earliest days, the company has incorporated a focus on fun and love—for both passengers and employees—into its unique management style. Southwest flight attendants dress casually in khakis and polo shirts. Pilots wear WWII–era replica leather jackets. Comfortably dressed employees are happier and more relaxed, which leads to happier and more relaxed passengers. Luv Nuts are served instead of meals on shorter flights and have become a company symbol for in-flight fun.

Passengers on a Southwest flight might hear flight safety instructions in the form of a song—sung by one of the flight attendants—if a particular employee feels like singing. One employee sang Happy Birthday to a passenger, Elvis style, over the public address system.[2] This relaxed and open working environment has encouraged customer service agents to hold holiest sock contests and to encourage passengers to make faces at ground crews while waiting to board the plane.

This behavior may seem unprofessional to an employee of a traditional airline. But the employee who would look down on these antics is exactly the type of person Southwest does not want to hire. "We look for a sense of humor, a sense of service," says Colleen Barrett, president and chief operating officer and chairman Kelleher's right-hand woman. "We don't care if you're the best pilot in the USAF, but if you condescend to a secretary, you won't get hired."[3]

The positive corporate culture starts at the top at Southwest. Kelleher once heard that mechanics on the graveyard shift couldn't attend the company picnic, so he held a late night barbecue, which featured him and pilots as chefs. Kelleher or Barrett personally send notes to employees for births, deaths, marriages, and promotions. (More than 1,000 husband–wife teams work for Southwest.)

Management's generosity extends beyond employees to customers. Kelleher once read a letter from a teacher whose students had never been on a plane. He invited the entire class to fly to Austin for free for a tour of the capital.[4]

Southwest management firmly believes that employees who genuinely care about each other and the company take extra steps to ensure customer satisfaction. Along with the ideal of hard work, Southwest executives want employees to conduct business in a loving and understanding manner.

Southwest offers employees competitive wages and benefits and in 1974 was the first airline to offer a profit-sharing plan. Employees now own 13 percent of the company's common stock. The company contributes 16 percent of its pretax operating income to its profit-sharing plan.[5]

## An Educated Employee Is a Valuable Team Member

The more employees know about their corporation, the better equipped they are to provide valuable input. To encourage a better understanding among employees of the various functions of the company, Southwest implemented the Walk a Mile program. Through the program, Southwest employees experience issues of other departments, which facilitates a company-wide understanding of the many airline functions and what it takes to be profitable. This encourages effective

[2]Kitchen, Patricia, *Newsday*, March 7, 1999.
[3]*Chief Executive Magazine*, July 1, 1999.
[4]*Chief Executive Magazine*, July 1, 1999.
[5]*Chief Executive Magazine*, July 1, 1999.

communication and real teamwork, which is especially important among pilots and ground and flight crews.

The Culture Committee, formed in 1990, aims to continually reinforce the "Southwest Spirit." With representatives from all areas of the company, from flight crews to executives, committee members promote the ideals of profitability, low cost, family, and fun.

## Behavior Affects the Bottom Line

All of these behaviors may satisfy employees and make great material for news articles. But when it comes to the bottom line, does this dynamic management style motivate employee behaviors that really pay off for Southwest? After all, the company is in business to make a profit.

- *Southwest posted seven consecutive years of record profits.*

In early the 2000s, when major airlines were filing for bankruptcy and upstart independents such as Southeast and Independence were folding, Southwest was one of the only profitable airlines. The airline won the U.S. Department of Transportation's "Triple Crown" awards for best on-time performance, fewest customer complaints, and fewest mishandled bags. It has maintained the best cumulative baggage handling record among all major U.S. airlines since September 1987 when the Department of Transportation began tracking and reporting these statistics. In addition, Southwest[6]:

- Was profitable for 28 consecutive years, a period that included two major industry downturns.
- Has the most enviable profit record in the industry, with the smallest number

of employees per aircraft and the most customers served per employee.

- Since 1972, it has been an outstanding investment. An investment of $10,000 in 1972 would have been worth more than $12 million in 2005.
- Received over 225,000 resumes in 2000; hired 1,700 new employees, bringing the total number of employees to over 30,000.
- Planes have a turnaround of approximately 20 minutes, even with today's airline growth, carry-on luggage, and airport congestion.
- Has ranked number one in fewest customer complaints for the last nine consecutive years.

Southwest's focus on employee satisfaction has enabled it to deliver on customer satisfaction and, as a result, excel in an increasingly competitive industry. Such satisfaction enables companies like Southwest to weather difficult times as well. For example, in 2005 a Southwest plane suffered an uncommon crash at Chicago's Midway Airport, skidding off a runway and into a passing car. In a subsequent story in *USA Today*, Southwest was complimented on its handling of the situation by crisis communication experts: "Southwest's safety record has been a major selling point," said one. "Any company that creates a cushion of goodwill with all its stakeholders before a crisis occurs will survive a crisis better than a company that hasn't done that in advance. And nobody has done a better job of that in the country than Southwest."[7]

Perhaps a better compliment came from competitor Northwest Airlines. In a 2005 *Orlando Sentinel* article, a consumer-advocate columnist was wrapping up the best and worst performances of the just-ending year. The best response came from

---

[6]Kitchen, Patricia, *Newsday*, March 7, 1999, and Southwest's Web site.
[7]*USA Today*, "Southwest's 'Goodwill' Should Keep Fliers," December 12, 2005, p. 3B.

## THE MISSION OF SOUTHWEST AIRLINES

The mission of Southwest Airlines is dedication to the highest quality of Customer Service delivered with a sense of warmth, friendliness, individual pride, and Company Spirit.

### TO OUR EMPLOYEES

We are committed to provide our Employees a stable work environment with equal opportunity for learning and personal growth. Creativity and innovation are encouraged for improving the effectiveness of Southwest Airlines. Above all, Employees will be provided the same concern, respect, and caring attitude within the organization that they are expected to share externally with every Southwest Customer.

Southwest, which was involved in a fare-rebate discussion with a disappointed customer. Quoting a Southwest spokesperson, "Perhaps we didn't provide the correct information to (the customer) or perhaps she didn't know the correct way to ask for what she needed. Regardless of how it happened, we will quickly correct the situation and make sure (the customer) gets the refund she desires." Nominated for "worst response" by the columnist was Northwest Airlines, which, after denying a customer's request, said "Well, we're not Southwest Airlines."[8] ■

---

## QUESTIONS FOR DISCUSSION

1. In a tight labor market, it can be tough to find experienced employees—let alone ones that are willing to incorporate love and fun into their jobs. As manager of employee communications for Southwest, you are asked by the director of human resources to develop a recruiting plan using existing employees. What are some strategies you might suggest?

2. How would you handle the following situation: You are working late one evening in Southwest's media relations office and receive a phone call from the police. It appears two Southwest employees were robbed on airport grounds. How will you respond to:

   - Reporters questioning the company's ground security?
   - Employees' concerns with safety?
   - Calls for information from the victims' families?

---

[8]*Orlando Sentinel*, "The Good, the Bad, and the Truly Lame," December 30, 2005, p. 1E.

# Case 3-3  Creating a Collaborative, Employee-Driven Vision for the Future: Atlantic Southeast Airlines*

Typically, a CEO articulates an institution's vision. The CEO might involve senior management in the process or put together a team of senior leaders and consultants to wordsmith their ideas, but the final product nine times out of ten, comes down from the top. Many argue that this is what leadership is about and how it should be done.

Atlantic Southeast Airlines (ASA), an Atlanta–based regional airline formerly owned by Delta Air Lines, chose to do it differently, taking the unusual approach of involving employees from the ground up in the revision of the company's vision and guiding principles. Management's rationale was that *"all members of the company would 'own' the vision . . . would understand the guiding principles so well that they could easily apply them to their own roles in the workplace."*

## Situation Analysis

ASA, originally formed by three visionaries in 1979, became a wholly owned subsidiary of Delta Air Lines in 1999. The airline immediately laid out a five-year plan with the goal of becoming, in its words, "the best regional airline." At the helm was President Skip Barnette, a 29-year Delta veteran who had spent seven and a half years of his career as a "ramper," loading bags as the first rung on his corporate ladder. He knew

the business from the ground up, and he knew that empowering his people was the key to success.

By 2004, ASA's 25th year in business, the company had experienced rapid growth, an influx of new employees, and was in the middle of a tremendous culture shift. With these changes came the typical "growing pains": communication breakdowns between work teams, the need for technological upgrades to operate more efficiently; and stressed employees attempting to keep up with all the changes. Adding to the complications was the struggle of working under a parent company with a very different culture (Delta) while trying to maintain a separate identity and culture as a regional airline.

Barnette saw this as the perfect time to launch an updated vision and set of guiding principles, with the help and input of employees. He also saw an opportunity to simultaneously evaluate communications company-wide and involve employees in finding solutions for improvements.

## Research First: Two-Way Communication in Process

ASA's corporate communications department worked closely with behavioral public relations and research consultants to design research that would:

---

*Thank you to Deborah Nash of ASA Airlines, Kent Landers and Gina Pesko Laughlin of Delta Air Lines (formerly of ASA), and Robin Schell of Jackson Jackson & Wagner for their insight and work on this case.

- Improve communications
- Engage new employees while "re-engaging" seasoned employees
- Gauge employee morale
- Improve the current rewards and recognition system
- Lay the groundwork for the revision of the company's vision and guiding principles

A series of 25 focus group sessions involving every employee group—from pilots to gate agents to mechanics—enabled facilitators to talk personally with over 150 employees. Supervisors helped to identify potential focus group participants. Those candidates then received an invitation letter from President Barnette, a symbolic communication that stressed the importance of the research. Sessions were held in five of the airline's main facilities, which were selected specifically for their geographic distribution, hot spots, access from other facilities (so employees could come in for a group), and employee schedules. This meant facilitating some group discussions at 9 P.M. for the mechanics checking in on the night shift. This was another symbolic communication—making the group discussions accessible and doing them on the employees' home turf, if possible. In addition, consultants interviewed 21 managers one-on-one.

The goal for both the focus groups and the one-on-one discussions was going *beyond problem identification to solutions.* Participants could vent about what was wrong, but then they had to really think about how to *fix* the problems. Each group yielded dozens of suggestions for improving communication and motivating job performance.

Finally, the consultants did a third-party review of all written communication, including a review of ASA's Web site and intranet. They also reviewed existing research to identify trends to explore in conversations with employees.

## What Makes ASA Special: Identifying the USP

Employees identified many communication issues typical to a company in rapid-growth mode. Supervisors were overloaded, causing communication breakdowns. All employees were experiencing one-way communication overload; plenty of information was received, but it wasn't always understood. Employees appreciated the opportunity to give feedback and participate in two-way communication forums and wanted more of it. Lateral communication systems were weak. This meant that there were fewer opportunities to communicate and understand overall goals such as "on-time arrivals" from everyone's perspective and more tendencies to participate in the "blame game" (it's the pilot's fault because . . . ).

Employees could see that a shift from command-and-control style management to an open and participatory culture was happening, but more progress needed to be made. They talked openly about the rewards and recognition program, identifying simple motivators, such as "notes from supervisors," "new uniforms," and "meals on holidays," and urged systems that recognized team performance as well as individual performance. For a holiday, ASA management had sent around a company-wide "thank you" with a box of cookies for each employee. In almost every focus group, this came up as an example of how employees *didn't* want to be thanked: *"We don't need two 50-cent cookies in a $3 box!"*

Employees were in universal agreement about the things that made ASA different and special, or its USP (Unique Selling Proposition). Across the board, they talked about having pride in their work and the ability to "change on a dime" to get things done efficiently and effectively. They talked about the ASA family, the loyalty they felt for ASA, and the passion they felt for the work they did. They talked about their ability to deliver personalized service; flight attendants gave examples of knowing their regular customers by name. These comments served as the foundation for the newly adopted vision and guiding principles.

## The Power of Feedback and Immediate Action

The senior management team received a briefing from the consultants on their overall findings and recommendations just three weeks after the last focus groups were completed. From there, findings were carried back to the *individual work groups* so those divisions and work teams could immediately begin making improvements. A few examples:

- The company made *at-home intranet access* available within 60 days, addressing concerns of timeliness and access for its transient workforce.
- The CEO began making *regular visits to the pilots' lounge* and appearing on the night shift, becoming more accessible and visible to those employees with an irregular work schedule.
- Various divisions adopted *rewards and recognition programs* to supplement the corporate reward program. These

ranged from Wal-Mart gift cards to lunches brought in for winning teams.

- ASA implemented a *cross-divisional shadow program*, so a gate agent could shadow a baggage-handler, and vice versa, to get a better understanding of each other's jobs and the problem solving required.
- Mechanics finally got the *new, more functional uniforms* they wanted!
- ASA added more *two-way communication forums*, including "lunch with Skip" for a rotating cross-section of employees and "Ask the Manager" calls with members of the senior management teams.

## Building the New Vision and Guiding Principles

A cross-section of 12 ASA employees, including the CEO, supervisors, and frontline employees, spent a full day discussing the research results and articulating a revised vision statement and set of guiding principles. A testament to how well they did: Their draft was adopted by the senior management team with very few changes.

The draft then went back to *everyone who participated in the research* (newly identified opinion leaders), along with an update of the communication improvements that

**ASA *aspires* to be the most *trusted* and *respected* regional airline in the eyes of our customers, team members, shareholders and competitors by:**

- Showing every customer our passion for safety and personalized service
- Attracting and developing team members who contribute to the success of the ASA family
- Creating a fun and rewarding culture that recognizes the value of individuals and teamwork
- Being flexible and efficient in everything we do

**GUIDING PRINCIPLES**

- We all work as one team that serves our customers
- We take pride in our work and hold each other accountable
- We treat each other and our customers with dignity, trust and respect
- We listen and respond to each other and our customers
- We empower our people to make a difference
- We share ideas and involve team members in decisions
- We embrace the ability to question and challenge

*I'm Committed to ASA's Success!*

had been made since the focus groups two months ago. The focus groups brainstormed ways to make the rollout of these statements as visible and meaningful as possible.

## Strategy: Fall Rollout to Complement 25th Anniversary Activities

Because the summer was dedicated to celebrations of ASA's 25th anniversary, the senior management team purposely waited until the fall for the rollout of the new vision and guiding principles, piggybacking on a management meeting for the initial unveiling.

Because the old statements had been worn around the necks of employees on a lanyard, Corporate Communications recommended sticking with that behavior and added the additional step of having employees sign off on their cards to indicate they had read and understood it.

In addition to the lanyard cards, the following strategies and tools were developed:

- Regular *postings* on the Internet and ASA's intranet.
- *Adoption of "vision leaders"* who would keep the momentum going year round.

This idea came from focus group discussions and was piloted at the Baton Rouge facility, using such techniques as regular on-site recognition, bulletin boards acknowledging and honoring "vision" behaviors, and regular small-group discussions.

- An *employee video* featuring participants in the focus groups who described what the vision meant to them in their own words.
- A *manager briefing book* with talking points and likely questions and answers.
- *Vision Week* which was dedicated to discussions of the new vision.

## Outcomes

One year after the audit, an employee-engagement survey was conducted that included new questions based on the vision and guiding principles. Among the findings:

- **Over half** (53 percent) said they had had a discussion with their team about the vision.
- **Two-thirds** (66 percent) said that the new ASA vision reflects values that are important to them. ■

## QUESTIONS FOR DISCUSSION

1. What are some other ways you might have measured the *behavioral impact* of the communications audit research if you were a member of the Corporate Communications department?

2. One of the themes from the research was that ASA employees felt they were not always speaking with one voice because Delta Air Lines had such a different corporate culture. What are some strategies you might have put in place to help them with better and more seamless communication with their parent company, while still maintaining a unique identity?

3. In the research, employees talked about what was important to them as far as rewards and recognition. The case mentioned some of the ways that Corporate Communications changed the program to reward team efforts and thank people in meaningful ways. Most of these changes involved increased *internal recognition*. What programs or ideas do you have about ways to thank employees *externally*, involving the customers they are serving in the process?

4. What do you see as the pros and cons of building a vision/mission statement for an organization in this fashion? Would you recommend doing it the way ASA did or going with the more traditional top-down approach? Explain. What if your CEO wanted to promulgate his or her own vision? How would you present the alternative?

# Case 3-4   Kodak Communicates One-on-One with All of Its Employees*

The early 1990s were troubled times for Kodak. Pressed by changing technologies, international competition, and fickle consumer behavior, the Rochester, New York–based photo giant found itself struggling to maintain its legendary leadership in consumer photography.

In 1993, Kodak hired CEO George Fisher to lead a turnaround. He and his management team undertook an aggressive campaign to make Kodak more competitive and performance driven. The backbone of this campaign was a "one-on-one" communication strategy designed to increase morale and productivity. Kodak evolved this strategy of speaking one-on-one with its 100,000 employees around the globe to resolve a problem it uncovered in late 1994: Employees were unclear about what was expected of them and their business units during a time of rapid change.

Though Fisher got broad employee approval, opinion surveys showed employees were confused and unable to see the big picture. "It's obviously difficult to build a performance-based culture if we fail to share expectations for performance with those charged with delivering the results," Fisher said.

As a result, the decision was made that managers and supervisors throughout the organization would meet quarterly with their work groups for a face-to-face briefing. The idea was that if everyone was supposed to pull together in the same direction, they had to have an idea of where the company stood at points along the way and understand how their unit's goals tied in with those of the overall company.

Corporate performance information, including financial results as well as customer and employee satisfaction, would be communicated, providing a context for local unit information. These categories aligned with the company's three key publics: employees, customers, and shareholders. Managers, from Fisher on down, were supposed to align their personal and unit goals to contribute to company goals around these three measures. The briefings would also provide opportunities to educate employees and managers about significant business news and key performance indicators.

Two-way communication was key at this point as well, giving people the ability to ask questions. Today the program, called *Snapshots*, continues to bring supervisors and managers together with employees for regular face-to-face communication.[1]

Since its beginnings, the program has undergone a number of changes and enhancements to make it more user-friendly and dynamic and to keep it up-to-date. For example, after Fisher's tenure, content was changed to reflect goals that were relevant under the new CEO. In 2002, a total redesign added:

- Context about external economic and competitive trends
- Key goals/initiatives going forward

*Thank you to Christopher Veronda, manager of communications initiatives for Kodak for has invaluable assistance in the preparation of this case study.

[1]Snapshots comprises a PowerPoint file with talking points, along with a short (3–4 minutes) self-playing module highlighting corporate successes across the globe.

- Templates, so units could easily include local information
- Presenter talking points and transitions preprogrammed for the slides so the presentation was more "ready to use" by managers

Perhaps most important, more images and graphics were included in the presentation and the quarterly news section was replaced by a new feature: "Reasons to Believe." Probably the most popular and widely used feature of Snapshots, this section includes pictures and related news items about new Kodak products, awards, and major contracts. Good news related to Kodak's efforts in environmental, community, and employee programs also is included.

In the past few years, the company has been undergoing perhaps its biggest and most critical change as it transforms itself for the fast-paced digital imaging world. The Snapshots team continues to upgrade the presentation package to meet the changing needs of presenters and audience members.

For example, for the year-end 2005 package Reasons to Believe was reworked into a self-playing slide module with music (running about 3 minutes). It included the same news as included in the static slides, but gave presenters an upbeat way to end the Snapshots meeting. Early reaction was enthusiastic. In fact, Kodak's communicators in China converted the module to feature local successes.

### Research on the Importance of One-on-One Communication

Before beginning the snapshots program, Kodak completed extensive research, the results of which helped structure the effort. Some of the results included:

1. **Employees prefer direct interaction with supervisors**. Such interaction significantly increases understanding and reinforces the leadership responsibility of supervisors.

2. **Employee surveys revealed skepticism and lack of confidence** in Kodak managers, indicating a pressing need to rebuild their credibility both as messengers of company information and as leaders guiding the direction of change.

3. Two-thirds of production, technical, and clerical **employees relied on outside sources**, such as local news reports, for company information. The leading sources for professional employees were supervisors and the company newspaper. This is not atypical for the circumstances: Kodak is a big company in a relatively small city. Corporate news is big news and is covered heavily by the local media.

4. The communication roll-out of major benefit reductions in the fall of 1994 was an important test of the face-to-face approach. **For the first time, Kodak used direct management conversations to reach all U.S. employees with this news**.

5. Post roll-out surveys of nearly 3,000 employees showed that **84 percent felt the meetings were a good way to communicate this information and 74 percent understood why the changes were being made.** Just as important, the process helped put a face on local leadership throughout the company.

### Objectives of the Snapshots Program

The objectives of the Snapshots program are as follows:

1. Establish a communication infrastructure that helps employees see the big picture in a way that (1) fosters management credibility and (2) mitigates negative surprises.

2. Enable employees to understand Kodak performance expectations and act to achieve company objectives.

3. Clarify corporate and unit goals by answering "What does this mean to me?" and "What actions should I take?"
4. Stimulate regular, two-way symmetrical communication between supervisors and employees.

## How It's Done

The snapshots program includes the following components:

1. **Cross-disciplinary teams:** Employee communicators work with contacts in human resources, finance, corporate research, and Kodak business units to develop information for each package.
2. **Employee Communications creates the Snapshots package**, which includes briefing charts and bullet-point scripts, for managers worldwide. An Employee Communications team member creates all the charts in PowerPoint and works on the slideshow for the Reasons to Believe module. In recent years, more effort has been placed on providing a "news" section along with the standard measures for each quarter. The news section includes topics of worldwide interest/impact, for instance, Kodak's consumer digital strategy, introduction of Kodak's new president, an update on Kodak's online services business, and so on.
3. **Quick cycle time is a priority**, so briefing packages are prepared and approved within three days of receiving quarterly performance measures. The package is posted on the company's intranet, which is a big time and cost saver.
4. **Grassroots pull** is created by "watch-for" messages in Kodak's employee media.

5. **Managers/supervisors are expected to meet face-to-face with employees** to present Snapshots information, but they are given a high degree of discretion in how they choose to do this. In fact, managers are encouraged to make local news and activities a priority of the meeting.

## Results

Evaluation was built into the original process, including quarterly attendance reports and postmeeting employee opinion surveys. Key early findings included:

- **Attendance at voluntary briefings** went from 57 percent of employees to 81 percent in the first year. At many sites it approached 100 percent. These gains are a vote of confidence in the program. Five years into the program, 88 percent of employees attended a Snapshots session regularly or occasionally.
- **Communication survey results** have been strongly positive. Employees agreeing that Snapshots "helped me understand the company better" jumped from 71 percent in the first quarter to 81 percent by the second quarter. In 1999, 80 percent said the meetings provided useful information about the company's performance and 70 percent said the meetings helped them understand how Kodak is performing against its goals.
- **Opinion surveys** tracked gains in employee confidence in Kodak management. Employees agreeing "Kodak is well managed" jumped from 29 percent in 1994 to 49 percent at the end of 1995 a 20 percentage point increase. At Kodak Park, the principal manufacturing center, where attendance is among the highest in the company, the increase was 23 percentage points from 29 to 52 percent.

*Today evaluation is more anecdotal. With more than a decade of formal evaluations, Employee Communications is comfortable sending a note to gather current feedback.*

Kodak managers eagerly anticipate the regular Snapshots briefings. "I use the Snapshots material every quarter to have a group meeting with all (my) employees globally," says one Rochester–based manager. "The meeting also includes an update on our (division) organization. I think the corporate information is easy to understand and I do get to address questions from the group as a result of the information being shared. If people were unable to attend the meeting, they can see the Snapshots information and our group's update on our internal team room. The format is good."

Kodak's new focus has paid off in the marketplace as well. As of 2006, Kodak was the industry leader in digital camera sales in the United States and other key markets and first worldwide in home Snapshot printer sales. A year earlier (2005), Kodak's revenue from digital products comprised a majority of the company's business for the first time.

Profits, however, remain elusive in the highly competitive photography industry, but Kodak is continuing the face-to-face communication as a primary weapon. "One thing that has happened is that the CEO (now Antonio Perez) has spent time meeting with different employee groups" says Christopher Veronda, manager of communications initiatives for Kodak. He says, "In facing this challenge of transforming the company, face-to-face communication is more important than ever." ■

---

## QUESTIONS FOR DISCUSSION

1. In today's "wired" world, why is face-to-face communication a better option than a broadcast e-mail, fax, or voicemail?
2. How does effective communication affect morale?
3. How can a communication program address problems created by falling stock prices, dwindling market share, or even layoffs?
4. Do you see a correlation between the attendance at briefings and the people who say they have a better understanding of the company?
5. How would you prepare line supervisors to best communicate with those reporting to them?

## PROBLEM 3-A WHAT PRICE "GOOD" EMPLOYEE RELATIONS?

Safeplay, Inc., has competed in the sports and recreation equipment market for more than 25 years. The market is hotly contested.

One of the programs for employee morale and productivity long used by Safeplay has been the retention of former athletes of national repute on its payroll at each of its five manufacturing plants. Although the athletes are part of the personnel department staff, they are made available by the public relations department for news interviews, to conduct sports clinics at schools, and to sit on committees for newsworthy civic events.

One of the Safeplay plants is located in the small city of Westward, which has a population of 20,000 and is located on the outskirts of a metropolitan city. This plant, with an average of 900 employees, specializes in leather items such as baseball gloves, golf gloves, basketballs, footballs, soccer balls, and leather carrying bags for sports clothing.

This plant has a former professional baseball star on the payroll as an assistant personnel manager. He is good copy on occasion, can speak with authority about the products, and directs a recreation program for employees.

## A Tolerant Attitude

At Safeplay plants and in sales offices, there is some pilferage of products by employees. Company policy is that any employee removing company property from the premises without authorization is subject to dismissal. So far this policy has never been invoked where products are concerned. The unspoken attitude of management is much the same as exists in many consumer product companies, particularly those that make food, confections, or inexpensive clothing items. It is tolerant, treats it quietly as a minor cost written into the price of products, and looks the other way rather than confront employees, with the risk of possible repercussions if someone is falsely accused. Put another way, management reluctantly concludes that the cost of a baseball mitt taken home in a lunch pail or paper bag to a kid on occasion is not high if employee turnover is low and working enthusiasm is high.

As a means of trying to discourage pilferage, Safeplay offers employees a discount on any products they buy from the store in the personnel office, and on the 10th birthday of any employee's child the employee can select any product priced under $20 and take it home free.

## Tolerance Abused

Recently, however, the "mysterious disappearance" of sports items has gone beyond the boundaries of normal pilferage and management tolerance. Whole containers of items in the stockroom and in the shipping area have disappeared. Inventory records have apparently been doctored.

Obviously distressed, the home office has sent in a private detective agency. The agency's preliminary investigation and analysis are disturbing. It appears that there is an organized thievery ring involving as many as 25 of the Westward plant's employees. It appears, also, that the former athletic star on the payroll is somehow involved, but to what extent is not clear. Someone on the inside, not yet identified, deals with an outside "fence," and someone else on the inside, also not yet identified, handles the payoff to all the cooperating employees. Some of the involved employees are members of the union, and some are in the office "white-collar" jobs.

## The Decision Process

At an executive decision-making meeting, you, as director of public relations, have been called in, along with the director of personnel and a company lawyer from the home office. The three of you have been asked to assess the repercussions if the town's police are called in and legal action is taken. You are asked to offer any other resolution that would "better serve the interests of all involved."

The lawyer says that as soon as an airtight case can be accumulated, including photographs and eyewitness accounts of products being removed, being transported to a "fence," and an actual money transaction completed, she favors appropriate law enforcement action and legal redress against those involved.

The personnel manager prefers, he says, to bring charges only against the leader or leaders inside and all those involved on the outside. He prefers to handle the cooperating employees individually, possibly allowing some sort of plea bargaining to keep the employees the company considers of real value on the payroll. He feels this approach will adequately frighten all employees, halt the activity, and avoid having to replace some trained and competent employees.

It is your turn to speak, using whatever notes you have taken while the others stated their positions. What is your view, taking into account the impact not only on internal relations, but on other publics directly or indirectly involved—including families of employees involved, neighbors, and the community generally, local law enforcement, news media in the trade, the Westward community, and shareholders of Safeplay, Inc.? Are there others?

What actions, and in what sequence, would you propose and why?

How would you deal with the recommendations of the lawyer and the personnel manager without setting up an adversary situation?

## PROBLEM 3-B KEEPING MERGER HAVOC AT BAY

You are the vice president of public relations for a computer manufacturing company. The CEO called you and the vice president of human resources in for a meeting. Your company is planning to merge with another computer manufacturer.

You are aware of the havoc mergers inflict on employees. You also know that unhappy, disgruntled employees don't perform their tasks as well, can damage customer relationships, and can ultimately wreak havoc on a company's profits. You are worried about how to present this merger to the employees.

Communication with employees currently is done through an intranet site called "What's Happening." It's read by most employees, but not regularly as not all have access to a computer. A newsletter goes out periodically—at least quarterly, but more often if needed. The CEO meets with upper management weekly to be informed of goals and how well they're being met. He is a friendly, people kind of person, not afraid to speak before large groups, and thinks well on his feet. He enjoys the weekly meetings with upper management. He has from time to time thought about being more available to all employees but till now neither the time nor the motivation has been enough to bring that about.

The CEO has said he does not want anyone to lose his or her job. Some may need to be retrained but no one will be let go. The merger will take place in two weeks but the timeline for blending the organizations will be over several months.

He is asking that you and human resources work out the employee communication details and report back to him in two days.

Put together the key messages you want delivered to employees, and who will deliver them and how. Also plan the timing of the messages in conjunction with when the merger will actually take place. If you plan to use two-way communication, through what vehicles will employees communicate and to whom? Who will respond to their comments and questions? Is there a way to measure effectiveness?

# CHAPTER

# 4

# Community Relations

A community is a social organism made up of all the interactions among the residents and the organizations with which they identify. As a social organism, a community can take pride in its scenery or in its high school basketball team; it can be factionalized on the basis of who lives on which side of the railroad tracks, or who is well-off or poor; it can be a heterogeneous collection of suburban residents drawn together only by a common desire to escape living within a metropolitan area.

It is necessary for organizations to live by the community's ordinances and social mores. Permits must be sought to expand facilities, dig up utilities, change traffic flow, or even to operate at all.

A neighborhood, town, city, or state is obviously a human community. Like organizations, they require positive interrelationships among all members in order to function smoothly and efficiently. Because a company, hospital, school, or other organization would have difficulty operating effectively in a community that is disrupted or inefficient, it is necessary for them to accept the responsibility of corporate citizenship.

Therefore, mutual trust engendered by positive public relationships is essential in order for both the community and organizations located there to function in a reasonable manner. A community is not merely a collection of people who share a locality and its facilities.

## THE OLD-FASHIONED VIEW OF COMMUNITY RELATIONS

Traditionally, employers have tended to regard their relationships with home communities as being extensions of their employee relations. The idea was that employees who were treated decently would go into the home communities singing the praises of their employer. In this traditional viewpoint, employers felt that their dollar payroll, their local tax payments, the occasional loan of a facility for a meeting, and the annual contribution to the United Way discharged their community obligations.

Their attitude seemed to say, "Look what we are giving: jobs, taxes, meeting facilities, and charitable donations." Employers who held this view tended to assume that with little more than a snap of their fingers they would be provided the practical necessities for efficient operations: streets, sewers, water lines, power and telephone, police and fire services, recreational areas, health care centers, schools, shopping centers, residential areas, cultural and religious facilities, and all the rest. The viewpoint tended to say, "These are what we are entitled to in return for what we give. The community owes us these."

This attitude has changed. Employers now know that they must have more than a general concern for the efficiency and adequacy of community services for themselves and for their employees. They have learned that they must become involved in specific community decisions and actions concerning fiscal policies; honesty in public offices; attracting new businesses and holding older ones; planning for the future; and generating the enthusiasm of volunteers in charitable, cultural, fellowship, educational, recreational, business, and patriotic endeavors. In general, they must apply the collective talents of the organization to the community in which it operates. The combination of these concerns involves having representatives in the policy-making structure of the community, sometimes directly and openly, sometimes behind the scenes.

- Community relations, as a public relations function, is an institution's planned, active, and continuing participation within a community to maintain and enhance its environment to the benefit of both the institution and the community.[1]

## COMMUNITY ISSUES

**Community relations (CR)** work is a dynamic aspect of public relations. If there were no other reason, the changing physical and social makeup of communities would make it so, but there are many other contributing factors. Among them, few people stay in the communities where they are born. Families move not once, but several times. Community communications programs must deal with this constant turnover of residents. Also, employers move. Sometimes they move from a congested central city area to a suburb. When they move, both areas are disrupted. A manufacturer may move a headquarters or a manufacturing facility from one city to another, mortally wounding the economy of one and perhaps starting a boom in the other. Branches of businesses and institutions are opened in areas of growing population and closed in areas that are shrinking or that are poorly managed. A new interstate highway bypasses a community formerly dependent on travelers for its trade. Undesirable elements get control of government. A community also undergoes change when there is a movement for reform or rehabilitation.

Almost all the needs of a community as a desirable place to live and work can be placed into 10 categories:

1. Work for everyone who desires it
2. The prospect of growth and new opportunities
3. Adequate competitive commercial enterprises
4. Competent municipal government with modern police, fire, highway, and other services

---

[1]Wilbur J. Peak. "Community Relations," in *Lesly's Handbook of Public Relations and Communications*, Chicago: NTC/Contemporary Publishing, 1998, p. 114.

5. Educational, cultural, religious, and recreational pursuits
6. Appropriate housing and public services
7. Provision for helping those least able to help themselves
8. Availability of legal, medical, and other professional services
9. Pride and loyalty
10. A good reputation in the area and beyond

## THE ROLE OF PUBLIC RELATIONS

Public relations work of a basic nature is involved in at least nine areas of an organization's community relationships:

1. Issuing news of interest to the community and providing top officials of the organizations with information on the status of community relations
2. Representing the organization in all sorts of volunteer activities, including fund drives—and getting employees to do likewise
3. Managing the contributions function—giving donations if a corporation, raising funds if a nonprofit organization
4. Counseling management on contributions of employees as volunteer workers or board members; arranging for use of facilities and equipment by community groups
5. Functioning as the organization's intermediary with local governmental, civic, educational, and ad hoc groups concerned with reform, social problems, and celebrations
6. Planning and helping to implement special events such as ground breaking or dedication of new facilities, change in location, anniversaries, reunions, conventions, or exhibitions
7. Preparing advertising or position papers aimed at residents or local government as needed or desirable
8. Preparing publications for distribution to resident groups
9. Planning and conducting open houses or tours as needed or desirable

With the dynamics of change mentioned earlier, public relations work is becoming less concerned with "routine" and more with the unusual: controversies between factions in the community; activism on social issues; and dealing with calamity, crisis, and governmental regulations as they affect the local community or as they are echoed in local ordinances affecting an organization.[2]

## CAN COMMUNITY RELATIONS BE THE CORE
## OF PR PROGRAMMING?

Yes, community relations can be the core of public relations programming because it sets the tone of what an organizations stands for—not in words (rhetoric) but in actions (behavior). Today, how organizations conduct themselves in the communities

---

[2]For an example of a sudden and drastic change in local relationships, see news accounts of the oil spill of the *Exxon Valdez* in Alaska in March 1989.

where they do business is driven by two factors that make it more than just "getting the house in order":

1. Instant communication, encompassing burgeoning information networks that go far beyond news media data gathering. It has the capacity to capture and transmit home behavior far and wide.
2. Global competition and the "global village" have created interest in such information, at least by competitors, activists, government agencies, and others who have reason to broadcast it.

Three strategic levels need to be planned:

1. **Defensive:** guarding against negative acts, or acts of omission
2. **Proactive:** being a leader in positive acts that appeal to key publics
3. **Maintenance:** finding ways to retain relationships with publics not currently key, but still able to influence a company's reputation by forthright expression of their perceptions of it

This approach is far different from "doing nice things for the community." Assigning community relations to indifferent or inexperienced staffers because it's "easy" no longer suffices—and of course misses the centrality of community relations today.

## TWO TYPES OR LEVELS OF PROGRAMMING EMERGE

Standard community relations involves basic, arm's-length, "good corporate citizen" activities that reach out, invite in, create awareness, and let facilities be used. For example:

1. **Membership network**, assigning, "official" representatives to all important community groups
2. **Speakers bureau**, placing talks to key groups on topics vital to the organization
3. **Make facilities available**
4. **Open houses**, visitations, tours
5. **Programs around holidays**
6. **Service on boards** of directors
7. **Take part** in public events and back "must-support" causes

The second level of community relations involves becoming part of the fabric of the community by placing people throughout its planning and decision-making networks:

1. **Ambassador or constituency relations** programs
2. Hold regular **opinion leader briefings** or idea exchanges
3. Set up local **community relations advisory boards**
4. **Employee volunteer programs**
5. **Community research**, jointly with a college perhaps
6. **Social projects** that tackle the real community needs as seen by your key publics
7. **Make expertise available**

Neither list is exhaustive, but the two suggest the differences in the types. In most cases, some of both levels are useful.

### Other Considerations

Employee volunteerism has so many serendipitous benefits that it raises the issue of **spouse, family, and retiree** participation. Those organizations that do involve them generally report expanded impact and a widening network.

**Feedback databanks** may be the biggest opportunity, capturing what is heard and observed from opinion leaders and community members in a formal way. Use of databanks is *really* listening to the community for invaluable information, which is instantly actionable through community relations programs.

## SUCCESSFUL COMMUNITY RELATIONS ARE PLANNED, ORGANIZED, AND SYSTEMATIZED

In community programs there should be five considerations:

1. **Targeting**
   - Which *groups* in the community must be targeted?
   - What *behaviors* need to be motivated?
   - What specific *activities* will achieve this motivation?
   - What *information* must be gathered and assessed before starting?

2. **Participate or own**

   If your reputation needs improving, working on projects with accepted partners can use their reputation to pull yours up; if yours is good, projects you can own offer more benefits and visibility without any dilution.

3. **Here versus there**

   Should a program be based within the organization, or should it be an outside program? Should it take place on-site or off-site?

4. **"Official" versus employee volunteer activities**

   If the latter, how will the organization get credit? Should employees be able to do some volunteer work "on the clock"?

5. **Reaching opinion leaders**

   What design will assure that this critical goal is met?

## TURNING WORKERS INTO GOODWILL AMBASSADORS

People trust people, so turning employees into ambassadors within the community is an effective way to be known, spread goodwill, and develop relationships. Because it wanted to develop its community relationships, Shell Chemical's Geismar site in Ascension Parish, Louisiana, did an opinion poll of 600 residents. The poll showed that when it comes to news about the plant, people tend to trust nonmanagerial plant workers. Asked who they would believe in matters regarding a chemical plant's impact on health, safety, and the environment, 68 percent said they would believe plant workers "a lot" or "some." Only medical doctors and the federal EPA got more favorable ratings. This data was used to leverage a program to keep employees better informed of the company's activities—turning workers into goodwill ambassadors both inside and outside the plant.[3]

Employee ambassadors can be used to build solid community relations programs in four ways:

1. Using speakers bureaus to get information out to local opinion leaders
2. Employee participation in volunteer or outreach programs
3. Direct opinion leader contacts, sharing news and gathering insight and feedback
4. Sponsored memberships (where employees are designated to belong to and attend a specific group's activities on behalf of the organization)

## REFERENCES AND ADDITIONAL READINGS

Arnstein, Caren. "How Companies Can Rebuild Credibility and Trust." *Public Relations Journal* 50 (April 1994): 28–29.

Bagin, Don, and Donald Gallagher. *The School and Community Relations*, 7th ed. Needham Heights, MA: Allyn & Bacon, 2000.

Brion, Denis. *Essential Industry and the NIMBY Phenomenon.* Westport, CT: Quorum, 1991.

Burke, Edmund. *Corporate Community Relations: The Principle of the Neighbor of Choice.* Westport, CT: Praeger, 1999.

Chynoweth, Emma, et al. "Responsible Care: Listening to Communities: What Do They Want to Know?" *Chemical Week* 153 (December 8, 1993): 68–69.

*Corporate Community Relations Letter* published by The Center for Corporate Community Relations at Boston College, www.bc.edu/cccr.

Cutlip, Scott, Allen Center, and Glen Broom. "Corporate Philanthropy." Chapter 14 in *Effective Public Relations*, 8th ed. Upper Saddle River, NJ: Prentice Hall, 1999.

Frank, Helmut, and John Schanz. *The Economics of the Energy Problem.* Joint Council on Economic Education, 1212 Avenue of the Americas, New York, NY 10022. Pamphlet.

Hunter, Floyd. *Community Power Structures.* Chapel Hill, NC: University of North Carolina Press, 1953. A Community Relations classic.

Hussey, John. "Community Relations," in *Experts in Action Inside Public Relations*, 2nd ed., ed. Bill Cantor and Chester Burger. White Plains, NY: Longman, Inc., 1989: 115–125.

Kruckeberg, Dean, and Kenneth Starck. *Public Relations and Community: A Reconstructed Theory.* Westport, CT: Greenwood, 1988.

Lerbinger, Otto, and Nathaniel Sperber. "Community Relations." Chapter 6 in *Manager's Public Relations Handbook.* Reading, MA: Addison-Wesley, 1982.

Lundborg, Lolls. *Public Relations in the Local Community.* New York: Harper and Row, 1950. Continues to be definitive. By the public relations staffer who advanced to CEO of Bank of America.

*Making Community Relations Pay Off: Tools & Strategies.* Washington, DC: Public Affairs Council, 1988. Tells how companies are meeting the test of effective community relations.

McDermitt, David. "The 10 Commandments of Community Relations." *World Wastes* 36 (September 1993): 48–51.

O'Brien, Paul. "Changing Expectations of Community Relations." *Executive Speeches* 8 (October/November 1993): 33–36.

*pr reporter* Vol. 41 No. 49 (December 14, 1998). "Hyundai's 'Blind Date' with Community Improves (Part 2)": 2.

*pr reporter* Vol. 41 No. 48 (December 7, 1998). "'Blind Dates' with Communities Don't Work; Steady Courtships Do": 2–3.

*pr reporter* Vol. 41 No. 35 (September 7, 1998). "Even Superior Community Relations Not

---

[3]*pr reporter* Vol. 42 No. 34, August 30, 1999. "Shell Chemical's Employee Ambassadors Add Personal Element to Community Relations—and Help Assure Plant Survival," pp. 1–2.

Beyond Reach of Entrepreneurial Trial Lawyers—But It Can Defeat Them": 1–2.

*pr reporter* Vol. 36 No. 28 (July 19, 1993). "Can Community Relations Be the Core of Public Relations?": 1–2.

*pr reporter* Vol. 36 No. 4 (January 25, 1993). "Model for Employee Participation and Outreach Programs": 1–2.

*pr reporter* Vol. 35 No. 15 (April 13, 1992). "Inviting the Public Inside Is Effective and Unexpected Way to Deal with Community Issues": 3.

*The Public Relations Body of Knowledge.* New York: PRSA. See abstracts dealing with "Community Relations."

Rich, Dorothy. "Business Partnerships with Families." *Business Horizons* 36 (September/October 1993): 24–28.

Skolnik, Rayna. "Rebuilding Trust." *Public Relations Journal* 49 (September 1993): 29–32.

-------------------------------- C A S E S --------------------------------

# Case 4-1 A Classic: Chemical Industry Takes Responsibility for Community Concerns

## Trade Association Takes the Initiative

The American Chemistry Council (ACC) is the trade group for the chemical industry. Its members represent 90 percent of the industrial chemical productive capacity in the United States. Dues are based on a percentage of a company's chemical sales.

Chemical companies must be constantly innovative to remain competitive in today's global marketplace. Like most trade associations, ACC helps members stay abreast of issues and techniques. It provides assistance in complying with laws and regulations. ACC also offers **leadership training** and **task force groups** to develop skills and knowledge in the managerial, legislative, technical, and communications areas.

> Over the years, Responsible Care's[1] focus has evolved from a measure of process to one of improved performance. After initially focusing on shaping our companies' operating behavior practices and reaching "Practice-in-Place," we have stepped up our commitment to Responsible Care®. Our industry is now dedicated to a vision of no accidents, no injuries and no harm to the environment.
>
> TOM REILLY, CEO OF REILLY INDUSTRIES

> We have said all along that we are not asking the public to *trust* us. We are asking everyone to *track* us, to monitor our performance and make suggestions that will help us improve.
>
> FRED WEBBER, PRESIDENT, AMERICAN CHEMISTRY COUNCIL

As public awareness of environmental health and safety issues has increased over the past few decades, the chemical industry has been scrutinized by activists, regulators, and consumers more closely than ever before. As environmentalists make louder protests, legislators respond with more stringent regulations.

Under the Superfund Amendments and Reauthorization Act (SARA), also known as the Emergency Planning and Community Right-to-Know Act, chemical manufacturers and other organizations are required to inform employees and the community about the nature and hazards of the materials with which they work.[2]

As pressures from legislation mounted and NIMBYists[3] began paying closer attention to environmental issues in their communities, the chemical industry realized that it needed to reach beyond one-way communication of its side of the story. It needed to do three things:

---

[1]Responsible Care® is a copyright of the American Chemistry Council. Thanks to Lisa Grepps, APR, Manager of Strategic Communications for Responsible Care® for providing extensive updated information on this program.
[2]Bernard J. Nebel. *Environmental Science*. Upper Saddle River, NJ: Prentice Hall, 1990, p. 290.
[3]*Not In My Back Yard*. An update is *NOPE (Not On Planet Earth)*.

1. *Listen to and recognize the perceptions and fears* of the public, especially neighbors of chemical plants.
2. *Own up to any performance problems.*
3. *Take action* to correct problems and address perceptions.

## Proactive Response to Public Concerns: Responsible Care®

ACC created an initiative in the United States called *Responsible Care®* in 1988 (see Figure 4-1). Modeled after a Canadian Chemical Producers Association program, *Responsible Care®* couples environmental, health, and safety improvements in individual plants with invitations for industry and public scrutiny. Many observers believe this to be one of the best strategic public relations programs, although the industry does not acknowledge it as such.

An integral part of the Responsible Care® program is its **six Codes of Management Practices** (see Figure 4-2). These codes established priorities for operating chemical plants. ACC places reduction of emissions, reduction of the waste that facilities generate, and sound management of

FIGURE 4-1   Shown here is the symbol of Responsible Care®

**Responsible Care®**
*Good Chemistry at Work*

*Source:* (Courtesy of ACC.)

1. **Community Awareness and Emergency Response Code (CAER)**

   to reduce potential harm to the employees and the public in an emergency as well as bring the chemical industry and communities together

2. **Pollution Prevention Code**

   to improve the industry's ability to protect people and the environment by generating less waste and minimizing emissions

3. **Process Safety Code**

   to prevent fire, explosions, and accidental chemical releases

4. **Distribution Code**

   to reduce employee and public risks from the shipment of chemicals

5. **Employee Health and Safety Code**

   to maximize worker protection and accident prevention, through training and communications

6. **Product Stewardship Code**

   to ensure that the design, development, manufacture, transport, use, and disposal of chemical products is done safely and without environmental damage

**FIGURE 4-2** The six Codes of Management Practices turn guiding principles to practical application

*Source:* (Courtesy of ACC.)

remaining releases and wastes at the top of its priorities.

According to Richard Doyle, vice president of Responsible Care® at ACC,

Responsible Care® calls for continuous improvement by the chemical industry in health, safety, and environmental performance. Responsible Care® is not a quick fix or an overnight cure. It is not a public relations program. It is an ongoing process, and a call for action. . . . Its ultimate goal remains to *create a dialogue with constituents in order to educate and obtain input into how the chemical industry can most effectively improve its performance in a manner that is responsive to the public.* [Emphasis added.]

Responsible Care® is *proactive public relations.* Rather than waiting for an accident to occur, or the public to become fearful or upset, it actively *invites* people to learn which chemicals are produced at a plant, how the plant is operated, and what protective measures are in place should an accident occur.

Studies have shown that *fear* of an unknown event is more powerful than an actual *bad occurrence.* In a study of a group known to have latent tendencies for developing Huntington's disease, the majority of those whose genetic tests showed they would most likely develop this incurable malady felt that knowing was beneficial. "Better to know than be always wondering." Those that knew they were likely to get the disease reported their quality of life and psychological health was better than those for whom testing was inconclusive.

This holds true for knowing and communicating about chemical risks as well. Most people can handle truth better than being left in doubt. Open communication shows respect for people by treating them like responsible adults. However, the Huntington study also indicates that all people do not react the same when learning of risks. About 10 percent had trouble adjusting to the news, even when it was good (i.e., they would probably not develop the disease). Apparently for some, just handling the change or believing the test is accurate was more impactful than the relief. As always, no rule fits everyone.[4]

Responsible Care® is composed of 10 elements:

1. Guiding Principles: followed by every member and partner company
2. Codes of Management Practices: environmental, health, and safety guidelines
3. Dialogue with the Public: to identify and address public concerns
4. Self-Evaluation: annual reporting on a company's implementation of the Codes
5. Measures of Performance: to view progress of Responsible Care®
6. Performance Goals: company-specific goals reported on annually
7. Management Systems Verification: independent review of companies' implementation of Responsible Care®
8. Mutual Assistance: company-to-company dialogue
9. Partnership Program: helping companies to participate in Responsible Care®
10. Obligation of Membership: to participate in Responsible Care® and follow these elements

ACC member companies adhere to a list of 10 guiding principles about safe plant operations and proper public communications. Figure 4-3 illustrates these principles.

## Responsible Care®'s Target Audiences

The goal of Responsible Care® is to continuously advance the level of chemical industry performance, demonstrating commitment to a better, safer world. This message is targeted to:

- The chemical industry
- Teachers and students
- Employees
- Federal and state officials
- The media
- The general public
- Plant neighbors
- Local and national interest groups
- Supply chain customers

## Building Public Relationships

### Activities to Reach External Audiences

ACC member and partner companies use a combination of one-way and two-way communication activities to invite external publics to communicate with their local plants. One-way (or information transfer) efforts include:

- **Brochures** featuring shelter-in-place messages and explanations of Responsible Care®
- **Annual Responsible Care® reports** that target the business community, as well as community stakeholders, and report on the company's environmental, health, and safety performance
- **ChemicalGuide.com** Web site featuring member and partner company Web sites detailing products and outreach activities, as well as Responsible Care® performance
- **Advertisements** on the local level
- **Community newsletters** sent to plant neighbors to keep them informed about the company and its activities

---

[4]*pr reporter* 36, May 3, 1993, pp. 2–3.

1. To seek and incorporate public input regarding our products and operations.
2. To provide chemicals that can be manufactured, transported, used, and disposed of safely.
3. To make health, safety, the environment, and resource conservation critical considerations for all new and existing products and processes.
4. To provide information on health or environmental risks and pursue protective measures for employees, the public, and other key stakeholders.
5. To work with customers, carriers, suppliers, distributors, and contractors to foster the safe use, transport, and disposal of chemicals.
6. To operate our facilities in a manner that protects the environment and the health and safety of our employees and the public.
7. To support education and research on the health, safety, and environmental effects of our products and processes.
8. To work with others to resolve problems associated with past handling and disposal practices.
9. To lead in the development of responsible laws, regulations, and standards that safeguard the community, workplace, and environment.
10. To practice Responsible Care® by encouraging and assisting others to adhere to these principles and practices.

**FIGURE 4-3   ACC member companies adhere to a list of 10 guiding principles about safe plant operations and proper public communications**

*Source:* (Courtesy of ACC.)

Two-way (or relationship-building) efforts include:

- **Community advisory panels** (CAPs), groups of citizens with diverse backgrounds and feelings toward the chemical industry. CAPs are sponsored by local chemical plants and encouraged to voice community concerns with industry representatives. Well-run CAPs provide dialogue between the plant and the community. To date, ACC members and partners sponsor nearly 300 CAPs across the country with great success. One example is the LeMoyne (Alabama) Community Advisory Panel, which works to improve emergency response service to the local community and sponsors an annual "Responsible Care® Night" at member company plants to help residents understand the initiative.
- **Hazardous material drills** involving plants and local emergency responder groups. These exercises help improve knowledge and response time in the event of an incident. For more information, visit www.transcaer.org.
- **Responsible Care® fairs/days/open houses** are sponsored by the plants or CAP groups. These events are opportunities for the community to tour the plant and learn about its operations.
- **Inviting state legislators and local and national activist leaders to speak at association meetings** and sending ACC delegates or scientists to meetings of environmental, regulatory, and community groups.

## Activities to Change Behavior of ACC Members

To maintain ACC membership, companies are required to implement Responsible Care® guiding principles and codes of management practice. More than 1,000 executives and managers have attended ACC workshops on implementing the codes for Responsible Care®. Many have found creative ways to reach their new objectives. For example, some have tied managerial bonuses to achieved objectives. Others use peer pressure of recognition to motivate and support the Responsible Care® initiative.

As codes are implemented, ACC requires every company to report its progress along the way. As of 2001, 110 members or approximately 95 percent of companies that have been implementing the initiatives for five or more years are at full implementation of the six codes of management practices.

## Evaluation: External Publics

The National Association of Public Environmental Communicators commended Responsible Care® for its one-way and two-way communication vehicles.

## Evaluation: Internal Publics

### Reductions in Chemical Emission

ACC members reported that total releases (occurring when a chemical is discharged into the land, air, or water) declined from 381 million pounds in 1988 to 139 million pounds in 1998. Air releases dropped more than 69 percent. Water releases were cut by 75 percent, and chemicals sent to landfills were reduced by 74 percent. Underground injection of chemicals was cut by 39 percent. Off-site transfers (excluding off-site recycling and recovery) decreased 74 percent.

### Self-Evaluation

The ACC Responsible Care® initiative includes a self-evaluation process. Member companies are required to furnish ACC with an annual report of their progress in implementing the Codes of Management Practices. They have shown significant gains in Process Safety, Distribution, Community Awareness, and Emergency Response.

Although these results show improvements, ACC recognizes the fact that company self-evaluations are subject to challenges of credibility. ACC is now identifying additional code measurement systems that continue to meet objective public scrutiny.

## Performance Measures

Performance measures exist to demonstrate the progress being made through Responsible Care® and are used to help drive performance improvement throughout the membership. The performance measures include Community Awareness and Emergency Response, Pollution Prevention, Process Safety, Distribution, Employee Health and Safety, and Product Stewardship.

### Performance Goals

Member and partner companies are asked to:

- Establish at least one goal for a Responsible Care® performance result
- Make steady performance improvement toward that goal
- Publicly communicate the goal(s) and progress toward meeting that goal(s)
- Annually report to the Council the established goal(s), progress, and public reporting mechanism

This case demonstrates the trend of public relations programs to *begin with responsible action* by organizations, with public relations practitioners playing a key role in *design and strategy*. The *communications and relationship-building activities* then follow to gain recognition for the responsible action. ■

## ESSENTIAL 2

When the American Chemistry Council began its Responsible Care® program in 1988, the purpose was to first ensure that all Council members were meeting standards of quality in areas such as environmental protection, worker safety, pollution control, and the like. The idea at the time was to head off touchy public relations problems with a proactive effort that required every member to monitor and report progress on a number of sensitive fronts. One area not directly addressed in Responsible Care® was public outreach. The founders of the program said 'track us, don't trust us," but few of the resources dedicated to Responsible Care® went to public education.

The program, which is still in place, continues to thrive. But regular monitoring by ACC officers reveals some interesting facts: The chemical industry continues to lag behind other industries in public acceptance. "The favorability of the chemical industry always trailed other, similar industries," said Elizabeth Curwen, manager of communication for the ACC.

To address this problem, the ACC initiated two pilot "good chemistry" campaigns in Massachusetts and Louisiana, and out of those efforts came a program deployed in 2005. Dubbed "essential 2," its message is "Chemistry is essential to every aspect of everyone's lives."

Whereas Responsible Care® was a behavioral public relations program—working with stakeholders to "show" them how the industry was doing rather than just "telling" them—"essential 2" uses a traditional public relations approach. The program includes a wide range of customary public relations tactics—education, paid advertising, publicity, special events, and employee communication.

Appropriately, the program kicked off with employees of member companies. "You'd think the employees would be our number-one supporters, " Curwen told *PR News*, "but they were as beleaguered as the rest of America."

To address this critical problem, the ACC selected campaign coordinators for each of its 129 member companies. These representatives became the conduit through which passed up-to-date information on the industry and examples of how chemistry and chemicals make life in America that much better. An employee-focused Web site was also launched.

Bolstered by strong, positive feedback from member companies, the ACC took "essential 2" public in 2005. Working with Ogilvy PR Worldwide, the campaign centers on the areas of American life in which chemistry plays a vital part. That chemistry is "essential 2" safety, health, innovation, the economy, and the environment is the message transmitted through traditional advertising, publicity, and the Internet. The effort was budgeted at $35 million for the first two years.

David Fowler, creative director at Ogilvy & Mather, who helped create the program, says "essential 2" was designed "with modern life in mind. The more we looked at the facts, the more we realized that products that come from chemistry aren't just nice—they are essential: medicines, silicon chips, clean water, and cellular telephones. They make modern life modern."

In getting the "essential 2" message out, the ACC borrows liberally from major public events, such as NASCAR races, the Indy 500, holidays, and other regular events. Once dubbed "brand standing," using such events to showcase products and services is now a top public relations tool.

Although the program is too young to gain empirical data about its success, Curwen is confident the trends are moving upward. "Our members quickly saw the value of this," she says.

Meanwhile, Responsible Care® continues to serve its purpose, something that's not lost on those administering "essential 2." "We still don't want any releases into the environment, no chemical spills," Curwen said. "The industry's performance is still part of our message."

------------------------------------------------------------

## QUESTIONS FOR DISCUSSION

1. Richard Doyle, then ACC vice president of Responsible Care®, said the initiative "is not a public relations program." What did he intend to convey? He said Responsible Care® is a performance improvement initiative and that ACC's members are striving for public input into this process. What do you think he meant, and how can this goal best be achieved? Do you think the community advisory panels in neighborhoods around facilities are beneficial?

2. To what extent can a voluntary performance improvement initiative by private industry forestall government legislation and regulation on environmental matters? Explain your position.

3. What else could ACC do to attain higher credibility for Responsible Care® with:
   • The public
   • Its own members
   • Associated industries
   • Legislators and regulators
   • Activist groups

4. How could it measure an increase or decrease in credibility?

5. List other industries whose products or operations engender fear. What steps are you aware of that each is taking to allay public apprehension? How does Responsible Care® compare with what these industries are doing?

6. Imagine yourself living across the street from a chemical plant. List all the feelings you can think of that you might have about the plant—positive, negative, or neutral. What specific actions would representatives from the plant need to take to address your feelings?

7. Draft a letter from a chemical plant manager to those living near the plant announcing introduction of the Responsible Care® initiative.

# Case 4-2    Community Relationships Maintained During Hospital Closing*

Throughout the 1980s and early 1990s, business and the government trimmed whatever fat there was from the healthcare system. In 1997, Congress passed the Balanced Budget Act in an attempt to reform Medicare and trim waste from the system. But cuts went billions of dollars beyond expectation. The healthcare system was in a financial crisis. Health premiums weren't paying for the cost of services. Hospitals were being squeezed by managed care companies having their own financial troubles. One consequence was the closing of hospitals.

## Mercy Hospital–Detroit's Struggle

The east side of Detroit is among the most troubled urban areas in the United States, struggling with a multitude of social and economic challenges. Mercy Hospital–Detroit was an important anchor in this neighborhood, not only providing access to healthcare, but also security, employment, leadership, and a place for social interaction. It relied heavily on Medicare, Medicaid, and other government sources for its business—nearly 80 percent of its total admissions.

In the early to mid-1990s, Mercy Hospital–Detroit found it increasingly difficult to maintain its fiscal health; operating losses were supplemented by the hospital's parent company, Mercy Health Services (MHS).[1] Then, in 1997, the Balanced Budget Reconciliation Act severely reduced

Medicare and Medicaid reimbursements. The already struggling hospital was devastated by the cuts. Losses of $1.5 million per month began to mount. The federal and state funding cuts similarly affected operating margins at Mercy's other hospitals. The MHS Board was faced with system-wide financial constraints that put the system's bond rating at risk. Operating losses at Mercy Hospital–Detroit totaled nearly $100 million from 1990–2000.

In the hope of finding a buyer, a series of discussions with major Detroit health systems ensued in 1999, but all were facing the same circumstances: increasingly ill patients with no health insurance and decreasing reimbursements from the government. The decision was made to close the hospital in December 1999. Mercy Hospital–Detroit quickly became a national example of the evolving healthcare crisis in the United States.

## Several Public Relations Issues Emerged

- How can the hospital close without giving the impression of abandoning the city and its poorest residents?
- Is it possible to close the hospital while still maintaining the excellent reputation of MHS and its sponsor, the Sisters of Mercy?
- How can Mercy coincidentally acquire a similar-sized hospital in a predominantly white suburban community without attracting major criticism and, worse yet, accusations of "racism"?

---

*Thank you to Stephen Shivinsky, APR, vice president of corporate communications and public relations at Trinity Health for this case study.
[1] Renamed Trinity Health after a May 2000 merger.

## Research

Preparations began when Mercy Hospital–Detroit commissioned a research study to obtain community opinion and attitudes. The study showed that parent company MHS was held in high esteem and that the local community not only counted on Mercy Hospital–Detroit but saw it as an entitlement for the community.

Meanwhile, the commitment to the community from the Sisters of Mercy and the MHS Board led MHS management to conclude that it should donate the 10-year-old building to the community. Instead of simply selling the hospital campus to a developer for commercial use, MHS decided the hospital should be converted as a long-term community asset to enhance neighborhood revitalization, and the new owner(s) and users should share the mission and values of the hospital's parent, MHS. Additionally, MHS decided to keep a presence on the hospital campus by earmarking $2 million for a primary care clinic for the uninsured. In doing so, Mercy supported its mission of "care for the poor and underserved" while seeking a new owner for the larger block of property and buildings.

The next step was a major study in early 2000—just after the announcement of closure—consisting of personal interviews with 198 Detroit community and opinion leaders, including elected officials, clergy, and major business and social service agency representatives, to obtain ideas about how to "do the right thing" and "give back" to the community, rather than simply close the hospital and move on. The personal interviews provided valuable input on specific community needs, possible organizations that met the criteria as a new owner, and communication tactics for most effectively reaching the important audiences of key community leaders and area residents, many of whom are without transportation

or telephones. The interviews also helped crystallize other audiences to target:

- Mercy Hospital–Detroit employees, medical staff, board members, and volunteers
- Mercy's leadership group (40 top management personnel nationwide) and other corporate office employees
- Community religious leaders
- Local physician leaders
- Regional and national partners
- Major insurers
- Archdiocese of Detroit and Bishops in all MHS markets
- Michigan's governor and staff
- Detroit's Mayor and key aides
- The Wayne County Executive and key aides
- Detroit City Council
- Trade and healthcare consortia
- 99,000 residents in the primary service area

## The Public Relations Plan

A public relations plan was developed to reach these audiences using a variety of tactics—not relying on advertising—including specific ways to obtain their input and feedback. Tactics in the plan included e-mail; a telephone hotline; staff and community town hall meetings; targeted letters to volunteers, community leaders, and others; the hospital newsletter; editorial board meetings with Detroit's two daily newspapers, weekly business newsmagazine, and African-American weekly; formal closure notices in community newspapers; direct-mail letters; and news releases, fact sheets, and backgrounders.

The **key messages** to communicate were: "Mercy can no longer tolerate this level of losses or be supported by others within the Mercy system," "Mercy is 'doing the right thing' by donating the property to help meet community needs," and

"Mercy continues its ministry for the poor with a new primary care center for the uninsured—investing $2 million per year to make that happen."

## Plans Were Executed with Precision

Plans began with a carefully implemented effort to obtain balanced stories—as early as September 1999—about the difficult financial situation and the possibility that Mercy Hospital–Detroit may close. This was followed with a series of editorial board meetings with Detroit's two dailies, the weekly business newsmagazine, and African-American weekly. Similar meetings were later held with community leaders and the Detroit City Council. The generally fair and favorable editorials and news coverage resulting from the meetings helped educate Mercy's key audiences and would later help them understand the reasons for closing.

Media coverage reached a crescendo in January 2000 and continued through March 2001, including NBC Nightly News and several national trades. A total of 10,000 letters were mailed to residents' homes within three eastside ZIP codes. All audiences received the news of Mercy Hospital–Detroit's closing and, although disappointed that Detroit's east side would lose an acute care hospital, they were generally understanding of the situation.

Excluding a regulatory requirement to place a "Public Notice" advertisement in local newspapers, no other form of advertising was used to reach the audiences.

## Evaluation

In late 2000, the Mercy Hospital–Detroit building was donated to a multiservice community organization (SER Metro) and a Catholic organization serving youths and families (Boysville). Other new tenants on the former hospital campus include Mercy Primary Care Center to serve the uninsured, the National Council of Alcoholism and Drug Dependency, Head Start, Child Care Coordinating Center, the Detroit Fire Department, and McCauley Commons' independent housing. The revamped campus promises to continue providing a positive, major impact in the community. Balanced media coverage told the story fairly. Personal interviews with a sample of 20 (from the list of those previously interviewed) were extremely positive. Internal meetings were equally positive. Employees from Mercy Hospital–Detroit, many of whom would be without jobs, gave Mercy–Detroit's CEO a standing ovation after he explained the closing and transfer of the hospital.

The final test came when MHS announced the purchase of St. Mary Hospital, a 300-bed hospital in the Detroit suburb of Livonia, only four months after closing the inner-city Detroit hospital. Without the effective public relations program on the closing of Mercy Hospital–Detroit, the announcement to acquire a new hospital in a predominantly white suburb could have caused significant editorial scrutiny and community backlash that would surely damage MHS' reputation (just one month after its merger with another major national health system to create Trinity Health) and hamper its future growth. All internal and external audiences met the announcement of the St. Mary Hospital acquisition, except for minor exceptions, with support and encouragement.

Today, Mercy Primary Care Center continues to operate in one of the most impoverished areas of Detroit. It provides a range of primary care services, regardless of ability to pay. In 2005, it served more than 6,200 patients, providing medication, lab tests, limited radiological studies, physicals, preventive care and health education, management of acute and chronic diseases, pelvic exams and pap tests, enrollment into medical plans, social services, and limited specialty care to uninsured, low income patients. Mercy Primary Care Center also has a Specialized Personal Assistance program that provides clothing, showers, and laundry services for homeless persons. It provides about 150 showers a week and processes 300 loads of laundry a month.

Mercy Health Care, now known as Trinity Health, contributes up to $2 million a year in salaries, operations, and donations to keep the center open. ■

--------------------------------------------------------------

## QUESTIONS FOR DISCUSSION

1. You are the public relations director of the closing hospital. Your public relations plan calls for a community town hall meeting. Some people in the community don't have phones or computers. How will you alert everyone about this meeting? When will you hold it? How many times? Who will attend from the hospital? What is your goal for the meeting and how will you achieve that? Put together a plan addressing these issues.

2. Many depend on the hospital for their own and their children's health needs. The plan calls for input and feedback from the community. What will you do with their feedback? What if your CEO is unwilling to listen?

3. Take as an example the hospital closest to where you live. Who do you think are the opinion leaders for that hospital? Make a list and identify them by their position in the hospital, how they would be contacted and what the message strategy would be.

# Case 4-3 The Struggle for Nuclear Power

The environmental movement had its beginnings in the 1960s and 1970s, originally in protest of the nuclear power industry. Since that time, the movement has broadened its concerns, becoming involved in efforts to curb air, water, and ground pollution; global warming; overpopulation; and more. Many of the tactics used today by the environmental movement are the same as those it used in the 1970s.

The building and expansion of nuclear power plants over the last 25 years has pretty much dried up for numerous reasons. Activist actions and demands have driven up the costs of nuclear power projects. According to the Office of Nuclear Energy, Science and Technology, barriers to the deployment of new nuclear power plants include significant cost and schedule uncertainties associated with the new untested licensing processes for siting, licensing, and operating new nuclear power plants and the high capital cost of existing certified design. No new nuclear plants have been ordered in the United States for more than 25 years, but the strategies and tactics of the activists who protested these plants live on in most activists movements today.

In light of current global political situations, energy production will most likely become the focus of activists once again. Therefore, it is critical to understand where these strategies and tactics originated and consider how both sides of these issues may proceed in the future.

Seabrook Station became a national symbol of the nuclear power debate in the 1970s and 1980s. Located in Seabrook, New Hampshire, 40 miles north of Boston (see Figure 4-4), it was built on New Hampshire's 17-mile North Atlantic coastline in an extensive salt marsh area. During the prolonged construction and licensing process, Public Service Company of New Hampsphire (PSNH)—the original owner—encountered persistent opposition from various sources.

- Initially, opposition came from environmentalists who were concerned about the potential impact a "once-through" water cooling system would have on ocean temperature. Among other issues, they were worried about possible irreparable damage that warming ocean waters would have on the biological populations in and under those waters.
- As plant construction progressed, a broader section of the community became increasingly concerned about the safety of the reactor and the proposed evacuation plans.
- The cost of the plant and its possible effect on the region's electricity rates sparked additional opposition. Increased power costs were perceived as an obstacle blocking industrial development and the prosperity of northern New England.

Perhaps the first sign of problems for Seabrook Station occurred when the proposal to build came before various official boards. The illustrated model showed the containment unit, with a proposed height of 250 feet, mostly hidden from view by trees. But redwoods don't grow in New England!

FIGURE 4-4    Seadbrook Station, located near the seacoast in Seabrook, New Hampshire

*Source:* (Courtesy of Seabrook Station.)

- Some citizens protested the plant because they doubted New Hampshire's need for a new power source.

Seabrook Station encountered delays as activists started demonstrating. The opposition intervened in the Nuclear Regulatory Commission's (NRC) adjudicatory review boards. The legal case was led by the Seacoast Anti-Pollution League (SAPL), while other grassroots activists spearheaded by the Clamshell Alliance led protests. The Clamshell used grassroots organizing, group decision making, and affinity networking against public or private projects felt to be disruptive to an area. Its activities ranged from peaceful demonstrations to forceful attempts at site occupation with mass arrests.

After nearly 18 years of licensing, construction, and regulatory review, Seabrook Station began regular full-power operation on August 19, 1990. "We realize that we may never be able to satisfy the core group of people who do not support nuclear power," said Richard Winn, Seabrook's communications counsel at that time, "but we do not ignore them either." Through the years Seabrook Station has become more sensitive to the needs and concerns of its publics. At that time, according to Winn, Seabrook was doing something that a nuclear power plant does not have to do—that is, focusing on "the sorts of things that don't make electricity," such as community relations, public education, and environmental information.

## The Opposition

The Audubon Society opposed Seabrook Station before safety became an issue— before Three Mile Island. Its concern was environmental. When Seabrook changed the design of its cooling systems in order to prevent interference with the ocean, Audubon withdrew its opposition. Today, Seabrook is partnering with the Audubon Society and NH Fish and Game to build an osprey nest on its site in the hope of attracting a pair of nesting ospreys.

After the Three Mile Island and Chernobyl accidents, safety become the main concern of opposition. Seabrook opponents did include many gate-bashers, the form of opposition that comes to mind where nuclear power is concerned. But many other activists sought a different route to get their message heard. Issues of opposition ranged from complete rejection of nuclear power to the location of Seabrook Station.

The Clamshell Alliance, one of the most visible opposing organizations, went door to door in towns affected by Seabrook Station to gather support for protest. They also staged large, nonviolent and occasionally somewhat violent demonstrations.

Some real estate agencies and banks were opposed to Seabrook. Individuals in these fields joined other activist groups. In general, they were opposed to the possible drop in real estate value.

The Seacoast Anti-Pollution League (SAPL), a small group of dedicated volunteers, legally pursued Seabrook's perceived lack of safety. Their purpose at that time was "to work toward the deferral of the proposed nuclear plant at Seabrook.[1] Members, in conjunction with their attorney, Robert Backus, worked through the NRC's judicial system to improve the evacuation plan. SAPL believed that the initial plan was not adequate to meet the needs of the neighboring communities. Indeed, only three roads— all two-lane—lead away from the beach area adjacent to the plant, where on a summer Sunday as many as 100,000 people congregate for swimming and other beach activities.

Now that Seabrook is on line, SAPL strategies still emphasize the risks associated with living near a nuclear power plant. SAPL works in coordination with the Massachusetts-based Citizens within a 10-Mile Radius (C-10) to monitor the levels of background radiation to see if any additional radiation is being emitted from Seabrook Station. Their efforts are directed toward discovering if there is a correlation between increased levels of radiation and increased health problems in the area.

SAPL members often visit local schools to speak about the dangers of nuclear power, and they set up question-and-answer booths at university fairs and other events. SAPL also responds to NRC regulation changes distributed by the Nuclear Information and Resource Service. Members receive newsletters encouraging them to write letters to the editors of local newspapers in an effort to notify people about how these regulatory changes affect the general public. To this day, some dedicate their lives to opposing nuclear power.

## Financial Troubles Plague Seabrook

As a result of the mounting costs of Seabrook, PSNH was forced into bankruptcy. The company became financially strained when New Hampshire legislators passed the CWIP (Construction Work In Progress) law, which forbade the utility from

---

[1]Henry F. Bedfore, *Seabrook Station*. Amherst, MA: University of Massachusetts Press, 1990, p. 67.

---

**IDENTIFYING THE SEABROOK PUBLICS**

The Seabrook communications staff identified important publics for Seabrook.

**Internal Publics**

- All Seabrook Station employees who live in communities around the plant site
- Employees who do not live in the area

**External Publics**

- Massachusetts and New Hampshire residents living both inside and outside the Emergency Planning Zone

- Local and national news media
- The financial community

Seabrook community relations staff targeted, in the 23 New Hampshire and Massachusetts towns, public and private schools, day-care facilities, police and fire departments, local officials and opinion leaders, local media, advocacy groups, large (over 50 employees) and small businesses, chambers of commerce, network organizations such as the Lions and Rotary clubs and the local United Way, and citizens living within the 22-mile radius.

---

including the cost of the plant's construction in consumer electric rates until the power was turned on. This law delayed the economic burden on New Hampshire citizens but added to the utility's interest costs on millions borrowed to finance construction.

Construction ceased temporarily in 1984. Then New Hampshire Yankee (NHY), a division of PSNH, took over the project and with the Seabrook Joint Owners[2] (other power companies with an interest in the plant) reaffirmed determination to complete Seabrook. People from PSNH were moved into top position at New Hampshire Yankee.

## Developing Strategies

NHY's community relations team focused on Seabrook's publics in the seacoast area (see *Identifying the Seabrook Publics*). The

public relations team initially used reactive programming to address the opposition's concerns and to resolve the opposition's concerns and to resolve cognitive dissonance.[3] They used one-way and two-way communication techniques to address these goals.

## One-Way Techniques

1. Created a series of hard-hitting ads featuring Seabrook employees offering words of reassurance (see Figure 4-5).
2. Distributed a "safety kit" consisting of information on Seabrook, waste management, radiation, and safety systems.
3. Circulated *Energy,* a community-targeted newsletter, between 1988 and 1989 to all publics in the emergency area. The articles focused on issues related to energy.

---

[2]Originally, Seabrook Station was jointly owned by a large number of companies with PSNH holding the largest percentage of ownership. In 2002, Seabrook was sold to FP&L Energy.

[3]The theory of cognitive dissonance, first put forth by Leon Festinger in 1947, suggests a human desire for consistency between what people know and what they do. Any conflict creates a disturbance. See Glen Broom, Allen Center, and Scott Cutlip, *Effective Public Relations,* 8th ed., Toronto, Ontario: Prentice Hall Canada, 1999.

# Geryl Jasinski, Quality Assurance Engineer At Seabrook Station, On Her Job And Her Commitment To Safety.

**~Seabrook station**

A SAFE INVESTMENT
IN OUR ENERGY FUTURE

This message is brought to you by New Hampshire Yankee.

**FIGURE 4-5 Example of ads featuring a NHY employee and "The Lesson of Chernobyl"**

*Source:* (Courtesy of Seabrook Station.)

## Two-Way Techniques

1. In 1986, NHY formally invited the surrounding community to tour the nuclear plant. More than 7,000 people from the surrounding New Hampshire and Massachusetts communities attended this event.

2. Seabrook Station's Science and Nature Center (see Figure 4-6) allows viewers to explore nature and science simultaneously. The Center displays information about electrical generation and contains an ocean aquarium 260 feet below sea level. A total of 30,000 people visit the Center annually.

3. According to NRC regulations, the state must inform the public in the 23 affected towns about emergency and safety procedures. NHY took this one-way task and made it into a two-way strategy. Public relations staff created a calendar decorated with photographs of the seacoast and mailed copies to all homes in the area. The

**FIGURE 4-6   A brochure of the Science and Nature Center**

*Source:* (Courtesy of Seabrook Station.)

calendars include public notification information, including which radio stations broadcast emergency bulletins and instructions. Employees hand-delivered calendars to approximately 4,000 of the 7,000 small businesses in the area. Only 2 percent of those businesses rejected the information.

Seabrook did encounter some heated public opposition to the evacuation plan, and that attracted a lot of media attention. Some schools were unhappy with the proposed evacuation plans because teachers would be required to stay with their classes even though their instinct would be to rush to their own families. These perceptions of the proposed evacuation plan's shortcomings forced many towns to reject the emergency procedures.

4. Communicators representing Seabrook met with school superintendents and business executives to educate them about emergency planning. They also developed relationships with Massachusetts emergency medical squads and fire departments.

5. NHY communications approached the media proactively. If a siren that had nothing to do with Seabrook

sounded off in a surrounding town or if a rumor about Seabrook was circulated, NHY called the media before the media called them.

These efforts helped Seabrook Station achieve on-line status. NHY won its contested case before the NRC's adjudicating boards.

## The Need for Proactive Measures

Seabrook public relations teams did not stop once the plant was on line. "We did the things we needed to do to get our license according to the rules and regulations. And then we went a step farther to be proactive and adopt a policy of 'management of expectations' for our community relations efforts," wrote Richard Winn.

Seabrook utilized strategy to build one-on-one relationships. Now that the plant was up and running, those relationships needed to be maintained. According to Seabrook research at that time, the greatest percentage of people were not definitively for or against nuclear power. Therefore, public relations staff believed it was vital that the public feel comfortable about contacting Seabrook whenever there was a concern.

## Reinforcing Relationships

NHY took measures to reinforce the relationships it had established.

1. NHY continued to send out an Emergency Plan Information Calendar to all of its external publics. The calendar consists of 33 pages of emergency planning and safety information.
2. The Science and Nature Center was made accessible for school and community-based field trips. The Center provides hands-on exhibits featuring energy and environment and the Owascoag Nature Trail—approximately 1 mile of preserved woods and marshlands with a variety of plants and animals.

3. NHY established a local hotline for citizens in surrounding communities to call and inquire about specific problems and concerns.

## Focusing on the Community

In 1991, Seabrook Station employees and volunteers participated in several community-oriented events and activities. The community relations department initiated at least one new program encouraging community involvement each quarter.

1. Employees participated in the Lion's Camp Pride, a summer camp facility offering educational and recreational overnight programs to children with special needs. Volunteers installed docks, stained and painted buildings, and cleaned and set up bunkhouses.
2. Employees participated in the seacoast's Seafood Festival. They raised money at the event by selling popcorn and donated all proceeds to My Greatest Dream, an organization that benefits terminally ill children.
3. Volunteers participated in Coastweeks, a nationwide celebration of the nation's coastal areas. NHY cleaned up Hampton Beach, a New Hampshire state park about two miles from the Seabrook plant.
4. Time and building materials were donated to Action Cove Playground, an innovative playground in West Newbury, Massachusetts. The children's area was designed for explorative and imaginative play.
5. NHY founded a local Project Homefront, an effort assisting families whose relatives were called to serve in the Persian Gulf War. A total of 163 volunteers offered services and assistance in transportation; auto, electrical and plumbing repair; carpentry; and babysitting. Employees also donated $1,135 to this project.

Other community endeavors aided organizations such as Wish Upon a Star, which provides anonymous Christmas gifts to needy children, and the Girl Scouts of America. According to Martha Netsch, Director of Communications for the Swift-water Girl Scout Council, the Girl Scouts frequently visit Seabrook Station's Science and Nature Center, work with staff on scout education programs about solutions to today's energy problems, and recognize the Science and Nature Center as support for young women interested in mathematics, science, and technology.

Seabrook encourages employees to become involved in local civic organizations and in local government. Many are on town and city boards, volunteer emergency medical squads and fire departments; Rotary, Lions, and Kiwanis clubs; or are active in school organizations. Every year employees serve as judges at local science fairs.

## Through the 1990s, Into the Twenty-First Century

In 1992, control of Seabrook was bought by Connecticut-based Northeast Utilities, which earlier took over bankrupt PSNH. Legislation was passed in 2000 that deregulated the energy industry. It required those who distributed energy to divest themselves of energy sources that produce power. Thus, Seabrook was sold again in 2002 to FP&L Energy, a Florida energy provider that set up a separate energy-producing company from its delivery side. It promptly dismantled the second cooling tower on site. Although management has changed, very little else has.

Some activist groups continue to exist, though most are now peaceful in their approach. According to SAPL's Joan and Charles Pratt, both SAPL and C-10 work as watchdogs. Their mission is to make sure Seabrook complies with NRC regulations. The Citizens Radiological Monitoring Network acts as a support group that focuses on how to live with potential hazards. Its goals are to monitor every air and water emission from Seabrook, to hold Seabrook socially accountable for every emission, and to expect a responsible attitude from the station itself. All these awareness groups keep a close eye on Seabrook.

Despite the controversial issues, Seabrook employees, for the most part, maintain professional relationships with activist groups. There are still a small number of people opposing the plant who remain very reserved and refuse to speak to anyone who works at Seabrook Station. The plant's community relations department believes it is in their best interest to deal cooperatively with these groups.

The Seabrook Station Communications Team noted at the time, "A subtle community relations shift occurred at Seabrook Station as the plant became more accepted and proved itself to be a good neighbor. Initially, the value of a solid community outreach program in large part was to help support the plant's efforts to get licensed and begin generating power. Now that Seabrook has done that, our community outreach is just as important now as it ever was. In many ways, our community relations activities have become more of an extension of our own employees' personal lives and commitments to their neighborhoods."

The Seabrook Station Science and Nature Center, its "most valuable PR outreach vehicle," continues its efforts to educate people about nuclear energy. The Center also affords the opportunity to inform visitors about the many initiatives taken by the Station that helped transform a town dump into a thriving ecosystem.

## Evaluation

Has Seabrook Station prevailed in the court of public opinion? In one sense, it has in that it is now an accepted part of the community.

Seabrook Station continues its two-way communication efforts by upholding its good neighbor policy, offering ongoing educational information to the public, and through the involvement of its employees in their neighborhoods and community organizations—becoming Seabrook Station's ambassadors. However, according to the Office of Nuclear Energy, Science and Technology, "Until nuclear power becomes an energy solution once again, we won't know for sure if Seabrook and its string of owners have done enough with stakeholder education and relationship building to be successful in building new plants." ■

---

## HISTORY OF SEABROOK STATION

### 1960s

- Plans for a nuclear plant in New Hampshire developed.

### 1972

- Two-unit power plant proposed for Seabrook, New Hampshire.

### 1973

- Application for construction permit filed. Concerns about environment arise.

### 1977

- The Clamshell Alliance and others form and mount protests; 1,400 people are arrested.

### 1978

- Peaceful demonstration on site is suggested to "The Clam" by an area public relations counselor, Isobel Parke, as more effective than another protest; 30,000 people attend an energy fair on plant grounds. No one is arrested.

### 1979

- Three Mile Island incident causes Seabrook to reconsider its design. Safety features and more emergency planning are added. Activists express concern through demonstrations.

- Interest rates skyrocket. Construction delayed because of financing difficulties.
- CWIP (Construction Work In Progress) law passed; causes more financial strain.

### 1984

- Changeover period. New Hampshire Yankee, a division of PSNH, takes over in June to manage completion of construction, licensing, and operation of the plant.
- Construction is temporarily suspended for three months.

### 1986

- Election year. Candidates' success depended on whether they were for or against Seabrook.
- Paul McEachern, Democrat, defeated by incumbent Republican governor John Sununu, over the CWIP issue.
- Construction of plant completed (July 31).
- Nuclear Regulatory Commission issues license for testing of reactor.
- Chernobyl disaster in USSR.
- More safety concerns and activist demonstrations.
- Massachusetts Governor Michael Dukakis, representing the six Massachusetts towns near Seabrook, pulls his state's support and vows to fight the plant's opening.

**1988**

- Public Service Company of New Hampshire (PSNH) files Chapter 11 bankruptcy in January.
- Atomic Safety and Licensing Board, an arm of NRC, approves state of New Hampshire's emergency response plan for the towns surrounding Seabrook.

**1990**

- NRC issues full-power operating license in March, and power is generated for the first time in May. Power level reaches 100 percent in July.

**1991**

- U.S. Court of Appeals rejects appeal of the NRC's decision to issue an operating license in January.
- Massachusetts Governor William Weld directs state officials to begin cooperative emergency planning with New Hampshire Yankee in March.
- U.S. Supreme Court lets the lower court's decision stand to uphold the NRC's licensing of Seabrook Station in October.

**1992**

- PSNH is acquired by Northeast Utilities. Seabrook operates at 77.9 percent of generating capacity for the year.

**2000**

- Seabrook Station celebrates its tenth anniversary.
- Acknowledged by the industry as one of the best-run nuclear plants in the nation.

**2002**

- Facility sold to FP&L Energy

## QUESTIONS FOR DISCUSSION

1. What responsibilities does a business have to the community, if any?
2. Should a business that produces a controversial product or service have obligations that surpass legal and regulatory mandates? Why or why not? Does your answer depend on whether the product (or production of the product) is potentially hazardous or lethal to the environment or humans?
3. Seabrook offers an informational phone line for communities and employees to call whenever questions or concerns arise. This phone line accommodates the local towns surrounding Seabrook Station. Do you think this phone line would be more effective if it were a national 800 number, thus making it available to all U.S. residents? Why or why not?
4. Develop some strategies that could strengthen the messages or effectiveness of the remaining opposition.
5. Develop some proactive and reactive strategies that Seabrook will need when decommissioning the plant, disposing of the spent fuel rods, and if the radiological emission risk correlations show that the plant has become dangerous.

# Case 4-4   Nuclear Waste Goes Down the Drain

Every day people all across the country choose to do things that have a certain degree of risk—crossing the street, driving a car, flying in an airplane, bungee jumping, or eating foods they know do not constitute good nutrition.

What happens, though, when someone else controls the risks we face? Do we ask our friend to pull the car over so we can get out? Never fly unless we pilot the plane? What happens if an organization wants to take a risk in a community, such as dumping low-level nuclear waste, even if it may be smaller than the risks we take in everyday life?

More and more, organizations are facing strident opposition to their plans from groups and coalitions opposed to taking on more risk. Grassroots environmental concerns have fostered attitudes such as Not In My Back Yard (NIMBY) and Not On Planet Earth (NOPE) to limit any sort of activities viewed as at all risky. Yet, in many cases, organizations need to assume some risk in order to run their business, produce products, adhere to government standards, or make a profit.

Risk management deals with explaining and persuading a risk-averse public to allow the execution of necessary actions that may carry some risk (see Figure 4-7). But risk communication is more than explanation or persuasion. It must be process-oriented to allow interaction between the opposing groups—the public, proponents, experts, and regulatory officials—and allow each to identify the true issues at stake from its perspective. Only then can the average citizen form an intelligent judgment.

## Is Risk Communication a Different Ball Game?

As technology has changed, so have the type and amount of risks we face. Public reaction to risk can be varied, depending on each individual's mind-set and experiences. Each person perceives risk in his or her own personal context and with his or her own established biases for or against that risk.

In 1983, the National Research Council (NRC) completed a study on managing risk, leading to a report entitled *Risk Assessment in the Federal Government: Managing the Process*. Raised in this study was the realization that with risk management comes a new kind of communication, risk communication. The NRC chartered a committee, the Risk Perception and Communication Committee, to research how to communicate risks effectively to the public. The committee found that explaining risks in a logical manner was not effective for convincing a risk-averse public that the risks were nothing to worry about. People evaluate risks contextually, and their *perception* of that risk motivates their behavior.

## One Example

For many years, the city of Albuquerque, New Mexico, had an ordinance forbidding anyone—except hospitals and radiation treatment clinics—from disposing of low-level radioactive wastes in the city's sewer system. Low-level radioactive waste covers anything that may have been contaminated by radioactive materials, such as equipment, clothing, tools, and so on.

ANNUAL NUMBER OF DEATHS PER MILLION PEOPLE

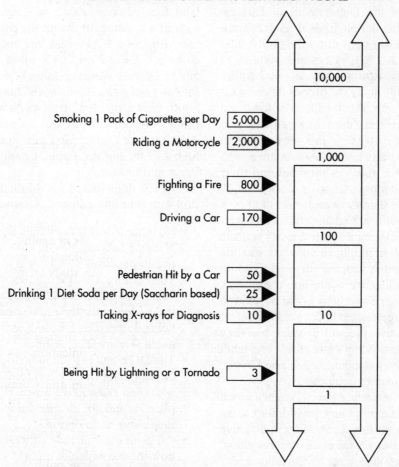

Source: Adapted from Schultz, W.,G. McClelland, B. Hurd, and J. Smith (1986), *Improving Accuracy and Reducing Costs of Environmental Benefits Assessment.* Vol. IV. Boulder: University of Colorado, Center for Economic Analysis.

WARNING! USE OF DATA IN THIS FIGURE FOR RISK COMPARISON PURPOSES CAN SEVERELY DAMAGE YOUR CREDIBILITY (SEE TEXT).

**FIGURE 4-7**   **One tactic used by risk communicators has been to make risk comparisons in order to communicate the extent of the risk. But making quantitative risk comparisons with voluntary risk has proved illogical and damaging to the organizations who employ this tactic. Demonstrating it visually is more effective**

*Source:* (Courtesy of the Chemical Manufacturers Association. From Vincent T. Covello, Peter M. Sandman, and Paul Slovic, *Risk Communication, Risk Statistics and Risk Comparisons: A Manual for Plant Managers* [Washington, D.C.: CMA, 1988].)

In 1991, Sandia National Laboratories (a facility of the Department of Energy, DOE) and Inhalation Toxicology Research Institute (ITRI) petitioned the city to dispose of its waste in the city sewer systems, as the hospitals were already allowed to do. Sandia initially made the proposal because it wanted to dump 50,000 gallons of low-level radioactive water (used to shield nuclear reactor fuel rods) into the sewer system. Radiation experts assured Albuquerque residents that the risk was minimal and their tap water had more natural or "background" radiation in it than the wastewater did.[1]

An amendment to change the city's sewer-use ordinance was put before the city council. The change would have allowed anyone licensed to use radioactive material to dump low-level radioactive waste into the sewers. Though more organizations would be allowed to dump, more stringent limits would be set on how radioactive the waste could be. They would be able to dump waste at only one-tenth the radioactivity standards established by the Nuclear Regulatory Commission.

After investigating, the city council found that its ordinance or any amendment to an ordinance regarding discharging radioactive wastewater does not fall under its jurisdiction. These regulations are set by the federal government through the Nuclear Regulatory Commission and DOE. Thus Sandia as a federal laboratory could ignore the city ordinance and dump anyway—that is, if its managers thought this was acceptable public relations policy. They did not, however, so the issue went to public debate.

## A Vocal Opposition

Citizen opposition was immediate and outspoken. A group named People's Emergency Response Committee (PERC) began to organize. PERC was formed a year before the emergence of this issue, when those involved first became aware of Mayor Louis Saavedra's attempt to change the city's sewer-use ordinance. It is an ad hoc coalition of citizens' organizations made up of Hospital and Healthcare Workers Union 1199, Citizens for Alternatives to Radioactive Dumping, the South West Organizing Project, New Mexico Public Interest Research Group, the Albuquerque Center for Peace and Justice, Sierra Club, and the Labor Committee for Peace and Justice.

PERC immediately established its position with four fundamental statements:

- No other industries including Sandia National Laboratories should be allowed to dump radioactive wastes in the sewers.
- The existing Albuquerque sewer ordinance should be strengthened to control and monitor the radioactive wastes being dumped by hospitals and other medical treatment facilities.
- The DOE and private industries must develop long-range plans for dealing with their radioactive waste. These plans should not include dumping in the sewers as an option.
- All plans must include strategies on how these companies and the DOE will reduce the *generation* of radioactive waste in the first place.

Representatives of the group were at the first hearing regarding the change. They were concerned that the issue was more than obtaining permission to dump 50,000 gallons of waste. They saw it as a ploy to allow any business in the future to rid itself of radioactive waste. Concerns were raised about the water's path. Would it enter the Rio Grande and then affect towns downstream from Albuquerque? This was not a risk that the citizens of Albuquerque and the surrounding towns were prepared to take, PERC felt.

---

[1]Background radiation is naturally occurring radiation that accounts for more than half of the radiation we are exposed to. It is generated from cosmic rays, naturally occurring elements such as uranium, and radioactive chemicals in the body.

## PERC's Tactics

One communication tactic that PERC utilized was to publish a newsletter entitled Radioactive Pipeline to establish its position. Its focus was on the risks that residents perceived: that this could contaminate Albuquerque and that there was no telling if Sandia and the others could be trusted. This newsletter helped PERC get its message out to make people aware of the situation. The newsletters and flyers PERC distributed urged the citizens of Albuquerque and surrounding areas to take action and voice their concerns at community and city council meetings. Postcard campaigns were mounted by distributing preprinted cards so that citizens could easily send them to local city councilors expressing opposition to this ordinance. A petition drive was started, gathering more than 7,000 signatures.

## Obstacles for Sandia

Media coverage was not helpful for Sandia, either. While officials were explaining how safe the water was in one article, other articles in the newspaper reported some of Sandia's sewer violations and mismanagement of radioactive materials by DOE.

City council meetings were packed with citizens who came to voice their outrage. Sandia arranged for two radiation experts to speak in an attempt to reassure people of their physical safety, but this expertise did not address the underlying issues that made up a major part of this controversy.

- Many Americans have a **lack of trust** for the federal government and those organizations that are a part of it. When, or if, stories concerning federal mismanagement and secret nuclear tests are uncovered, the public will remember them later.
- The effects of radioactive wastes are not completely understood. Some effects will not be apparent for a very

long time, and this **uncertainty** is difficult for anyone to deal with.
- Many people already have **biases** against anything nuclear, especially if it is near where they live.
- Albuquerque residents were concerned with what this initial dumping would mean for the **future.** They were asking themselves: What else would be dumped, and how often would it happen?

## The Sandia Side of It

Sandia's public affairs department did make an attempt to educate the public about this risk to try and allay public fears about radiation and radioactive materials. Some of their activities included:

- Organizing some of the public meetings to create the opportunity for citizens to voice their concerns and get questions answered.
- Reaching out to public officials and leaders who showed opposition to the proposal to give them the facts of the issue.
- Making public affairs people available for any and all questions that the public had about the issue.
- Arranging for television interviews with radiation experts to disseminate to the public the facts of radiation.

## Can There Ever Be Agreement?

On November 5, 1991, the Albuquerque City Council voted against the proposal to change the city ordinance. The Council then formed a study committee to review important questions about radioactive dumping and offer recommendations in six months. Two years and two research studies later, the city council finally consented to the disposal of the wastewater in the sewer system.

For Sandia National Laboratories, the task of disposing of its waste became an ordeal. A simple task of applying for a permit had become an extended three-year controversy.

For all affected organizations, the question remains: What will we do with our low-level radioactive waste? Wha. is often overlooked is the benefits that nuclear science offers. Do we abolish nuclear science altogether? NIMBYists demand that disposal not be done where they live. Where else, then? Will there ever be an acceptable alternative? For public relations practitioners, the challenge of communicated risk will only become greater as technology advances.

## Yucca Mountain—An Unresolved Risk Management Problem

While Sandia National Laboratories was eventually successful in obtaining permission to dispose of its wastewater in the city sewer system, another Department of Energy (DOE) proposal for the disposal of radioactive materials continues to remain unresolved. The Yucca Mountain case is further complicated by issues of alleged environmental racism and the right to protect culturally sacred sites.

In 1982, Congress passed the Nuclear Waste Policy Act that set an objective framework for government officials to study and evaluate multiple potential repository sites for nuclear waste in the United States. The DOE faces the task of finding a geologic repository to permanently store 77,000 metric tons of high-level radioactive waste that is temporarily being stored at various locations around the country. About 90 percent of this waste is from commercial nuclear power plants; the remainder is from government defense programs.

The Nuclear Waste Policy Act Amendment of 1987—nicknamed "Screw Nevada Act" by residents there—(1) eliminated all but one of the potential repository sites, Yucca Mountain in Nevada, and (2) directed the DOE to study only that location for site suitability. The Amendment stressed that if, at any time, the Yucca Mountain site is found unsuitable, studies of the site will be stopped immediately. If the studies are discontinued, the site will be restored and the DOE will seek new direction from Congress.

Yucca Mountain is located 100 miles northwest of Las Vegas and sits on the western edge of the DOE's former nuclear-weapons test site. The proposed repository would sit 1,000 feet below the top of the mountain and 1,000 feet above the ground water.

In 1992, Congress passed the Energy Policy Act, which required the Environmental Protection Agency (EPA) to develop site-specific radiation protection standards for Yucca Mountain to protect public health and the environment from harmful exposure to the radioactive waste that would be stored there. The Nuclear Regulatory Commission (NRC) is responsible for implementing the standards set by the EPA. Ultimately, the NRC would be responsible for establishing the process for deciding whether Yucca Mountain meets the EPA's standards.

---

### CAN KIDS IMPACT YUCCA'S OUTCOME?

Billed as an educational program only, the DOE has a kid-friendly area as part of its Yucca Mountain Web site. It has taken a mascot—"Yucca Mountain Johnny"—into the Nevada schools as an educational tool. DOE spokesman Craig Stevens says, "Yucca Johnny teaches hydrology, geology, and earth science." Opponents compare Yucca Johnny with another, now maligned, symbol. Says Shelly Berkeley, a U.S. Representative from Nevada, "Yucca Mountain Johnny is the Department of Energy's Joe Camel. And the product he's peddling is just as toxic."

From the beginning, the State of Nevada has firmly opposed the plan and is prepared to file lawsuits through all steps of the process if Yucca Mountain is recommended as the permanent repository site.

The state is supported in its opposition by more than 200 environmental groups.

Primary concerns with the plan to make Yucca Mountain the permanent resting grounds for the country's nuclear waste are:

---

### PR MESSAGES SET RISK PERCEPTIONS, AND RISK IS EVERYWHERE

All communications have become risk communications. Therefore, the rules for dealing with hazardous waste and cancer fears should be applied to every communication—to employees, shareholders, stakeholders, and customers, and surely to regulators, government entities, and the body politic.

Why? Because today publics are interested in two things: What can you do *for* me? And what, if I'm not careful, might you do *to* me? That second query—people's natural skepticism raised to new levels by today's troubled economy and quality-of-life—adds a risk perspective to every message or appeal.

#### INFLUENCING PEOPLE'S PERCEPTION OF RISK

Risk communication is proactive. Its goal is to improve knowledge and change perceptions, attitudes, and behaviors of the target public, write Leandro Batista and Dulcie Straughan, of the University of North Carolina at Chapel Hill.[1] They note, however, that changing risk perception—a necessary step for behavior change—is complicated. It can be:

1. *Objective:* product of research, statistics, experimental studies, surveys, probabilistic risk analysis, or

2. *Subjective:* how those without expert or inside knowledge interpret the research or the situation—which is based on their values and particular levels of experience and knowledge.

Thus, experts and lay people build different mental models that lead them to interpret risk activities differently. One does it objectively, the other subjectively.

#### FORMAT OF THE MESSAGE

The format of the risk message forms the risk perception. For example, radon and asbestos have a 25-fold difference in *actual* risk to the population, but generate only a slight difference in *perceived* threat. The inaccuracy of people's perceptions of the relative risks of radon and asbestos can be explained by the similarity of the format of messages conveying the risks involved. Regardless of the actual content of the message, the idea that is usually conveyed is that "this is a technical area that you probably won't understand, but there is a *danger here*." In other words, people will have similar responses to messages that are expressed in similar formats, even though the information may be different. Public relations teams can apply their knowledge of this aspect of human nature to formulate effective messages in a systematic way.

1. Each risk has its own identity (or risk perception), which is a specific combination of subjective risk factors (see box),

(*continued*)

*(continued)*

or, as Neil Weinstein and Peter Sandman call them. "Outrage Factors."[2]

2. Some combination of these outrage factors leads people to be more upset about hazard X than hazard Y.

3. Not all factors are relevant for all risks and there is no trade-off among factors—scoring high on one factor will not compensate for a low score on another (the noncompensatory model).

---

### SUBJECTIVE RISK FACTORS

| Less Risky | More Risky |
|---|---|
| voluntary | involuntary |
| familiar | unfamiliar |
| controllable | uncontrollable |
| controlled by self | controlled by others |
| fair | unfair |
| not memorable | memorable |
| not dreaded | dreaded |
| chronic | acute |
| diffused in time and space | focused in time and space |
| natural | artificial |

---

Factors are either on or off in the overall perception of that risk.

4. Therefore, it's important to understand the underlying dimensions that affect the perception of a particular risk—how the outrage factors combine to form a risk perception.

5. Messages should not be formulated until these underlying dimensions are understood.

A final concept to keep in mind is the one that governs the decision-making process: With health or environmental risks, people will modify their behavior if a highly threatening situation exists (or is perceived to exist). Thus a minimum standard, or threshold, is set for risk acceptability. If a risk is greater than the threshold, action occurs; otherwise the status quo is preferred. In all probability, this concept is as true for risks of being overcharged, getting fired, or losing on investments as it is for nuclear discharges.

Peter Sandman's formula for identifying risk has become widely used by public relations practitioners: HAZARD + OUTRAGE = RISK PERCEPTION.[3]

[1]"Dimensions Influencing Risk Perception: The Case of Lung Diseases." Unpublished paper, n.d.
[2]Neil D. Weinstein and Peter M. Sandman, "Predicting Homeowner Mitigation Responses to Radon Test Data," *Journal of Social Issues* 48, 1992.
[3]Peter Sandman, *Responding to Community Outrage: Strategies for Effective Risk Communication,* Fairfax, VA: American Industrial Hygiene Association, 1993.

---

(1) The threat of earthquakes in the proposed area which could cause leakage. Since 1976, more than 600 earthquakes of 2.5 or more on the Reichter scale have occurred within a 50-mile radius of Yucca Mountain. In 1992, a 5.6 earthquake occurred on a previously unknown fault at Yucca Mountain. (2) There is evidence, uncovered by the Los Alamos Department of Energy Project in 1998, that Yucca Mountain would not comply with guidelines regarding ground water flow. Data regarding rainwater infiltration of Yucca Mountain would have called for the immediate disqualification under set guidelines. However, Yucca Mountain was not disqualified. When the nuclear industry found that two of the DOE requirements were going to be violated,

they lobbied Congress to change the suitability guidelines.

In November 1998, the opposition held a news conference. Many political representatives and members of consumer organizations and environmental groups introduced a petition from more than 200 groups opposed to the plan. They urged the DOE to "follow the law, disqualify the site because it could not meet the environmental guidelines under the current law." Despite the opposition, the evaluation of Yucca Mountain continues. In August 1999, the EPA released draft radiation protection standards for Yucca Mountain. It gave a preliminary approval of Yucca Mountain as a safe disposal site. After issuing its report, the EPA accepted written comments and held public hearings around the country "to ensure public involvement in the decision-making process."

In December 1999, a policy revision proposal for Yucca Mountain was released by the Federal government. The proposal eliminated safeguards regarding water flow on the mountain. Nevada Senator Henry Reid said the change contradicted Energy Secretary Bill Richardson's original goal that science, not politics, would drive the decisions regarding the disposal of nuclear waste.

In April 2006, the DOE sent proposed Yucca Mountain legislation to Congress that would "fix Yucca" once and for all. The DOE announced in an April 4, 2006, news release that the new legislation included a comprehensive set of provisions that "will facilitate licensing and construction of the geologic repository and will lead to the safe, permanent disposal of spent nuclear fuel and high-level radioactive waste deep within the mountain." It also stated that it would eliminate the current 70,000 metric ton cap on disposal capacity and streamline NRC licensing process.

However, the legislation was halted despite, as the *Las Vegas Sun* reported, a "near-perfect alignment of powerful interests. The Bush administration is the most pro-nuclear administration in decades. Republicans control both houses of Congress and the nuclear industry is pushing hard to get the project moving again."

Activists have continued to control this issue, although the industry has been working hard. The *Sun* reported that Charles Pray, co-chairman of the U.S. Transport Council's Yucca Mountain Task Force, increased his travel budget by $10,000 in 2006 to rally nuclear power generating states to the cause.

## Environmental Racism Is Involved

Opposition also comes from Native American rights groups and, more specifically, the Western Shoshone Nation, because Yucca Mountain is a place of spiritual significance to the Shoshone and Paiute peoples. The Western Shoshone Nation contends that the government has no right to use the land since it was guaranteed to them by an 1863 treaty (18 Statutes at Large 689). Corbin Harney, a Western Shoshone spiritual leader, says "Even the mere study of the site is a violation of the treaty. The Shoshone people want the DOE off their land and their mountain restored to them."

Based on the history of the interaction of the United States government with Indian tribes, mistrust of the government is deeply instilled in most Native Americans. In their view, another treaty violation and further dismissal of native participation in the process simply validates and exacerbates this mistrust. Many Native American and environmental groups believe that Native American lands are specifically targeted for nuclear waste disposal by the federal government and that these actions can be defined as environmental racism. According to Grace Thorpe of the National Environmental Coalition of Native Americans, the following factors make native lands an easy selection for governmental agencies:

- The lands are some of the most isolated in North America.
- The lands and the populations are extremely impoverished.
- The tribes are politically vulnerable.
- Their tribal sovereignty can be used to bypass state environmental laws.

A review of the government's Yucca Mountain Project Web site (www.ymp.gov) indicates that the spiritual concerns and land rights issues of the Western Shoshone Nation are given little, if any, consideration. Under a section entitled "Preservation through Conservation," the site states "the U.S. Department of Energy works to protect important cultural resources at the site . . . through the Yucca Mountain Project's Cultural Resources Program. As part of the Cultural Resources Program, delegates from the Project have met with tribal leaders . . . to gather cultural data for the Program." Although this Program professes to endeavor to protect the "archaeological, botanical, and cultural resources," there is no mention of the spiritual nature of the land or acknowledgement of the 1863 treaty and, therefore, the alleged illegality of the presence of the Project in the Yucca Mountain area. In fact, the Web site states "Nearly all of the land surrounding Yucca Mountain is federally owned."

Although the Yucca Mountain repository was originally scheduled to open by 1998, numerous technical and political delays have advanced that date. Spencer Abraham, Secretary of Energy, was expected to decide in 2001 whether to recommend to President Bush that Yucca Mountain be established as a nuclear waste repository site, but that decision was further postponed by the September 11 terrorist attacks. The attacks put the safety of transporting nuclear waste from one location to another under further scrutiny. However, in January 2002, Secretary Abraham announced that he would recommend to the president that Yucca Mountain be used as a nuclear waste storage site. The president will then decide whether to recommend the site to Congress for approval. If approved, the DOE must apply for licensing from the Nuclear Regulatory Commission. The license would then permit the DOE to construct the facility and begin waste disposal in 2010. ■

## QUESTIONS FOR DISCUSSION

1. If you were a public relations practitioner working at a local hospital that was dumping low-level radioactive waste into the sewers, what would you have counseled management to do during the Sandia attempt to gain authorization to dump its waste? Why would you recommend that?

2. Would it have been possible to convince the citizens of Albuquerque to allow the dumping of radioactive waste in the sewers? Why do you believe this? What tactics could Sandia have used to allay the fears of the public?

3. Why was PERC successful in gathering so much public support? What did it do differently than Sandia?

4. If you were the EPA's public relations director, what would you do to reach the opposition and communicate about the risks involved at Yucca Mountain? Do you think it's possible to reach a win-win solution? If so, how? Or must the government strong-arm its plan into place? If it pushes through its plan, what do you think will be the consequences?

# Case 4-5 Grassroots Efforts Save a Historic Piece of Land

In the summer of 1995, a for-sale sign was placed on a small parcel of open but developable land in the heart of historic downtown Exeter, New Hampshire. Almost immediately, a small group of concerned citizens began a grassroots effort to purchase the land and keep it as open space for everyone to enjoy. It was on this land that the original Town House of Exeter stood. And it was there, on January 5, 1776, that New Hampshire declared its independence from Great Britain—the first of the colonies to do so.

A total of $150,000 was needed to purchase this last parcel of open space in historic downtown Exeter. The grassroots effort had three phases:

1. Gathering over 50 signatures on a citizens' petition to place a warrant article before town meeting for $70,000 toward the land's purchase price.
2. Gaining a yes vote for the article at town meeting. This was a real challenge because the taxpayers union had won two-thirds support for changes in town government that it felt would restrain expenditures.
3. Raising, in three months, matching funds from private donations. This effort was a public-private partnership.

## Public Relations Tactics

This grassroots effort successfully used the following tactics:

- **The information campaign began early to give those most likely to be interested a heads-up without alerting the opposition.** Soon after the for-sale sign appeared, the historic Perry-Dudley House, located next to the open space, participated in a townwide open house tour. This provided an opportunity to talk with visitors about the importance of the adjoining open space. A flier handed out to over 250 visitors outlined the issue and suggested action steps, such as calling their selectman to express support for saving the open space.
- **A broad spectrum of well-respected opinion leaders in the community were chosen to be members of the organizing committee.** Their connections and credibility helped to support the cause.
- **The committee concentrated on those most likely to offer support**—especially helpful when there are limited resources. They did not waste time trying to convert others. To gain support for the upcoming vote at town meeting, a mailing was sent to organizations most likely to be supportive: Exeter Historical Society, Conservation Commission, an area land trust, a local museum, and friends of the organizing committee—including a local walking club (of which one of the steering committee was a member) and a senior citizens community known to have strong environmentally aware residents.

  Brief talks were given to local organizations such as the Chamber of Commerce and the Rotary. Personal visits were made to the chief of police and to the fire department—both situated opposite the open space.
- **The organizing committee was open and upfront with likely objections. This weakened the force of the opposition.** Through one-on-one research, the committee anticipated opposition from the

newly formed taxpayers association, especially its concern that creating a park on the open space would remove the land from the tax rolls. The tax implications were explained in a flier sent to selected town residents and made available at the town meeting where the issue was discussed.

The leader of the taxpayers association opposed taking the land off the tax roll. On another project, however, he expressed support for the concept of the public–private partnership. Park proponents used the communication strategy of asking that his group remain at least neutral in discussion of the warrant article, since opposition was discourteous to fellow citizens willing to make the effort to raise private matching funds for this public–private partnership.

This soft tactic worked. The leaflet produced by the taxpayers association advised its members to oppose almost every warrant article up for vote at the town meeting, but omitted the park issue—even though it required the largest amount of money.

- **Despite negative predictions, the committee did not give up**—hoping that events over which they had no control might tilt the balance in their favor. Organizers had hoped for a small turnout with their supporters carrying the day. But due to special items on the agenda, the meeting was larger than anticipated. Many of the supporters for the open space were in their 60s, 70s, and 80s. Organizers had relied on the advice from town officials that the meeting would probably be a short one, over by lunch.

However, the contentiousness of the taxpayers association prolonged the discussion of the early items on the agenda, which made a lunch break necessary. Would the supporters for open space return after lunch? They did. Some of the taxpayers association supporters melted away because the two items on which they felt most strongly (and lost) were dealt with early in the agenda. The order of the agenda (which unexpectedly was changed) was extremely helpful to the open space cause. Without this change, the taxpayers association would have stayed to the bitter end.

All the articles adding to the town budget passed. The open space article was the last money article on the agenda. It came up at about 4 P.M. Shortly before the opening speech, the organizers decided to amend the article. This was a risk but it served them well in presenting a case for a downward cap on the amount of money requested. Rather than asking for $70,000, it was amended to ask for half the negotiated purchase price, not to exceed $70,000.

As expected, selectmen and the speakers from the floor raised the negative aspects of taking property off the tax roll. The committee's three speakers were brief and avoided going into the kind of detail, especially financial, that usually confuses and leads to disaster in town meeting situations. Feeling that the meeting was ready to vote, the "cleanup" speaker decided not to speak, knowing well that many good causes have talked themselves to death. The initial voice vote was indecisive. A hand vote showed the motion carried by a safe majority of 106 to 78. Given the inauspicious environment of the voters and the opposition of the selectmen, the committee was pleasantly surprised.

- **The committee avoided the media because organizers were uncertain of the media's stand on the open space issue.** During the period of town elections, an initial visit was paid to the editor of the local paper. His support seemed uncertain, especially since he gave editorial support to the successful bid for office by the leader of the taxpayers association. No news releases or media interviews were given until after town meeting. This avoided giving the opposition a target.

During the fund-raising period, the committee also worked "under the media radar" until one-third of the money was raised. Then, members of the media were given an informational kit and two members of the committee were designated to act as spokespersons for the fund-raising committee.

- **Fund-raising audiences were carefully targeted.** Forty potential donors able to give $5,000 or more were targeted for personal calls by members of the committee who knew them. Letters were sent to 2,100 taxpayers with property valued over $100,000. Others were invited to participate through a sign posted on the open space and an advertisement in the local newspaper. Gifts from more than 400 individual donors, businesses, and foundations raised more than $163,000—this did not include the $70,000 from the town of Exeter. Money remaining after the sale of the land was used for beautification of the park and the establishment of a maintenance fund.

- **Fund-raising materials were carefully matched with the values of the community.** They were simple, no pictures, one-color ink on white or colored paper, no gloss, and designed to use one first-class postage stamp.

The half-acre public park was purchased, completed, and dedicated 18 months after the plan to create the park began. It is simply landscaped with low-maintenance perennial flowers, trees, and bushes that bear spring flowers and offer shade in the summer and rich color in the fall. Brick walkways, benches, and a picnic table make it an inviting green space for people to enjoy (see Figure 4-8). ■

**FIGURE 4-8   Fully landscaped, the park offers a quiet respite for local citizens**

## QUESTIONS FOR DISCUSSION

1. Consider the efficacy of a "stealth" campaign. What conditions must be present for a stealth campaign to be the best option?

2. Was the inclusion of "opinion leaders" on the steering committee beneficial? Why? How?

3. Evaluate the tactic of not attempting to convert those opposed to the park. Is this a risky move? Why? What can be done to reduce any risk this strategy carries?

4. Evaluate the role "small-town America" played in this campaign. Would these same tactics succeed in New York? Los Angeles? Your hometown? Why?

5. What could proponents have done if the opposition and media took a vocal, opposing stance to the park?

# Case 4-6   One Company's Battle Resurrected in a Hollywood Movie: What Is the Best Defense?

Having your company name featured—or even mentioned—in a Hollywood movie starring top-name actors is a public relations practitioner's dream, if the focus is positive. But what happens when your company is portrayed negatively?

W. R. Grace faced this challenge when *A Civil Action*, a movie starring John Travolta and Robert Duval, opened on Christmas Day 1998. You may remember the case. It was the subject of a book also titled *A Civil Action* published in 1995 based on a lawsuit involving W. R. Grace. In the suit, Grace was accused of contaminating drinking water in the Boston suburb of Woburn. The case gained national attention after the book became a bestseller. Unfortunately for W. R. Grace, that attention was resurrected with the release of the film three years later. How W. R. Grace handled the situation is the focus of this case.

## A Company with Deep Roots

W. R. Grace is a $1.6 billion global supplier of specialty chemical, construction, and container products. The company was founded in 1854 in Peru by William Russell Grace, and relocated in 1865 to New York City. In 1880, Grace was elected mayor of New York City for two terms, and in 1885, he accepted the Statue of Liberty from the people of France.

Over the years, the company expanded, and the Grace name became well known around the globe. In 1914, the Grace National Bank was established, later to become Marine Midland Bank. That same year, Grace sent the first commercial vessel through the Panama Canal. Later that decade, Grace Line passenger ships were drafted into war service to ferry troops.

## The Stage Is Set

From 1960 to 1988, Grace operated a machine manufacturing plant in Woburn. In the early 1980s, a leukemia cluster was discovered in the town. The families of those who died of the disease filed a lawsuit accusing W. R. Grace and a second firm, Beatrice Foods, of polluting the town's water supply with industrial solvents. They believed the chemicals contaminated their drinking water and caused the deaths of many innocent people.

W. R. Grace admitted to dumping some chemicals, including trychloroethylene (TCE), in an area of Woburn but adamantly denied that the chemicals entered the families' water systems. The legal case created a controversy in the community and heartache for the families involved for many years. In the end, the families received an $8 million settlement, although W. R. Grace claimed no responsibility for the deaths. The companies are today engaged in a 50-year, $70 million clean up.

## A Valuable—But Costly—Lesson

Grace received much criticism from professionals for its public relations strategy during the Woburn case. It strongly asserted its innocence throughout the trial and refused to talk about the case publicly. It chose instead to focus efforts on cleaning up the polluted sites and building relationships with the community. Unfortunately, the company's efforts didn't include some key publics. "We did a bad job of communicating with employees, and paid a heavy price for it," explained Mark Stoler, former director of environmental safety and health at W. R. Grace. "We also made mistakes in not addressing the concerns of community and government agencies."

According to Stoler, Grace was determined to use the lessons learned from the Woburn trial to build relationships with employees and government agencies. The company set up social responsibility programs with local schools and provided training and equipment to help the fire department better respond to hazardous materials handling. In the years following the Woburn case, the Environmental Protection Agency praised W. R. Grace's efforts as setting "a new standard for accelerating the pace of Superfund cleanup."

## The Case That Wouldn't Die

But the case was not closed in the eyes of the media. In 1998, 12 years after the Woburn trial ended. Disney announced the upcoming release of *A Civil Action*. The film would be based on a book of the same name about the Woburn trial. The book, written by a previously unknown author, Jonathan Harr, became a bestseller.

When W. R. Grace executives found out about the planned movie, they tried to contact Disney producers to give them their side of the story—to point out what they perceived as untruths in the book, and to promote their progress in making amends with the Woburn community. Grace representatives said they received no response from Disney representatives.

## A Media Campaign Is Born

Grace public relations executives felt they had no choice but to launch an offensive against the movie, especially in light of their previous mistakes. "We didn't talk for 10 years," explained Stoler. "Under these circumstances, we felt we had to stand up and say something."

Grace employed several tactics to prevent or counteract potential negative publicity the movie might generate:

- CEO Paul Norris sent a letter to the press giving his opinion of the movie—but he did this before he even saw the movie.
- The company developed a Web site titled "Beyond A Civil Action: Woburn Issues and Answers."
- Press kits were distributed at the movie's opening in Los Angeles and New York.
- Grace representatives appeared on talk shows and in newsrooms to tell the public about the company's efforts to clean up the environment.
- A glossy, 30-page press kit was mailed to newspapers, magazines, and radio and TV stations around the country.

Grace attempted to "get ahead" of the issue and provide the media with information on its activities since the case was settled, hoping to generate attention on the positives rather than the negatives. Unfortunately, it neglected an important public relations tenant: *Understand the opposition's strategy before making a move.*

Subsidiaries of the other company in the suit, Beatrice Foods (which disbanded after the trial), chose to sit back and wait it out. Interestingly, Beatrice Foods was barely mentioned in the media coverage. Boston Herald reporter Dan Kennedy, who covered the trial for years, said Grace overreacted to the film. "They're really almost an afterthought in the film," he said in a *Boston Globe* article following its release.

## A More Effective Approach

Perhaps Grace would have been well served to more thoroughly determine exactly what it was up against. The company focused little attention on two of its key publics: Woburn residents and its own employees. Through pre- and post-focus groups, could the company have assessed its publics' opinions on the film and developed a more targeted path of action? Its hands-off approach motivated key players to retry the case in the media, who, thanks to the information provided in Grace's press kits, were more than willing to listen.

In a similar case, Dow Corning was deep in the silicone breast implant controversy (see Case 10-4) when the company learned of a made-for-television movie about it. After determining the film contained inaccuracies, they decided to take a stand. Dow communicated with all of its publics, and focused particular attention on the hometown community. It organized a town meeting at the local high school where the company's CEO, president, and bankruptcy counsel commented on the situation, and then opened the floor to questions. The executives stayed until every question was answered.

## Another Chapter

Just six months after the release of the movie, W. R. Grace found itself involved in yet another confrontation with citizens in one of its operating communities. Residents in a Cambridge, Massachusetts, neighborhood felt the company's measures to contain the release of asbestos during the construction of a hotel, two office buildings, and a retail space were inadequate. For years they had been trying to persuade W. R. Grace to investigate and clean up the contamination and abandon its plan to develop the area. "The problem is," said City Councilor Kathleen Born at a meeting on the issue, "W. R. Grace does not have a trust relationship with this community." ■

------------------------------------------------------------

### QUESTIONS FOR DISCUSSION

1. Environmental issues like those addressed in the Woburn and Cambridge incidents have become hot topics. What are some of the behaviors driving the key players on both sides of these situations?

2. Your public relations firm was hired by W. R. Grace to handle the company's strategy around the release of *A Civil Action*. What are some of the situational factors that would have been important to evaluate before developing a plan?

3. Keeping those issues in mind, what would be the main objectives of your plan, and what tactics would you use to achieve them?

4. List the positive steps, then the negative ones, W. R. Grace took in this case, and be prepared to defend your decisions.

## PROBLEM 4-A Helping Isn't Always Easy

You are a member of a civic organization that has 300 members locally and is the local chapter of a national organization. Most of the membership is well educated and falls into the middle- and upper-income brackets. The local organization has a reputation of civic involvement—working for better schools, increased voter registration, and equal rights for minorities and women.

About 18 months ago, the executive committee made a presentation to the organization on illiteracy in your city. Studies show that 25 percent of the adult population is "functionally illiterate." By the year 2001, the number of functional illiterates is projected to reach more than one-third of the population. Although the problem is spread throughout the population, the percentage of minorities in this group is high.

Soon after the executive committee's presentation, the organization votes to establish a literacy council for adults in the city. The primary function of the council is to solicit and train volunteers to act as tutors and match these persons with individuals wanting to learn to read and write. The organization is able to generate heavy news coverage of the council and public service announcements about the need for tutors and students. Despite the coverage, very few persons have volunteered to tutor, even fewer persons have requested the service.

Because of your expertise as a communicator, the organization has asked you to become involved in this program. Your review of the program indicates there is general agreement among individuals that something has to be done, but no one is quite sure what. Your organization sets an objective of obtaining and training 50 volunteer tutors and matching these with 50 students in the next six months.

As a well-trained public relations professional, you recognize that your organization has fallen into the trap of believing that widespread and positive publicity will influence behavior. You agree to help the cause but stipulate that research is essential to discover why the program hasn't taken off.

Describe how you will design and budget (in time and money) a research program to give you the information necessary to implement a successful recruiting program for students and tutors.

## PROBLEM 4-B ADJUSTING TO A CHANGE IN COMMAND

For 10 years, George Loyal has been a one-person public relations department at Siwash, a college of 3,500 students in Ohio. They have been 10 good years in terms of George's working conditions. There has been plenty of publicity material to pump out, and there has been cooperation on the part of news media.

A main factor assisting George has been the attitude of the Siwash College president. He takes an open stance publicly. He is articulate, handsome, and personable. He has been effective in attracting quality faculty, activating alumni support, and adding notable trustees who have been important in raising funds and making sure that Siwash is favorably regarded by legislators in the state capital.

But all these good things seem to have come to an end. The president was struck down by a massive heart attack and suddenly passed away. The trustees moved quickly to name a successor, who turned out to be a senior member of the Siwash faculty. He is a professor of anthropology, a scholar who is well published, quiet, and nonpublic.

The new president, in the month since his selection, has not informed George that he is not going to be active in alumni affairs, visible at sports events, or available to talk with news media whenever they want him to. He spends most of his time closeted with a few of the older faculty members. His secretary seems to feel that her job is to protect him from intrusions or outside visitors. He has not sent for George or sent him a memo about any specific job to do or any change in his responsibilities.

George's work has almost come to a standstill except for routine news releases. He frankly is not sure where he stands. The cooperative relationship he has had with news media seems to be threatened. The director of alumni relations is as baffled as he is. Two trustees have quietly indicated that they are stepping aside rather than stand for reelection when the time comes. The local sports editor has tipped George off that the newspaper's managing editor plans to ask for a meeting with the new president soon if he doesn't "come out of his shell."

The question before George is, What options does he have in trying to preserve the gains in public relations attained during the past 10 years?

1. What would be the most effective way of establishing a proactive relationship with the new president?
2. What would be your overall strategy for maintaining the college's relationships with its important stakeholders?
3. Given the personality of the new president, what role would you allot to him in maintaining the college's reputation?
4. How would you gain support for this strategy?

## PROBLEM 4-C BRINGING THE COMMUNITY TO CONSENSUS

You are an employee of a public relations firm that focuses on raising money for the fine arts. A large client of the firm wants to find funding in order go relocate the city's largest Center for the Arts within a yet-to-be-built state-of-the-art facility. You meet with your peers and discuss taking on this large assignment.

There are several key factors to consider; most important is how the community will react to such a change. The Center's current home is legendary, dating back to when the city was first built. It has held many memorable performances. Parents love to bring their children to the plays and musicals that are performed there; many enjoy its opera and classical music performances. Film festivals and dance performances have also been presented there.

However, the Center is old and in need of repair. Estimates for the needed repairs and for long-term upkeep are high. This client feels it would be more financially sound to build a new facility than to pour more money into the old building. The advantages for building a new Center—state-of-the-art acoustics, up-to-date technology, expanded and more comfortable seating, etc.—weigh greatly against the community's desire to keep the old building and find funding to repair it in future years. There is also the matter of convincing the board of directors. Some of the members are in favor of keeping the old building and feel that, historically, it is too valuable to abandon.

Knowing that you need to sway opinion within the community as well as the board of directors, how would you begin? What information do you need and how would you get it? What specific audiences would you target? Which audience must you reach first? How do you propose to reach all the various audiences? How would you use two-way communication in your plan? Would opinion leaders work here? If so, how would you find them? Consider also the future use of the current building. How can that become part of your plan?

# CHAPTER

# 5

# Investor Relations

Financial investment is no longer the purview of the wealthy alone. With the advent of the IRA, 401(k), ESOP (Employee Stock Ownership Program), and online trading, the body of investors has swollen with middle-class wage earners looking to a more secure future. These people follow the market with the same fervor as traditional institutional investors and probably suffer more over the ups and downs of the market than any high rollers.

One aspect of financial affairs that increasingly affects the national mood is U.S. investors' evaluations of the corporations in which they have invested. The major measurements are dollar sales volume, profit, the increase or decrease in interest or dividends paid, and whether the price of the stock or bond has increased or decreased from the original purchase price. Other factors include the rank of the company among competitors in its field and what percentage of dividends is paid in comparison with the purchase price.

Experts in the financial world who make a living, and sometimes a fortune, by analyzing and trading equities for themselves and for customers have to be aware of changing conditions in the money supply, raw material prices, international monetary affairs, national economies around the world, and much more. They use sophisticated measurement tools such as stock market trend lines, a company's management capabilities, debt to asset ratio, and several others.

In addition, there is the element of government finance—borrowings by the Treasury Department, municipalities, or state agencies in the form of bonds or debentures.

Today, with stock market news and international monetary or economic status constantly reported and talked about, public relations practitioners also must keep abreast of these topics. A small percent of practitioners will specialize in investor or financial relations. However, *all* practitioners need to be familiar with the economic climate and its impact on the organizations they represent—corporate, governmental, or nonprofit.

## THE PUBLICLY OWNED CORPORATION CONCEPTUALIZED

In the U.S. business system, as an ideal, the publicly owned corporation's mission, performance, and behavior represent the consent granted, and the consensus of views held, by all those who have a stake in its financial success. This concept embraces shareholders, employees and their pension fund, community neighbors, suppliers, and certainly customers. On the sidelines, appropriately, are those associations and governmental agencies designated to encourage, oversee, referee, or discipline in the name of all taxpayers, or the voters. In this idealization, publicly owned corporations might be seen as instruments of a people's capitalism. In actuality, such a concept is simplistic and does not exist, for these companies quickly take on the personalities of those who manage them—competitive, greedy, self-serving, or just the opposite.

A publicly owned business is created and managed to be profitable and to be competitive with others that sell the same product or service. In order to get started at all, there must be capital or credit and a product or service for which a market is perceived or waiting to be created. Prudent use of capital and skill in producing and marketing the product or service become the province of a small group that manages the enterprise day by day. Survival comes first. Beyond that, growth, diversification, and expansion make up goals that fuel ambition and drive all participants on the payroll. Profit, what's left over after all expenses are paid, makes everything else possible.

Given these realities, it is simply not practical for all those who have a stake in the outcome of an enterprise to take an active part in a forum for major decisions or as links in the decision process. Apart from being largely inaccessible, the stakeholders of a publicly owned corporation are too diverse in their self-interests and in their views of what a business should do, except for a few public issues such as quality of environment, to rally and force action. Given the realities, it should not be surprising that profit, and the power it brings, frequently leads to excesses, abuses, and corruption. These bring investigation, prosecution where indicated, and regulatory measures to preclude recurrence, in the name of the ultimate public interest.

## REALITY HAS A LONG HISTORY

Corporations are not ordained by Mother Nature but are a creation of the state. Until the early 1800s, someone starting a business had no "corporate shield," but put all his or her assets at risk. If the business failed, the owner was personally responsible for all debts to the point of personal bankruptcy. Because this situation discouraged the formation of new business, laws were enacted allowing for the formation of **corporations**—business entities in which shareholders risk only the amount of their investment.

What the state creates it can regulate. Regulatory measures started a long time ago. In addition to regulations in interstate commerce mandated by the U.S. Constitution, the federal government began to institute more stringent controls over business. In 1890, the Sherman Antitrust Act was passed, aimed at concentration or monopoly within several industries. This act was supplemented by the Clayton Act in 1914, and in the same year the Federal Trade Commission Act set up a mechanism to keep channels of interstate trade open to competition. The 1929 stock market crash and the Great Depression of the 1930s stimulated legislative and regulatory actions in the investment area. First was the Securities Act of 1933, requiring a corporation to publish a prospectus (a preliminary printed statement that describes an enterprise and is distributed to prospective investors) when it prepares to sell securities to the public. Then came the Securities Exchange Act of 1934, creating the Securities and

Exchange Commission (SEC) and dealing with the conflict of interest involved when a corporate official reaps personal financial gain on information not known to the public. Rule 10b-5 in 1942 tightened the act, prohibiting fraudulent and deceptive practices in the purchase or sale of securities.

## THE MATURING OF FINANCIAL PUBLIC RELATIONS

In spite of the Teapot Dome scandal and other problems stemming from over-control of many economic areas by the so-called robber barons, financial public relations didn't spring up in the 1920s, but publicity specialists such as Ivy Lee and Ed Bernays were called in at that time for their expertise.

Financial relations in the 1930s was recognized by employers as a useful communications element, but secondary to the publicity and special events that supported marketing efforts as the economy struggled out of the depression. It gained no ground in the pecking order and earned no particular voice in the decision process during World War II, when the corporate focus was on employee morale to achieve the productivity necessary to arm the Allies and on war bond sales to finance the effort. After the war, with so much pent-up consumer demand to be satisfied, it was hard not to be successful and keep stockholders satisfied, so financial relations specialists were not needed.

A financial relations breakthrough came in the 1960s, in a classic situation of insider trading, where a single news release was deemed by a court to be the critical factor in whether the investing public had been misled (see Case 5-1). Out of the case came—in the determination by the SEC, the New York Stock Exchange, and corporate officials—that financial communications were important and could create or obviate legal liabilities for the corporation. Shingles labeled "Financial Public Relations" appeared by the thousands. Qualified practitioners began to sit in on the financial decision-making process of their corporations.

## AT THIS JUNCTURE

Corporate growth has become almost a religion in U.S. industry. The means of getting to heaven has involved huge investment in research and technology, diversification of products and services, acquisitions, mergers, conglomeration, and multinationalization. From these actions has come an increasing concentration of corporate ownership among a few thousand very wealthy individuals, investment funds, and banking and insurance interests, both U.S. and foreign. Boards of directors of huge corporations have been woven in a crisscross pattern of a few thousand individuals whose views of the system are similar and whose posture is dependably reactive when the system comes under criticism of any kind.

In the 1970s and into the 1980s, conditions were not reassuring for the small investor or average wage earner. Inflation helped wages but hurt buying power. Borrowed money for car or home was at high interest rates, mortgaging the future. Available jobs for traditional functions shrank as corporations went abroad for cheap labor and automation displaced people. Savings decreased or disappeared for a great many.

In the latter 1980s, conditions were ripe for the rich to get richer and for the high-rolling risk takers and arbitrageurs to find market manipulation and insider trading irresistible. The mood seemed to be that "anything goes if you don't get caught." Each new rumor of a corporate raid takeover, issuance of junk bonds, or bit of privileged information spurred speculation.[1]

Black Monday came in October of 1987. It was a rude awakening as the market's Dow Jones average plummeted some 500 points, taking with it some of Wall Street's big dealers. In the wake, a Tender Offer Reform Act was proposed as an amendment to the Securities Exchange Act of 1934. Too little, too late.[2]

Things quieted down, but not completely or permanently. In 1988, another case made financial headlines when a young trainee in Morgan Stanley's mergers and acquisitions department was alleged to have fed material information to a wealthy Hong Kong customer, who then traded on that information, garnering $19 million in gains. Then for the next several months it seemed each week brought a new Wall Street scandal, making the names of such men as Michael Milken and Ivan Boesky infamous.

The 1990s saw the government, through the SEC, get tough on insider trading issues. With an outpouring of public comment—nearly 6,000 comment letters and the vast majority from individual investors in favor of adopting Regulation Fair Disclosure (Reg FD)—the SEC adopted the ruling. Reg FD's intent is to end the special relationship that existed between public companies and analysts and brokers—to level the playing field for *all* investors. Prior to Reg FD, analysts and brokers often received information from companies that was material to investment decisions but was not shared with the general public. As one comment letter noted: "The explosion of the Internet provides ways for information to reach all investors. Analysts are one way, and in the past they were the principal conduit. But now that's changing."

On October 23, 2000, the new ruling took effect with cries from the analyst community that it would chill communications from companies. In fact, it has both promoted and inhibited corporate communications. A survey by the National Investor Relations Institute of its membership finds that 28 percent are providing more information to investors than before the new rule, 48 percent are issuing about the same amount, and 24 percent are providing less information. NIRI is concerned about that 24 percent. Further study is needed to determine the reasons and what can be done about it.

By the beginning of the twenty-first century, in light of all preceding activities, one would have expected to find investors more careful, regulators more attentive, and

---

[1]Elliot D. Lee. "Takeover Predators Now Share the Prey," *The Wall Street Journal*, April 29, 1988. Article lists takeover activity at the time, including Campeau Corp. buying Federated Stores for $6.6 billion and GE acquiring Roper Corp. from Whirlpool. William Celis, "Low Stock Prices Spur Takeover Flurry," *The Wall Street Journal*, March 1, 1988, revealed six takeover transactions in a single day, totaling $5.4 billion in assets. Among those involved were Homestake Mining, Media General Inc., and USG Corp. A chart showed total value of transactions increasing from $10 billion the first two months of 1987 to $28 billion in the same period of 1988.

[2]George Getschow and Bryan Burrough. "Pickens, Acting Bitter, Finds Takeover Game Isn't Much Fun Now," *The Wall Street Journal*, April 5, 1988. Detailed profile of Texas oil man T. Boone Pickens, who said in 1983 he wanted to take over Gulf Oil Corp, later decided not to go ahead, but made a $518 million pretax profit when speculators bid up the price of Gulf stock on the basis of his intent. In 1988, he was weary and bitter, lashing out at investment bankers, advisers, local and national news media, and many others.

managers more ethical. Yet, some of the biggest corporate failures due to poor management practices, corrupt ethics, and questionable financial methodologies have led to financial ruin for many investors. The excesses of such organizations as Enron, WorldCom and Tyco have led to further regulation. The Sarbanes-Oxley Act sought to rectify some of the problem areas. Some feel it hasn't done enough—others feel it went too far. The SEC continues to seek out and prosecute senior managers when they step over the line and play havoc with investors' nest eggs. In 2006, Ken Lay and Jeffery Skilling of Enron fame were both found guilty and sentenced to years in prison. (Lay died suddenly in July 2006, thus vacating his guilty verdict and throwing civil suits against him into disarray.) Bernard Ebbers of WorldCom was already serving his time while Dennis Kozlowski of Tyco was busy fighting on appeal. Martha Stewart had also served her time and was back on network television as if nothing had happened. The question is now, and will always remain, what is the role of the public relations practitioner to the organization and the stockholders when shady dealings are at work?

NIRI's survey also found that, prior to the new ruling, 60 percent of its member companies were providing full public access to their conference calls to discuss quarterly earnings results and guidance. After Reg FD, 89 percent are doing so, mostly through Webcasts. Eighty-four percent of companies are notifying investors and the media of their upcoming conference calls in a news release, 75 percent post a notice on their company's Web site, and 55 percent are using "push technology"—directly notifying interested investors who want an e-mail alert.

The one-on-ones between companies and analysts and investors are continuing, according to NIRI's survey, contrary to the fear that these might be severely cut back for fear of violating Reg FD. However, there is important information, much of which is nonfinancial, that companies can and should discuss with analysts and investors. This nonfinancial information offers important measurements of a company's well-being, which can directly affect the bottomline. Analysts may have to do more work now with Reg FD. No longer can they be guided in their analysis by the companies. Information will be distributed equally. Knowledge and the ability to analyze data are key.

## AN ENVIRONMENT OF STRONG VIEWS

Financial relations present a worthy challenge to the practitioner. As prime audiences, you have millions of small investors fighting to be on an equal footing with those who "control" the market (such as pension funds, mutual funds, and other money managers) and leaders of publicly owned corporations who can make decisions that are helpful or harmful, choosing short-term expedients or long-haul public interest. Then there 'are the regulators—and the ever-inquiring media, economists, and legislators—who can make and change the rules.

The positive views small investors have of the corporate world stem in part from good news such as dividends or appreciation in the value of their investments, bullish forecasts by corporate and investment spokespersons, and profiles of company leaders portraying them as intelligent, honest, and planning for future success.

Their negative views are formed in part by information in proxy statements about lavish executive salaries, bonuses, and stock options not based on the health or performance of the corporation. Investors read news items about costly indulgences

---

**A LANGUAGE OF ITS OWN**

A generation ago, practitioners had to learn new financial semantics. Terms such as *privileged information, conflict of interest, insider trading, timely and adequate disclosure, due diligence*, and *a material fact* became part of communications as well as legal language.

An infusion of words appeared during the late 1980s and early 1990s. Practitioners needed to understand *arbitrage* and *arbs, junk bonds, payment in kind (PIK), green mail, raiders, programmed trading*, and *hostile takeover*.

Today, new lingo continues to emerge on the Street, for example, Regulation Fair Disclosure (see page 99).

---

such as private aircraft, executive dining rooms, limousines, club memberships, and junkets, all in the name of incentives or customer relations, that are recovered in higher prices for the products or services. And they are not reassured when such free-spending corporations, unable to compete with foreign products, run to the government for protection.

Large investors—directors chosen to guide the corporations and the people hired to manage the businesses—constitute a relatively small audience with some deeply ingrained convictions in common. They claim that the system works well. Criticism or threats of regulation tend to harden their positions and to render spokespersons less flexible rather than more open and accessible. When challenged, this posture provides an example of the *artificial censorship principle*. At times, unwelcome criticism or questions concerning economic matters are labeled as expressing an unacceptable political viewpoint—thus the strategy or tactic of *changing the issue*.

- The role of the corporate financial relations specialist or consultant tends to be that of *interpreter and mediator* between the prime audiences. He or she usually comes on as a moderate or neutral in economic and political philosophy. The position requires skill and objectivity in representing the average investor, the middle-class unsophisticated citizen, while representing private enterprise and conservative views publicly.

Among the intervenors financial relations must take into account are the financial news media, those who run and support nonprofit institutions such as education, and those charged with making and enforcing the securities laws.

## THE SPECIFICS OF THE FUNCTION

The financial public relations role can be summarized as:

- Communications strategy appropriate to management goals in investor relations
- Preparation of public literature, including reports required by law and establishing press contacts
- Managing relationships with the financial community, including analyst meetings, tours or visits, and so on

Among the specific situations requiring communication are:

1. A company goes public, splits its stock, or arranges added financing.
2. A corporation wishes to make a tender offer to acquire another corporation, to merge with another corporation, or to head off or oppose an unwanted offer. An acquisition or merger may result in a change of identity such as name, logo, headquarters location, or ownership.
3. A timely announcement is needed for significant new products, services, expansion, or acquisition, which might affect the price of the company's stock.
4. Periodic reports of financial results are issued, including an annual report.
5. Arrangements are required for meetings with investors and for public reports of proceedings, including the annual meeting—and, in some enlightened corporations, an employee annual meeting.
6. Special literature is required, dealing with a corporation's philosophy, policies, and objectives; its history or anniversary; and its scope, "identity," or "culture." Any of these may also be the subject of advertising.

## REFERENCES AND ADDITIONAL READINGS

Berkeley, Alan. "Stand by for Change: The Future of Investor Relations." Address at University of Texas, April 30, 1987. Synopsis in *pr reporter* 30 (August 17, 1987).

Berle, A. A., Jr. *Power Without Property*. New York: Harcourt, Brace and World, 1959. A classic book.

Cheney, Richard. "What Should We Do About Takeovers?" *tips & tactics, pr reporter* 25 (supplement, April 6, 1987).

Cutlip, Scott, Allen Center, and Glen Broom. "The Practice: Business and Industry." Chapter 14 in *Effective Public Relations*. 8th ed. Upper Saddle River, NJ: Prentice Hall, 1999.

Dobrzynski, Judith. "The Lessons of the RJR Free-for-All." *BusinessWeek* (December 19, 1988). Raises and answers questions about the battle for RJR Nabisco.

"Four Barometers Analysts Apply in Measuring Management Performance." *Investor Relations Update* (October–November 1992): 15. Summary in purview, supplement to *pr reporter* (February 15, 1993).

Holliday, Karen Kahler. "Understanding Investor Relations." *Bank Marketing* 24 (August 1992): 22–25.

Leeds, Mark, and Bruce Fraser. "Why Wall Street Matters." *Management Review* 82 (September 1993): 23–26.

Lees, David. "A Strategy That Pays Dividends." *Management Today* (March 1994): 5.

Lerbinger, Otto, and Nathaniel Sperber. "Financial Relations." Chapter 7 in *Manager's Public Relations Handbook*. Reading, MA: Addison-Wesley, 1982.

Metz, Tim. *Black Monday: The Catastrophe of October 19, 1987 . . . and Beyond*. New York: William Morrow, 1988. A chronology of the stock market drop of 500 points and theory concerning the mystery of it.

Miller, Eugene. "Investor Relations." Chapter 11 in *Lesly's Handbook of Public Relations and Communications*. 5th ed. Chicago, IL: NTC Business Books, 1998.

Moore, Philip. "Ciba Takes Investors into Account." *Euromoney* (September 1993): 37–38.

National Investor Relations Institute offers a wealth of information, including *IR Update*, a monthly newsletter. National Investors Relations Institute, 8045 Leesburg Pike, Suite 600, Vienna, VA 22182; 703/506-3570; www.niri.org.

The *Public Relations Body of Knowledge*. New York: PRSA. See abstracts dealing with "Financial and Investor Relations."

Seely, Michael. "Hit the Financial Bull's Eye with Well-Aimed IR Programs." *Corporate Cash Flow* 14 (July 1993): 26–30.

------------------------------C A S E S------------------------------

# Case 5-1    A Classic: On Wall Street, Inside Information Is Profitable

For nearly 30 years after the enactment of the Securities Exchange Act in 1934 prohibiting manipulation and deception in the financial world, the role of public relations in stock transactions was not taken seriously by corporate management and the relevant sectors of the Securities Exchange Commission (SEC). As a result of a landmark court case involving Texas Gulf Sulphur Company, the role of public relations changed drastically.[1] This case is definitive in understanding some of the problems and requisites in the performance of financial relations.

- At the heart of the case was a single news release drafted by a public relations consultant and the vice president of Texas Gulf. The manner in which the news was released to the media raised questions of whether the content was deceptive.

### Precedents

Until 1942, inside trading, or using private information, had not been outlawed. Questions of integrity or ethics went largely unasked publicly until the Sherman Antitrust Act was passed in 1890. Even after the Securities Exchange Act was passed in 1934 and Rule 10b-5 was made public, the laws were not enforced and went untested for two decades.

Since the depths of the Great Depression, the SEC has tried to prevent insider trading. Insiders—anyone with facts or news not yet released to the general investing public—have a distinct advantage until that knowledge is available to the public. Thus, insiders are in a position to "cash in" on that information to the detriment of the investor who might buy or sell shares absent the information known only to insiders. The Securities Exchange Act of 1934 was written to forbid insiders from benefiting from information unique to them.

Section 10 of the 1934 Securities Exchange Act, and Rule 10b-5 promulgated by the SEC in 1942, state that persons may not "make any untrue statement of material fact or . . . omit to state a material fact" that would have the effect of misleading in connection with the purchase or sale of any security.

*A precondition would be that a person did, in fact, possess information whose disclosure or nondisclosure could have an effect on the value of a security. Thus, "insider" information, the disclosure of such information, and the purchase or sale of securities are mutually involved. Private gain is implicit.*

---

[1]The name was subsequently changed to Texasgulf. In 1981, the company was acquired by the French corporation Elf Aquitaine Inc. for $5 billion and then purchased by Potush Corporation of Saskatchewan in 1995 for more than $800 million.

## The Texas Gulf Sulphur Case

The Texas Gulf Sulphur (TGS) scenario started with some late 1950s exploratory activities for minerals in eastern Canada.[2] Aerial, geophysical surveys over a large expanse of land were made until potential drill sites were selected. The people who participated in the surveys included:

- **Richard D. Mollison**, a mining engineer and later a vice president of Texas Gulf Sulphur (TGS)
- **Walter Holyk**, a Texas Gulf geologist
- **Richard H. Clayton**, an electrical engineer and geophysicist
- **Kenneth H. Darke**, a geologist

They selected a segment of marshland near Timmins, Ontario, that showed sufficient promise to indicate a survey on the ground. This land was not owned by TGS. One of the first problems was to get title or drilling rights, via an option from the owners. Contact with the owner of part of the desired area was first made in 1961.

Eventually, in mid-1963, some land was acquired and drilling began in November. On visual inspection, the sample—obtained by diamond-core drilling—seemed to contain sulphides of copper and zinc.

On Sunday, November 12, 1963, Darke telephoned his boss, Walter Holyk, at his home in Connecticut with an optimistic report. Holyk called his boss, Richard D. Mollison, nearby in Old Greenwich, and later that evening called Dr. Charles F. Fogarty, TGS executive vice president, also nearby in Rye, New York. Holyk, Mollison and Fogarty subsequently went to the site—called the Kidd 55 tract—to see for themselves. The group concluded that the core was indeed promising and should be shipped to Utah for chemical assay.

## A Lid on the Information

Pending the results, they wanted the acquisition program for other desired land in the area to proceed as quickly as possible. They knew obtaining rights might be difficult. To facilitate matters, TGS president Claude O. Stephens instructed the group to keep the unconfirmed results a secret . . . even to other officers, directors, and employees of the company. Following traditional prospecting and camouflage customs, the first hole was marked and concealed, and another one, *barren*, was drilled and left in sight.

## Calendar of Events: 1963–1964

- November. Seven TGS employees were the "keepers" of significant information. In the same month drilling began,

---

[2]The narrative and facts that follow were gleaned from some of the same sources that formed public opinion during the period when the events in this case took place. Among the sources are a complete text of the court's opinion in *SEC v. TGS*, 446 F2d 1301 (2nd Cir. 1966); an article by John Brooks. "Annals of Finance: A Reasonable Amount of Time," in *New Yorker* magazine, November 9, 1968 (and from a critique of the John Brooks piece provided by TGS public relations consultant William H. Dinsmore); *The Wall Street Journal* articles, "Big Boards Expands, Tightens Standards on Timely Disclosure of Corporate News." July 18, 1968; "Texas Gulf Ruled to Lack Due Diligence in Minerals Case," February 9, 1970; "Rise Detected in Use of Inside Information to Make Stock Profits," October 31, 1972; "Most Executives Say They Won't Give Insider Data to Analysts," August 16, 1968; "New Structure Prompt Firms to Revise Policies on Disclosure of News." October 9, 1968; and "Rules on Disclosure Don't Bar Exclusive Interview, Cohen Says," October 9, 1968; and "No Comment—A Victim of Disclosure," *New York Times*, August 25, 1968. Also helpful was an analysis provided to officers of Motorola, Inc., by its legal counsel, entitled "Corporate Information Releases." We also drew on several references in issues of the *Public Relations Journal, PR News, pr reporter*, and other business and professional publications. An appeals brief for the defendants was requested of attorneys but was not received.

and Fogarty, Clayton, Mollison, and Mrs. Holyk bought TGS stock totaling 2,050 shares at $17 to $18 a share.

- "One of the most famous instances of insider trading was Charles F. Fogarty's purchase of Texas Gulf Sulphur shares during 1963–64. Forgarty, an executive vice president of Texas Gulf, knew that the company had discovered a rich mineral lode in Ontario that it couldn't publicize before concluding leases for mineral rights. In the meantime, Forgarty purchased 3,100 shares."[3] His "investment" yielded about $300,000 profit in 2006 dollars.
- December. The chemical assays of the test core came back, largely confirming the TGS estimate of copper and zinc content, as well as discovering a silver content. TGS scheduled the resumption of drilling in March.
- January–February. Inside informers and those they gave "tips" to owned 8,235 shares. At this point there were also 12,300 calls (options to buy a specified amount of stock at a fixed price) to buy TGS stock.
- February. The company issued stock options to 26 of its officers and other employees, 5 of whom were the insiders on Kidd 55. The option committee and the company's board of directors had not been made aware of the find.
- March 31. The company resumed drilling.

After further drilling of three more holes by April 10, there was evidence of a body of commercially minable ore. (The accuracy of the estimate later came into contention between SEC experts and TGS officials.)

## Leaks and Rumors

By this time, there had been enough activity at the Kidd site that rumors of a possible major ore strike were circulating in Canada. A press item on February 27, in the *Northern Miner*, reported rumors of Texas Gulfs "obtaining some fat ore indications" from its work north of Timmins. On March 31, Texas Gulf invited the publication to visit and see the exposed, barren site for itself, and a date was set for April 20. Then on April 9, the *Toronto Daily Star* and the *Globe and Mail* carried stories. The *Globe and Mail* headline read, "Wild Speculation Spree on TGS: Gigantic Copper Strike Rumored." The phone lines and the conference rooms at TGS headquarters, 200 Park Avenue, New York, were busy on April 10. According to John Brooks, writing later in the *New Yorker* magazine:

> President Stephens was sufficiently concerned about the rumors to seek advice from one of his most trusted associates, Thomas S. Lamont, senior member of the Texas Gulf board . . . and bearer of a name long venerated on Wall Street. Stephens asked what Lamont thought ought to be done about the "exaggerated" reports.
>
> "As long as they stay in the Canadian press," Lamont replied, "I think you might be able to live with them." However, he added, if they should reach the papers in the United States, it might be well to give the press an announcement that would set the record straight and avoid undue gyrations in the stock market.[4]

## Public Relations Called In

The stories in Canada were picked up and printed on Saturday, April 11, by such U.S.

[3]David D. Haddock, "Insider Trading: The Concise Encyclopedia of Insider Trading," in *The Concise Encyclopedia of Economics*.
[4]J. Brooks, *Business Adventures*, New York: Weybright and Talley Division, David McKay. Originally published in "Annals of Finance," *New Yorker* magazine, November 9, 1968.

media as the *New York Times* and the *New York Herald Tribune*, with the rumor of a major copper strike. Robert Carroll, a Doremus & Co. public relations consultant, helped Dr. Fogarty, the executive vice president, draft a news release over the weekend, and it was released at 3:00 P.M. on Sunday, April 12, to appear in Monday morning's papers.

## News Media and Stock Market React

The Monday *New York Herald Tribune*, an important financial medium, headlining its story, "Copper Rumor Deflated," quoted passages from the TGS press release and hedged on the optimism in its earlier story out of Canada.

On the New York Stock Exchange, TGS stock price on April 13 ranged between 30⅛ and 32, closing at 30⅞. When compared with an $18 high in November the $30 price represented a 65 percent rise in five months. Meanwhile, the internal, nonpublic reports from Timmins became so rosy that an official announcement confirming a major ore strike was readied for April 16.

There was a problem in the synchronization of communications. A reporter for the *Northern Milner*, a Canadian trade journal, had interviewed Mollison, Holyk, and Darke and had prepared an article confirming a 10-million-ton strike for publication in his April 16 issue. The story, submitted to Mollison, was returned to the reporter, unamended, on April 15. Separately, a statement drafted substantially by Mollison was given to the Ontario minister of mines for release on the air in Canada at 11:00 P.M. on the 15th, but was not released until 9:40 on the 16th. Also, separately, in the United States an official statement announcing a strike of at least 25 million tons (2½ times the Canadian trade-journal story) was read to the financial press in

New York from 10:00 to 10:15 A.M. on April 16, following a 9:00 A.M. directors' meeting. The news showed up on the Dow Jones tape at 10:54 and on Merrill Lynch's private wire 25 minutes earlier at 10:29, another peculiar circumstance.

## The Trial and Appeals

An SEC complaint indicated that company executives had used privileged information to trade in the company's stock before the information had been disclosed publicly. In May, the complaint was argued before Judge Dudley B. Bonsal of the Southern District Court at Foley Square, New York. He ruled in favor of all the defendants except David M. Crawford and Richard H. Clayton, who had engaged in TGS stock purchase after the first press release on April 12 and before the second one, on April 16, was public knowledge.

The lower-court judge dismissed the case against the defendants who had purchased stock prior to the evening of April 9, on the grounds that information they possessed was not "material," that their purchases or tips to others were educated guesses or hunches, and that executives should be encouraged to own shares in their own company. As for trading by insiders following the April 16 directors' meeting, and whether they had waited a "reasonable time" for the disclosure to become public knowledge, the judge decided the controlling factor was the time at which the release was handed to the press, not when it appeared on the Dow Jones stock market tape.

## Public Relations Involvement

The trial court judge gave a big lift to the public relations profession because a public relations consultant had been involved. The judge

## THE PRESS RELEASE: APRIL 12, 1964

New York—The following statement was made today by Dr. Charles F. Fogarty, executive vice president of Texas Gulf Sulphur Company, in regard to the company's drilling operations near Timmins, Ontario, Canada. Dr. Fogarty said:

During the past few days, the exploration activities of Texas Gulf Sulphur in the area of Timmins, Ontario, have been widely reported in the press, coupled with rumors of a substantial copper discovery there. These reports exaggerate the scale of operations, and mention plans and statistics of size and grade of ore that are without factual basis and have evidently originated by speculation of people not connected with TGS.

The facts are as follows. TGS has been exploring in the Timmins area for six years as part of its overall search in Canada and elsewhere for various minerals—lead, copper, zinc, etc. During the course of this work, in Timmins as well as in eastern Canada, TGS has conducted exploration entirely on its own, without the participation by others. Numerous prospects have been investigated by geophysical means and a large number of selected ones have

been core-drilled. These cores are sent to the United States for assay and detailed examination as a matter of routine and on advice of expert Canadian legal counsel. No inferences as to grade can be drawn from this procedure.

Most of the areas drilled in Eastern Canada have revealed either barren pyrite or graphite without value; a few have resulted in discoveries of small or marginal sulfide ore bodies.

Recent drilling on one property near Timmins has led to preliminary indications that more drilling would be required for proper evaluation of this prospect. The drilling done to date has not been conclusive, but the statements made by many outside quarters are unreliable and include information and figures that are not available to TGS.

The work done to date has not been sufficient to reach definite conclusions and any statement as to size and grade of ore would be premature and possibly misleading. When we have progressed to the point where reasonable and logical conclusions can be made, TGS will issue a definite statement to its stockholders and the public in order to clarify the Timmins project.[1]

[1]From the appeals court opinion, *SEC v. TGS*, 446 F.2d, 1301 (2nd Cir. 1966).

decided that because corporate executives had sought the advice of public relations counsel, they had exercised reasonable business judgment.

As for the news release itself, a major point of contention in the hearings was whether it was encouraging or discouraging to investors. A Canadian mining security specialist said that they had had a Dow Jones (broad tape) report that TGS "didn't have anything basically." A Midwest Stock Exchange specialist in TGS was "concerned about his long position in the stock" after reading the release. TGS defense attorneys contended that the financial

media had been at fault in not publishing the full text of the controversial release. The trial court stated only, "While in retrospect, the press release may appear gloomy or incomplete, that does not make it misleading or deceptive on the basis of the facts then known."

## The Complaint Moved Up the Court Ladder

The SEC appealed all dismissals, and the case was argued in the court of appeals. In essence, the appellate decision reversed the lower court's findings on the important issues, except for the convictions of Crawford and Clayton, which were affirmed.

The case was remanded to Judge Bonsal of the lower court for the "appropriate remedies." He:

- Ruled that Texas Gulf Sulphur Co. and its executives failed to exercise "due diligence" in the April 12 news release.
- Ordered certain defendants to turn over to TGS profits made by trading on inside information.
- Issued injunctions against Crawford and Clayton, barring them from further purchases or sales based on "undisclosed" information.
- Denied a request by the SEC that TGS, as a corporation, be enjoined from issuing false, misleading, or inadequate information, pointing out that there was no "reasonable likelihood of further violations."
- Because there was no "reasonable likelihood," did not issue injunctions against Darke, who had left the company; Holyk, chief geologist; Huntington, a TGS attorney; Fogarty, then president of TGS; and Mollison, a vice president.
- Noted that Coates, a director, had paid $26,250 in an approved settlement, including $9,675 said to be profits to several "tippees," and that Crawford returned "at his cost" the stock he purchased.
- Assessed paybacks of $41,795 from Darke personally and $48,404 for his "tippees," $35,663 from Holyk, $20,010 from Clayton, and $2,300 from Huntington.[5]

## Some of the Echoes

In the immediate wake of the TGS settlement, several predictable measures were taken to avoid a repetition. Publicly owned corporations reexamined their practices of disclosing financial information to be sure they were in compliance. The New York Stock Exchange expanded its policies regarding timely disclosure and issued new pages for its company manual.

Financial news media, somewhat defensively, placed responsibility for the published information on the corporate sources of such information without permitting those sources to control what was published. While insisting on the media's right to edit financial releases according to the news values perceived in them, some comments by financial editors suggested that corporate practitioners constituted obstacles rather than facilitators in getting out all the relevant facts.

Corporate financial relations people, for their part, undertook with notable success to exercise a more important and outspoken role in corporate decisions regarding the "what, when, and how" of significant information to be released publicly via press or controlled media. This meant a seat in management councils for financial relations people when decisions were made regarding whether a particular item of information was newsworthy and whether it was capable of influencing the value of the corporation's shares in the stock market. This also meant attendance at meetings with groups of analysts where material information might inadvertently be introduced, calling for immediate broad disclosure.

New counseling shingles were hung out, with the words "Financial Public Relations." The trade literature abounded with analyses of the risks and requirements implied by the TGS case.

---

[5]Extracted from the opinion rendered in 65 Civ. 1182 by Judge Dudley J. Bonsal, United States District Court, Southern District of New York, February 6, 1970.

## Relevance to Public Relations Practice

With the dollar stakes involved in the stock market so large today as to seem almost fictional, the day-by-day practice of public relations may seem remote or unrelated. It is neither.

Every large corporation, bank, brokerage firm, charitable foundation, and other financial institution has public relations counsel or staff. The professionals providing counsel and implementing the communications involved in financial affairs can qualify legally as "insiders." They can be found guilty, as individuals, of knowingly releasing financial information that is false, deceptive, or misleading or of trading on privileged information. In court cases, it has been evident that financial relations practitioners are not in the clear by pleading "I only did (or said) what the client told me to." Practitioners must make reasonable efforts to verify facts disseminated. "Hold harmless" clauses no longer constitute a shield.

Although TGS didn't create the financial relations industry, its aftershocks certainly drew clear guidelines for practitioners. A law that had been on the books since 1934 now had some teeth, and those who understood the new circumstances were sure to be more valuable to their employers than ever before.

Perhaps more important, however, were the precedents established by the TGS rulings. From that day forward, every publicly held company knew (or should have known) that the SEC requires:

- Full and complete disclosure of every material fact in a timely manner
- A complete ban on insider trading
- Corporate and personal responsibility of public relations counsel

These tenets would be the backbone of what is now the highest-paying segment of the public relations profession—investor relations. ■

---

## QUESTIONS FOR DISCUSSION

1. Drawing on the information in the case, and having the benefit of knowing how it all came out, what should the public relations executive have counseled TGS officers to do differently, or to communicate publicly, at some point before TGS executives were found to be trading in the stock?

2. Apart from the TGS case, try a different situation. Suppose that a weekly financial magazine column "Tips and Rumors" regularly got into some people's hands a day before each issue of the magazine came out, and some of the stocks mentioned were suddenly traded heavily and run up in price. Suppose also, it turned out that a clerical person in the magazine's public relations department privately had been giving an advance rough draft of the column as a favor to a friend at a brokerage firm. Neither that clerk nor the friend at a brokerage firm traded or made any profit. As you understand SEC's Rule 10b, who is legally liable? Put another way, where does common sense tell you the responsibility for the privacy of material facts belongs?

3. Objectively, was the initial TGS news release about the ore strike at Timmins misleading on the basis of what was known *at the time the news was released?* Or did it go only as far as a cautious, prudent management was willing to go for fear of overstating and getting in trouble for that? Or, what else does your objective evaluation say might have been the determining consideration?

**4.** A reputation for being honest in economic matters, civil in social relations, and honorable in character has long been said to be a precious and fragile possession. And the reputation of communications people is generally perceived by critics and supporters alike as being a reflection of those they serve and associate with. If we accept both premises, how can we stay clean and honorable, earn a good living, and advance in a career when we are cast in an atmosphere that many moralists, historians, intellectuals, journalists, and some government officials describe as a "moral morass"?

# Case 5-2   Bankruptcy: Communicating for Future Success*

Nothing strikes fear into investors like the possibility of bankruptcy in a publicly held company. Under bankruptcy law, investors are the last consideration in the distribution of assets of the bankrupt entity. In the Enron collapse, for example, some $80 billion in shareholder value was lost, including more than $2 billion held by Enron employees and retirees. That value will never return.

But not all bankruptcies involve liquidation. Many struggling companies find relief in bankruptcy, taking advantage of the shelter of Chapter 11 to reorganize, absent the pressure of creditors or—commonly—legal verdicts that would otherwise prevent a company from continuing daily operations. This case addresses the reality of bankruptcy and the need for effective communication throughout the process.

When a company files for bankruptcy, it is using an important management tool for effectively operating an enterprise. Executives have the expectation that the bankruptcy "remedy" will help protect their business at a time when they've exhausted other options and are operating beyond their current financial capabilities.

Companies and people who file for bankruptcy protection are not "bad," but they might be looked at negatively if they fail to meet the public's demand for effective and timely communication. Everyone who is affected by the bankruptcy filing, including employees, customers, shareholders, and suppliers, want to know how they will be impacted. They want straight answers. They shun rhetoric, complicated phrases, and smokescreens.

Customers want their deliveries; employees want their jobs and paychecks; shareholders want a return on their investment; and suppliers want to be paid. And, the media want to report the facts. It's really quite simple.

Bankruptcy communication, like all crisis communication, requires credibility. Although there is nothing wrong with saying, "I don't know," it's important to add the phrase, "but I'll get back to you as quickly as I can with the answer." Then, live up to your word. Don't guess and don't go beyond the information currently available.

Some issues in a filing cannot be answered or resolved immediately. Telling a "white lie" that will satisfy the questioner in the short term (e.g., "The check will be sent next week") will probably result in a long-term loss. The cardinal rule of crisis communications—and a bankruptcy is generally considered a crisis—is always tell the truth. There are no exceptions.

Many companies today have a crisis communications plan that details actions to be taken when something goes wrong. Typically, the plan addresses manufacturing or packaging errors, a regulatory investigation, a lawsuit, an accident, or a boycott. No one anticipates bankruptcy, however, and it often isn't included in preplanning efforts despite the keen public interest and media attention filings receive. Although every crisis situation is different, each demands the same basic response—proactive contact with all concerned constituencies on a continuing basis.

*Appreciation to James B. Strenski, APR, chairman, and James R. Frankowiak, APR, president, Public Communications Inc., Tampa, Florida, for their assistance in preparing this case.

When a filing is imminent, public relations professionals must think about the key messages that need to be conveyed and anticipate what questions are likely to arise. Before the various constituencies are notified, answers should already be in place. The most credible spokesperson for each public should be designated and thoroughly briefed. Other company executives must know who the appropriate spokespersons are and refer inquiries to them. It's important to be rumor-sensitive so that misinformation is quickly corrected. Keep an ear to the street—especially Wall Street.

Conditions will change during court protection proceedings that will have an impact on the communication plan. Public relations professionals need to be proactive so that new information, whether good or bad, is communicated before important audiences read it in the newspaper.

Examining recent bankruptcy communications programs can provide valuable insights.

## Harvard Industries

Harvard Industries, a large, publicly held original equipment manufacturer of automobile components sought protective action because of serious losses at its Doehler-Jarvis subsidiary, which manufactures manifolds, transmission housings, and other castings. Strategically, the subsidiary offered good long-term potential, but continuing losses made it impractical to realize that potential in the short run.

The company's public relations counsel, PCI, developed a comprehensive communications plan in the event Harvard's board of directors determined a Chapter 11 filing was necessary. This was done in advance of the board's ultimate decision to seek Chapter 11 protection. The key message was that Harvard Industries planned to submit a reorganization plan quickly and that operations would continue uninterrupted.

A commitment for $175 million in debtor-in-possession financing would help assure continued operations while under court protection.

A planned rehearsal was scheduled for constituent leaders, plant managers, controllers, and human resource representatives just before the court filing. Once court action was taken, the company disclosed the action to the SEC, as required under the SEC's "full and complete disclosure" tenets.

Tailored versions of letters signed by the CEO were faxed to all key audiences, including customers, investors, employees, and suppliers. A news release and a question and answer document were enclosed. Hard copies were mailed as a follow-up. Selected customers were visited personally, and a series of toll-free telephone lines were established for individual stakeholder groups.

A strong emphasis was placed on monitoring constituent questions and concerns so that responses could follow quickly. Daily call logs including the nature of the call and the call-back telephone numbers were shared with senior management. Media calls and article clippings were monitored by the public relations firm with response suggestions made to the CEO. Follow-up communications with suppliers also utilized a telephone hotline.

Employee meetings were held to address concerns. Employees were offered the opportunity to submit anonymous questions to management. Reorganization updates were posted throughout the court protection period.

The company is working aggressively with creditors to develop a feasible plan of reorganization. Stakeholders are updated periodically. When Harvard is ready to reestablish its leadership role as a leading industrial manufacturer, all stakeholders will know it.

## Celotex Corporation

Celotex Corporation, a major building materials manufacturer for domestic and international markets, filed for bankruptcy protection in 1990 due to the threat of asbestos litigation. Its public relations council, PCI, was asked to assist senior management with the development and implementation of a comprehensive communication plan to support the company's filing. At the time of the filing, Celotex consisted of two divisions: an affiliated research and development capability and an international sales and marketing affiliate.

Celotex had 26 manufacturing facilities across the United States, plus regional sales offices, all networked via e-mail communications. The company employed nearly 3,000. In many of the company's plant locations, Celotex was a dominant employer and purchaser of local goods and services.

The communication plan, which was constructed with the participation of senior management representing finance, purchasing, human resources, sales and marketing, and corporate communication, identified and considered the special communication needs of every Celotex stakeholder. The plan set the stage for proactive communication initiatives throughout the nearly seven-year period of protection and beyond.

Key milestones during the company's period of protection were communicated in advance with all stakeholders. Toll-free numbers were established, and call backs took place within 24 hours. Special editions of the company's publication, *IMAGE*, were produced and distributed to support the communication program, and comprehensive rumor-monitoring systems were established for internal and external stakeholders. Misinformation was corrected as quickly as possible.

When appropriate and necessary, senior management supported communication activities by telephone and in person. The company worked diligently to ensure that all stakeholders were updated on any steps related to the bankruptcy. Having a stakeholder read about an important process milestone in the newspaper or seeing it on television was simply not acceptable.

Senior executives visited all company locations each year and held candid conversations with employees. Those staff members wishing to submit questions and concerns anonymously were encouraged to do so by calls to the toll-free lines. When it became apparent that many stakeholders had similar questions or concerns, the company produced materials to address those issues. The period of protection was marked by a series of ebbs and flows related to the future of Celotex.

The outcome of similar bankruptcy cases in the recent past had been less than favorable. Through hard work and good fortune, Celotex achieved consistent, record-setting sales and revenues in the final years of its protective period. Management began to plan for the company's future.

Although Celotex had done well operating under protection, it became apparent that the new Celotex would have to better position itself to effectively compete in the marketplace. In late 1996, less than six months before emerging from protection, Celotex consolidated its divisional structure into a single operating unit for enhanced customer service and staff productivity. The company's R&D, international, and former corporate parent all became part of the new Celotex.

The Celotex story relied on the same basic strategies that helped other companies in similar situations: Recognize information needs of all audiences, be the sole source of related information, provide a solid way to express concerns and questions, and respond immediately. Rumors and incorrect information were not tolerated. Proactive communication with all stakeholders on a continuing basis became the rule for Celotex.

*(Editor's note: When Celotex emerged from bankruptcy, ownership was vested with a trust that was to manage its assets in such fashion that future asbestos claimants would have access to funds to pay individual claims. The trustees determined the best course of action would be to sell the assets of the company to the highest bidder, and that was done.)*

Bankruptcy communication parallels other corporate crisis situations in that it demands proactive, continuing contacts with different groups. Yet, it is almost always unanticipated and therefore not included in many crisis plans. Paying close heed to corporate bankruptcy success stories offers valuable lessons in today's complex business climate. ■

----------------------------------------------------

## QUESTIONS FOR DISCUSSION

1. Why would a company that is not totally failing want to declare bankruptcy?
2. Does the stigma of bankruptcy damage a company's reputation and business?
3. How does bankruptcy affect a publicly held company's relationship with the SEC?

4. How can a reputable company "take bankruptcy" and avoid its legitimate debts and obligations? Is this good public relations?
5. How does communication at a company in bankruptcy differ from that of a healthy company?

# Case 5-3   A City Divided: SDG&E Takeover*

In a society in which organizations must recognize the interest of stakeholders as well as stockholders, investor relations often goes far beyond stock issues and earnings reports. This abbreviated case shows how public many topics once reserved only for stockholders have become.

The late 1980s left California in a serious recession. The real estate and banking industries suffered miserably, thanks to falling property values and the savings and loan associations scandals. Southern California Edison, a power utility headquartered in Rosemead, a suburb of Los Angeles, experienced financial difficulties and was a victim of a depressed economy. The population growth of Los Angeles had begun to slow, but San Diego, served by San Diego Gas & Electric, was the fourth-largest-growing city in the United States. Edison, the larger of the two utilities, licked its chops at the thought of eating SDG&E for dinner in a hostile takeover.

On July 26, 1988, Edison pounced on SDG&E with a hostile takeover bid of $2.03 billion in Edison stock. SDG&E officials initially resisted the offer, continued to reject the augmented bids of $2.1 billion and $2.15 billion, and eventually asked the state to stop the Edison takeover attempt. Suddenly on November 30, SDG&E directors turned enemies into allies and embraced an Edison proposal of $2.5 billion.

City officials and civic leaders of San Diego were unnerved. Mayor Maureen O'Connor and several civic leaders challenged the merger. There was even discussion of a municipal takeover of SDG&E. SDG&E dropped out of the greater San Diego Chamber of Commerce. Two board members at SDG&E resigned in protest of the merger. Rumors circulated that SDG&E officials were being offered positions by Edison, and a poll revealed that San Diegans opposed the Edison/SDG&E merger by a two-to-one margin.

## Groups Promoting the Merger

Three groups were promoting the merger.

1. San Diegans for the Merger, a so-called grassroots organization funded by Southern California Edison, was an "impartial" front group composed of stockholders and SDG&E employees (current and former) who felt that the merger would improve stock value. San Diegans for the Merger distributed literature and held informational meetings.
2. Southern California Edison.
3. Members of management and the board of directors at San Diego Gas & Electric.

## Groups Opposing the Merger

Four groups opposed the merger.

1. The Coalition for Local Control (CFLC), a diverse organization representing business interests, environmental and consumer issues, and organized labor concerns, was created in early 1989 when the president of The Greater San Diego Chamber of Commerce, Lee Grissom, persuaded Gordon Luce of Great American Bank to form a merger opposition committee from both public and private sectors. The CFLC was funded by

*We thank Nuffer, Smith, Tucker, Inc., public relations counsel, for the information provided for this case.

contributions from concerned citizens and vehemently opposed the merger. Subsequently, the group launched a public relations campaign against it.

2. San Diego Mayor Maureen O'Connor, the spearhead of the opposition, gained more respect than she had previously enjoyed by defending the independence of SDG&E. She was a major spokesperson against the proposed merger.

3. City Attorney John Witt and his legal staff.

4. The majority of employees at San Diego Gas & Electric.

## The Coalition for Local Control

The CFLC was headed by executive director Bob Hudson, who coordinated the talents and skills of a diverse group of people to unite against Edison. This coalition was formed "to convince the majority of the PUC [Public Utility Commission] members [three of five] to rule against the merger through a groundswell of opposition."[1]

## A Broad-Spectrum Coalition Brought Together Unlikely Bedfellows

The conservation coordinator of the San Diego chapter of the Sierra Club, the business manager of the International Brotherhood of Electrical Workers #465, a mayor from the nearby city of Chula Vista, the executive director of the Utility Consumers Action Network, a public relations professional, and many others worked together to represent San Diego in a fight for the control of SDG&E. They adopted a vision statement that was accepted by the entire coalition by June 19, 1989.

*If we are successful San Diego would have preserved its quality of life and controlled its own destiny.*

- SDG&E will remain healthy, local, and investor-owned.
- SDG&E will be supporting the community with civic leadership and philanthropic support.
- SDG&E will provide economic vitality and responsiveness to the community.
- SDG&E will enhance its record of effective management.
- SDG&E rates will continue to be competitive with other Southern California utilities.

## Key Messages from Southern California Edison

In its struggle against the mayor and the CFLC, Edison argued that:

1. The merger would prove cost-effective by eliminating duplicative functions (e.g., billing departments, public relations departments, and so on).

2. The community would benefit from price advantages, namely a promised 10-percent rate reduction.

3. The environment would be saved because SDG&E and Edison wouldn't need to invest in and construct new power facilities.

4. The merger would benefit shareholders. who would partake of the savings.

## Key Messages from CFLC

CFLC countered with its own arguments:

1. A relocation of the utility's central headquarters to Rosemead would create a loss of corporate presence in San

---

[1]For setting rates and ruling on other issues, the PUC is often the agency that decides whether something is in the best interest of the public.

Diego. The city had just lost Pacific Southwest Airlines corporation, and there was speculation that another loss could psychologically damage San Diego's independence.

2. Downsizing and transfers in both companies could sacrifice between 1,000 and 1,600 jobs.

3. The pollution level of Los Angeles could increase even further.

4. The magnitude of the combined utilities would be reminiscent of the 1930s, when utility trusts had to be broken up.

## Both Sides Take Action

Edison and its front organizations spent more than $2.2 million on advertising and publicity campaigns, pamphlets, and flyers.

---

**FIGURE 5-1    The CFLC devised its strategy by prioritizing which decision makers would be most receptive to its message**

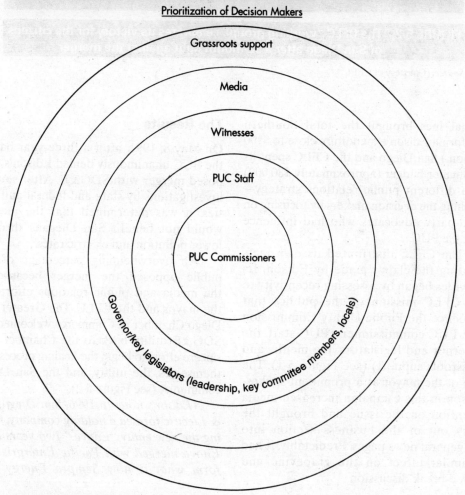

Prioritization of Decision Makers

Grassroots support

Media

Witnesses

PUC Staff

PUC Commissioners

Governor/key legislators (leadership, key committee members, locals)

*Source:* (Courtesy of CFLC.)

**FIGURE 5-2** The CFLC "working group" celebrates its victory for the citizens of San Diego after a 32-month fight against the merger

*Source:* (Courtesy of CFLC.)

(Legal fees brought the total Southern California Edison expenditure close to $100 million.) San Diego and the CFLC spent its far smaller budget (approximately $80,000) on a different public relations strategy—reaching the decision makers by focusing on third-party advocates who had influence with the PUC.

The CFLC distributed its own facts refuting the claims made by Edison. Its activities began by assessing receptivity to the CFLC mission of the publics that influence the Public Utility Commission (the PUC commissioners, PUC staff, the governor and legislators, the media, and grassroots support) (see Figure 5-1). The role of the mayor as a prominent spokesperson in this campaign increased media attention on the issue and brought the story out of the business section into the general news pages. Predictably, it had a similar effect on the grapevine and coffee-break discussion.

## The Results

On May 8, 1991, after a three-year battle, the PUC unanimously denied Edison's proposed merger with SDG&E. After several investigations by state and federal authorities, it was determined that the merger would not benefit San Diegans through lower pollution and electric rates.

An overwhelming percentage of the public opposed the merger because of the media and public relations efforts by the mayor and the CFLC. The Greater San Diego Chamber of Commerce welcomed the SDG&E utility back to the Chamber in a sincere effort to begin the healing process for themselves, the utility, and the San Diego community (see Figure 5-2).

*(Editor's note: In 1996, San Diego Gas & Electric formed a holding company, naming the new entity "Enova." Two years later, Enova merged with Pacific Enterprises to form what is now Sempra Energy. San*

*Diego Gas & Electric is one operating division of Sempra, which is headquartered in San Diego.*

*"Keeping San Diego Gas & Electric in San Diego was the whole purpose in fighting*

*Edison," said Kerry Tucker, of Nuffer, Smith and Tucker, strategists for the Edison fight. "It wasn't about being merged; it was more about being moved. Sempra is based in San Diego, so there was no problem with that merger."* ■

--------------------------------------------------------------

## QUESTIONS FOR DISCUSSION

1. Was it fair to SDG&E stockholders, who might have benefited financially by selling their stock in the proposed takeover, for other parties to intervene? Why or why not?

2. Make a point-by-point case, pro or con, on a situation in which people who own shares in a company nonetheless have a voice in its destiny. Justify your position with comparative examples in other areas of public policy.

3. Compare the key messages from CFLC and Edison. How are they dissimilar or similar? What is the specific strategy behind each of the messages? What publics might find each appealing or persuasive?

4. How was the public served in this case?

5. How ethical was Edison's decision to fund San Diegans for the Merger?

# Case 5-4 A Classic: Established Relationships Save a Landmark Company

Of all the crises that can strike an organization, probably none is as threatening as a hostile takeover attempt. Sometimes one company wants to acquire a competitor or a firm that will add new markets or products. Often the raider has neither the intention nor the capability of operating the company. The objective is to obtain its asset value by selling off the company in pieces. In most takeovers, some dismembering, layoffs, or budget cutting must be done in order for the raider to pay off debt incurred to purchase the target company.

The final decision whether to allow a takeover rests with the stockholders. In an earlier time, they were largely individuals whose purpose in investing was to earn dividends and hope the stock would appreciate in value so they could sell it at a gain for their retirement. Such "little investors" have been replaced by giant investment funds managed by shrewd professionals with sophisticated computer programs to guide their decisions. They work for mutual funds, pension funds, and other large-volume investors with billions of dollars that they must "keep working" for the benefit of their shareholders or members.

Under pressure to "grow" a pension fund's assets as large as possible, so that it will be able to meet commitments to retirees, investment managers "play the market," searching for maximum profits while guarding against any possible loss. As a result, their decisions can be ruthless. The slightest downturn in a company's fortunes may cause some investment managers to quickly sell large blocks of its stock.

However, when it appears that a stock may rise, they will buy large amounts and do what they can to keep the stock price going up. One of the best ways to make a "killing" has been to accumulate the stock of a company targeted for takeover. Invariably, the price of acquiring the company is at a high premium over the normal trading value or actual worth of its stock. Price per share may rise 50 percent or even more during the bidding battle among rivals vying to take over the company, as each makes a tender offer to the stockholders at increasingly higher prices. It is really an auction, with each stockholder free to sell shares to the bidder of choice.

Faced with an unfriendly takeover, management and the board of directors must first decide whether it is in the present shareholders' best interests to sell. The best management teams and directors will also take into account the effect on stakeholders as well as stockholders, including employees and the community. If the raider is after asset value, planning to break up the company, they may conclude that operating the company will give better long-term value to shareholders, while selling it off piecemeal provides merely a one-time gain.

Then management must devise a defense to thwart the raider. By and large, such defenses are the *product of public relations*. In some cases, this means trying to convince the stockholders not to sell their shares to the raiders. In the case that follows, it meant persuading state legislators to pass new laws that make it difficult for raiders to accomplish their aims.

## A Premier Company

Before it became Target Corporation, the business was known by a variety of corporate monikers, including Dayton-Hudson's (1969–2000) for its two flagship store chains. During the 1980s frenzy of takeover madness in the retail trades, Dayton-Hudson/Target became a takeover target. Dayton Hudson Corporation (DHC), headquartered in Minneapolis, was *one of the five largest retailers in America, with sales of over $18 billion annually*. It was also one of those rare companies that, almost from its inception, had been an innovator and leader. This is how James Shannon described DHC in the Minneapolis *Star and Tribune* at the time of its takeover troubles:

In the 1880s and early 1890s, George Draper Dayton was a banker in Worthington, Minnesota. In that capacity he began to buy real estate in Minneapolis. In 1895 the original Westminster Presbyterian Church at the corner of 7th and Nicollet in Minneapolis burned to the ground. Because of the economic panic of 1893, the vacant lot (really an empty hole) at that site went unsold for more than a year. At the urging of his Minneapolis business conferees, Dayton in 1895 bought the land and constructed the store that today is the keystone of the Dayton Hudson retail chain.

Known originally as the Dayton Co., and privately owned by the family of George Draper Dayton, the company went public in 1967. Now known as the Dayton Hudson Corp., its 1986 sales exceeded $9 billion. By 1993 Dayton Hudson Corporation had expanded to 33 states and operated 892 stores, including Target, Mervyn's, Dayton Hudson, Lechmere, and Marshall Field's, the famous Chicago-based department stores. It has 34,000 employees in Minnesota.

Ever since the company was privately owned by the Dayton family it has given five percent of its annual pretax profits to worthy causes in communities where it has significant presence. In 1986 it contributed $20,718,500 to the arts and to social-service programs nationwide, half of them in Minnesota.

In a community nationally known for its corporate support of the arts, social services, and education, the Dayton Hudson Corp. is the flagship for dozens of other publicly and privately held corporations committed to the proposition that a successful company has an obligation to be a good corporate citizen. In 1984 the University of California School of Business Administration named Dayton Hudson "the best managed company in America." As the first recipient of the Vanguard Award (for corporate social responsibility), Dayton Hudson was cited for its "unusual dynamism . . . entrepreneurial zeal . . . and its uncompromising ethical standards."

The company's 1983 Management Perspectives program, a participatory activity that attempted to identify and pass along for future use its corporate culture and values, determined that DHC's goal was to "be premier in all we do."

## The Raid Begins Suspensefully

In mid-June 1987, after several weeks of unusually heavy trading in its stock, Dayton Hudson learned that it was the target of an unfriendly takeover. But who was the raider? Writers in the *Wall Street Journal* and other media speculated it was this one, then that one—but the company didn't know for sure. Rumors of a takeover attempt—and the escalating stock price that inevitably accompanies it—resulted in an extremely dangerous situation: Within a three-week period, nearly 30 percent of DHC's stock changed hands, making the situation so fluid that someone could have taken control of the company at any time.

As a company statement issued via press release stated, "That means 30 percent of our stock is owned by people who have had it less than 15 days. They could care less about our customers, our employees or our communities. We have every reason to believe those shares moved from stable institutional investors to speculators, short-term investors and what are called arbitrageurs [a person working in a brokerage firm who trades in stock on speculation]."

Under SEC regulations, whenever a stockholder accumulates five percent of any company's stock, it must report the fact. However, through various tactics, the purchaser may take as long as a year before making the report. Realizing the danger, management began taking steps to defend the company. In addition to usual activities, such as having investor relations staff scrutinize activity in the stock and media relations staff monitor news coverage, special steps were taken:

- CEO Kenneth Macke sent a memo to all corporate staff warning them not to speculate or comment on the situation, since that could fuel rumors (and the stock price); he also reminded them that the official spokesperson for the corporation was its vice president of public relations (VP-PR), Ann Barkelew.
- A task force was assembled to study what others had done in such situations, investigate all available data about the most likely raiders, and review new laws passed by some states to deal with hostile takeovers; included were representatives from public relations, investor relations,

public affairs, law, and outside consulting firms.
- On the morning of June 17, 1987, Macke set a meeting of the crisis team for 2:00 P.M. Its members were himself as CEO, the president and COO (chief operating officer), the CFO (chief financial officer), the general counsel, and the VP-PR. The objective was to determine action and timing "assuming I receive the five percent letter" today. Specific agenda items included: What actions are required? What actions are recommended? Will we have a press release and, if so, what will it say? Who will notify all concerned parties?

As speculation about a takeover and a possible raider swirled around the company, Barkelew fell back on established policy to handle the hundreds of media, stock market, and other inquiries. She reported to Macke: "I continue to stand on our corporate policy of no comments on rumors or speculation of this nature . . . and, except for the rumors, we know of no reason for the fluctuations in our stock price or trading volume."

## Seven Days in June

The task force established the objective: "To build support for a special legislative session to enact tougher anti-takeover laws that would provide greater protection for all Minnesota-incorporated public companies." June 18, the day after the action and timing meeting, Macke requested and got a meeting with Governor Rudy Perpich. He briefed the governor at 3 P.M. on the situation—using a script and briefing paper prepared by public relations—and asked him to call a special legislative session to pass the new law.

Considering that the regular session of the legislature had ended only recently, and that special sessions are costly and unpopular, this was a bold move. It meant that the governor and legislative leaders had to be completely convinced of the severity of DHC's situation—and of the possibility that it could happen to other Minnesota concerns. This, in turn, meant that public relations and allied departments had to generate massive amounts of materials in an exceedingly short period.

When Macke went to meet Perpich, much of this material was already in his hands, thanks to late night and weekend work by public relations staff and its consulting firms.

At 8 P.M., Governor Perpich met with legislative leaders to rally support for the special session. He told the press afterward, "We will not act hastily but we will not hesitate to act to protect a good Minnesota company that provides about 34,000 jobs to Minnesotans." The news conference was held at 10:30 P.M., prompted by leaks about an imminent takeover bid, reported the *Star and Tribune.*

The next day, June 19, the raider communicated its intention to seek control of DHC. This action prompted two events: (1) June 20 news reports spread the fact widely and gave emphasis to another fact, that the suitor, Dart Group Corp. of Landover, Maryland, "had already attempted hostile takeovers of six other retailing firms," as the *St. Paul Pioneer Press* reported, and (2) DHC launched an intensive effort to win the public, other corporations, and legislators to its side. That day alone these events were staged:

- Macke met with editors in the morning, then appeared on a public affairs television show in the evening.
- In the afternoon he met with business and community leaders at DHC headquarters.
- A letter to the company's 34,000 employees in the state, over Macke's

signature, asked for their active help "to support our state legislators in enacting tougher antitakeover laws that will provide us and other Minnesota companies protection from stock market raids and other abusive tactics."

- Dayton Hudson Foundation called 200 community and arts organization leaders to a meeting at the Children's Theatre, where audience members urged the crowd to write or call their legislators and the governor, in order to protect the $9 million the company provided through its foundation that year to nonprofit groups in Minnesota.
- General Mills, Honeywell, and other prominent companies headquartered in the state issued supporting statements to the legislature and the media, as did the Minnesota Business Partnership, comprising chief executives of 75 of the state's largest companies.
- Backgrounders, question-and-answer pieces, in-depth discussions of the pros and cons of the legislation, data on Dart (including an unflattering *Fortune* article depicting it as a predatory outfit whose operating practices took advantage of suppliers and customers), and other material was widely distributed. The material brought forth substantial editorial support from state media in the days following.

Meanwhile, standby advertisements were prepared, ready to run if public opinion shifted against the special session. One pictured Dayton's Department Store's Christmas teddy bear, used for several years as a holiday premium and known as Santabear, with the caption "Who'll get custody?" A shopping bag stuffer was entitled,

"A special session to keep Minnesota a special place." Even a glossary of terms used in takeovers was developed, explaining words and phrases such as *arbitrageur, white knight*, and similar jargon.

Survey research was undertaken both as a planning guide and, when results proved favorable, as a lobbying tool. Telephone interviews were conducted over the weekend in order to have information available when the decision about

calling a special session was being made (see Figure 5-3).

## The People and Their Elected Officials Decide

As the week of June 22 began, DHC representatives visited cities and towns across the state seeking support. An employee rally was held, and massive media coverage continued. On Tuesday, key legislative committees met

---

**FIGURE 5-3    The results from the telephone interviews**

Minnesota Resident Attitudes Toward a Special Session of the Legislature That Would Consider Changing Minnesota Law to Make Hostile Takeovers More Difficult

Question: "The Governor has announced that he may call a one day special session of the legislature that would consider changing Minnesota law to make hostile takeover of Minnesota companies more difficult. Which of the following statements best describes your feelings toward a special session to change the Minnesota law?"

| | | Gender | | Place of Residence | | Political Affiliation | | |
|---|---|---|---|---|---|---|---|---|
| | All Residents | Male | Female | Seven County Metro | Out-of-state | Democrat | Republican | Independent |
| I'm in favor of changing the law to protect Dayton Hudson from a hostile takeover. | 7% | 6% | 7% | 6% | 8% | 6% | 6% | 6% |
| I'm in favor of changing the law to make hostile takeovers more difficult as long as the law applies to all Minnesota corporations, not just Dayton Hudson. | 78 | 76 | 81 | 82 | 72 | 85 | 77 | 79 |
| I'm not in favor of a special session to consider changing the law. | 12 | 15 | 9 | 10 | 15 | 6 | 15 | 12 |
| Don't know | 3 | 3 | 3 | 2 | 5 | 3 | 2 | 3 |
| Total | 100% | 100% | 100% | 100% | 100% | 100% | 100% | 100% |
| Number of Respondents | (772) | (384) | (388) | (515) | (257) | (222) | (158) | (346) |

*Source:* (Courtesy of Dayton Hudson Corporation.)

FIGURE 5-4   Dayton Hudson Corp. leader Kenneth Macke, left, addresses special legislative hearing. Next to him is Representative Wayne Simoneau

*Source:* (Courtesy of *St. Paul Pioneer Press & Dispatch,* Mark Morson, photographer.)

to hear testimony, including Macke's (see Figure 5-4). It appeared that sentiment was favorable toward the antitakeover law and the special session necessary to enact it. But for quick action, enough votes must be available to suspend the rules—rarely an easy proposition. Some committee members were not convinced, feeling that too much protection of current management could be as harmful in some cases as unfriendly takeovers.

As Governor Perpich considered whether to call the session, a freak occurrence brought yet more attention to Dayton Hudson's stock. A Cincinnati investment manager and member of a prominent family made a bid for DHC shares at a higher price than Dart was offering. After frantic trading, plus efforts to identify the validity of the offer, the New York Stock Exchange halted

trading in DHC shares for 2 hours. In the end, the bid turned out to be bogus—another public relations challenge management had to contend with, and at the worst possible time.

Wednesday night, the governor called a 1-day special session for the next day. He had insisted that House and Senate leaders reach agreement. After the usual compromises and political posturing, plus adding some features of their own to the bill, they told Perpich they were ready to go into session.

When the vote came on Thursday, June 25, the House passed it 120 to 5, the Senate 57 to 0. The governor signed it into law that evening. The *Pioneer Press* lead next morning told the story:

The prospect of a department store chain rallying a state government to save it from a corporate raider, doing it all over 7 days in June and with barely a whisper of opposition, would probably be seen as long odds by folks from other states.

Dayton Hudson Corp, accomplished that in Minnesota Thursday with stunning swiftness by cashing in on customer goodwill built up over decades, the clout of 34,000 employees, a small army of top state lobbyists and the assistance of groups that have received millions of dollars in contributions.

By any yardstick it was a boggling show of clout.

Thus ended one of the swiftest crisis responses ever witnessed. In spite of (or perhaps because of) the severity of the case, within a 7-day period Dayton Hudson was able to plan, execute, and succeed in a hostile takeover defense—thus becoming the only major takeover target to escape unscathed until that time. But the work wasn't over for public relations staff.

### Saying Thank You

Illustrating the attitude that built positive public relationships for the company over

**FIGURE 5-5** Santabears greet visitors to the IDS Center's Crystal Court at lunchtime with a message encouraging them to sign a huge thank-you banner to Minnesota from Dayton Hudson Corp. The *Minneapolis Star and Tribune* recorded the public response

*Source:* (News photo by Tom Sweeney, Staff Photographer.)

many years and enabled it to orchestrate such a rapid response to crisis, DHC put as much creativity and energy into expressing appreciation to its supporter as it had into the campaign. Some highlights:

- Life-size Santabears, wearing "There's no place like home. Thanks Minnesota" sandwich boards, greeted downtown visitors (see Figure 5-5).
- Employees signed a giant "Thanks Minnesota" banner, which was then placed in Minneapolis' major downtown center for others to add their names, before being sent to the governor (see Figure 5-5).
- "Thanks Minnesota" buttons were worn by employees, after Macke appeared at an employee ice cream social and thank-you party wearing one.
- All employees received a letter from the chairman thanking them, urging them to pass their appreciation along to public officials and customers,

then noting that only by redoubling efforts to make the company even better would they be truly free of raiders.

- Ads were placed, as well as publicity, and personal thank-you letters from Macke went to legislators.
- The next issue of the company's internal newsletter, *Courier*, reprinted Macke's remarks at the ice cream social, in which—by name—he thanked each headquarters employee who had taken part in the effort.

The takeover case generated 3,600 inches of newspaper coverage. *Corporate Exposure* newsletter, which tracks media coverage of companies, found Dayton Hudson in first place for the period—but also reported that the dominant tone of reportage was favorable to DHC.

After the legislation was passed, Dart Group quietly sold its holdings in Dayton Hudson. ■

----

## QUESTIONS FOR DISCUSSION

1. In its various subsidiaries that operate stores across the country, Dayton Hudson has 168,000 employees. Why was it important to keep them informed of the Minnesota legislative effort? How would you have done it?
2. Dart Group Corporation had been the subject of unflattering news reports about its operations and reputation. Generally, the raider was depicted as profit-hungry and a haggler with its suppliers. How might this depiction have affected various publics in the DHC takeover attempt? How might it have affected other DHC stockholders? Legislators? Editors and reporters? Employees? Management? Communities in which the company operates? What motivations in each

group would Dart's reputation have stimulated?
3. The new Minnesota law allowed corporate managements to take the effect on stakeholders as well as stockholders into account when deciding whether to accept a takeover bid. Without this provision, managements are apt to consider only whether the deal is good for shareholders. Is it fair and sound social policy for employees, customers, communities, local governments, and other stakeholders to be considered when they have purchased no stock? What investment do they have? Why should they be considered?
4. What influence on the case, if any, do you think the bogus offer had? Did it make matters better or worse for DHC?

## PROBLEM 5-A CAN AN ANNUAL REPORT PLEASE EVERYONE?

Preparation of the annual report for a publicly owned corporation is probably the most frustrating, if not the most difficult, communications literary task generally assigned to the corporate communications staff. This statement is true whether the job is handled internally or with the aid of outside counsel.

As the "report card" of management to those who own the company as shareholders, and to those in the financial community who can influence others for or against owning shares, it is an ultrasensitive and personal document. In many cases it is an ego trip for the head of the firm, for the top financial officer, or for officers hoping one day to become CEO.

The top official, when the company has had a good year, both competitively and in operating results, may want a lavish four-color booklet. The senior financial officer may prefer one or two colors (the second being silver or gold), demonstrating prudence as well as success. The heads of operating divisions, wanting to broaden the circulation to customers and prospects, may want lavish product or service pictures, particularly of the products or services of their particular division or subsidiary. The director of personnel will probably want pictures showing how happy the employees are at their jobs. Systems analysts will want their latest cost-reducing equipment shown. If the corporation is international in scope, the export department will want to emphasize "hands across the seas."

Shareholders who may receive dividends of $1 per share of stock may receive an annual report that costs $1 to $2 per copy to produce, not counting the time to put into it by executives and members of the communications staff. In many corporations, thinking about the next year's report starts as soon as one year's annual report has come out and been distributed, feedback has been received, and the annual meeting of shareholders has taken place. Given the high vanity quotient involved; the diversity of views within a corporation; the inherent "competition" for attention, recognition, and prominence among corporate divisions; and possibly financial results that are not the best, public relations has its work cut out for it.

Persuasion, compromise, and reconciliation are needed. See how you would go about this task: Select a corporation and acquire an annual report. Assume that you have to plan for the next year's report.

1. What questions will you ask and what research will you do before you start your basic strategic plan for the report?
2. Your research indicates the desirability of some major changes in the content and design of the report. Draw up a formal outline of your approach, including:

   - Overall theme in words and graphics (with your rationale)
   - Table of contents indicating obligatory information
   - Preliminary concepts for cover and layout
   - Photography needs or other visual techniques with costs
   - Printing costs, including number of copies
   - A timetable with deadlines

3. How will you suggest reducing the cycle time required to produce the annual report?

## PROBLEM 5-B HERE COMES THAT MAN NADER, AGAIN

The article, "Ralph Nader's group nominates 10 companies for Hall of Shame," appeared in the national newspaper *USA Today*. The companies earned a place on the list based on their "unethical conduct, narrowness of vision, lack of foresight, and unwaveringly steady focus of the short-term bottom line."

You are newly hired, a business school graduate with an emphasis in public relations, in the shareholder relations section of a department in one of the 10 companies named in the news story.

After the story appeared, there were a few well-chosen expletives expressed in your company regarding Nader and his associates, but there was no request from senior financial officers or top management that any responsive or reciprocal action be taken. Your immediate boss asked nothing of you, and the vice president for public relations made no request of him. The position of your employer, apparently, is much the same as the "cool-it" posture of GM when Nader's Campaign GM was on. There is a new development, however.

A letter has come in, addressed to Director of Shareholder Relations. The letter includes these passages:

> My husband was a successful businessman. His success is the reason I am able to live comfortably on my investments, one of which is ownership of 1,000 shares of your stock. I might say that I own more of your stock than some of the people on your board of directors.
>
> Having more of my money invested in your stock than some of your directors who get paid fees concerns me somewhat. But my major concern is that you do things that invite attention and distrust because they appear unethical, illegal, short-sighted, or just plain greedy, and contrary to what investors and consumers are entitled to expect. Isn't this a legitimate reason to question the justification for the huge salaries, bonuses, and stock options you give yourselves?
>
> I know I have the alternative of removing my funds from the company and investing them elsewhere. The news article, however, suggests that the standards you set for your conduct, and your performance, are typical of all big business. That leaves me no place to go except to foreign businesses, or to government with demands that they regulate you more strictly, or take over your industry and run it for the benefit of everyone. Frankly, your speeches complaining about regulation leave me a bit cold.
>
> Isn't it high time that those in business take the lead in self-discipline so that government and everybody else will have real leadership to follow?

This letter has been passed down the line, and it stops with you. The note of instruction on it reads: "We may get a bundle of letters pretty much like this one. Upstairs [the president's office] they want a reply, to be signed by the president. Let's see what you can come up with."

1. What will you do before you fire up your computer to write the letter?
2. Write a draft of the letter with a cover sheet explaining to the president the rationale for your approach.

## PROBLEM 5-C PLANNING THE ANNUAL MEETING WITH A TWIST

You work for the corporate communications department of a major corporation in California. Your duties vary on what projects come up, but your focus as of late has been internal. As a function of your job, your department is responsible for arranging the annual meeting of shareholders. Your corporation has decided to merge with another leader in the industry and the company has decided to release this information at the annual shareholder meeting.

Planning the annual meeting is a large task to take on, but with the added information that will need to be communicated, you realize that you have a huge job on your hands. This merger will have a significant effect on many aspects of the corporation. First, it will be a larger operation. As you are already a leader in the industry, this merger will put your company at the top and possibly put it in the *Fortune* 500. Second, the company will expand its services and products and will have to make changes internally to support the new business that it will be taking on. Job descriptions will need to be changed as well as departments consolidated so that they may become more cohesive as to what their new concentration will be. Third, many jobs will be eliminated from both companies to complete the final merger. Some of the company's shareholders are employees; some of them might lose their jobs in this process.

Knowing all of this, how will you communicate this information to shareholders at the annual meeting? Would you make a presentation to employees separate from shareholders and allow them to voice their concerns? What media outlets would you use to relay this information to the public outside of the company? In what sequence would you release this information?

Public relations practitioners often play the role of interpreter or mediator in situations like these. What recommendations will you make to the CEO that might help her present this news in a positive light?

# CHAPTER

## 6

# Consumer Relations

"Who are the three most important publics?" asks an old trick question. The answer is "customers, customers, and customers." If you don't succeed in attracting and then building continuing relationships with them, you'll be out of business and nothing else will matter.

During the rise of marketing as a cure-all in the mid-1980s, this view frequently prevailed in corporations. Hospitals, universities, public agencies, and even churches adopted marketing as a response to the increasing competition for people's interest and dollars. On balance, the marketing revolution was helpful to many organizations—particularly large or very successful companies, which had often forgotten that it is the customer who pays the bill, and to nonprofit entities, who often treated users of services as a nuisance to their routine, rather than the reason for their existence.

Ironically, while this trend reestablished a key point of public relations philosophy, it sometimes pushed public relations departments into a secondary role to marketing. A much-debated point was whether public relations is a part of marketing or vice versa or whether they are both essential strategic services and thus equal factors.

The question was prominent because marketing became a part of organizations that traditionally did not use marketing concepts. Hospitals in particular began marketing their "products" in an effort to gain their share of the healthcare market. Their patients began making it clear they did not want to be sold health care, and hospitals retreated—putting the function back into perspective.

Marketing and public relations share some fundamental concepts. These include analyzing market opportunities (research), selecting target markets (publics), developing a marketing mix (communication and action plan), and managing the marketing effort (evaluation).

The sharing of these concepts illustrates the close working relationship of the two fields. Despite these similarities, keep in mind that marketing is ultimately product-specific or service-specific. Public relations is so much broader a discipline. *pr reporter* illustrated the differences, stating that public relations as a strategy does four things marketing cannot do:

- Public relations is concerned about internal relations and publics.
- Public relations cares about noncustomer external publics and the environment in which the organization operates.

- Public relations operates on the policies of human nature (what makes the individual tick), whereas marketing focuses on consumer behavior (purchasing and economics, often expressed in number-crunching research).
- Public relations may work to stabilize or change public opinion in areas other than products.[1]

In the 1990s and into the twenty-first century, the functions have come close together, as demonstrated by the dominant customer relations strategy: relationship marketing. As the name suggests, this approach adopts public relations principles such as personalized, one-on-one dialogue regarding marketing of products and services.

The buyer–seller relationship concerns every public relations department and every public relations counselor. Ideally, the role of the public relations counselor is to help create conditions of understanding so that the objectives of sellers can be attained by satisfying needs of consumers. As a landmark conference between public relations and marketing leaders concluded,[2] public relations must both (1) help motivate purchases and (2) create a hospitable environment for the organization to sell product and services.

## HISTORICAL BACKGROUND

Starting in the late 1940s, following an almost universal base of hardship during the Great Depression, consumer "wants" were for material possessions, labor-saving devices, convenience, ease, and luxury. To producers and sellers, these were seen as consumer "needs." In the succeeding decades of increasing prosperity and affluence, it followed that if a product or service could be sold, it "deserved" to be sold. If a desire for it could be induced, it was what the people "wanted." Wants translated with adept interpretation into needs. A hula-hoop, a Frisbee, a pair of jogging shoes became "needs" for wholesome recreation or health.

For product and service sellers, the 1950s were happy times, as they were for marketing, promotion, advertising, and publicity personnel. The economy was based and dependent on increasing consumption. Trading in one's car annually, building a summer home, discarding clothes for each fashion change, engaging in fads, buying on time with credit cards, maintaining a big mortgage, stocking a basement with appliances, using hair tonics and electric shavers—these were "marks of distinction." Buying was promoted as though it were patriotic. Communications served these times well, especially when television came on the scene to give printed and audio media rough competition.

In this set of conditions, it was inevitable that sellers would stretch the boundaries of quality, service, and safety in products and services. They would exceed the limits of truth and accuracy in their claims and would abuse the privilege of using the public media. On occasion, through inadequate concern for quality, they would kill and injure some people and alienate many others.[3]

---

[1]*pr reporter*, Vol. 27, January 2, 1984, p. 3.
[2]"A Challenge to the Calling: Public Relations Colloquium 1989" held at San Diego State University on January 24, 1989, sponsored by Nuffer Smith & Tucker.
[3]For further insight, see Earl W. Kintner, *A Primer on the Law of Deceptive Practices*, New York: Macmillan, 1971.

The first significant government restraint in the 1960s came in the Kefauver-Harris Drug Act in 1962. Through the decade, other federal laws were passed, involving abuses in packaging, labeling, product safety, drugs, and truth in lending. Regulatory agencies became more active and aggressive.[4] A presidential assistant was appointed to represent and help protect the consumer. A tough adversary relationship was established for business.

Meanwhile, business approaches to the consumer were shifting. "Share of mind" superseded "share of market" for many national product advertisers. Programs spoke more about "benefits" and "value." Publicists were engaged more in concepts to sell "an idea," "industrial statesmanship," "a good company to do business with," or the "philosophy" or the "personality" rather than the sheer pleasure of owning the product or enjoying the service.

In public relations programming, there was an increasing shift to use of public service hitched to marketing. Recipes were provided for home economists; commemorative events were tied to products; dinosaur models went on exhibit; cars were tested by the loan of one to each family in a small town; a blimp roamed over public events, aiding national telecasts. The introduction of a new line of sports equipment endorsed by a celebrated athlete might be accompanied by a personal appearance. On tour, the athlete might sign autographs in stores, be interviewed by local writers on controversial sports subjects, be photographed at bedside in children's hospitals or wards, and conduct free clinics on sportsmanship at a local school.

- Today this approach has become the rule: People want to be *served*, not sold.

Further business response to growing consumer protectionism and advocacy came in the activation of ombudspersons, 800 numbers, understandable warranty statements, devices for improved listenership and response, calls to customers to check satisfaction after purchase, quick settlement of injury claims, and product recalls. This attitude gave even more importance to public relations and its implementation, but it did not stop all the abuses.

Television commercials were louder by several decibels than entertainment broadcasts. Among the largest advertisers were makers of products that were the most profitable but among the least necessary to human survival or uplift—cosmetics, liquor, and tobacco, to name a few. Going into the 1970s, consumer disenchantment with sellers, their wares, and their words expressed itself as more awareness of alternatives and here and there a boycott.

In 1970, Federal Communications Commission (FCC) Commissioner Nicholas Johnson raised and answered his own question of alternatives. "How can we make life in the corporate state more livable and more human?" His personal approach was to plan an "ideal day." In it he found fundamental elements to be love, beauty, contemplation of some kind, personal analysis, creative expression, contact with nature, and some participation in the support of one's life. He included such measures as riding a bicycle; throwing away expendable things in the house; and using bicarbonate of soda for toothpaste, gargle, mouthwash, burn ointment, stomach settler, room freshener, fire extinguisher, refrigerator cleaner, children's clay, and baking powder—at less than 25 cents a box.

---

[4]Early cases of FTC intervention and decisions include Carter's Little Liver Pills in the 1950s and Geritol in the 1960s. There are many more recent cases.

He jotted down his thoughts on the basic elements of life. One of his observations was that "when people live their lives in ways that take them too far from these basic truths, they begin to show up in the rising statistics indicating social disintegration, crimes of violence, alcoholism, drug addiction, suicide, mental illness, and so forth."[5]

## THE LINK BETWEEN REPUTATION AND MARKETING

In the 1980s, a new rash of crises shared the front page; they involved violence, drugs, greed, pollution, and lack of integrity. Business has adjusted to this situation. Advertising and publicity talk about reforestation, human dignity, education, rehabilitation, and "caring." Projects and speeches focus on safety, health, and the minority, neglected, and handicapped groups in society.

There are other problems. Conglomeration and divestiture tarnish traditional identities. What happens when Armour, not only a prestigious name on a pound of bacon but a landmark at the Chicago stockyards and a family intertwined for generations in the culture and society of the city, is swallowed into a bus company, also with a well-known name, Greyhound? Or when Twinkies becomes a product of International Telephone and Telegraph?

Multinationalism is another matter. Does anything significant happen in consumer relationships when a company that has proclaimed its "loyal American heritage" goes abroad to manufacture because wages are lower?

Savvy consumers make buying decisions based on how companies run their businesses, according to a 1995 survey by public relations firm Porter/Novelli.[6] Five major influences on buying habits were (1) product quality, (2) the company's method of handling consumer complaints, (3) the way a company handles a crisis in which it *is* at fault, (4) challenges by a government agency about product safety, and (5) accusation of illegal or unethical trading practices. Communication with consumers began moving from a product or service focus to information about how the organization operates and what values guide its decisions.

The first decade of the twenty-first century might see reputation become an even stronger element in the marketing mix. A sophisticated new generation of consumers, subjected to a constant barrage of marketing since their youth, will be looking for real distinctions between competing products.

As "social networking" or "buzz marketing" continues to grow, the reputation of a company and its brands will play an even greater role in the word-of-mouth communication around products and services.

## THE ROLE OF PUBLIC RELATIONS

Technically, both marketing and public relations support the sales function. "Nothing happens until a sale is made," says an old bromide. The difference is that marketing is totally engrossed in selling, whereas public relations is more holistic. It supports sales to

---

[5]Nicholas Johnson, "Test Pattern for Living," *Saturday Review,* May 29, 1971.
[6]*pr reporter,* October 2, 1995, pp. 3–4.

customers, but also is concerned with relationships with all other stakeholders of the organization.

Originally, public relations supported sales almost exclusively through media publicity, promotional events, and consumer information programs. The objective was to make people:

1. Aware of the product or service in the first place
2. Knowledgeable about the benefits and advantages of the particular product or service
3. Constantly reminded and reinforced in favorable feelings toward the product or service

Such activity ties in with advertising and authenticates product claims. Media used include newspapers, magazines, radio, television, features, photos, planned events, sponsorship of sports or musical activities, and many other venues for promotion. These are one-way communication vehicles touting the name and claims of the product or service.

Although the emphasis on marketing pushed some public relations departments back to this role, the changing conditions of the marketplace also brought forth several new activities, such as:

1. Forming user groups (as computer makers did) or customer service departments (as some automakers and utilities did) to personally build customer loyalty
2. Adopting customer satisfaction programs in which the entire organization is focused on delivering not just a product or service but also the quality and personal interactions consumers expect when making a purchase (as retailers, utilities, and brand manufacturers did)
3. Concentrating the publicity and promotion activities on taking customers away from competitors (which the beer and cigarette makers state as their primary reason for publicity and advertising)
4. Protecting the reputation of the product or service, and of the organization, in a period of consumer activism, government regulation, competitive predation, global marketing, and similar conditions that bring a continual bevy of public issues to bear on every organization and industry

## CUSTOMER DELIGHT REPLACES CUSTOMER SERVICE

Yet even as organizations trimmed and shaped themselves to meet their customers' needs and values, two problems surfaced: (1) how to discipline and motivate the organization (and its employees) so it (2) delights customers who then become regular, repeat, and loyal.

Grant Medical Center (GMC) of Columbus, Ohio, succeeded in satisfying its customers by involving its employees. Out of its experience evolved a four-step customer satisfaction model.[7] GMC found its emergency room was ranked in the

---

[7]"Action Research Unites Staff and Management in Satisfying Customers," *pr reporter,* May 23, 1994, pp. 1–2.

third percentile in terms of satisfying customers—97 percent were doing better than GMC. The process undertaken to correct this involved:

- Phase 1: Staff held brainstorming sessions to draft a model of a satisfied customer from the viewpoint of those who deliver it, and the barriers that prevent them from delivering it.
- Phase 2: The staff then went to customers to learn what they want. This research gave them a model of what satisfies customers designed by customers and a baseline of data on which to measure future progress.
- Phase 3: These results were taken to senior management for prioritizing as to what could get done today, in several months, and not at all. Results were revealed to staff and they began to frame the recommendations. What resulted was a matrix divided by customer, any required action, who is responsible for implementing it, and the current status.
- Phase 4: Ongoing evaluation to make sure operational changes are happening, tracking survey data, and continuing to update the plan.

Results of this process were dramatic. GMC's customer satisfaction ranking climbed. Senior management, convinced of its success, expanded it.

Further proof of the importance of customer service is shown in recent research of a major national company. It found that 64 percent of surveyed customers were perfectly satisfied with the product or service, but changed because of the way they were treated. Seventy percent chose a particular organization, not because of its product/service (which they know they can also get elsewhere), but because of how they were treated.

Organizations that compete for customers know that the goal has shifted to *delighting customers*—the ultimate competitive edge. Even if competitors satisfy customers, your organization can prevail by delighting them. Elements in designing a customer delight program include:

1. **The Promise:** A plainly stated vision of benefits for customers. Take care that these benefits are not undermined by employee actions or by ad copy that promises the moon.
2. **Customer Expectations:** These arise chiefly from (a) your actual promise, (b) competitors' delivery of delight, and (c) customers' perceptions of service quality in general.
3. **Delivery:** The gap between promise and delivery is frequently huge. Management must recognize that frontliners—those who actually serve the customers—are not the bottom rung of the organization, but its most important resource. Keeping those frontliners motivated means using teamwork, continuous training, employee evaluation and reward systems, and a method for measuring customer delight.
4. **Aftermath or Maintenance:** This is where reputations are sealed as shown by the classic study[8] that shows satisfied customers tell 4 or 5 others, while dissatisfied customers whose cases are not resolved tell 10 others.

---

[8]*pr reporter,* November 9, 1981.

## REFERENCES AND ADDITIONAL READINGS

Aaker, David. *Managing Brand Equity.* New York: Free Press, 1991.

Broom, Glen, and Kerry Tucker. "Marketing Public Relations: An Essential Double Helix." *Public Relations Journal* 45 (November 1993): 39–40.

Crispell, Diane. "What's in a Brand?" *American Demographics* 15 (May 1993): 26–32.

Cutlip, Scott, Allen Center, and Glen Broom. "Consumer Affairs and the 'Marketing Mix.'" Chapter 14 in *Effective Public Relations.* 8th ed. Upper Saddle River, NJ: Prentice Hall, 1999.

Davidson, Kenneth. "How to Improve Business Relationships." *Journal of Business Strategy* 14 (May/June 1993): 13–15.

Degen, Clara, ed. *Communicators' Guide to Marketing.* New York: Longman, 1990.

Feeman, Laurie. "Direct Contact Key to Building Brands." *Advertising Age* 64 (October 25, 1993): S2.

Felton, John. "Consumer Affairs and Consumerism." Chapter 16 in *Lesly's Handbook of Public Relations and Communications,* 5th ed. Chicago, IL: NTC Business Books, 1998.

Hardesty, Monica. "Information Tactics and the Maintenance of Asymmetry in Physician–Patient Relationships." In D. R. Maines and C. J. Couch. eds., *Communication and Social Structure.* Springfield, IL: Charles C. Thomas, 1988: 39–58.

Harns, Thomas. *The Marketer's Guide to Public Relations.* New York: John Wiley & Sons, Inc., 1993.

International Customer Service Association (ICSA) has a variety of materials related to the total quality service process and encourages professional dialogue in the achievement of customer satisfaction. For more information, contact ICSA, 401 N. Michigan Ave., Chicago, IL 60611–4267; www.icsa.com.

Kotler, Philip. *Principles of Marketing.* 9th ed. Upper Saddle River, NJ.: Prentice Hall, 2000.

Lerbinger, Otto, and Nathaniel Sperber. "Consumer Affairs." Chapter 4 in *Manager's Public Relations Handbook.* Reading, MA: Addison-Wesley, 1982.

Mazur, Laura. "A Consuming Ambition." *Marketing* (January 13, 1994): 23–24.

McManus, John. "Disaster Lessons Learned: Customer's Lifetime Value." *Brandweek* 35 (January 24, 1994): 16.

Murphy, John. *Brand Strategy.* Upper Saddle River, NJ: Prentice Hall, 1990.

Ott, Rick. *Creating Demand.* Richmond, VA: Symmetric Systems, Inc., 1999.

*pr reporter* Vol. 43 No. 46 (November 20, 2000). "Relationship Marketing: What Precisely Is PR's Role? Creating the Environment, Counseling, Running the Show?"

*pr reporter* Vol. 37 No. 12 (March 21, 1994). "Elements on Making Your Organization Customer-Friendly."

*The Public Relations Body of Knowledge.* New York: PRSA. See abstracts dealing with "Marketing, Marketing Support, and Consumer Relations."

Rich, Judith. "Public Relations and Marketing." Chapter 14 in *Lesly's Handbook of Public Relations and Communications.* 5th ed. Chicago, IL: NTC Business Books, 1998.

Sanford, David, and Ralph Nader, et al. *Hot War on the Consumer.* New York: Pitman, 1969.

Wilcox, Dennis, et al. *Public Relations: Strategy and Tactics.* 6th ed. New York: Longman, 2000.

Zandl, Irma, and Richard Leonard. *Targeting the Trend-Setting Consumer.* Homewood, IL: Business One Irwin, 1991.

--------------------------------C A S E S--------------------------------

# Case 6-1 Firestone: A Recall Revisited*

> *"Those that fail to understand history are doomed to repeat it."*
>
> —JEAN JACQUES ROUSSEAU

Large production companies are in business to make a profit. However, when products fail and lives are lost much more than profit must be considered. In August 2000, Ford Motor Company took on the largest recall in history because of Firestone tires failing on the road. Many deaths and injuries were caused by the bad tires, and many lawsuits were filed against Ford and Firestone, but the greatest impact of the fiasco was on the public reputations of the companies involved. The media coverage was sensational, and everyone who owned a Ford Explorer was taking a close look at the tires. The situation was in need of a strong public relations response, but there was none to be found.

## A Little History

In the early 1970s more than 20 million Firestone 500 radials were sold to customers who then experienced problems and failures with the tires. They registered their complaints with Firestone.

Two years later, Firestone's director of development reported to top management that the design of the radial 500 was of "inferior quality." In 1975, Firestone did some "severe torture" tests in its R&D division and found that half of the tires did not pass the test. No report was filed or made public, because the government did not require one.

Firestone kept the information to itself and sold millions more 500s.

In 1976, numerous consumer complaints about tread separation were sent to the Center for Auto Safety. The complaints were then sent to the National Highway Traffic Safety Administration (NHTSA). Finally, in 1977 Firestone recalled only the 500s from the years 1973 and 1974. It stated that one of nine plants was having problems on the production line and that this was the cause of these failures. Firestone said that the 500s were a good tire and that only the ones from the specific plant were faulty. Company officials also said that any other problems with the 500s were due to improper inflation or abuse by customers.

The NHTSA decided to do some tests of its own. Random tire brands were tested for blowouts, tread separation, and distortions. The results showed that 46.4 percent of problem tires were the Firestone brand. The NHTSA planned to release the information to the public, but Firestone obtained a restraining order to prevent the release of the news. This caught the attention of the national media. Everyone wanted to know what Firestone was hiding.

Test results from the NHTSA were leaked to the Center for Auto Safety, and in March 1978 the Center released the information to the media. It became a media frenzy, with nearly every paper covering the story on the front page. In August 1978, Firestone was forced by the government to recall all the 500s. In the end, the 500s caused 29 deaths and 50 injuries.[1]

---

*This case was researched and written by Jason Rock, a public relations major at the University of Central Florida.
[1]"Firestone's Reluctant Recall." *PR Practices, Fourth Edition.* p. 276, Case 8-1.

## History Repeats Itself

Beginning in the 1990s, many tire failures and fatal SUV rollover cases were reported, causing the NHTSA to investigate. In mid-summer of 2000, Ford acknowledged the problem, igniting continuing legal battles concerning what Ford knew and when it knew it.

Ford and Firestone had a large crisis on their hands, much like the one Firestone had before. In August 2000, Bridgestone-Firestone announced a voluntary recall of 6.5 million tires, the largest recall to date. The information about the recall along with all other communication was put on the Firestone Web site.

The NHTSA was closely watching Ford and Firestone during the recall. After doing its own testing, the NHTSA supplied the media with an extensive list of tires that needed to be recalled. Ford chose to recall only the 15-inch tires, but not the 16-inch ones, as strongly suggested by the NHTSA.

It was not long before information was leaked that pinpointed the reason the tires were failing and the SUVs were rolling over. A missing layer of nylon in the tires was to blame for the rollovers and the many accidents. Jacques Nasser, CEO of Ford, said that Ford would do what needed to be done. However, Ford began to blame Firestone for the problem, and then Firestone blamed its employees at a plant in Illinois.

In September 2000, Firestone's public relations firm Fleishman-Hillard walked out saying, ". . . it became evident that we could no longer be of service to Bridgestone/Firestone."[2] Firestone named Ketchum as its new public relations firm after Fleishman-Hillard walked out.

John Lampe, CEO of Bridgestone/Firestone, said there was testing to be done

with all tires on the NHTSA's list, but for now it was recalling only the 15-inch tires. He offered free inspections to any who were unsure of their own tires. Throughout the next year, Ford and Bridgestone/Firestone communicated internally and searched for whom to blame. The majority of external communication to the public was through company Web sites and a handful of press conferences. Research on Ford SUVs and Bridgestone/Firestone tires continues, but there have been more than 200 deaths—not to mention thousands of injuries.[3]

## The Facts

In the 1990s, consumers experienced failures with their tires and after investigation and research the largest recall ever was conducted. By November 2001, more than 200 lives had been lost in Ford Explorer rollovers. Ford used its Web site to facilitate the recall and display written communications, because it was an inexpensive medium. However, Ford's Web site for the recall could not handle the flow of traffic the day the recall was announced. Within the first eight days, the site received some 5.1 million hits. The majority of people trying to get to the Web site were unable to because it was down for 11 hours due to the overload.

Ford, which is a U.S. company, was the first to jump on the consumer's side, with Nasser saying Ford would "stand behind and replace the tires." Bridgestone, a large Japanese company, owns Firestone. Japanese senior executives perhaps did not understand the difference between Japanese and U.S. cultures in a time of crisis. Tradition in Japan is that an issue will fade out of the news as soon as a public apology is given.[4] Therefore, Bridgestone/Firestone did its part

---

[2]"Is Firestone's Clock Ticking?" CNNfn, New York. September 8, 2000.
[3]"Ford Is in the Driver's Seat." *The Orlando Sentinel.* October 31, 2001. C1 & C7.
[4]"The Ford-Firestone." FindArticles.com. October 2000. Maryann Keller.

and apologized to its public in Japan. However, the United States has a different tradition when it comes to crisis—the public demands more than an apology. Firestone's sales dropped 50 percent after the recall, causing profits to drop by 80 percent.

Ford and Firestone have a long history together. Traditionally, new Ford vehicles come with Firestone tires. But Ford can choose another name brand of tires if it chooses to do so. Subsequently, Firestone has the most to lose. It makes much of its money selling tires to Ford. Thus, the crisis impacted Firestone's future more than Ford's.

The CEO of Bridgestone/Firestone, realizing that the company was losing in the court of public opinion, finally acknowledged, "We know that we have been slow in responding to public concerns, that we underestimated the intensity of the situation, and that we have been too focused on internal details." This was as much of an apology as Bridgestone/Firestone would make.

Firestone maintained that the Explorer was the problem, and ties between the companies were severed. Meanwhile, the case continued in the courts of law and of public opinion. Ford won a few lawsuits against Firestone and is using that money to do more research on why the tires failed more on the Explorers and not so much on other SUVs. Consumer legal actions were expensive for both companies.

This public relations issue is still playing out for both companies. They have become victims of their own actions.

## The Perceptions

The media is the public's eye in such situations. Before the recall took place, there were frequent images of SUV rollovers on the nightly news, creating national awareness of the problem with the Firestone tires. Consumers saw the damage first hand

because of videotapes and still images of the horrific rollovers. Death tolls and injury numbers were growing as the recall became public. Lawsuits were filed and investigations began.

Owners, aware of the many accidents and lawsuits pending against Ford and Firestone, were checking their own Fords to make sure the tires were not part of the recall. As consumers were rapidly shaping their opinion about Ford and Firestone, little was being done to address consumers' concerns.

The media were unsure of whom to blame. The NHTSA's test results were published, and consumers were pointing fingers at everyone. The media kept the public up to date on the recall and the court decisions. Rollovers and injuries continued to happen, and each one made the news. Ford and Firestone could be found on news and investigative shows on a regular basis.

Other tire companies capitalized on the information vacuum. Goodyear offered information about Firestone's recall on its Web site. In addition, competing local tire businesses offered consumers free tire inspections.

Ford had actually communicated well internally and had made some good decisions (see Figures 6-1A and 6-1B). Initially, the public viewed Firestone as the culprit, but with more research needed, Ford might have been to blame also. As a whole, the public was confused, but consumers knew to stay away from Ford and Firestone. The public was also entangled in the blame game, hoping for someone to blame who could then fix the problem. That hope began to wane, however, as the former partners parted and pointed fingers at each other.

## Public Relations Impact

Public relations is supposed to play a major role in a crisis such as a recall, but Ford and Firestone didn't appear to be up to speed with

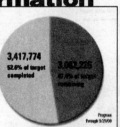

## FIGURE 6-1A   Ford explained recall procedures via pamphlets and brochures

*Source:* (Courtesy of Ford Motor Company.)

the consumer-sensitive lifestyle of the new millennium. Firestone could have learned its lesson from the first recall. Learning to deal with the media, not blaming consumers, and working with the NHTSA were problems not addressed at that time—nor in the later crisis. News coverage in the papers during the first recall read, "The success of a corporation nowadays depends not only on how it makes and markets its products, but also how it is perceived by the public." Society has progressed since the 1970s, and more important now than the court of law is the court of public opinion. This concept seemed lost on Firestone.

It is understandable that the Japanese company, Bridgestone, did not understand American public relations. However, being a company that conducts much of its business in the United States it should have been able to handle communication in the U.S. market.

# Key Tire Information

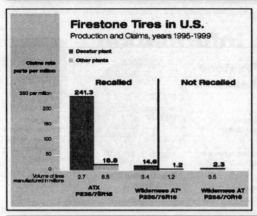

### Firestone Tires in U.S.
Production and Claims, years 1995-1999

■ Decatur plant
▨ Other plants

**Recalled**       **Not Recalled**

### Should other Firestone tires also be recalled?

Ford has analyzed Firestone's tire field data. This is what Ford has found:

Firestone tires not included in the recall are performing at world-class levels.

Although tread separations are rare events, they occur much more frequently among the recalled tires. Firestone ATX P235/75R15 tires are much more likely to fail than Wilderness AT P235/75R15 tires. All P235/75R15 ATX tires are being recalled.

Virtually all Wilderness AT P235/75R15 tires included in tread separation claims were built at Firestone's Decatur, Ill. plant, and these tires are also being recalled.

## Firestone Tire Pressure on Explorer: 30 psi

Ford now recommends 30 psi tire pressure for Firestone tires on Explorers to help simplify the recall issue for customers.

- Explorer performs well with a tire pressure rating of 26 psi on Goodyear tires.
- For 10 years, Firestone warrantied 15-inch Explorer tires at 26 psi.
- Firestone recently specifically requested that we change the Explorer recommendation to 30 PSI. Ford agreed in order to avoid confusion.
- However, this still does not address the root cause of the Firestone tread separations. The investigation continues.

Ford is recommending a change in Firestone tire pressure for Explorer and Explorer Sport Trac vehicles.

Previously recommended tire pressures:

|  | Explorer FRONT | Explorer REAR | Explorer Sport Trac FRONT | Explorer Sport Trac REAR |
|---|---|---|---|---|
| P235/75R15 AT | 26 psi | 26 psi | 28 psi | 35 psi |

**NEWLY RECOMMENDED TIRE PRESSURE:**

|  | Explorer FRONT | Explorer REAR | Explorer Sport Trac FRONT | Explorer Sport Trac REAR |
|---|---|---|---|---|
| P235/75R15 AT | 30 psi | 30 psi | 30 psi | 35 psi |

### WHAT CAN WE TELL OTHERS?

Verify if tires are affected by the recall at:
- Ford hot line         1 800 660 5719
- Ford e-mail inquiry    tireinquiry-ford.com
- Ford Web site          www.ford.com

**IF TIRES ARE AFFECTED:**
- Contact your Ford, Mercury or Firestone dealer for a tire replacement appointment.

**ALWAYS FOLLOW THESE SAFETY GUIDELINES:**
- Wear your safety belt.
- Check tire pressure regularly with a gauge.
- Check tires for excessive wear, cuts, punctures, etc.
- Rotate your tires as recommended in your vehicle manual.

**FIGURE 6-1B   Ford provided to consumers information about recalled Firestone tires**

*Source:* (Courtesy of Ford Motor Company.)

Ford didn't communicate much more effectively. Much of the news from Ford was released to the media and also posted on the Web site. However, the communication that did take place was not done in a timely manner. Because of this, many of the public's opinions were shaped and finalized before the recall could take full effect. Ford was too late and therefore unable to control the agenda and set expectations. Competitors were only too eager to offer information on the situation as well.

## Lessons Learned

Ford and Firestone could have done many things differently before, during, and after this became an issue of public concern. In a consumer-based society, just getting bad tires off the road is not enough. The lost relationships between customers and the two companies are going to be difficult to rebuild.

Neither company seemed to have a plan in place for dealing with such a crisis. The scenario of a possible recall should have been addressed before it happened. No one was "expecting the unexpected." Deciding whom to blame should take a back seat to fixing the problem.

Both companies should have focused their efforts on (a) fixing the problem; (b) focusing the agenda on this solution; and (c) providing consumers with a realistic timetable for the solution to be in place and working.

Absent this, the companies are left with an agenda set by the media and the government—something that no company wants to endure—and the unrealistic expectation that the problem should have been resolved yesterday. ■

------------------------------------------------------------

## QUESTIONS FOR DISCUSSION

1. Compare/contrast the situation Firestone faced in 2000 with the similar situation of 1975.
2. How does Ford's involvement in 2000 change the scenario?
3. Discuss Firestone's decision to recall only the 15-inch tires. Was that a good "PR" move?
4. Recalls occur daily in the automotive industry. Why do you think a total recall was such a sticking point with Ford and Firestone?
5. Discuss the role the internet played in Ford and Firestone's communication strategy.
6. How did Japanese ownership affect this case?
7. Why do you think the PR agency for Firestone quit in the middle of this?

# Case 6-2 Texas Cattlemen Versus Oprah Winfrey

On April 16, 1996, Oprah Winfrey, host of America's top syndicated talk show, featured a former cattle farmer named Howard Lyman, who was invited as part of the Humane Society's Eating with Conscience Campaign. On the show, Winfrey and Lyman discussed the Bovine Spongiform Encephapathy (BSE) disease—a deadly disease that had been found in British cattle. Just a month before the show, the British government had announced that 10 of its young citizens had died or were dying of a brain disease that may have been a result of their eating beef from a cow sick with mad cow disease, a similar dementia. An article in *The Nation* magazine quoted a scientist who headed the British government's Spongiform Encephalopathy Advisory Committee saying that millions of people *could* be carrying the disease, and that it is fatal and undetectable for years. When it does appear, it emerges as an "Alzheimer's-like killer."

In the Winfrey interview, Lyman compared BSE with AIDS and raised the possibility that a form of mad cow disease *might* exist in the United States. He also explained that the common practice of grinding up dead cows to use as protein additives in cattle feed *may have* contributed to the outbreak of BSE.

Winfrey seemed clearly shocked by what Lyman said. At one point she asked. ". . . you say that this disease could make AIDS look like the common cold?" Lyman replied "Absolutely." Winfrey replied. "It has just stopped me cold from eating another burger."

The audience applauded in approval. But Wall Street did just the opposite: The price of cattle futures dropped and remained at lower levels for two months.

The cattle industry was enraged at Winfrey and Lyman for what they viewed as defamatory and libelous remarks. Texas rancher Paul Engler of Amarillo, Texas, along with a group of other beef ranchers, immediately filed a $12 million lawsuit against Winfrey her production companies, and Lyman, claiming they violated the Texas disparagement law, otherwise known as the "veggie libel law." Passed in 1995, the law attempts to protect farmers and ranchers against false claims about their products that could unnecessarily alarm the public and hurt industry sales. According to the law, the plaintiff must prove two things: that the statement(s) made were false, and that the person who made them knew they were false.

There has long been an adage advising against making war against "those who buy ink by the barrel" and it should be extended to those who have hours of television time at their disposal every week. While the case against Winfrey and Lyman proceeded through the courts of law, it really heated up in the court of public opinion.

Battle lines were drawn early and included comments from industry groups such as the National Cattleman's Beef Association and the American Feed Industry Association supporting the cattleman and consumer groups venting via publications ranging from *USA Today* and *The Nation*. Issues such as "free speech" and the First Amendment to the Constitution were bantered about against those who would prevent "economic havoc caused by sensational and untruthful reporting by the media."

The ranchers, and the city of Amarillo, were not fully prepared for a battle with Oprah Winfrey on either front. When the trial dates were set, Winfrey put her national popularity and fame to work, moving her show to Amarillo to "avoid interruption" of her daily taping. Once there, she continued her daily shows while her crack legal team fought the battle in court.

With each airing, the American public was reminded once again that the show was in Amarillo because its host was being sued by Texas cattlemen who didn't like her opinion that she would not eat hamburger again. Cast in that light, the legal effort was disparaged without even so much as a mention. Public opinion was clearly in the corner of the popular talk show host.

Legally, things were not going much better for the plaintiffs. Lyman's opinions were just that—opinion—even if misguided opinion. Winfrey's declaration was just that—her vow that she would not again eat hamburger meat. Proving those statement to be false would be difficult because they were personal opinions. The legal grounds for the suit, even under a law established to protect agriculture from disparaging comments, seemed weak.

Consumer groups said the laws prevented critics from making any statements that might anger the food and cattle industry. An article in *USA Today* the week before the trial reported "Critics say the laws, enacted as consumers concern over food safety is at an all-time high are an effort to squelch debate on public health issues." According to the magazine *The Nation,* "Winfrey had the right to broadcast it and hamburger lovers have the right to know it . . . even if Winfrey's program gave a one-sided perspective on things, cattlemen have obvious remedies: They could have published and disseminated point-by-point critiques of Lyman's statements, they could have challenged him to open public debates and they could have hired the best experts money could buy. After all, the

meat industry already spends hundreds of thousands of dollars a year hawking its products; its opinions and promotions and celebrity spokespeople dominate the commercial airways."

The jury found the defendants not guilty. Right after the verdict, the president of the National Cattleman's Beef Association said in a statement "The good news for the American consumer from this trial is that all the scientific experts testified that America has the safest beef in the world."

The Winfrey/Cattleman episode clearly shows the peril of confusing legal and public relations issues. Under libel and slander laws (to which the veggie law is similar) legal redress is limited and difficult to achieve. Proving statements false is one thing; proving state of mind of the speaker is another. Courts tread lightly on such slippery slopes, and appellate courts are even more careful. Initial verdicts rarely make it through the appeals process, meaning remedy in the courts of law is illusive, indeed.

The court of public opinion, however, is another thing. When individuals or industries have a grievance with public utterances, the better avenue of remediation is usually via public opinion. Here the public relations practitioner is the "attorney" and the affected publics are the "jury."

As the apple industry did when attacked by media driven by the Natural Resources Defense Council in the Alar "scare,"[1] the cattle feeders might have used the "facts" to their advantage in a public relations response to the Winfrey/Lyman assertions. The facts are BSE is not the equivalent of AIDS, nor does it "make AIDS look like the common cold." (Editors note: The common cold is still much more common and less fatal than AIDS.)

[1]See Case 7-2.

The cattle-feeding industry might have called in favors from its end-users—McDonald's, Burger King, Wendy's, etc. The popularity of Winfrey's show is unquestioned, but millions of American consumers are satisfied customers of hamburgers every day. This personal experience will prevail over the opinion of even the most famous celebrity.

In the end, the cattlemen did get across a message that American beef is safe—if anyone was listening. In the end, Winfrey's show and its popularity remain intact. The American consumer still buys hamburger meat in copious quantities. The City of Amarillo still stands, even if its mayor at the time had to confess, "I didn't realize the depth and breadth of Winfrey's popularity."

The American public has a relatively short memory. This issue, like most others, can and did pass without lasting damage—the lesson to be learned in handling similar cases in the future. ■

-----------------------------------------------------------

## QUESTIONS FOR DISCUSSION

1. Assess the wisdom of legally challenging a national icon such as Oprah Winfrey. What are the pros and cons?
2. Comment on Winfrey's strategy of moving her entire broadcasting operation to Texas for the period of the trial. What was she hoping to accomplish? Did she succeed?
3. What limits are there to First Amendment rights?
4. What other ways could the Texas cattlemen have considered to handle this issue?
5. Do American consumers adopt or change behaviors based on what they see on a television show?

# Case 6-3 A Classic: Tylenol Rides It Out and Gains a Legacy

The Tylenol tragedy, Johnson & Johnson's responsive reaction, the product's reissue and comeback, and the nation's applause, add up to a classic case study of how a corporate crisis can be dealt with using effective public relations strategy.

This story has been told in a variety of special and public media. It has been interpreted for its merits in the practice of management, marketing, and public relations, and for the blend of what is admirable in all three.[1]

In 1982, some Tylenol capsules, laced with cyanide, were discovered to be the cause of seven persons' deaths in the Chicago area. It was discovered that the packages had been tampered with, and the cyanide added by a person, or persons, unknown. In 2007, the crime remains unsolved. All supplies of the product in stores nationwide were pulled off the shelves by the parent company, Johnson & Johnson, at a cost exceeding $50 million. After due time and investigation, the product was reissued in tamper-resistant containers, and a sealed package of capsules was offered free to consumers who had discarded the suspect supplies in their possession. The company became a champion of tamper-resistant consumer product packaging.

In the echoing events, Tylenol recovered more than the share of market it had held before the tragedy. The company gained credibility, public trust, and esteem.

The Food and Drug Administration of the Department of Health and Human Services (HHS) tightened its regulations regarding packaging (see Figure 6-2).

## Practical Realities

It is relevant here to set "what-if" questions aside in favor of a realistic situation analysis. Why was it that Johnson & Johnson, specifically, was able to weather this storm—indeed, to turn adversity into gain? Among the factors that appear instrumental:

1. The company benefited from a long history of success and service in a field of "beneficial" and "worthwhile" healthcare products.
2. The company took pride in its public visibility and its reputation for integrity.
3. The company benefited by having had a strong founder who believed that "the corporation should be socially responsible, with responsibilities to society that went far beyond the usual sales and profit motives."[2] High ethical standards were set in place early on to be continued as a tradition or as a legacy.
4. There was a credo, a "For this we stand" on paper, on which succeeding generations of executives have built and interpreted in terms of changing times and challenges. The

---

[1]For accounts that address these issues further refer to *pr reporter,* February 13, 1983; *Public Relations Journal,* March 1983; *Public Relations Review,* Fall 1983; "The Tylenol Comeback," Johnson & Johnson, undated booklet; "Tylenol's Rebound," *Los Angles Times,* September 25, 1983; "Tylenol Deaths Still a Mystery," Associated Press, September 26, 1983; and "Tylenol's Miracle Comeback," *Time,* October 17, 1983.
[2]Lee W. Baker, *The Credibility Factor,* Homewood, IL: Business One Irwin, 1993, p. 54.

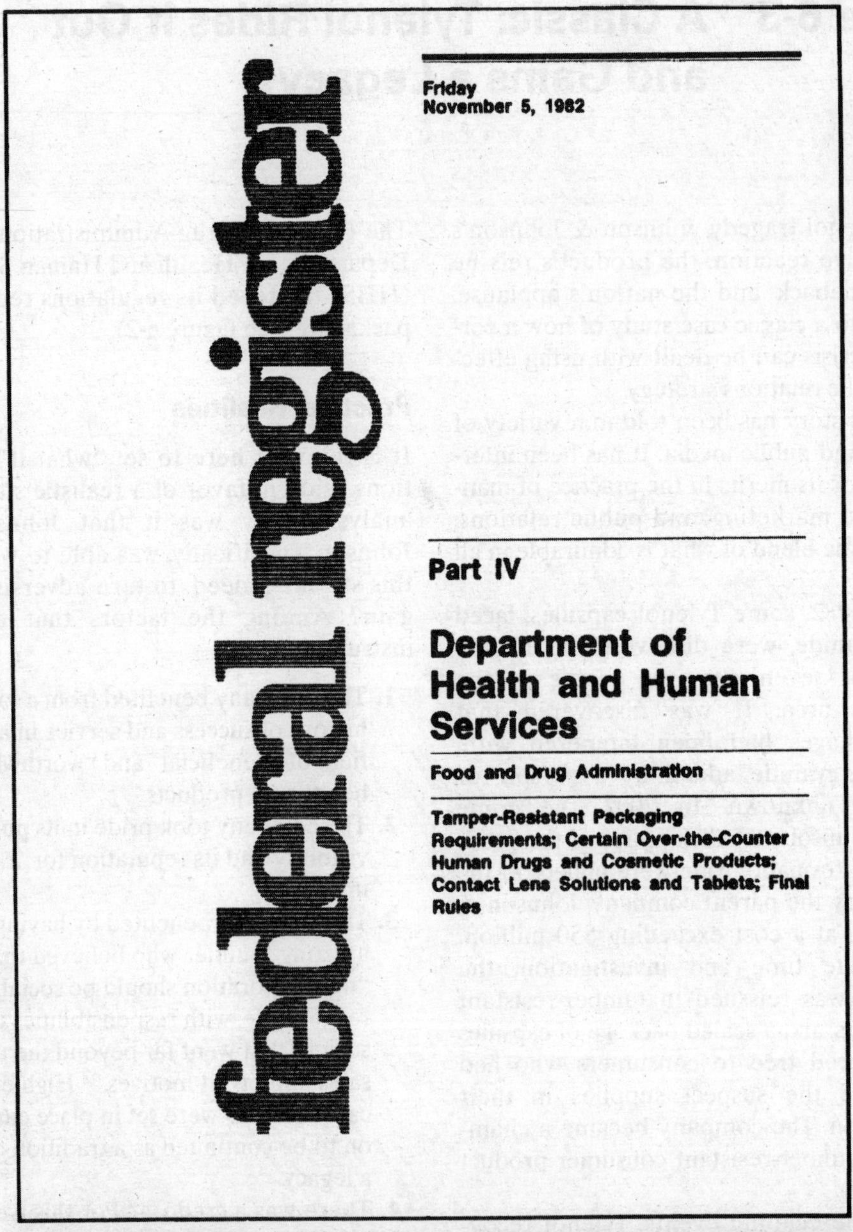

**federal register**

Friday
November 5, 1982

Part IV

## Department of Health and Human Services

**Food and Drug Administration**

Tamper-Resistant Packaging
Requirements; Certain Over-the-Counter
Human Drugs and Cosmetic Products;
Contact Lens Solutions and Tablets; Final
Rules

FIGURE 6-2   Tylenol case leads to federal regulation on tamper-resistant packaging

*Source:* (Courtesy of The Food and Drug Administration.)

# Our Credo

We believe our first responsibility is to the doctors, nurses and patients,
to mothers and all others who use our products and services.
In meeting their needs everything we do must be of high quality.
We must constantly strive to reduce our costs
in order to maintain reasonable prices.
Customers' orders must be serviced promptly and accurately.
Our suppliers and distributors must have an opportunity
to make a fair profit.

We are responsible to our employees,
the men and women who work with us throughout the world.
Everyone must be considered as an individual.
We must respect their dignity and recognize their merit.
They must have a sense of security in their jobs.
Compensation must be fair and adequate,
and working conditions clean, orderly and safe.
Employees must feel free to make suggestions and complaints.
There must be equal opportunity for employment, development
and advancement for those qualified.
We must provide competent management,
and their actions must be just and ethical.

We are responsible to the communities in which we live and work
and to the world community as well.
We must be good citizens — support good works and charities
and bear our fair share of taxes.
We must encourage civic improvements and better health and education.
We must maintain in good order
the property we are privileged to use,
protecting the environment and natural resources.

Our final responsibility is to our stockholders.
Business must make a sound profit.
We must experiment with new ideas.
Research must be carried on, innovative programs developed
and mistakes paid for.
New equipment must be purchased, new facilities provided
and new products launched.
Reserves must be created to provide for adverse times.
When we operate according to these principles,
the stockholders should realize a fair return.

*Johnson & Johnson*

**FIGURE 6-3   The well-publicized credo**

*Source:* (Courtesy of Johnson & Johnson.)

credo was brought out during this episode for the world to see (see Figure 6-3).

5. In its relations with employees, neighbors, investors, customers, and government agencies, there was a candor consistent with competitive and financial security. Company spokespeople—including the CEO—showed leadership and authority.

FIGURE 6-4  Employees got the word fast in company publications. This is the cover of a booklet that Tylenol published to keep employees informed about the situation

*Source:* (Courtesy of Johnson & Johnson public relations.)

6. There was a recognition of the public interest and its legitimate representation by news media. Information, whether good or bad, was forthcoming as rapidly as it developed (see Figure 6-4).
7. The corporate public relations function was part of management, participating in the decision process and in the implementation when communication was involved.
8. There were mechanisms for feedback from constituent publics, and a high value was placed on public input.

These virtues, some of which derived from the company's history, graced the behavior of Johnson & Johnson in its emergency. This is not to say that their behavior was without agonizing, great risk, or debates within the management task force set up to make decisions (see Figure 6-5).

## Johnson & Johnson Was Not Alone

In the crisis, public attention was focused heavily on Johnson & Johnson, the parent company, which took over for its McNeil Consumer Products subsidiary, which makes and sells Tylenol. However, many other entities were involved, some in a major capacity. It is instructive to look at the public information actions of one of them, the Food and Drug Administration (FDA).

**FIGURE 6-5   The corporation used news, such as this news conference, as well as ads to communicate with the public**

*Source:* (Courtesy of Johnson & Johnson.)

Over a period of several days the FDA's press office was busy keeping the public informed about this incident. Constant communication about this crisis characterized its behavior. It issued several updates about the initial recall of 93,000 bottles of Tylenol on September 30, 1982. In addition, it reported on the total national recall of the drug that Johnson & Johnson installed five days after the first local recall. Finally, on November 4, the FDA released its new uniform standards for nonprescription drug manufacturers in providing tamper-resistant packages. This constant flow of information from an objective third party helped to quell any consumer panic.

## Dealing with a Sequel

Four years after the first poisoning episode, there was a recurrence. In February 1986, a stenographer in Westchester County, New York, died of cyanide poisoning from Tylenol capsules that had been purchased at an A&P store in Bronxville. Johnson & Johnson, well-prepared for the crisis, halted capsule manufacturing and offered to refund or exchange all capsules on the market for tablets or caplets. A few days after the stenographer's death, five poisoned capsules were found in a Woolworth store. Johnson & Johnson took action to withdraw Tylenol capsules entirely from the market at a cost of $180 million, which covered "inventory handing and disposal, *and communication expenses* to reassure consumers of the safety of noncapsule Tylenol." The action fitted the public image of Johnson & Johnson, and the news media coverage was positive.

By the late 1980s, competition in the pain-easing medicine business returned to normal. Entries such as Advil (American Home Products), Ecotrin (Smith Kline), Bufferin (Bristol Myers), Anacin (Whitehall), Panadol (Sterling), and some others matched and countermatched each other's claims in consumer media advertising and publicity to get a bigger piece of the very large and profitable market. If the tragic incident befalling Tylenol was a negative for the product, that didn't show in a 1986 poll of consumers about the same time as the second incident. Some 76 percent of those queried said they thought the company had done enough to ensure that its products were not tampered with. Apparently, much of the public had come to realize that isolated acts of violence and terrorism cannot be totally avoided.

## The Public Mattered

The importance of corporate responsibility to the public is illustrated vividly by the Tylenol crisis. Although the company did not specifically have a plan before to deal with crises such as this one, its commitment to the credo "the first responsibility is to the customer" helped Johnson & Johnson to bounce back and contain the tragedy without sacrificing credibility. "Johnson & Johnson developed and geared activities to protect and communicate with its customers, to react to their fears, and provide what consumers needed."[3] A study conducted by Johnson & Johnson emphasized the importance of recognizing a responsibility to the public and maintaining positive public relationships. Companies that gave special attention to the public and their needs enhanced their profitability.[4]

James Burke, then chairman stated, "I think the lesson in the Tylenol experience . . . is that we as business men and women have extraordinary leverage with our most important asset—*goodwill*—the goodwill of

---

[3]Eileen Murray and Saundra Shohen, "Lessons from the Tylenol Tragedy on Surviving a Corporate Crisis," *Medical Marketing and Media*, February 1992.
[4]*pr reporter*, Vol. 27, February 6, 1984, p. 3.

the public. *If* we make sure our enterprises are managed in terms of *their obligations to society,* that is also the best way to defend this democratic capitalistic system that means so much to all of us."[5]

## Almost Above It All

Regaining its competitive lead was not the only positive result for Johnson & Johnson. In 1986, the Council on Economic Priorities gave the company its "American Corporate Conscience Award." In that same year, a public relations exclamation point was added by then-public relations vice president Lawrence Foster who authored a book entitled *A Company That Cares,* honoring

the c_____
Throug_____
received_____
ing two m_____
Economic P_____
corporate soc_____
2000, the "Bes_____
award from The _____
both 2000 and 2001_____
the World's 100 Best-_____
by *Industry Week* magaz_____
dent that the Tylenol bra_____ ained
its reputation as a safe p_____ because
Johnson & Johnson successfully launched numerous Tylenol-based remedies since the late 1980s. The company reported $53.3 billion in sales in 2006. ■

---

## QUESTIONS FOR DISCUSSION

1. Business is said to be a game of hardball most of the time, and competitive success requires that the cards be played close to the chest. The pharmaceutical business is no exception. How, then, can you defend Johnson & Johnson's traditional adherence to a "do-gooder" credo written by its founder or the open and candid way the company went about dealing with the problems posed by a small number of poisoned Tylenol capsules in Chicago?

2. Tylenol is a product of the McNeil Consumer Products wing of Johnson & Johnson. When the deaths occurred, the parent organization moved in and took over both responsibility and spokesmanship. What are the pros and cons to that strategy as far as the CEO and the communications people in McNeil are concerned? What about the news media?

3. Although the functions of marketing and public relations are often confused

as one and the same, or as part of each other, what do you see as distinguishing one from the other? Use this case as an example.

4. Which of the following conclusions do you feel can properly be drawn on the basis of your personal familiarity with the Tylenol incident?

a. The episode (diminishes/enhances) Johnson & Johnson's claim to competitive leadership in its industry.

b. The episode illustrates that marketing and public relations are (much the same/different) in values and priorities.

c. The episode shows that having a sterling character can (help/hinder) the bottom line.

d. Public relations (has/does not have) a significant voice in the decision process during a crisis when big money is at stake.

---

[5]Ibid.

# Intel Pays High Price for Losing Focus

Getting customers to try a product is important. But maintaining their loyalty is just as vital—if not more so—to a business' bottom line. It's a relatively well-known fact in the management world that it takes five times as much to attract a new customer as it does to keep an existing one.

Intel Corporation spent years—and millions of dollars—convincing consumers that its microprocessor chips are the brains of personal computers. With its campaign, "Intel Inside," the company managed to make its brand a household name in regard to computers. By 1994, 80 percent of personal computers contained Intel chips.

Dell computers, especially, benefited from the "Intel Inside" campaign, rising to the top of the PC industry as an "Intel-only" competitor. By the end of 2005, Dell was the global leader in PC manufacturing, with revenues in excess of $55 billion.

Intel, too, was doing well. At the close of 2005, Intel revenues had grown from $20 billion in 1996 to more than $38 billion, with sales to Dell and HP comprising about 35 percent of its business. Another 60 percent went to Asia, where most electronic manufacturing takes place.

But after spending so much time and money winning over customers, the company, made up mainly of engineers and mathematicians, failed to take the next step—keeping customers happy.

## Release of the Flawed Pentium Chip

In the spring of 1993, Intel released its Pentium series of chips—the company's most advanced microprocessor. About a year later, the company began receiving complaints from some high-tech users concerned with erroneous calculations. About the same time, the company discovered that the chip contained a flaw—a bug that affected complicated computations. Believing that the flaw affected mainly high-end theoretical math problems and that there was no impact on the average personal computer user, Intel decided not to alert customers about the problem. Until October 1994 (18 months later) when a new chip was designed and distributed, Intel continued to sell the flawed chip.

On October 30, 1994, a mathematics professor at Lynchburg College in Virginia reported the problem in an Internet message. The story spread quickly, at first through the computer industry, then among the general public. Intel's initial reaction was mainly defensive. Company spokespeople claimed the problem was so minor that it would affect a computer's calculations only once every 27,000 days (or more than seven years). They also pointed out that most computer chips by their very nature have some type of flaw or bug when they are released. Experts acknowledged the truth in that, but admonished Intel for failing to let the public know about the flaw and letting customers make their own decisions as to whether it was a big deal.

## Intel Takes a Defensive Stance

For weeks, Intel maintained its defensive position. The company had the facts on its side and thought the facts mattered. Intel engineers didn't know that it's how the facts are presented and perceived that matters. In that light, it offered a replacement chip *only* if consumers could prove that the flaw affected them.

For several weeks, Intel managers held 8 A.M. daily meetings to work on the crisis. Each member of the group reviewed news stories that covered the Intel issue and discussed reports that contained information from sales representatives in the field and from the customer hotline set up to handle customer questions. The group met again at 5 P.M. each day, sometimes staying until late in the night. After two weeks, calls to the hotline slowed down. Intel executives began to think the worst was over.

## IBM Deals a Deadly Blow

In reality, the worst was yet to come. On December 12, IBM announced that its scientists determined that the flaw could affect users much more often than Intel claimed. As a result, IBM suspended shipments of computers containing Intel chips.

The news stunned Intel. In a *New York Times* article, Intel's then-CEO Andrew Grove said that was when he started to realize "an engineer's approach is inappropriate for a consumer problem."

In addition to the IBM announcement, consumer advocacy groups were concerned:

- Attorneys general in two states asked Intel to level with customers.
- The Gartner Group, a well-known and respected consulting group, said companies would be wise to put off purchasing computers containing Pentium chips.
- On the Internet, where news of the flaw was initially released, more than 10,000 messages were posted.
- Engineers and computer writers wrote harshly about Intel's reluctance to replace the flawed chip.

## An About-Face for Intel

On the Tuesday after the IBM announcement, Intel ran ads in major newspapers containing an apology for the way it had handled the flaw. It offered to send a new chip within 60 days to those who requested one and to help install the chip or pay to have someone do it.

Intel continued to dispute IBM's findings that the flaw would affect users once every 24 days instead of once every 27,000 days as Intel had claimed. Grove told *USA Today,* "We hope to convince them, engineer to engineer, that they're wrong." But some analysts thought politics were behind IBM's decision to stop shipments. At that time, top PC makers were concerned with Intel's dominance in the market. Some were busy developing their own chips.

Regardless, Intel was faced with a serious public relations crisis. From the beginning, CEO Andrew Grove spoke for the company. An engineer by nature, he told *USA Today* he was shaken by the episode. "I feel personally responsible for the decisions," he said. "These are harsh lessons to learn. We made a lot of mistakes. But we can't replay history."

Wall Street was immediately pleased by Intel's change in its replacement policy for the flawed chip and its public apology. Intel's stock was the second most actively traded stock that day, rising $3 to just over $61 a share. Explained Drew Peck of Cowen & Co in *USA Today:* "Rightly, analysts and investors see this as stopping the crisis."

## A High Price to Pay

If only the crisis could have been avoided. When the final figures came out in January, Intel realized how expensive its mistakes had been: It took a $475 million charge against its fourth quarter earnings to cover expenses incurred from replacing the flawed chip. Analysts had anticipated the charge would be between $50 million and $300 million. Fortunately for the company, net income fell just slightly for the year.

## Not Intel's Last Recall

In his book *Only the Paranoid Survive*, Andrew Grove wrote that this incident, Intel's first recall, was a defining event for the company. Since then, Intel has been forced to recall other products. It has also felt the pressure of consumers regarding product design.

The Pentium 4 was introduced in November 2000 *without* the controversial PSN (Processor Serial Number) that was in the Pentium 3. Its presence in Pentium 3 processors caused consumers to boycott Intel, because they feared an invasion of consumer privacy, according to the organization Big Brother Inside. Intel's push to be first in this market—to beat out its competition—is continually being tempered by consumers' needs and expectations.

In 2006, Intel and Apple announced new software (Boot Camp) that will permit Mac users to install Windows XP and thereby use Apple Computers as if they were Microsoft-based PCs. The technology that permits this revolution in computer usage is contained in Intel's microprocessors, which Apple began using in 2005 after a long relationship with Motorola. Thus, Apple, with Intel's help, is positioned to recapture some of the momentum currently held by Microsoft and PCs.

But, not long after the Boot Camp announcement, Dell announced it would begin using high-end microprocessor chips from AMD. Although this decision likely had little or nothing to do with the flawed chips, it is the first major departure by a major chip customer. Time will tell if this is a blip on the screen or the first step in a trend away from Intel's chips for high-end usage. ■

---

### QUESTIONS FOR DISCUSSION

1. How might formal research by Intel have helped the company's strategy?
2. What can go wrong with an "engineer's approach" to a "consumer problem"?
3. What value is there to the "engineer-to-engineer" approach?
4. When facts and perceptions clash, which usually prevails? Why?
5. Should Grove have acted as Intel's spokesman during this crisis? Why? Why not?
6. Do you think the $475 million cost of the recall influenced Intel's strategy? How?
7. Why did IBM "turn on" Intel (a valued supplier) during the crisis? What impact did that have on the outcome?

## PROBLEM 6-A Wine Bar Needs Positioning

"Berry's" is a wine bar in a southwestern U.S. city with a population of 400,000. In fact, it is the only full-fledged wine bar in the city. While many other bars serve wine, none specialize in fine wines of the United States and Europe as Berry's does. The fact that it is the only wine bar in the city is its problem. Although the city has ample well-educated middle-income people, wine has not developed a following as it has in some larger cities. Because no other wine bars are available, wine drinkers have become used to ordering wine at regular bars rather than at "specialty shop" wine bars.

Berry's location is good—downtown near some fine hotels and in an area that is being revitalized, further emphasizing the upscale image. The interior is pleasant and has wine vaults for persons who want to store their wine there and have it available whenever they come into the bar. All of these vaults have been rented.

The wine bar has been open for only six months. It has a good lunch business, but needs a better evening business (especially during the week).

The total budget for creating new business is only $11,000. Mr. Berry comes to you because he knows you have just opened your own communications firm. He says, "I know it's not a lot of money, but it's a lot for my business. I can't afford to just buy ads—what do you suggest?"

Consider what type of research you would use to determine how to manage customer satisfaction—how to attract new customers and how to retain the loyalty of existing ones.

On the basis of your research, prepare a one-year strategic marketing plan that prioritizes your publics and uses a mix of one-way and two-way communication activities with evaluation methods built in. Provide a budget that allocates the $11,000 between research and customer relation activities.

Finally, what issues should Berry's be speaking out on, considering the enormity of alcoholism and driving-while-intoxicated problems, so much in the news today? Think about how to position Berry's as a socially responsible drinking establishment.

## PROBLEM 6-B Good Intentions, Bad Results

Earlier this year, when you graduated from college, you were fortunate. You had a job waiting for you at Bart's Cartmart Inc., the largest distributor of motorized vehicles and accessories in Amarillo. The firm's slogan is, "Speed Up with Us!" Bart (Cartwright), the owner, happens to be your father. That saves having to work your way up. Besides, you've already helped out summers, when you weren't using one of the products playing golf, cruising off-road, or mowing the lawn.

This job has great promise. You're an only child, and your Dad has long had in mind that you would be taking over the business some day. In preparation, you majored in marketing, minored in public relations, and took several elective courses including one in business law.

To start you out full-time, your dad put you in charge of customer relations. It has been fun and challenging. This first year, you've devised a follow-up program in which you or an assistant called on each customer a week or so before the warranty period for the product purchased expired. You asked whether anything was needed by the customer that you could supply within warranty. Customers praised and liked that attention. And you've had Bart's Cartmart sponsor the winners' awards in one of the major competitive events at the annual Stock Breeders' Exhibition (motor vehicles as well as plaques and ribbons, of course).

This week, the Annual Harvest Festival is on, and acting on a request from the committee running it, you have loaned six used golf carts for the festival events.

Your father has been most tolerant about your activities. He obviously wants you to enjoy your job and to relish growing with the company. At the same time, Bart is no softie. He came off a farm and up in business the hard way. He knows what he wants and is determined to get it. At times he can be tough, if he feels he has to, and even dictatorial.

When you got to work recently, you were handed a morning newspaper by the receptionist. In it there was a story about a 12-year-old boy, the son of a local farmer and Harvest Festival official, who was driving one of your carts around late yesterday afternoon for fun. Something happened, and the cart tipped over on his leg, mangling it, with possible permanent damage. The kid, in the hospital, told his parents, and they told the newspaper reporter, that he "didn't know what happened." He was "just going along fine," when he felt a bump and he couldn't turn the steering wheel. Next thing he knew, the cart was headed for a big harvest machine. He tried to turn the wheel, but it wouldn't work and he became jammed between the cart and the machine. The newspaper carried a head shot of the boy. He was cute. The story indicated that the cart had been borrowed from Bart's Cartmart.

You sought out your father immediately. He said he'd gotten a call from the newspaper late in the evening, but there was no reason to disturb you. He had called the boy's father and mother, with whom he was acquainted, to express concern and sympathy. They were very upset. When he'd mentioned to them that these heavy carts weren't really made for handling by little kids, the father had made some critical remarks about lending out used carts that might have something wrong with them.

"I don't like it," your father said to you. "People don't react reasonably when their own flesh and blood is involved. I doubt we've heard the last of it." You asked him what you could do. Should you send someone in the shop with a trailer to bring the cart back and have it inspected, send the boy a book to read, arrange to retrieve all the loaned carts, or what? "We shouldn't touch that cart," your father said, "not until I can talk to our lawyer. Just sit tight for a few hours, and we'll know where this thing is going."

Within the hour, a lawyer representing the injured boy and his family called the company to say he had requested that local authorities "impound" the cart, and indicated he would want to talk with Bart soon. Also within the hour, your father had talked with the company's lawyer, the agent of the firm handling the company's insurance, and with a person at the police department who said they would hold the cart. Your father's lawyer, he said, would be talking with the legal department of Rundo, the manufacturer of the carts.

Before the day was over, you and your father talked again in some detail. "This is the kind of thing you dread in a business like this," he told you. "And with so damn many ambulance-chasing lawyers around, good intentions and fair dealing don't always come out the way you had in mind. With the newspeople looking for things to blow up into headlines, I can see this thing heating up into a court case and a local issue where people who should be minding their own business stick their noses into ours and choose up sides."

You assure your father that the good intentions in loaning the carts will come out in the end and that if you're open with the newspeople they'll be fair in whatever they write or say. He says, "We'll see. If you have any ideas as this thing goes along, come tell me. I'll welcome them. But don't go off half-cocked talking with others in the newspaper, the Festival Committee, or the next door neighbors. Come see me first."

Obviously, you are anxious to help, to apply what you learned in four years, and to retain the conviction that if you treat others fairly, that's what you get in return.

Given the four-step planning process, and the aforementioned events, what might you set as your objective, your strategy, and your main tactics in helping resolve the problem before it boils over into the community and into a courtroom? What might you recommend to your father regarding the do's and don'ts of customer and community relations in the future, and communications about those relations?

## PROBLEM 6-C TURNING CUSTOMER COMPLAINTS TO CUSTOMER DELIGHT

Eagle's Wings Airlines is a young company that flies no-frills flights within the United States. You work for its public relations department. Winter holiday time is approaching and flights are booked but customer complaints are increasing. For now, the cheaper ticket prices are keeping reservations high, but if the level of complaints continues, customers will be lost. In fact, you have just been informed that Eagle's Wings has been named the worst in customer service. The number of customer complaints has been piling up on your desk. Flights continually arrive and depart late due to the inefficiencies of airport crew members and the on-flight crew has received poor ratings because of rudeness.

To add to this pressure, flight attendants and pilots are complaining about being overscheduled. They want time off to enjoy the holidays at home with their families, not in some remote location as they wait for a flight back—a result of poor scheduling, which has been happening more frequently.

The number of customer complaints is growing as are employee complaints. You do not have responsibility for human relations but you can see that it impacts customer relations. The head of human relations is very busy and understaffed but she has agreed to meet with you tomorrow. In the meantime, you need to get a plan formulated because you can't afford to further antagonize customers. In fact, you want to delight customers. How will you do that knowing what you know about this situation? What is your immediate plan of action?

Then put together a one-year strategic plan to build consumer relationships outlining possible problems and solutions. Put into action an evaluation process that will help you to gauge the minds of your consumers as well as your employees. This will make it easier for both sides to communicate what they like, don't like, and would like to see improved. You hope this will bring about improvements and repeat customers, which will help business in the long run.

# CHAPTER

## 7

# Media Relations

The biggest misunderstanding in public relations concerns the mass media: what its role and power really are in modern society and how important media relations is in building effective public relationships.

Many practitioners still go to the extreme of *equating* public relations with publicity. So, unfortunately, do some managers. Others find contemporary journalism so unbalanced in its emphases and its audiences so fractionated that, except in unusual circumstances, they prefer to avoid the media. Fortunately, many scholarly studies have given us an objective look from which to devise workable strategies. They find that:

1. **Media influence is cumulative and long-term.** A single news report, even if covered by media across the country, or an item in a single medium, even if it's the evening news, usually causes little if any behavior or attitude change. But when many media cover a subject over the years, perhaps expressing a viewpoint on the topic, whole generations can be influenced. For example, most of us have no personal experience whatsoever with communism, yet we strongly oppose it—because all our lives it has been a subject portrayed in a negative way in our media.

2. **The main power of the media is to make us aware**—of products, services, companies, and ideas—and to provide information about them. By itself, awareness rarely moves us to action or even shapes an opinion. But as a first step in the decision-making process, it is vital. If we don't know something exists, we can't do anything about it. Scholars call this the *agenda-setting role of the media.* (See Figure 7-1.)

3. **The media concentrate on reporting bad news**—the errors, accidents, and scandals of human society. As an early American political figure said, "In a republic based upon public opinion, it is necessary to excite a spirit of inquiry—to furnish public men with information of their errors."[1] Today, this statement is true not only of elected officials but of all executives and all organizations as well. As educator Scott Cutlip said, "There are no private organizations today, even if they are totally owned by one or a few persons, because all must abide by the rule of

---
[1]William Plummer, U.S. Senator, several times governor of New Hampshire and historian, in an article titled "To the People," published widely, May 23, 1820.

FIGURE 7-1 Even members of the media, such as the creator of this popular cartoon, recognize the changes that have occurred in news gathering and dissemination

# Calvin and Hobbes

## by Bill Watterson

public consent." But research shows we prefer to hear about bad news, rather than good news, by a factor of seven to one. In their own marketing interest, then, it follows that the media would feature bad news. It's what their customers demand.

Clearly the challenge is to create relationships with journalists and media figures—as with *all* publics—that will permit them to rely on our organizations when we are the focus of interest. If reporters and editors have learned that they can trust an organization and its public relations staff, they are likely to (a) report on the information of which we need to make our publics aware and (b) give us a fair chance, or at least balanced reportage, when we're on the hot seat.

Though the generalized relationship between journalists and practitioners may forever be characterized as adversarial, we must remember that the two professions share one basic tenet—the First Amendment—and in pursuit of protecting this license, we are united.

## WORKING WITH THE MEDIA

An important part of the practitioner's job often is working with the media. This relationship depends on practitioners providing information that newspeople consider to be of public interest—is it newsworthy?

A close and friendly working relationship is relatively easy between small or local organizations and the community, trade, or professional media. In such situations, and there are many thousands of them, the media have small staffs and need "free" news-gathering help. Public relations practitioners provide it.

- That word *media* still puzzles. It is plural. Newspapers in Cincinnati are the local print *media,* but the *Cincinnati Post* is a *medium.* Yet we often use this plural word as a collective noun and so treat it as if it were singular. How often do we read "media is" rather than "media are"? Further complicating the lexicon of public relations is that *all* communication forms are also called media. Technically, we ought to differentiate between the *news* media or *mass* media (radio, television, newspapers) and *communication* media (newsletters, group meetings, speeches, letters, videos, and so on). This chapter deals with the former.

Personalized, mutually supportive relationships have become extremely difficult, however, between the mass media and the giant enterprises and institutions. Both entities tend more and more to conglomeration and automation, as the former bends to exposé journalism and the latter turns to controlled advocacy—and as animosity grows between the private and public sectors.[2]

---

[2]Ben H. Bagdikian, *The Media Monopoly,* Beacon Press, 1997. When first published in 1983, 50 corporations owned most of American media. According to *Advertising Age* (August 20, 2001), the top 10 leading media companies in 2000 were AOL Time Warner, Viacom, AT&T Broadband (AT&T Corporation), Walt Disney Company, NBC-TV (General Electric Company), Gannett Company, Cox Enterprises, News Corporation, Tribune Company, and Clear Channel Communications. These rankings were based on the net revenue generated from each company's U.S. media properties.

The old image of "press relations" with a publicity-seeking "flack" wining and dining an underpaid newsperson is passé. Most major media have ethics codes that prohibit their journalists from accepting favors. The notion that it is helpful to have a buddy or a relative as a reporter, columnist, editor, publisher, news director, or producer is no longer always true. It can be suspect or even function as a handicap, particularly as media ethics codes become more common.

---

## VIDEO NEWS RELEASE INVESTIGATION: A SOLUTION IN SEARCH OF A PROBLEM

The *news release* has been around as long as the practice of public relations. Beginning as a *press release*, this ubiquitous document has long been accepted as the way public relations practitioners communicate with the media.

Originally, press releases were prepared as closely to the journalistic format as possible, the thought being that if a release was well written the newspaper would use it pretty much as is. That turned out to be a pipe dream, but the format continued, becoming a *news release* when broadcast journalism came to the fore.

In the 1970s, savvy practitioners realized a new form of release for broadcast might be more effective—a news release developed specifically for television. Called the *video news release* or VNR, it was the electronic equivalent of the print news release. Built to resemble the standard TV news report, the VNR carried the same information as its print cousin, but did so in such a way that a TV station could pick up the visuals as well as the audio track. When stations did avail themselves of the VNR, it was (and is) up to the station to identify the source of the information and the accompanying visuals. However, not all stations did (do) so, thus creating problems for practitioners who use VNRs to gain access to televised news.

The self-appointed consumer watchdog group Center for Media and Democracy (CMD) has labeled VNRs "fake news" and issued a stinging report based on the findings of a CMD survey condemning those who would issue or use them.[1] "Local TV broadcasts—the most popular news source in the U.S.—frequently air VNRs without fact-checking, conducting their own reporting, or disclosing that the footage has been provided and sponsored by big corporations," said a press release accompanying CMD's report. (*Editor's note: Not all VNRs come from large corporations. Many non-profits and governmental entities use them, as well as some small corporations.*)

The CMD survey examined 77 stations over a 10-month period that aired unidentified VNRs. The public relations publication *Tactics* (PRSA, June 2006) noted that the survey represented less than 1 percent of the total VNR market. However, CMD's report and other concerns about VNRs have led the FCC to take a closer look at the practice.

So, just how serious is this problem? Not as serious as CMD thinks, but certainly abuses have (and do) occurred. Most VNRs report favorably on the sponsoring

---

[1]Diane Farsetta and Daniel Price, "Fake TV News: Widespread and Undisclosed," PRWatch.Org, April 6, 2006.

*(continued)*

*(continued)*

entity. Some do not clearly identify the "report" as being part of a "release." However, most broadcast outlets recognize that "supplied" information will represent the interests of the supplying entity. That's true regardless of the format—news release or VNR. If the *Tactics* estimate is accurate, then over 99 percent of VNRs are appropriately identified so viewers can make an educated decision about the validity of the information. As Kevin E. Foley, president of KEF Media Associates (producers of VNRs) said in the same issue of *Tactics*, the fact that VNR are supplied information doesn't invalidate the strength of the material. Important information can be relayed via VNRs, even thought it represents the point of view of the supplier.

What does all this mean for the public relations profession? It means practitioners must provide newsworthy information to the media and be totally transparent about its source. It is still up to the media—print or broadcast—to appropriately identify the source. Historically, print media have picked up information from news releases and included it in news articles. Lately, many major print outlets have added words such as "said in a prepared statement" to indicate the medium had not spoken directly to the source.

It seems like broadcast media could do the same—scroll a line or mention the source in the audio—without the FCC or the CMD getting involved.

## THE FUNDAMENTALS

Stripped down to basics, the mission of the news media is to inform audiences quickly, accurately, and fully on matters in which audiences express an interest and on matters that affect them significantly, whether or not the audiences have expressed interest, or are even aware.

In simple terms, the mission of the public relations function is to build working relationships with all of an organization's publics. When appropriate, doing so may require making use of news media when viewpoints or activities are newsworthy.

Along with the opportunity and capability possessed by journalists and public relations practitioners to shape public opinion go the obligations of truth and accuracy, under the law. A high degree of ethical responsibility involving moral standards and integrity is implicit in serving the ultimate best interests of the public.

The freedom of the news media to inform the public and to interpret information without bias is assured by the First Amendment to the Constitution. Abuse of that freedom could lead to loss of credibility with the audience, loss of revenue from advertisers, and public censure. Thus, while news prerogatives are jealously guarded, journalistic education and practices emphasize self-discipline. News media, owned privately and operating competitively for profit, are admittedly careful. When they interject their own views, they are expected to label them as "editorial," "opinion," "analysis," "commentary," and so on.

The public relations function comes under the freedom of speech provision in the First Amendment. Practitioners have the choice of telling their story in paid space or time or offering it as news, subject to editing or rejection by the media. The penalties for abuse of free speech rights by a private organization can be loss of supportive constituents such as shareholders, employees, neighbors, customers, members, or donors, as the case might be. Then, too, there is monitoring by the FCC, FTC, and other federal agencies, as well as professional and trade societies. Within the professional practice of public relations, the penalties can be expulsion from membership to professional groups such as the Public Relations Society of America (see Chapter 10) or exposure by the news media. The penalties to the individual practitioner for being "clever" in manipulating facts, being "devious" in dealings with journalists, being "unavailable" when sought by the media, or being "unauthorized as the spokesperson" for an employer can be reaped in loss of credibility and integrity in the eyes of the media and consequently loss of some functional value to the employer. The sword has an edge on both sides of the blade.

## A DIFFICULT, DELICATE TASK

The practitioner serves two masters. One is the employer. The other is the public interest. Often, the news media stand between the two. The practitioner travels a precarious and rather thin line. The employer wants his or her best foot put forward in public. There are bound to be times when public exposure can be damaging to a campaign, a product, or a reputation. At these times, employers would prefer no publicity. Then there are times when the truthful and accurate response to a press inquiry is simply not known (the facts have not been ascertained). There are times when an organization's policies, or legal or competitive considerations, give precedence to its "privacy" over the "public's right to know." At such times, the forbearance of the media is desired—but rarely forthcoming.

If a practitioner is not able to handle the flow of information so that favorable news is covered and adverse news is at least treated fairly, the practical value of the practitioner to the employer is somewhat limited. However, practitioners must make it clear to employers and clients that they cannot control the media.

## GUIDELINES THAT HAVE SURVIVED

Although, as we said earlier, it is risky to draw generalizations about media relations, a number of guidelines are widely followed.

1. Start with a sound working knowledge of the methods and the technology involved in gathering potential news, evaluating it, processing it editorially, and putting it into the best format and mode for newsprint, magazine, and broadcast electronic media. Be able to fit into the process.
2. Be sure that the employer has a designated spokesperson available on short notice. It may be you.
3. Have spokespeople be as candid as possible in response to inquiries—within the limits of obvious competitive and national security and of compassionate consideration for those hurt by the news.
4. Play the percentages, as in a long successful partnership, taking the instances of bad news in stride with a record of good news coverage achieved.
5. Continuously educate and train employers and spokespeople on how to handle themselves when in contact with news media.

6. Generate good news situations as a track record to offset instances of undesired news. Do not simply wait defensively for bad news.
7. Advocate an employer's views on public issues among the organization's natural constituencies and in the news media receptive to them.
8. Expect the unexpected and be prepared for it. In particular, have a crisis or disaster plan for every foreseeable circumstance.

## CONSIDER CREATING A "SURGICAL" MEDIA STRATEGY

Because there is no evidence that visibility in the media motivates behavior or influences attitudes and because more managements are expecting behavior change or motivation rather than merely wanting to dump information on unwilling publics, a new media strategy is needed.

A "surgical" strategy means just what the term implies: placements in exactly the right media for your purpose. It requires knowing which media your target publics actually read, watch, or hear. Assumptions are dangerous, so intelligence work is needed. In issue cases or legislative support, it may mean targeting a single key person and placing a story in the medium she reads (or has clipped for her). A single such placement is worth a folder of untargeted clips.

Example: You're working on a regulatory matter and senator Jones from Louisiana is key. Don't expect her to see, be shown, or believe what the *Washington Post* or *New York Times* write. Place something in the *New Orleans Times-Picayune,* however, and you can rest assured the staff will clip it for her—because it was also seen by her constituents. Give the story a local angle, or a local person, and that's good surgical media use.

## STRATEGY FOR THE NEW CENTURY

In today's environment, people want to be served, not sold; involved, not told. Where do the media fit in when reaching out to and involving these stakeholders? Here's a five-point strategy:

1. **Build relationships face-to-face.** Earning trust through relationships motivates behavior. Ironically, when a relationship is formed, people will accept and pay some heed to your communications.
2. **Make internal publics top priority**—inreach before outreach. Only satisfied employees can deliver customer delight.
3. **Consider an "under-the-radar" approach to bypass media.** As journalists become entertainment-oriented voyeurs and media credibility and reach continue to decline, rarely can media help, even if disposed to do so. They can hurt, because in skeptical times it is easy to sow doubt, and bad news travels the grapevine fast. Instead, go direct to key publics, and don't make yourself overly visible since that may attract media snooping.
4. **Use accountable, focused, measurable programs.** Once called "soft," these public relations programs incorporate value-adding efforts. Strategic philanthropy, value-added and cause-related marketing, and loyalty programs are prominent

examples. The former "we're just nice people" approach never jibed with other organizational behaviors and was not trusted.

5. **Expand research**—far beyond statistical surveys. Research has gone beyond lip-service to be the backbone of programming and strategy setting. Top research techniques are participative: focus groups, panels, Delphi studies, and gap research.

Public relations practitioners know now that one-way information transfer is insufficient. We must pursue the ideal of two-way dialogue. Involving stakeholders and offering them service information or events is the key.

## BLOGS: A NEW TWENTY-FIRST CENTURY MEDIUM

During the height of the 2004 presidential campaign, Dan Rather, longtime anchor of CBS News, reported on recently surfaced documents that significantly questioned President George W. Bush's service in the National Guard during the Vietnam era. Not sufficiently verifying that these documents were authentic, CBS and Rather reported their content as fact. It was the blogs, those now-ubiquitous sources dedicated to politics and news, that torpedoed the story and Dan Rather at the same time.

- A **blog** (a portmanteau of **web log**) is a website where entries are written in chronological order and commonly displayed in reverse chronological order. "Blog" can also be used as a verb, meaning *to maintain or add content to a log*. Blogs provide commentary or news on a particular subject such as food, politics, or local news; some function as more personal online diaries. A typical blog combines text, images, and links to other blogs, web pages, and other media related to its topic. The ability for readers to leave comments in an interactive format is an important part of many blogs. Most blogs are primarily textual, although some focus on art (artlog), photographs (photoblog), sketchblog, videos (vlog), music (MP3 blog), audio (podcasting) or sexual in nature (Adult blog), and are part of a wider network of social media. In May 2007, blog search engine Technorati was tracking more than 71 million blogs. *Source:* (Wikipedia.)

Within minutes of the story's release, bloggers were examining the documents, researching 1970's typewriters, and reporting that the documents must have been forged. The speed with which bloggers report makes for a powerful tool. Consider that most of these blogs do have a political bent and make an effort to expose, discredit, or promote particular points of views.[3]

---

[3]BetOnIraq.com, "How the Blogs Torpedoed Dan Rather," January 2005.

It was the blogs persistency that caused the story to explode for CBS and Dan Rather. Rather finally acknowledged more than a week later that there were serious questions as to the authenticity of the documents used in the story.[4] As a result of using these manufactured documents, whether he knew it or not, Rather's credibility was seriously damaged. Shortly thereafter he left as anchor of CBS News.[5]

## REFERENCES AND ADDITIONAL READINGS

Cutlip, Scott, Allen Center, and Glen Broom. "Media Relations." Chapter 9 in *Effective Public Relations,* 8th ed. Upper Saddle River, NJ: Prentice Hall, 1999.

Dilenschneider, Robert. "Use Ingenuity in Media Relations." *Public Relations Quarterly* 37 (Summer 1992): 13–15.

Evans, Fred. *Managing the Media: Proactive Strategy for Better Business* and *Press Relations.* Westport, CT: Greenwood, 1987.

Foundation for American Communications (FACS) is an organization that seeks to improve mutual understanding between major American institutions and the news media. For more information write: Foundation for American Communications, 85 S. Grand Ave., Pasadena, CA 91105; 626/584-0010; facs@facsnet.org; www.facsnet.org.

Freedom Forum offers a variety of programs and publications exploring the field of mass communication and technological change. It funds two independent affiliates, the Newseum (Arlington, VA) and the First Amendment Center (Vanderbilt University, Nashville, TN). For more information write: The Freedom Forum World Center, 1101 Wilson Blvd., Arlington, VA 22209; 703/258-0800; news@freedomforum.org; www.freedomforum.org.

Glynn, Carroll, and Robert Ostman. "Public Opinion About Public Opinion." *Journalism Quarterly* 65 (Summer 1988): 299–306.

Greenburg, Keith Elliot. "Radio News Releases Make the Hit Parade." *Public Relations Journal* 48 (July 1992): 6.

Grunig, James, and Todd Hunt. *Managing Public Relations.* New York: Holt, Rinehart and Winston, 1984. See Chapters 11, 19, 20, 21, and 22.

Lerbinger, Otto, and Nathaniel Sperber. "Media Relations." Chapter 3 in *Manager's Public Relations Handbook.* Reading, MA: Addison-Wesley, 1982.

Lesly, Philip. "Publicity in TV and Radio." Chapter 25 in *Lesly's Handbook of Public Relations and Communications.* 5th ed. Chicago, IL: NTC Business Books, 1998.

Lukaszweski, Jim. *Influencing Public Attitudes.* Leesburg, VA: Issue Action Publications, 1993.

Marquis, Simon. "Media Speak: Mutual Respect Fosters Healthy Media Relations." *Marketing* (December 9, 1993): 21.

Mundy, Alicia. "Is the Press Any Match for Powerhouse PR?" *Business and Society Review.* (Fall 1993): 34–40.

Newsom, Doug, Dean Kruckeberg, and Judy Vanslyke Turk. "Communication Channels and Media." Chapter 11 in *This Is PR: The Realities of Public Relations.* 7th ed. Belmont, CA: Wadsworth, 1999.

Powell, Jody. *The Other Side of the Story.* New York: William Morrow, 1984. Media seen by a presidential press secretary.

*pr reporter,* Vol. 41 No. 18 (May 4, 1998). "Items to Consider in Creating a 'Surgical' Media Strategy."

*pr reporter,* Vol. 39 No. 28 (July 15, 1996). "Strategy Now: People Want To Be *Served,* Not Sold; *Involved,* Not Told."

*Public Relations Body of Knowledge.* New York: PRSA. See abstracts dealing with "Media Relations, Including Crisis Management."

*purview, pr reporter* supplement (April 4, 1994). The "new aggressiveness" in media relations; public relations learns new tricks.

Rafe, Stephen. *Mastering the News Media Interview.* New York: HarperCollins, 1991.

---

[4]WashingtonPost.com, "Rather Concedes Papers are Suspect," September 16, 2004, p. A1.
[5]CBSNews.com, "Dan Rather Statement on Memos," September 20, 2004.

Raley, Nancy, and Laura Carter, eds. The *New Guide to Effective Media Relations.* Washington, DC, Council for Advancement and Support of Education, 1988.

Reardon, Kathleen, and Everett Rogers. "Interpersonal Versus Mass Media Communication: A False Dichotomy," *Human Communication Research* 15 (2) (Winter 1988): 284–303.

Reilly, Robert. "Publicity." Chapter 6 in *Public Relations in Action.* 2nd ed. Upper Saddle River, NJ: Prentice Hall, 1988.

Shoemaker, Pamela, ed. *Communication Campaign About Drugs: Government, Media, and the Public.* Hillsdale, NJ: Lawrence Erlbaum Associates, 1989.

"Technology Transforms Media Relations Work." *Public Relations Journal* 49 (November 1993): 38–40.

Trahan, Joseph III. "Media Relations in the Eye of the Storm." *Public Relations Quarterly* 38 (Summer 1993): 31–32.

Trahan, Joseph III. "Building Media Relations During a Crisis." *tips & tactic,* a *pr reporter* supplement, December 14, 1992. Lessons learned from Hurricane Andrew.

Tucker, Kerry, Doris Derelian, and Donna Rouner. *Public Relations Writing: A Behavioral Approach.* Upper Saddle River, NJ: Prentice Hall, 1996.

Tucker, Kerry, et al. "Managing Issues Acts as Bridge to Strategic Planning." *Public Relations Journal* 38 (Fall 1993): 41–42.

Van Leuven, James, and Michael Slater. "How Publics, Public Relations, and the Media Shape the Public Opinion Process." *Public Relations Research Annual,* Vol. 3. Larissa Grunig and James Grunig, eds. Hillsdale, NJ: Lawrence Erlbaum Associates, 1991: 165–178.

Walsh, Frank. *Public Relations Writer in a Computer Age.* Upper Saddle River, NJ: Prentice Hall, 1986.

Wilcox, Dennis, and Patrick Jackson. *Public Relations Writing and Media Techniques.* White Plains, NY: Longman, 2000.

----------------------------------C A S E S----------------------------------

# Case 7-1   There's a Syringe in My Pepsi Can!

Large corporations are always potential targets for those who seek fame or fortune at the expense of those companies. In the summer of 1993, PepsiCo, makers of Pepsi-Cola and Diet Pepsi, among other beverages, found itself an unwilling subject in one of the most widespread news stories of the day, a story in which the PepsiCo was implicated in multiple claims of foreign objects being found in unopened cans of Diet Pepsi.[1]

This confidence crisis put the international soft drink company before the public in a way no company wants to be viewed. But the ensuing activities of the Pepsi response team, and the U.S. Food and Drug Administration, calmed the crisis and won for the company the coveted "Best of Silver Anvils" in the 1994 Public Relations Society of America competition.

## The Situation

On June 9, 1993, Tacoma, Washington residents Earl (Tex) and Mary Triplett reported finding a used syringe in a half-empty Diet Pepsi can. They turned the can over to their lawyer who contacted the county health department.

The next day, local television station KIRO aired a report of this incident, citing a Sudafed tampering just two years previously, and the fact that needles aroused concerns about AIDS. No other news medium covered the story that day.

The following day, June 11, a second needle claim was made in Washington, and the *Seattle Times* and other local media picked up the story, adding that in neither case had there been reports of injury resulting from the incidents.

On June 12, the Food and Drug Administration (FDA) did not recommend a recall, but did issue a five-state consumer alert, asking consumers to pour soft drinks, particularly Diet Pepsi, into a glass or cup before drinking. The next day, a New Orleans man claimed to have found a syringe in a can of Diet Pepsi, and by June 14, 10 more claims were reported.

Wire services and national broadcast media picked up the story as more reports came in. The coverage was second only to the Supreme Court nomination of Ruth Bader Ginsburg, as people reported finding syringes, sewing needles, pins, screws, a crack cocaine vial, and even a bullet in Diet Pepsi cans.

By June 16, claims had been reported in 24 states, including one from a reporter for the *Milwaukee Journal* who said she had no plans to sue Pepsi after finding a needle in a can of Diet Pepsi. Meanwhile, the *Los Angeles Times* and CBS reported the needle found by the Tripletts may have belonged to a diabetic relative. In one week's time, more than 50 incidents had been reported to the police, the FDA or the media. None, however, reported any illness or injury associated with the incidents.

---

[1]This case was prepared by University of Central Florida students Aimee Brownell and Troy Jewell under the supervision of instructor Frank R. Stansberry, APR, Fellow PRSA, now retired.

## The Facts

Throughout this seven-day nightmare, neither Pepsi nor the FDA could see any rational reason for the alleged incidents being reported. Soft-drink filling lines are high-speed, high-tech production lines in which empty, open aluminum cans are fed (upside down) down a conveyer at high speeds (1,200 a minute) to be filled. During this roller-coaster ride, the cans are cleaned with heat, water, and air before being inverted, passing through a closed filling filter/screen, and emerging filled and capped at the end. At no time is there an opportunity for foreign objects to find their way into the container, except during the brief time in the filling chamber. Further, the objects being reported are not those commonly found in a soft-drink plant or any other workplace.

The geographic spread of the reports was also difficult to understand. Canning plants are regional operations. The plant in Washington serves only five western states. Yet contaminants were being reported all across the county. These products were being produced by numerous canning operations so there was no direct link among them except for the brand of the product being produced, and the production process. Unless there was a concerted effort to tamper with Diet Pepsi, there was no reason to link the widespread reports to a single production problem. The FDA said continually it could find no connection from a production standpoint among the growing number of complaints.

PepsiCo, convinced its production operations were not at fault, decided against any recall of the products involved. PepsiCo President Craig Weatherup, taking the "point guard" position on the response team, said repeatedly in interviews that "there is no health issue" around the reports, citing the lack of any illness or injuries associated with the reports.

In a *Wall Street Journal* interview, Weatherup said, "We've gone through every can line, every plant, numerous records. All the evidence points to syringes going into the cans after they were opened."

## The Perceptions

"All the evidence" was lost on the news media and the consuming public, however. "When the national media juggernaut gets hold of something, and you're it," PepsiCo Vice President of Public Affairs Becky Madeira told a PRSA workshop a year later, "it's a public trial, and it's not much fun. This was a crisis without precedent."

Fueling the controversy were the continued reports of new contaminants found in Diet Pepsi. In city after city, residents came forth to press their claims of having found foreign objects in their cans of Diet Pepsi. Time after time, the familiar Diet Pepsi logo (being advertised at the time with the popular Ray Charles jingle punctuated by "Uh Huh") was being seen in the media with either an alleged contaminant object or a facsimile.

Weatherup continued the counterattack, saying he was "99.99 percent sure" the incidents were not related to anything under Pepsi's control. But sales slipped. Weatherup, in a follow-up report after the crisis had been put to rest, said, "The week of the hoax, sales dipped only 3 to 4 percent . . ." but 3 percent of Diet Pepsi's sales still represents millions of dollars. The perception crisis was real, indeed.

Adding to the difficulty in containing the spreading number of incidents was a 10-year pattern of substantiated and unsubstantiated product tamperings—some with fatal consequences. In 1982 (and later in 1986) deaths were reported from Tylenol capsules laced with poison (see Case 6-3). In 1986, rat poison was found in Contac (and other) products; glass fragments were discovered in Gerber baby food; and two people died in Washington after taking cyanide-laced Extra-Strength Excedrin. And there were the deaths of two people in Washington from ingesting Sudafed. The consuming public had reason to be concerned, as did Pepsi. With the number of soft-drink alternatives available, some consumers were opting for the competition.

## The Problem

The problem for Pepsi was how to stem the reports, show the safety of its products, and win back the customer loyalty, which had made Diet Pepsi the number two diet drink in the country.

Timing was important because the reports were mounting before the wildfire of news reports. "Speed is essential," said Madeira, "but so is accuracy. It is very dangerous to attempt to explain the cause of the crisis without facts that are corroborated from outside experts. In our case, the expert was the FDA."

The most important question was "Is there a health risk?" The FDA took the lead in answering this question, and almost immediately determined that, in the two Seattle-area reports, there was no health hazard or risk.

A second question involved the presence of syringes and needles in or around the filling process. Again, the FDA became the intervening public and determined, after an exhaustive examination of Pepsi's procedures and facilities, that the high speed and integrity of the filling lines made it impossible for any such object to find its way into the canning process. There was no internal tampering. Whatever was turning up in the cans had been placed there after the cans were opened. FDA Commissioner David Kessler agreed that there was no health risk from the tamperings and, most probably, no relationship between the alleged tampering reports popping up coast to coast.

The facts obviously weighed heavily in Pepsi's favor—the randomness of the reports, the security of the filling line process, the dubious nature of all the claims, the variety of objects being reported, and the fact that needles and syringes are never found in production-line situations under normal conditions. No one said there were any health issues resulting from the tamperings. There was no reason to think any of the reports had merit.

Perceptions, fueled by media reports, however, were just the opposite. Consumers in nearly two dozen states were lining up to claim contaminants were found in Diet Pepsi cans. Diet Pepsi cans were on television as much as Jay Leno—nightly. In fact, Leno and his peers were having a field day with the issue, poking fun at the difficult situation in nightly monologues. Editorial cartoonists also joined the spoofing by suggesting that everything from a power drill to the famous "missing sock" was turning up in Diet Pepsi cans. For a seemingly endless 96 hours, the Diet Pepsi scare was the nation's top news story. Something had to be done, and the Pepsi team mobilized and swung to the offensive.

## The Public Relations Impact

When the story first broke on June 9, Pepsi let the local bottler, Alpac Corporation, handle the media inquiry. Operating under the premise that the plant was secure, Alpac also had to investigate any possible way an object *could* have been introduced during the filling process. Working with local health officials and the FDA, Alpac assisted in the investigation and found nothing that would implicate the filling line.

The plant was opened to the media and the plant owner, manager, and quality assurance manager were made available to the press. All they were able to say at the time, however, was that the situation was unusual and that they would do everything they could to cooperate with local authorities to find the cause of the crisis.

But even these findings did not stem the tide of complaints filtering in or the growing media interest in the problem. Pepsi was going to have to get involved at the national level; the problem was more than Alpac's to solve.

Crisis coordinator Madeira identified four primary publics to be addressed:

- The news media
- Customers (those who purchased the product for retail sale)
- Consumers
- Employees and local Pepsi-Cola bottlers

The **public affairs department**, which Madeira directed, had a team of six media relations specialists prepared to respond to media inquiries and to provide regular updates of facts and developments. *One Clear Voice* was the key approach. A second team wrote and produced video news releases, audio-tapes, press releases, charts, and diagrams of the production process and photos for external and internal distribution.

**Consumer Relations** had 24 people manning the 24-hour toll-free hotlines, taking calls from consumers, hearing reports and comments, and monitoring public opinion as it developed.

**Scientific and Regulatory Affairs** assigned technical and quality assurance specialists to work with the FDA and local health departments to evaluate and track each complaint.

**Sales and marketing** personnel were responsible for maintaining relationships with its customers—supermarkets, restaurants, convenience stores, and others who sold Pepsi products to the consumer.

**Manufacturing** experts assisted the FDA and developed simple, easy to understand explanations of the filling line process for the news media and the public.

The **legal department** was involved at all stages of the reporting and communication process.

The entire effort was kept in-house as opposed to bringing in an outside crisis communication consultant.

Pepsi's response centered on four principles:

- **Put public safety first.** Look at the problem through the perspective of the public and address their concerns.
- **Find the problem and fix it.** Pepsi was convinced the problem was not within its production facilities, so it worked with the regulatory authorities to demonstrate the security of its plants, and to investigate and respond to all complaints.
- **Communicate frequently, quickly, and regularly.** Use both broadcast and print communication tools. Be honest, available, and informed about what the media need and be prepared to meet those needs.
- **Take full responsibility for resolving the crisis.** Pepsi realized quickly that this was a problem that the public expected it to help resolve. Pointing fingers at consumers or ducking responsibility was never an option even though most on the crisis response team felt the reports of foreign objects were hoaxes.

The chief weapon in the defusing of the crisis would be a compelling video news release showing exactly what happens on a can filling line and how difficult it would be to introduce any foreign element into a can during this process.

Television had brought the crisis into 100 million American homes and television would be Pepsi's best opportunity to expose the folly of the reports. On June 15, six days after the Tripletts said they found the syringe, Pepsi presented a dramatic look at an ordinary can filling line. The same consumers who had seen the Diet Pepsi cans with syringes now saw millions of the blue and red cans whirring by at the rate of 1,200 per minute. Image confronted image—and news programs picked up the video news release (VNR) in such numbers that soon nearly 300 million viewers had seen the footage.

That initial VNR and three subsequent ones presented the company's position that its production lines were safe and secure. Diet Pepsi was safe when it left the plant. Weatherup, continuing his role of spokesperson, appeared on a dozen major TV shows and the Pepsi public affairs team had conducted nearly 2,000 interviews within the week.

"Our strategy was to reassure the public that this was not a manufacturing crisis," said Madeira. "What was happening was not occurring inside our plants."

The strategy worked, assisted by some excellent support from the FDA and some good luck. A third Pepsi-Cola VNR contained images from an in-store surveillance camera that showed a woman trying to stick a syringe into a Diet Pepsi can while the cashier was not looking. Tampering with the food supply is a felony, and the woman was arrested. When the arrest was made, the VNR was released and the hoax began to crumble.

Many who had made claims against Pepsi began to recant their stories for fear of prosecution. In states across the country, arrest after arrest was made and reported by the media. Those who tried to profit at the expense of "big business" were located and apprehended. The media had gotten the message and were eager to highlight the consequences faced by the perpetrators. Weatherup continued his offensive and, as the number of arrests increased, claimed vindication for the Pepsi products.

By June 21, Pepsi was being defended and applauded in editorials and columns around the country and the FDA announced happily that "the hoax is over." A year later, 54 people had been prosecuted by the states in which they resided for their roles in the hoax, and all had been convicted. The *Milwaukee Journal* reporter had also recanted her claim but lost her job.

In newspapers across the country, Pepsi ran a clever ad stating "Pepsi is pleased to announce . . . nothing." The crisis was over.

## Second Guesses

Monday morning quarterbacks had a field day with the hoax and its many elements. Most of the second-guessing involved the timing of Pepsi's rebuttal. "I don't understand why Pepsi didn't explain everything on the first day," said Don Smith, the city editor of the *Seattle Post Intelligencer*, who was skeptical about the reports from the beginning. In spite of his misgivings on timing, Smith's evaluation of the Pepsi response was "they did fine."

Steven Fink, a Los Angeles-based crisis communication consultant, told the *Toronto Globe and Mail* that Pepsi had two crises—one of reality and one of perception. "The crisis of perception is that the company is not protecting the safety of their consumers. . . . If the public has the perception that the company was playing fast and loose with their safety, this will hurt the company in the long run."

The lack of a recall spurred some critics, too. Tylenol's swift (and expensive) recall of its products in 1982 left the impression that a recall was the linchpin of any product safety issue. Pepsi, however, saw no health or safety concerns resulting from its problems and opted against a product recall.

"The cost of a recall is a valid corporate concern," said Mayer Nudell, a crisis management consultant, "but they [Pepsi] have to weigh the short-term implications for the bottom line against the long-term corporate image and therefore market share and public receptivity and everything else. Very often, it's that long-term image that corporations sometimes lose sight of."

While Pepsi eschewed the recall, several retailers grew uneasy with the escalating furor and pulled the product from their shelves. Sheetz, a convenience store company with 250 stores in four mid-Atlantic states, pulled 16-ounce bottles of Diet Pepsi off its shelves after a West Virginia man reported finding a syringe. Other grocers and convenience stores from Iowa to Oklahoma followed suit. Kroger, the nation's largest food chain, offered customers a full refund on Pepsi products if they were uneasy after hearing the news reports.

Madeira concedes things might have been handled better, but points out "time was the enemy. It took us time to conduct the investigation in the plants, await FDA conclusions, and then get the information together to answer all the questions. The dynamics changed every hour. There is no standard crisis communication formula where you pull out your crisis readiness plan and implement it. You have to adapt your plan and process to the circumstances. In this case, this wasn't a product or public health crisis, it was a media problem. The more you saw that visual of the can and the syringe, the greater the concern became."

Looking back, she admits Pepsi did not expect that this would be a national story. "We have things that happen locally, and you do your job locally, and it's over and done with," said Madeira.

While that wasn't the case, few will argue with the success of the response. Sales dipped but soon recovered. Pepsi's positive relationships within the FDA paid huge dividends. In addition to using the FDA experts as counselors during the crisis, Pepsi was able to benefit from those same experts being powerful opinion leaders by speaking as third-party endorsers of the company's lack of culpability.

Pepsi's strong understanding of the news media and the experience built up over the years also contributed to the success. Even though Pepsi was the victim of a week-long media feeding frenzy at its expense, Madeira and her staff worked with reporters in getting the situation turned around. "Your only defense when your company is on trial in the media," she said, "is to be a participant in that trial." ■

------------------------------------------------------------

## QUESTIONS FOR DISCUSSION

1. Discuss the implications of Pepsi's strategy, specifically
   a. Putting public safety first
   b. Taking full responsibility for solving the problem
   c. Using the media to present its case
2. Differentiate between "solving the problem" and "solving the situation."
3. Evaluate Pepsi's decision not to order a product recall. What are the plusses and minuses of such a decision?
4. What options did Pepsi have on June 10, 1993? Did the company select the correct course of action? Why or why not? What other choices could the company officials have made?
5. Discuss the role of the FDA in addressing/solving the situation. Was

Pepsi's use of the FDA beneficial? Why? How?
6. Could this "crisis" have been avoided? How? Shortened? How?
7. Did the news media behave responsibly in reporting this story? Cite examples to support your answer.
8. Discuss the communication tools employed by Pepsi in solving the problem. Specifically evaluate the role of VNRs.
9. What was the "turning point" in Pepsi's resolution of this problem? Cite examples to support your answer.
10. When "perception is reality, facts notwithstanding," how can a company such as PepsiCo create new perceptions? Did the company succeed? Cite examples from the case to support your answer.

# Case 7-2 Alar and PR: Getting to the Core of the Apple Problem

This is the story of the fall and rise of the American apple industry in 1989. It serves as an excellent example of public relations' role in bringing about a change in public perception and in redefining the problem. This case was precipitated by a forceful public relations and publicity campaign that brought discredit and disfavor to apples and apple products. The ensuing problem was met by an equally forceful rebuttal campaign with the result that, today, apples are being consumed in normal fashion.[1]

## The Situation

Apples have been part of a healthful diet for centuries. An apple a day kept the doctor away. An apple for the teacher was appreciated, even if apple-polishing students were not. A favorite person was "the apple of my eye," and being "as American as apple pie" was as patriotic as one could get.

That's why the nation was shocked to hear, in February 1989, that people (especially small children) eating apples were jeopardizing their health. What had happened to change the shiny cure-all to a carcinogen? Alar and pr; *60 Minutes*, and the national media.

Since 1968, apple growers had used a chemical called daminozide (trademark Alar) to slow the ripening process and retain the red color. However, in 1985, scientists reported Alar and its residue, UDMH, could cause cancer in animals. Many growers stopped using Alar at that time[2] and in 1986 a self-designated public interest group called the Natural Resources Defense Council (NRDC) began a study of pesticides and resultant risks to preschool children.[3] (See Figures 7-2 and 7-3.)

The Environmental Protection Agency (EPA) began a regulatory process to consider banning the pesticide and, in early February 1989, announced that the process was being sped up, possibly as a result of efforts by NRDC. There was no rise in consumer awareness of Alar-related problems at that time.[4]

On February 26, however, the CBS show *60 Minutes* aired a segment entitled "A Is for Apple," which characterized the risk, especially to preschoolers, of getting cancer from eating apples and apple products as "intolerable."[5] It based the report on a white paper from NRDC, "Intolerable Risk: Pesticides in Our Children's Food."

NRDC followed the CBS report with a major news conference in Washington, D.C., the next day, augmented by regional news conferences in a dozen cities around the country.[6] In short, a major publicity effort had begun.

---

[1]Thank you to Steven Rub, a student at the University of Central Florida, who developed this case study under the direction of Frank Stansberry, APR, who retired from UCF in 2006.

[2]"Apples Without Alar," *Newsweek,* October 30, 1989, p. 86.

[3]"Intolerable Risk: Pesticides in Our Children's Food," a report by the National Resources Defense Council, February 27, 1989.

[4]"The Alar Scare: Rebuilding Apple Consumption During the Alar Crisis," a report by Hill & Knowlton (undated).

[5]*60 Minutes,* Transcript "A Is for Apple," broadcast February 26, 1989.

[6]*The Wall Street Journal,* October 3, 1989, an op-ed article on the Alar issue.

**Intolerable Risk:
Pesticides in our Children's Food**


**Summary**


**A Report by the
Natural Resources Defense Council**


**February 27, 1989**

FIGURE 7-2   The NRDC published a 141-page report in 1989 that examined
the types and amounts of pesticides that are in foods

*Source:* (Courtesy of the NRDC.)

National awareness of the "danger" of eating apples rose from virtually nil at the first of the month to 95 percent at the end of the month, as all news media jumped on this journalistically enticing story.

Faced with that type of public awareness and concern, the members of the International Apple Institute voluntarily stopped using Alar on their crops.[7] In June, Uniroyal, maker of Alar, announced plans to discontinue sales of the pesticide in the United States.[8]

Meanwhile, apple growers began to fight back. Spurred by the Washington State Apple Commission, the industry hired the public relations firm Hill & Knowlton (H&K), to mount the counterattack. H&K had been monitoring public opinion since before the first volley from NRDC. Its research showed that "purchase intent" for apples had gone into a "deep decline."

In its report, "The Alar Scare: Rebuilding Apple Consumption During the Alar Crisis," H&K noted that the media blitz

---

[7]*New York Times,* May 16, 1989, pp. 1, 19.
[8]*New York Times,* June 30, 1989, pp. 1, 11.

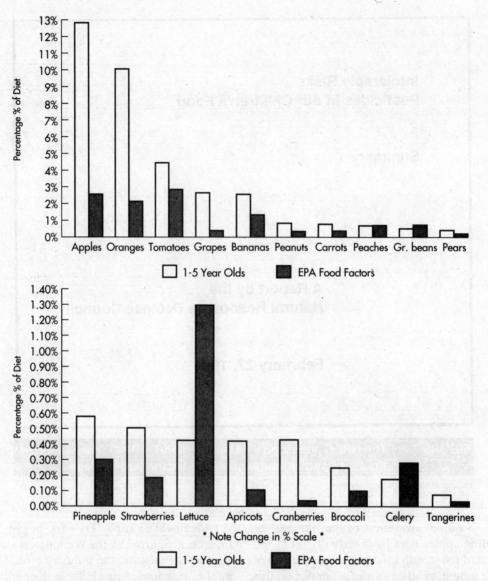

NOTE: Current preschooler consumption estimates were derived from the CSFII — *Nationwide Food Consumption Survey: Continuing Survey of Food Intakes by Individuals, Women 19–50 Years and Their Children 1–5 Years, 6 Waves,* 1985, and are average intakes of all forms (*i.e.* raw and processed) of each produce type for all children included in the 1985 Nationwide Food Consumption Survey. Food Factors were obtained from EPA, Toxicology Branch, Revised Average Food Factors, May 1, 1978.

**FIGURE 7-3    The report of NRDC examined pesticide intakes by children and noted the large consumption of apples by children**

*Source:* (Courtesy of the NRDC.)

from Alar's critics "led to a widespread panic, and a firestorm of negative reporting on the safety of apples. Moms across America began dumping apple juice down the drain. Cancer hotlines were deluged by calls from anxious parents. The message they were getting everywhere was 'don't feed your kids apples, it's not worth the risk.'"

The strategy for gaining back the lost confidence was threefold—to get the facts about the safety of apples to worried consumers; to discredit the NRDC report as "bad science," and to get key sources (government regulatory bodies, scientists, the medical community) to reaffirm apples' wholesomeness and nutritional benefits.

The plan worked; by fall 1989, per capita consumption of apples had returned to an all-time high, a trend that continues today.

## The Facts

The facts about Alar and apples are pretty clear. Alar is a plant growth inhibitor. Without Alar, apple growers will have to pick the crop four to six days earlier, before the apples drop. Thus, some varieties may go to market a little "green" and may lack perfect visual appeal. Shelf-life may also be affected.

Alar, as one of many products produced by Uniroyal, contributed only $4.6 million in sales at the time of the controversy, which accounted for about six-tenths of one percent of Uniroyal's total sales. It was not a major player in the overall sales picture.

Before 1985, about 35 percent of all "eating" apples were treated with Alar, including most red apples and some Golden Delicious. By 1989, the industry estimates of

Alar usage were between 5 and 15 percent.[9] Most growers stopped using Alar after EPA investigations in 1985.[10]

Risk factors from Alar-tainted apples are less clear. In a table released by NRDC as part of the "Intolerable Risk" report, apples fell at the midpoint of 26 fruits and vegetables rated by frequency of detectable levels of pesticides. Strawberries were ranked first (63 percent with detectable levels). Apples and spinach (29 percent) were in the middle, and corn and bananas (1 percent) were at the bottom.

Uniroyal continually said its pesticide was safe as used. Support for this position was widespread and broad-based. Canadian health officials noted pesticide residues only one-thirtieth of safety levels and commented that a child would have to eat 250,000 apples a day for Alar residues to impose a threat to health.[11]

In England, British health officials saw "no risk to consumers," noting that an infant would have to consume 150 times a normal amount to reach even a "no effect" level of UDMH.[12]

Even Consumer's Union, through its publication *Consumer Reports*, said, "Apples treated with Alar are not necessarily unsafe to eat, since daminozide itself has not been firmly shown to cause cancer."[13] Later, in a letter to the editor of another consumer's magazine, *Consumer's Research*, the editors of *Consumer Reports* acknowledged, "The statements that 'Apples are safe to eat,' and that 'The EPA should ban Alar' sound contradictory, but they are not." *Consumer Reports* further said that current data suggest that Alar, per se, probably is not a carcinogen, but that its breakdown product, UDMH, probably is.

---

[9]"Where the Daminozide Is," *Science News,* June 14, 1985, p. 169.
[10]"Law & Legislation," *Newsweek,* February 13, 1989, p. 65.
[11]"An Apple-Spray Scare," *Macleans,* March 20, 1989, p. N-8.
[12]"Upsetting the Apple Spray Cart," *Chemistry and Industry,* January 1, 1990, p. 2.
[13]"Bad Apples," *Consumer Reports,* May 1989, p. 287.

Thus, the risk is associated more directly with processed apple products than with raw apples (UDMH is released when apples are heated or otherwise processed). *Consumer Reports* saw the risk if UDMH levels rose to 45 parts per million and said, "While large enough to justify EPA regulatory concern, . . . there is no need for public panic over a risk this size."[14]

The federal agencies, EPA, Food and Drug Administration (FDA), and the U.S. Department of Agriculture, agreed to issue a joint statement on March 16, 1989, which said, "The federal government believes that it is safe for Americans to eat apples."[15]

Mothers and Others (a spin-off group from NRDC) said in a "fact sheet" that "chances are very slight that an individual child will get cancer from consuming apples or apple products," even when Alar was in use.[16] (See Figure 7-4.) And *Consumer Reports*, in a sidebar to its "Bad Apples" story,[17] tested 44 brands of apple juice for daminozide levels and found only four (all regional brands unique to the New York area) unacceptable.

UDMH, however, continued to pose a problem. *Consumer Reports* said, "The likely carcinogen is UDMH, which appears when juice from daminozide-treated apples is cooked to produce the concentrate from which commercial juice is made."

*This perception of danger, dramatized by major new outlets, was what caused the public to panic.* The impact on apple growers was immediate and substantial. Apple growers lost an estimated $100–150 million on the 1988 crop, which was being sold at the time. Most of this economic impact was felt in Washington State, where growers lost between $100 and $140 million on that year's crop. Washington supplies 60 percent of the fresh, or "eating," apples consumed in the United States.[18]

Apple juice sales in 1989 fell as much as 22 percent at one point and finished the year down about 14 percent,[19] while overall apple sales were down 20 percent for the year.[20]

## The Public Perception

The facts notwithstanding, the public was not buying apples. The media images of danger were too clear. For example, the *60 Minutes* story that kicked off the scare was entitled "A Is for Apple," but it showed a skull and cross-bones superimposed over a shiny red apple. The *Consumer Reports* story carried the title "Bad Apples."

Urged and directed by NRDC, actress Meryl Streep took to the airwaves and popular magazines to say she was "furious" to discover that two of her children's favorite foods, apples and strawberries, might be hazardous to their health because of Alar.[21] *Newsweek* entitled its report "EPA Is Looking for a Few Bad Apples."

The result was what publicist David Fenton described as "a sea of change in public opinion." *The Wall Street Journal* reported that "apples and apple juice have been going down garbage disposals all across the country." The school boards of

---

[14]*Consumer's Research*, July 1989, p. 28. Letter from editors of *Consumer Reports* in response to article, "Does Everything Cause Cancer?"

[15]"Fruit Fights," *The Wall Street Journal,* March 17, 1989, p. A-14.

[16]Mothers and Others, "Fact Sheet: Alar," undated.

[17]"Apple Juice: A Long Way from the Tree," *Consumer Reports,* May 1989, p. 293.

[18]Reuters, "Agencies: Alar Scare Nearly Over," *Orlando Sentinel,* November 4, 1989, p. 12.

[19]A. C. Nielsen and Co. report to Florida Citrus Commission, October 1989.

[20]"Avery's Uniroyal Ends Alar Sales in U.S.; Apple Product Imports Still Worry Critics," *The Wall Street Journal,* June 5, 1989, p. B3.

[21]"Ms. Streep Goes to Washington to Stop a Bitter Harvest," *People Magazine,* March 20, 1989, p. 50.

# Mothers & Others
for a livable planet

40 West 20th Street, 11th floor • New York, New York 10011

phone: 212-727-4474 • fax: 212-675-6481

# Fact sheet: Alar

*Mothers & Others is frequently asked about Alar, the chemical that was removed from the market in 1989 after a campaign by Mothers & Others and the Natural Resources Defense Council to call attention to problems of pesticides in children's food. Here, we address some of the facts and myths surrounding this controversial chemical.*

**Our children are safer with Alar off the market.** In 1989, public pressure led the manufacturer of Alar (which was used on apple crops to control growth and enhance apples' red color) to take the product off the market. The U.S. Environmental Protection Agency (EPA) later banned Alar for use on food products—*years after the agency first acknowledged the chemical's potential to cause cancer.* After concluding its review of the scientific data in 1992, the agency reiterated that Alar and its "breakdown" product, UDMH, should be classified as "probable human carcinogens," and that long-term exposure to Alar posed unacceptable risks to public health. (UDMH was formed when apples containing residues of Alar were processed into things like applesauce and apple juice.) Children eat significantly more apples and apple products, relative to their body weight, than adults do, and therefore received relatively greater exposure to Alar/UDMH. What's more, because their physiological systems are still developing, children are usually more susceptible than adults to the toxic effects of a contaminant. So children were *even more at risk* from exposure to Alar and UDMH than the general public—and are better off with Alar off the market.

**There is NO truth to the claim that a child would have to eat 28,000 pounds of apples a day to be at risk from Alar.** The chemical industry makes this claim based on high doses of UDMH fed to laboratory animals. Animals are routinely tested at very high doses, and a majority of the scientific community endorses the high dose method as a valid basis for regulating human exposure to chemicals, rather than waiting for actual proof of carcinogenicity in humans. However, the *human* risk from Alar was not based on the assumption that children would ingest an equal amount of UDMH as lab animals—risks to people are always figured on real exposure levels. In the case of Alar, exposure estimates were based on actual pesticide residue levels found on apples and on actual consumption data for pre-schoolers, which the USDA says is one ounce of raw apple and two ounces of apple juice per day.

**FIGURE 7-4    Mothers and Others distributed a specific fact sheet about the Alar chemical**

*Source:* (Courtesy of Mothers and others.)

New York City, Los Angeles, and Chicago, among others, banned apples from the lunch programs. (Fenton later said that effect was one not recommended by NRDC.)

The NRDC report highlighted the risk to children, who, because of their size and tendency to eat more fresh fruit than adults, seemed more at risk. "Children ingest so many apples for their size," Fenton said, "that the legal federal standard is unsafe." Reuters reported "Many consumers and school lunchrooms stopped buying apples," after hearing or seeing the report. "The negative messages about the safety of Alar and apples left the public unsure about what to believe," the Hill & Knowlton report said. "This led to a startling decline in intent to purchase apples."

The public was faced with cognitive dissonance—wanting to believe that apples were healthful, yet besieged by messages that apples would cause cancer. "The scare, though short-lived, was nearly everywhere," reports Lee Baker in his book *The Credibility Factor*.[22] People phoned the International Apple Institutes to see if apple juice should be disposed of in a toxic waste site!

Merchants, too, were worried. "Consumer reaction to the program [*60 Minutes*] was explosive, prompting many retailers to proclaim they would no longer sell Alar-treated apples or apple products." The International Apple Institute said at the time that consumers' concerns about the health effects of Alar had probably cost apple growers more than $100 million, a figure that proved to be conservative.

Competitors, however, were delighted. A representative of the A. C. Neilson Company reported to the Florida Citrus Commission that "lingering effects of the Alar scare" in 1989 helped orange juice widen its lead over apple juice as the fruit beverage of choice in American homes.

## The Public Relations Problem

Although the facts about apples and Alar weighed heavily in favor of the industry, the emotions were all negative.

The bulk of the communication, however, targeted apples and Alar in general—*without regard to the secondary role of UDMH*. Perception had been shaped in a way that left apples—all apples—tainted by association with the pesticide. Changing that perception was the challenge of the industry and its public relations counsel.

## The Public Relations Impact

Public relations techniques created the problem for the apple growers and processors, and public relations techniques helped get them back on their feet. David Fenton, public relations counsel to NRDC, outlined his program in a lengthy memo. In his memo, Fenton said that the situation was created "because of a carefully planned media campaign," based on NRDC's report "Intolerable Risk." Participation by actress Meryl Streep "was an essential element."

Fenton said that the goal of his campaign was to "create so many repetitions of NRDC's message that average American consumers could not avoid hearing it. The idea was for the story to achieve a life of its own, and to continue for weeks and months to affect policy and consumer habits." This goal, Fenton says, was met. "A modest investment by NRDC repaid itself many-fold in tremendous media exposure and substantial, immediate revenue for further pesticide work." Other revenue-producing elements of the program were "self-published book sales ... and a 900 phone number."

The timing of the campaign was to grant *60 Minutes* an exclusive "break," then to hold the Washington and satellite press conferences the following day. The *60 Minutes*

---

[22]Lee Baker, *The Credibility Factor*, Homewood, IL: Business One Irwin, 1993, pp. 120–127.

broadcast moved the needle of public awareness to 45 percent, while subsequent coverage moved it to nearly 95 percent. (But both numbers are highly questionable; for initial exposure to reach 45 percent of *any* public, to say nothing of the food-consuming public, is virtually impossible. The total audience for *60 Minutes* proved to be a tiny fraction of this group.)

Fenton played the "Streep" card a week later fanning the flames. Her group, Mothers and Others for Pesticide Limits, would lobby citizens to seek changes in pesticide laws and ask for pesticide-free products at retail outlets. Other celebrities joined the bandwagon as the story gained momentum. Schools began dropping apples from the menu; retail stores began rejecting Alar-tainted fruit. Alar was withdrawn from the market and the EPA, USDA, and FDA issued statements saying that apples were safe.

The media relations work done by Fenton and NRDC was thorough. In breadth and depth, the coverage generated and the resultant outcry met Fenton's goals. In fact, the media took the story so strongly that, to some, the coverage became advocacy rather than reporting of factual information or news. This is often the case in contemporary journalism, as audiences and advertising decline and coverage becomes more and more sensational in an attempt to recapture them.

At a Smithsonian Institution conference for environmentalists and writers, Charles Alexander, science editor of *Time* magazine, said, "I would freely admit that, on this issue, we have crossed a boundary from news reporting to advocacy." Later, David Brooks, editorial writer for the *Wall Street Journal*, wrote, "somehow the idea has gotten around that the environment isn't just a normal political issue, but a quasi-religious crusade. As a result, public discussion of the environment has been about as rigorous as one experts from a jihad. . . . The reporters who became advocates seem to think they are doing the environment a favor."[23]

Andrea Mitchell of NBC said, "Clearly, the networks have made that decision now, where you'd have to call it advocacy."[24] "Usually, it takes a significant natural disaster to create this much sustained news attention for an environmental problem," Fenton wrote in his memo. "We believe this experience proves there are ways to raise public awareness for the purpose of moving Congress and policy makers."

## The Apple Growers Respond

Apple growers would probably characterize the Alar scare as an "unnatural disaster." According to Hill & Knowlton, the producers of *60 Minutes* had promised the apple industry a "balanced look at the pesticide issue," but what occurred was later characterized by the *Wall Street Journal* as "fright wig treatment of Alar." Apples, not Alar, took the center stage.

With overnight telephone surveys, H&K followed the decline in apples' reputation. The public wanted to be assured that apples were safe before sales could rebound. What industry leaders hoped could be a low-profile response shifted into a higher gear. The truth would be the chief weapon.

While Washington State apples were hardest hit, and those growers would be the principal financial backer of the defense effort, it was decided that a national organization should represent the industry. Therefore, the International Apple Institute was identified as the nominal leader for the program funded by the Washington Apple Commission.

---

[23]"Alar PR," *Chemtech,* May 1989, p. 264.
[24]Ibid.

The strategy was threefold: (1) to get the facts out about apples' safety (and to separate apples from Alar); (2) to discredit the NRDC research as being based on old, discredited data; and (3) to get key influencers—government, scientific, medical—to stand up for the safety and nutritional benefits of apples and apple products.

Key publics were (1) governmental agencies, (2) industry insiders including growers, (3) the food industry including retailers and wholesalers, (4) the medical and scientific community, (5) schools, and (6) the news media.

The results were good. Consumer awareness of the Alar "danger" remained high, but by the third week of March 1989 (less than one month after the first *60 Minutes* broadcast) the decline in intent to purchase had reversed.

Sales bottomed out and began a slow climb upward until, by early May, shipments were "setting seasonal highs." By fall, per capita consumption of apples hit an all-time high. During the 1989–1990 apple season, the average American ate 21 pounds of fresh apples.

## Legacies of the Alar Debate

One of the legacies of the Alar debate was the passage of "agricultural disparagement" laws by at least 12 states. These laws, also called "veggie libel laws," establish liability if someone knowingly makes false and disparaging statements about perishable food products that result in damages. The state of Texas passed an agricultural disparagement law in 1995. This law was the basis of an unsuccessful lawsuit brought against talk-show host Oprah Winfrey in 1996 by Texas cattlemen for an on-air comment she made concerning beef.[25]

Opponents of the veggie libel laws say that the laws violate the First Amendment, stifle public debate, and discourage people from speaking out or filing complaints with government agencies. More than 15 states now have anti-SLAPP (Strategic Lawsuits Against Public Participation) laws in place, which prevent bringing a lawsuit based on an agricultural disparagement law. Anti-SLAPP legislation is not in response only to the veggie libel lawsuits but is a measure to prevent any meritless litigation that is aimed at suppressing free speech.

There continues to be numerous articles, studies and reports published that offer evidence that Alar is safe as well as unsafe. Representatives from both sides of this issue continue to resolutely maintain their positions.[26] Despite the removal of Alar from the marketplace in 1989, many in the food and chemical industry are committed to reiterating that the Alar "scare" caused an unnecessary panic and that Alar will always be synonymous with "hoax." As soon as one article appears that supports the harmlessness of Alar, another follows, documenting the hazards of the chemical. The apple industry carried out a successful counterattack to maintain the healthy image of apples. But advocates on both sides of the issue of Alar's safety continue to keep that debate alive in the media.

## Crops and Chemicals in 2007

The new "Alar" debate of the decade might be the genetic engineering of crops to make them more prolific and drought and bug resistant. Though there is little scientific research on the dangers in reengineering these crops, concern among many consumers is high. Thus, there is a steady increase in "organic"

---

[25]See Case 6-2 in Chapter 6.
[26]See "Ten Years Later, Myth of 'Alar Scare' Persists," Environmental Working Group report (www.ewg.org/pub/home/reports/alar/alar.html) and "The Alar 'Scare' Was for Real," Elliott Negin, *Columbia Journalism Review,* September/October 1996.

labeling in supermarkets. Milk is advertised as being "hormone free." Farmers and organic food markets are becoming more popular. All these options are, of course, more expensive for the consumer. Yet, perceptions of safety have increased their market share significantly. With continuing media coverage of concerns, food producers will be fighting these perceptions and defending their farming practices for years to come. ▪

-------------------------------------------------------------

## QUESTIONS FOR DISCUSSION

1. To carry out its work, a public interest organization such as NRDC must maintain a staff of administrators, scientists and researchers, lawyers, public relations practitioners, and others—as either employees or consultants. Because NRDC has no products or services to sell, in the usual sense, funds must be raised through memberships, contributions, and events to cover its budget. To what extent might this consideration influence the preparation, release, and promotion of a highly visible, controversial report such as the one on Alar? Do you think that the public that is the target of such campaigns—which are carried on by all public interest organizations as an important part of their *illusions*—is aware of this possible self-interest? If the public should be aware, whose responsibility is it to make them so?

2. Why would the public listen to an obvious nonexpert such as Meryl Streep on a scientific topic like this? Critics of such celebrity involvement in issues called her a "Hollywood toxicologist." Are you aware of any similar incidents?

3. Among its target publics, Hill & Knowlton listed the news media. Are the media a *public?* Or a communications *vehicle?* What are the strategy implications of according them status as a public?

4. Does David Fenton's campaign for NRDC raise any ethical issues? Check the PRSA code in the introduction to Chapter 10.

5. Is it possible that the attention focused on apples by the Alar scare played a part in the fact that Americans are now consuming the fruit in record numbers? Attempt to make a case for the position that it did.

# Case 7-3 GM Versus NBC: A Corporate Crisis of Explosive Proportions

"An error only becomes a mistake when you fail to admit it." Those were John F. Kennedy's words as he witnessed the infamous Bay of Pigs invasion of Cuba come to a disastrous end.

That statement will surely echo in the thoughts of former NBC News President, Michael Gartner, as he recalls the events connected to the *Dateline NBC* report on GM trucks. Gartner calls the aftermath of that broadcast "the worst week of my life."

## The Situation

On November 17, 1992, television viewers saw an old car being pushed by another vehicle along a narrow road in rural Indiana and colliding with a pickup truck—a collision sparking a fire that sent shock waves across the airwaves. This was the scene *Dateline NBC* broadcast that evening in a story showing a crash test of a GM truck that produced surprising results.[1]

The estimated 17 million viewers of that *Dateline NBC* program were likely shocked as they witnessed a General Motors C/K pickup truck bursting into flames after being hit in a crash test. The implication was clear; GM trucks were unsafe and should be recalled immediately.

ABC, CBS, and other media outlets subsequently broadcast similar newscasts citing NBC's material evidence and expert witnesses. If it were not for an outside tip, GM's battle might have been lost from the start. Pete Pesterre, editor of *Popular Hot Rodding Magazine*, wrote an editorial criticizing the *Dateline NBC* story. Soon afterward, a reader of that publication located a firefighter who had been present at the filming of the crash and had recorded his own video of the incident. GM's excellent relationship with the general media likely contributed to its acquisition of the firefighter's video.

There was only one concern on GM's part now—to clear its good name.

## The Facts

The NBC crash demonstration was a sham, rigged in every way from start to finish. The claims broadcast to millions were blatantly fraudulent. GM would have to embark on a meticulous investigation to research the facts of the NBC demonstration and expose the falsified report.

The ensuing actions of GM are unprecedented in American corporate history. Abiding by the old adage that says, "never pick a fight with a guy who buys ink by the barrel" would have seen GM letting this extinguish itself. Instead, they were taking on NBC, a Goliath in the media industry.

GM designated a unique team to tackle the crisis; it included one public relations professional, four attorneys, and two engineers. The team obtained the firefighter's personal video that proved to be the turning point of GM's efforts. The video clearly documented that the test was rigged. The prop

---

[1]This case was prepared by University of Central Florida student, Paul Smith, under the supervision of UCF instructor, Frank R. Stansberry, APR, Fellow PRSA, now retired.

trucks used in the broadcast were located at a salvage yard in Indiana, and the GM investigators purchased them for examination. In one of the trucks, a used model rocket engine was found and the gas cap was not present.

With the video revealing that the test took place under abnormal conditions, the evidence was quickly stacking in favor of GM. Between November 1992 and January 1993, four letters were sent to NBC by GM. In that time, they did not receive an adequate response or explanation. Even after threat of a lawsuit, NBC News President Michael Gartner continued to defend the network's claim, insisting the story "was entirely accurate."

In February 1993, GM filed a lawsuit against the National Broadcasting Company, charging that *Dateline NBC* had rigged the crash and falsely reported the results. GM was now fully in crisis mode.

## The Perceptions

The key public relations principle at work is that perception is truth, and the media creates that perception following a crisis. In most cases, the perception is established in the first few hours after an incident. Bill Patterson, head of crisis communications and media training practices at HMS Partners of Columbus, Ohio, has discovered that there is an unfortunate trend for most management teams at this stage of a crisis:

- Top management invariably says it is the public relations person's problem.
- Worse yet, the organization may have no PR person or staff to rely on or blame.
- The company may have a "crisis plan" but it turns out to be two pages with phone numbers of people to be notified.
- Management decides that it is "an internal problem" and endorses the stonewalling philosophy.
- The official policy is "no comment."

The trade journal, *PR News*, cites a survey that says 65 percent of the public interprets "no comment" as an admission of guilt. GM could have chosen to take no direct action and let the situation play out in the press, but once it established that its claims had merit, the team instead fought hard to defend the company's reputation.

Taking an adversarial approach to this media relations problem was never an option. Unlike doctors and lawyers, journalists have no official oversight committee, board, or organization. When one is offended or harmed by a doctor or a lawyer, a case can be made before a medical board or bar association. The first amendment clearly outlines freedom for the press so it has become nearly impossible to successfully sue them for libel or slander. This is the state of affairs GM would have to come to terms with in pursuit of fairness and accountability.

The perception of the questionable safety of GM trucks was only heightened when the National Highway Traffic and Safety Administration (NHTSA) opened an independent investigation of GM. Responding to public pressure, due in part to a well orchestrated campaign by NBC's attorneys, NHTSA launched this probe just one month after the initial broadcast. Consumer concern was at its highest level.

## The Problem

GM's crisis communications program was managed by two members of a recently reorganized communications staff: William J. O'Neill, then the director of communications for GM's North American Operations (NAO), and Edward S. Lechtzin, director of legal and safety issues for the NAO communications staff. Initially, O'Neill had, in fact, agreed that GM would participate in the original *Dateline NBC* program but had not been notified during the interview session about NBC's taped test.

Lechtzin's boss, GM General Counsel Harry J. Pearce, was selected to face off with the media. At the heart of the team's public relations effort would be a press conference, conducted by Pearce. The crisis communication team further made a conscious decision to target television as the key medium to deliver GM's message that they weren't going to settle for this. At GM, there was never any doubt that this deception should be publicized and as widely as possible. Briefed during an inaugural event for President Clinton, GM President Jack Smith told his public relations executives, "Don't overplay it, but do what's right."

A primary concern was to discredit NBC's supposed expert witnesses. The claims made by these individuals went to the heart of the case. It is no secret that adversary journalism relies on information from partisan or interested sources. That's no scandal in itself. Equally clear, though, is that unless the press brings a skeptical intelligence to bear on its partisan sources, as we see NBC did not do, its reputation will be at those sources' mercy.

What kind of experts did NBC use? Byron Bloch, for one, has a peculiar list of professional specialties. On one hand, he is a frequent network consultant on auto safety. When not doing paid media consulting, however, Bloch is perhaps the single best-known hired expert witness in injury lawsuits against automakers. He doesn't challenge reports that he lacks formal training in auto safety or engineering, and he acknowledged in a 1980 case that his résumé listed a degree he didn't have. Still, he's appeared in court to testify about alleged defects not just in cars but in products ranging from coffee pots to railroad cars.

Next there was Bruce Enz of The Institute for Safety Analysis (TISA). He frequently testified against GM and evidently against every other major car manufacturer in the U.S. market. He's not an engineer, nor, he says, are any of the 25 staff members of his institute, which is a for-profit organization.

Then there's Ben Kelley, another frequent witness. Kelley has enjoyed a successful career of providing crash-test footage to TV producers. When CBS's "Street Stories" questioned safety-belt reliability, it relied heavily on Kelley's Institute for Injury Reduction. Marion Blakey, head of NHTSA, flayed the resulting coverage as "factually inaccurate," not to mention that Kelley's group was founded and continues to be largely supported by a small group of trial attorneys. GM would have to scrupulously discredit the credentials and objectivity of the so-called safety experts. This objective headed the list of topics to be addressed in the press conference.

## The Public Relations Impact

Harry Pearce was scheduled to take the stage in the GM showroom at 1 P.M. on February 8, 1993. The only uncertainty now was what the media's reaction would be.

From the moment Harry Pearce stepped to the podium until the time he concluded more than two hours later, the assembled media personnel, numbering nearly 150 journalists and 25 camera crews, were mesmerized.

"What I'm about to share with you should shock the conscience of every member of your profession and mine, and I believe the American people as well," began Pearce. "I will not allow the good men and women of General Motors and the thousands of independent businesses who sell our products and whose livelihood depends upon our products to suffer the consequences of NBC's irresponsible conduct transmitted via the airwaves throughout this great nation in the November *Dateline* program. GM has been irreparably damaged and we are going to defend ourselves."

For the next two hours, calling on years of trial experience, Pearce systematically shredded any semblance of defense that NBC might have had. He concluded with a statement issued earlier in the day by NBC, "We feel that our use of those demonstrations was accurate and responsible." His reply was a challenge, as if to a jury. "Well, you decide that one, and that's going to prove your mettle within your own profession. It's sometimes most difficult to police abuse in one's own profession."

At the center of the Pearce press conference was a repeat of NBC's 55-second crash demonstration. After the replay of the segment, Pearce carefully commented on the credentials, or lack thereof, of NBC's so-called expert witnesses.

Ultimately, no source, not even the internal report generated by NBC after the affair, fully explained what the crashes of two aged Citations pushed into the sides of two Chevy pickups were supposed to prove. Certainly, it wasn't that the trucks were dangerous since the performance of the trucks impacted at 39 and 48 miles per hour respectively was superb considering the conditions. Even with the use of incendiary devices, the only fire produced was a 15-second grass fire caused by escaped gasoline from an incorrectly fitted gas cap. NBC's own investigative report summarized it best:

> We believe that the combined effect of the shot from the bullet car and the slow motion film creates an impression that the flames are about to consume the cabin of the truck. These images in the edited tape convey an impression quite different from what people saw at the scene. The fire was small, it did not consume the cabin of the truck, and it did not last long.

GM's news conference brought NBC to its knees. On the day after Pearce's press conference appearance, NBC initiated a negotiating session that lasted for 12 hours. GM would accept nothing less than a full public retraction of its prior broadcast.

On February 9, 1993, a day after the GM press conference, *Dateline NBC* co-anchors Jane Pauley and Stone Philips read a four-minute, on-air retraction that put the blame solely on NBC and apologized to GM.

In the aftermath, three *Dateline* producers were fired, the on-air reporter was demoted and reassigned, and ultimately, NBC News President Gartner resigned in humiliation. NBC agreed to reimburse GM all expenses incurred during the three-week investigation. In exchange, GM agreed to drop the defamation suit it had filed against NBC.

Following this incident, GM increased its public relations offensive to counter concerns about the safety of its trucks. It sought to show that the plaintiff's attorneys had a vested financial interest in nurturing the idea that the trucks were unsafe. Another consideration was that the experts were found to have been either financed by the plaintiff's attorneys or served as expert witnesses in mounting legal action against the company.

Seventeen-year-old Shannon Mosely had recently died in a fire when his GM pickup truck was side-impacted by a drunk driver. The *Dateline NBC* video was made in conjunction with the hearing of that case. The attorneys trying the case in Texas obviously stood to gain from testing that would implicate GM's trucks. With that in mind, the fact that the testing and production of that video was partially financed by a group of attorneys (the plaintiff's bar) indicates that this misrepresentation would afford the opposing legal team a very unfair and fraudulent advantage over GM's lawyers. All involved, of course, had not counted on such swift and effective public relations.

NHTSA still demanded that GM voluntarily recall its pickup trucks while it completed its own investigation. The company refused. In April 1993, GM sponsored briefings in which Pearce explained to key members of the media why the company wouldn't recall its trucks and why NHTSA's conclusions were false.

The Executive Summary of NBC's internal report concluded, "The story of this ill-fated crash demonstration and its aftermath is rather a story of lapsed judgment—serious lapses—by persons generally well-intentioned and well-qualified. And it is a story of a breakdown in the system for correction and compliance that every organization, including a news organization and network, needs."

## Ideal Public Relations Impact

An unprecedented effort resulting in the desired outcome could not fairly be called anything other than successful. Historically, there is really no standard to measure GM's actions. The company put together a unique response team that effectively handled all decisions in its public relations offensive. Even though the team reacted superbly in this matter, its effectiveness might have been maximized if a crisis plan outlining such a situation had already existed.

These members were selected after the onset of the crisis, and the president was briefed while on leave in Washington. Had there been a plan in place, GM's actions might have been swifter in mustering its team and delivering the fatal blow to NBC's fraudulent broadcast.

Another consideration is that GM did not necessarily have to dignify the report with a response and could have attempted to let it fizzle out in the media untouched. Many respected professionals still argue strongly in favor of this tactic. The writers and editors of Pat Jackson's *pr reporter* were some that shared in this school of thought during the events of this incident. Even though NBC reimbursed GM for all costs, the investigation lasted nearly a month and GM suffered $2 million in expenses while in pursuit of vindication. Not acknowledging the story might have seen the company arriving at the same results without incurring such high expenditures.

A truly proactive role would have seen GM conducting its own safety tests prior to putting a different product on the market. Certainly there are considerations regardless of where the fuel tank is located when it comes to various types of accidents, but the "side-saddle" design begs to have a side-impact test conducted before leaving the company open to the scrutiny it soon found. The company could surely have afforded a voluntary experiment by NHTSA when the new design was unveiled. Tests on record at GM could have readily dismissed NBC's claims as soon as they emerged as well as avoided the confrontation they ultimately had with NHTSA.

GM's excellent understanding of the media and its positive relationships with them came to the team's aid in this scare. Harry Pearce's trial experience was also key in establishing GM's innocence, but more importantly its perceived innocence in the court of public opinion.

## NBC Not the First, Just the First to Get Caught

An "electronic Titanic" is how Howard Rosenberg of the *Los Angeles Times* characterized it. It was heralded as an unprecedented disaster in the history of network news and considered the biggest TV scam since the Quiz Scandals. NBC was actually a latecomer to this sort of safety-exposé game, and it is believed that its decisions were made under cost-cutting pressures.

CBS and ABC were quoted by another *Los Angeles Times* reporter as having said, "Their standards forbid the sort of staging that got NBC into trouble." An investigation of past network auto-safety coverage reveals that both CBS and ABC have run the same sorts of grossly misleading crash videos and simulations, withheld similar sorts of material evidence, and relied on the same dubious experts GM discredited as being tied to the plaintiff's attorney.

In June 1978, ABC's *20/20* reported "startling new developments" showing that full-size Fords, not just the sub-compact Pinto, would explode when hit from behind. The network aired film tests from a UCLA demonstration in 1967 that showed researchers under contract with Ford simulating a rear-end collision into a Ford sedan at 55 miles per hour. The end result was the vehicle bursting into a fireball.

ABC insisted that it had analyzed a great number of Ford's secret rear-end crash tests, and anyone who owned a Ford of any kind was at risk of suffering the same outcome displayed in the film. If ABC had really analyzed those UCLA test reports, it had every reason to know why the Ford in the crash film burst into flames: There was an incendiary device under it. As the UCLA researchers explained in a 1968 report published by the Society of Automotive Engineers a decade before the ABC broadcast, one of their goals was to study how a crash fire affected the passenger compartment of the car; to do that, they obviously needed a fire. It clearly revealed that the testers had tried on multiple runs to produce a fire without an igniter and failed.

The coverage seen on ABC gave plenty of credit to the network's expert, Byron Bloch. He is the same expert from the *Dateline NBC* program and his defense in the GM case was very similar to the defense he gave concerning the ABC broadcast, "There was nothing wrong with what happened in Indianapolis. The so-called devices underneath the pickup truck are really a lot of smoke that GM is blowing to divert you away from any punitive damages." While NBC refused to acknowledge that the rocket engines started the fire, they did admit that they shouldn't have put them in and that their presence should have been revealed to the audience.

After NBC's downfall, Don Hewitt, CBS *60 Minutes* executive producer, was frequently quoted in the media that such things were unheard of at his show. "I'd be looking for a job tomorrow," he insisted if that happened under his watch. However, CBS already had a history of producing several similarly tainted reports on vehicles.

In December 1980, *60 Minutes* reported that a small army-style Jeep was dangerously prone to roll over, not only in emergencies but "even in routine road circumstances at relatively low speeds." The footage was of tests run by the Insurance Institute for Highway Safety and was produced in collaboration with a CBS film crew. It shows "CJ" Jeeps going through a series of standard maneuvers. From a distance, the audience watched as CBS repeatedly flipped the Jeep. In test run after test run, the camera shows J-turns and evasive maneuvers to avoid obstacles in the roadway all result in an overturned Jeep.

The catch is that the viewers might have benefited from knowing that the testers had to put the Jeeps through 435 runs just to produce eight rollovers. Make a car skid repeatedly and you predictably degrade tire tread and other key safety margins, Chrysler later said.

Also key in these tests is that the Jeeps were piloted by robot drivers who were turning the wheel through more than 580 degrees of arc in these supposedly "fairly gentle" maneuvers. In one case, the wheel was rotated more than five turns per second. An unrelated study by GM revealed that average drivers even in emergency conditions only turn the wheel around 520 degrees per second. The robot drivers in these tests were operating at rates from 1,100 to 1,805 degrees per second. Unless you plan on investing in a dangerously high-tech chauffeur, the conditions represented here were anything but real world.

NHTSA later found that the Jeeps had been loaded with weights in key areas and were shown under "abnormal test conditions and unrealistic maneuvers."

In March 1981, CBS produced an Emmy-winning *60 Minutes* segment revealing how the most common type of tire rim used on heavy trucks can fly off, killing or maiming bystanders. What their expert, Ben Kelley, failed to mention is that they had to shave off 70 percent of the rim and remove the locking caps before they could get it to separate from the tire. Again, this is the same Ben Kelley, supported by trial attorneys, who appeared in the GM program.

There is still another account of a *60 Minutes* attack on the Audi 5000 in 1986. "Sudden acceleration" had viewers puzzled by a car that was apparently possessed. What it was actually possessed by was a tank of compressed air or fluid attached by a hose to a hole that was drilled in the transmission.

The history of dubious safety journalism goes on and on in the other networks, but both ABC and CBS insist there was no wrongdoing on their parts at any time. This might leave NBC to be considered the moral front-runner. The network got burned, and it apologized, which is more than its rivals have done. Former NBC News head Michael Gartner secures his spot in infamy with this last statement. "I saw that I had been too ready to believe our so-called experts, without trying to find out who they were . . . I realized we were just plain wrong." ■

## QUESTIONS FOR DISCUSSION

1. Assess the value of positive relationships with the media to General Motors in handling its problems with *Dateline* and NBC.
2. Is "fighting back" a good strategy for media disputes in general? Why?
3. Do media reporters and producers have a responsibility to investigate their sources as well as to investigate the targeted organizations?
4. What other options might GM have considered in rebuttal to NBC/*Dateline?*

## REFERENCES

"A Chink in the Armor." Bill Patterson, Director of Crisis Communications and Media Training Practices, HMS Partners. www.media-relations.com/articles.htm.

"Crisis Advisor Says Only 10 Percent of Corporations Have Plans." *PR News* (October 16, 1995).

"Exposing the Experts Behind the Sexy Exposés; How Networks Get Duped by Dubious Advocates." *The Washington Post,* Sunday "Outlook" (February 28, 1993).

"It Didn't Start with *Dateline NBC*." *National Review* (June 21, 1993).

"The Most Dangerous Vehicle on the Road." *The Wall Street Journal* (February 9, 1993).

NBC self-generated internal report, "Report of inquiry into crash demonstrations broadcast on *Dateline NBC* November 17, 1992."

*The Practice of Public Relations.* 6th edition. Upper Saddle River, NJ: Prentice-Hall, Inc., 1995.

# Case 7-4   A Classic: Building Media Relationships That Pay

In the late 1970s, the domestic car industry was threatened by the rash of imports that flooded the country. The imports were fuel-efficient and better built than many American cars. These qualities, coupled with the economy that was hard hit by a suffocating recession, served to jeopardize the very existence of the three top U.S. auto makers. Chrysler was one car manufacturer that decided to fight back—but did not expect the media problems that would come along with the fight.

Chrysler Motors[1] had several problems at once. Its cars did not appeal to many buyers, and its sales lagged behind those of the two major competitors in the United States, Ford and General Motors. In 1978, the corporation was listed in *Fortune* as the year's "biggest loser," selling the "wrong kind of cars for the wrong kinds of buyers."

## Situation Analysis

*Fortune* magazine described Chrysler's problems in this way:

1. The demographics of Chrysler product owners showed that they were more conservative, older, blue-collar people less inclined to buy cars loaded with options, and people who got hurt first in an economic downturn.
2. Product engineering dominated the planning and marketing of cars.
3. Auto designs were considered "stodgy."

4. The corporation was on the move to non-automotive ventures around the world, many of which were not profitable.
5. Government regulations on mileage, safety, and emissions were things with which all manufacturers had to contend.[2]

Just at this downturn, Chrysler executives decided to launch a new product, the Dodge Omni, and its twin, the Plymouth Horizon. They were the company's first venture into the subcompact car line and also the first medium-priced cars with front-wheel drive manufactured in the United States.

The new products were introduced to the news media in two phases: The "long lead" preview for writers and editors of monthly magazines was held at the Chrysler proving grounds in Chelsea, Michigan. The "short lead" preview for daily newspapers, weekly news magazines, and radio and television stations was conducted in San Diego.

News kits timed for simultaneous release with the short lead preview were sent to all major U.S. daily and weekly papers, minority papers, and dealers.

Radio cassette actualities, featuring top sales executives and special feed from the preview site, were offered to all radio stations. Television networks were offered footage with and without sound, and a television crew was available on site for stations requesting special material.

---

[1] In 1998, Chrysler Motors merged with Daimler-Benz of Germany and the company was known as DaimlerChrysler. In 2007, the company was in the process of again separating the two, looking for a buyer for the Chrysler brands.
[2] *Fortune,* June 19, 1978, p. 55.

The crucial part of the introduction, however, was the test driving of the Omni and Horizon by the reporters and editors present at the short lead preview. Approximately 43 of them drove the cars from the proving grounds to their home cities.

Chrysler received extensive and glowing coverage from the news media. The News Analysis Institute, a Pittsburgh-based company hired by Chrysler, reported the publication of 904 news stories, totaling 16,646 column inches in newspapers with a combined total circulation of over 137 million. News/Sports Radio Network reported 12,888 radio broadcasts of the story to 136,022,600 potential listeners. About 78 television stations reported that they had aired stories and visuals to an average audience of 18,448,000. Glowing reports came from the automotive publications:

*Auto Week*: Hell of a nice car. Got a lot of favorable attention on the highway, especially from the foreign car guys. It's just what you need. Well worth waiting for.

*Car and Driver*: Fine little car.

*Automotive News*: It's a fine car, beautiful. Even at top speeds I was getting 31 mpg. Car handled fine.

*Auto World*: I was impressed. At 70, it handled beautifully. We averaged 31 mpg at the higher speeds. It's a beautiful little car.

*Motor Trend*, a magazine for automobile enthusiasts, gave the car its "Car of the Year" endorsement.

*Fortune* magazine reported that the cars had "scored well in the marketplace."

## Crisis Hits Six Months Later

On a Tuesday, six months after the introduction of the cars, Chrysler was conducting another of its long lead previews at its Chelsea proving grounds. Fifty-four monthly magazine editors and photographers from such diverse publications as *Hot Rod, Medical Economics*, and *Vogue* attended.

The entire public relations department was geared toward building a responsive two-way relationship with the news representatives. They coordinated product seminars, set up interviews, ensured that the writers were involved with ride and drive programs, and arranged models and props for special photographs.

*Consumer Reports*, a monthly product testing and rating magazine, turned down Chrysler's invitation to the long-lead preview, even though one of its reporters had attended a preview from another automobile manufacturer the week earlier.

Sometime in the afternoon that Tuesday, a reporter from the *Washington Post* called a Chrysler public relations executive: "I would like to get Chrysler's reaction to Consumers Union's finding your Omni/Horizon car unacceptable." (See Figure 7-5.) The question hit like a bombshell. The reporter insisted that the charge was true; having heard it from a reliable source within Consumers Union. He also said Consumers Union would hold press conferences to announce their findings the following day, in New York and Washington D.C. By late that afternoon, Consumers Union confirmed that the press conferences would be held, but refused Chrysler admission.

## Consumers Union's Charges Against Chrysler

Consumers Union's charges against Chrysler had been related to a test procedure that the Union said was performed routinely at auto proving grounds to check a car's directional stability: "ability to center itself and return to its original course when it is deflected abruptly from a straight path." The test is made by driving at steady "expressway" speed, turning the steering wheel sharply to one side and then letting go of the steering wheel with both hands.

**FIGURE 7-5    Photo from *Consumer Reports.* The new Chrysler cars are branded as "not acceptable," although earlier the cars had been rated very highly by the persons who had used the car**

*Source:* (Courtesy of Consumer Reports.)

The Union claimed that in such tests, most cars waver from side to side only minimally before returning to a course close to the previous one.

## Chrysler Swings into Strategic Action

At their Chelsea proving grounds, Chrysler's engineers immediately swung into action. The recreated the Union's test procedure while a television crew filmed the entire demonstration and made quantities of tapes. Meanwhile, the Consumers Union's press conferences were about to begin in New York and Washington, D.C., the following day. That evening, some news networks had already begun to inform the public of Consumers Union's charges against Chrysler's Omni and Horizon cars. But they balanced their coverage with a discussion of the excellent sales figures for the cars and their being awarded *Motor Trend's* "Car of the Year."

Wednesday, June 14, 1978; New York: Chrysler's executive was outside the Consumers Union's press conference, allowed admission only on the insistence of the media representatives who had learned of his presence. He was then allowed to share the podium with Consumers Union representatives.

Wednesday, June 14, 1978; Washington, D.C.: Chrysler's representative was denied admission to the press conference. He held his own sidewalk press conference after the Union's press conference.

In the meantime, the public relations staff was busy distributing tapes of the test demonstrations made the previous day to television news departments in New York and Washington, D.C., Chicago, and Detroit. The public relations staff had also been preparing for a barrage of questions, which came soon enough. Chrysler released statements forcefully denying the Union's charges, reminding readers that it had received praise from professionals and consumers alike. The statement was distributed to most U.S. news media. A radio actuality (sound bite) of the statement was also released to network radio news syndicates and key stations in the country.

There was more. An information kit on the complex subject of steering and handling was prepared for spokespersons staffing the telephones, so that they could respond intelligently and with One Clear Voice to general and technical media questions.

That same day, after the Consumers Union's press conferences, Chrysler held its own news conference at the Chelsea proving grounds. Detroit and network television and radio reporters, print journalists, and the long lead preview magazine writers were all present. Here again, the Union's test maneuvers were demonstrated. It was crucial to show that the Union's test was extreme and in no way related to real driving situations. In fact, one writer was overheard to say: "That's comparable to jumping out the second floor of your house, breaking a leg, and then accusing the house of being unsafe."

With its sound strategic planning and its immediate response (with proof) to refute the Consumers Union charges, Chrysler was able to garner some positive media reaction, demonstrated by these editorials:

> Consumers Union, which issued its report with great public fanfare — simultaneous news conferences in New York and Washington — ought to be darn sure it knows what it's talking about. We're not at all sure it does.[3]
>
> Anybody dumb enough to do this (the test) is probably certifiable, and anybody dumb enough to believe that it proves anything about a car's road ability or handling deserves to be working for Consumers Union. CU's motives may be squeaky clean, but we think they've soiled their treasured cloak of impartiality. The Omni/Horizon is as safe as the *Consumer Reports'* charges are irresponsible.[4]

The article in *Car and Driver* was given nationwide newspaper distribution through AP and UPI. Various network radio and television newscasts aired the editorial. Numerous national trade publications including *Automotive News* and *Advertising Age* published it.

Not only the national media were informed; public relations staff also made information available to the local media via video tapes and radio actualities distributed to Chrysler's 21 zone offices across the country. This information was also accessible to dealers.

Chrysler left no stone unturned. It petitioned the National Highway Traffic Safety Administration (NHTSA) and its Canadian counterpart, Transport Canada, to conduct their own tests of the Omni/Horizon cars.

Within a few weeks after the Consumers Union's charges, the two government agencies came forth with their own separate conclusions: Transport Canada, represented by a consultant and recognized automotive-handling expert from the International Standards Organization and the director of roads and motor vehicle safety in the Canadian Ministry of Transport, announced that "automotive specialists from Transport Canada had found that they handled in a normal and satisfactory manner in both obstacle avoidance maneuver tests and on the handling track."

NHTSA, after testings at both the Chelsea and Consumers Union proving grounds, concluded: "No evidence of a safety problem in the stability and handling characteristics of Chrysler's subcompact Dodge Omni and Plymouth Horizon."

Chrysler recorded both government agencies' endorsement on videotape and radio actuality statements with the corporation's chief engineer and sent them air

---

[3]"Unsafe or Unfair," *Washington Star.*
[4]"God Save Us from Our Protectors," *Car and Driver.*

express to New York, Chicago, and Los Angeles network offices. Radio actualities from interviews with the Canadian expert and the deputy administrator of NHTSA were sent to the *Voice of America, Armed Forces Radio*, and Canadian news outlets. These statements were also distributed over newswires throughout the United States. The statements were telegraphed to all 7,500 Chrysler dealers.

## When Public Relations Saves the Day

The News Analysis Institute analyzed the news coverage after the storm had blown over. In its finding, a negative story is one in which the greater part of the copy was devoted to criticism of the cars and a positive story has the Chrysler position dominating (see Figure 7-6). The Institute's report stated:

**FIGURE 7-6**   Summary and analysis by the News Analysis Institute of the coverage of the Omni/Horizon, which helped Chrysler evaluate its counter-media activity

## The *News Analysis Institute*

955 LIBERTY AVENUE   ●   PITTSBURGH, PA. 15222   ●   PHONE: (412) 471-9411

Analysis of
Consumers Union Report on
Omni / Horizon Handling Problems

|  | Stories Published | Space Secured | | |
|---|---|---|---|---|
|  |  | Column Inches | Newspaper Pages | Circulation |
| Favorable | 402 | 5,132 | 29.2 | 35,881,065 |
| Unfavorable | 342 | 4,815 | 27.4 | 22,928,866 |
| Totals | 744 | 9,947 | 56.6 | 58,809,931 |

|  | Pictures Published | Page-One Stories | Articles Running a Full - Page or Longer |
|---|---|---|---|
| Favorable | 61 | 38 | 2 |
| Unfavorable | 68 | 17 | - |
| Totals | 129 | 55 | 2 |

|  | Chrysler or Product Name Used in Heading |
|---|---|
| Favorable | 294 |
| Unfavorable | 224 |
| Totals | 518 |

*Source:* (Reprinted by permission of the News Analysis Institute.)

The results are unusual in two respects: Despite the negative nature of the event, Chrysler dominated the coverage in stories published, space, and circulation. Further, Chrysler's case was strongly stated in virtually all the unfavorable articles, and a Chrysler comment was usually introduced early in the article. Particularly effective in this respect was the executive's sidewalk conference outside Consumers Union's Washington headquarters and the placements of Chrysler's formal rebuttal. Also notable in positive news were the coverage of Chrysler's press test of Omni/Horizon and its rallying of auto writers to support its claims.

In evaluating how public relations saved the day, Frank Wylie, Chrysler's public relations executive at the time, cited two key "life-savers":

Most of the writers in major cities had already experienced the Omni/Horizon from their preview rides and local test drives. This *firsthand experience* helped to nullify or dampen the negative effects of Consumers Union's charges. This is perhaps succinctly summarized by one free-lance writer who had attended one of Chrysler's previews: "I think your letting people drive the cars away was the smartest thing you folks have done in a long time." [Emphasis added.]

The other vital "life-saver" was the preparation made by the public relations staff to answer all queries with *One Clear Voice*:

We tried to anticipate every question that we could in connection with the breaking news elements of the story and be prepared to handle them quickly and efficiently. We didn't want anybody hanging with overnight or weekend stories with unanswered questions.

The best evaluation tool, however, still is the final results of the public relations strategy during this crisis. Although sales figures plummeted immediately after the Union's charges, Chrysler believes that they would have remained that way if they had not reacted immediately and forcefully to counter the charges.

What's truly revealing happened at the dealers. The total sales of the two cars broke all of Chrysler's previous new car records during their first year on the market. Dealers sold every Omni/Horizon they had and could have sold more, had they had any more to sell. In addition, the two cars were all-time Chrysler leaders in capturing owners of competitive cars by establishing a "conquest rate" of more than 67 percent. Two out of every three buyers traded in another make of car for the Omni or Horizon.

In the final analysis, Chrysler's open and honest rapport and relationship with the news media combined with positive anticipatory action to the charges helped save it from an otherwise major media crisis. ■

------------------------------------------------------------

## QUESTIONS FOR DISCUSSION

1. During the Consumers Union flap, Chrysler dominated the news compared with its competitors. Though the reports contained some dangerous criticisms, is it possible all that this exposure actually helped the company? Explain why or why not.
2. Research has shown that the news media have limited effects on publics. How would you evaluate Chrysler's reaction to Consumers Union's charges in light of this statement?
3. What are some public relations or communications theories that you see in play in Chrysler's handling of the news media? Can you think of some other theories not used in this case that would have helped the sales figures for the Omni/Horizon cars to climb?

4. If you were in charge of managing this crisis, what are some strategic actions you would keep or abandon? Explain your answer in terms of public relations principles or communications theories, or both.

5. The News Analysis Institute found that the original introductory publicity for Omni/Horizon generated "the publication of 904 news stories . . . in newspapers with the combined total circulation of over 137 million people." How many potential customers read about these new cars?

# Case 7-5 Universal Studios Florida: Riding "Rat Lady" to Halloween Success*

## Situation Background

Universal Studios Florida (USF) opened its gates in Orlando in June of 1990 as a major player in the theme park industry (as USF grew and added a second theme park, *Islands of Adventure*, and a shopping/dining entertainment complex, *CityWalk*, it changed its name to Universal Orlando). In early 1991, USF had already set its sights on capitalizing on the resident market and building turnstile admissions during the traditional tourist off-peak periods.

The awareness-building plan was simple: USF would create an event for Halloween that would be so extraordinarily compelling that it would not only increase park visitation during the soft tourist October time period, but it would command a separate evening admission fee. During the daylight hours the theme park functioned as usual, but as darkness fell the park would be transformed into a morbid collection of haunted soundstages, "spooktacular" shows, and countless surprise guest encounters with the most realistic horror monsters Universal Studios makeup artists could conceive. Halloween Fright Nights (HFN) (later changed to Halloween Horror Nights) was born in concept, and the inaugural event was held for a four-day period, immediately prior to and including Halloween day. It was wildly successful and demonstrated that USF could "own" the Halloween celebration scene in Orlando as it had planned.

Building on great first-year attendance and guest enthusiasm, in 1992 HFN was expanded to begin much earlier in the month and include the two weekends (Friday through Sunday) prior to Halloween, plus the days immediately before Halloween and the holiday itself. The need for long-lead publicity to build public awareness of this expanded schedule presented an immediate problem. USF's public relations counsel was tasked with developing a publicity plan and immediately conducted a poll of newspaper reporters and TV news directors to determine where Halloween ranked for news story coverage. The result was unanimous—Halloween was considered a secondary holiday and as such would not become a newsworthy subject until the days immediately prior to Halloween (today, due to events like Universal Orlando's Halloween Horror Nights, Halloween has become one of the top-celebrated holidays in the United States). Reporters and news directors alike said only "extraordinary circumstances" would warrant Halloween news coverage so in early October, the period USF now needed the news placement.

## The Publicity Challenge

The publicity task was clear—create an extraordinary event to *compel* news media to cover the Halloween activities—however, the solution was not as immediately clear. A meeting was set with the USF entertainment and promotions department and public relations counsel to explore all the new scare-elements for HFN and determine what might be suitable as a showcase piece for publicity purposes. One element stood

*Appreciation to Joe Curley, APR, cofounder of Curley & Pynn Public Relations Management, Inc. (Orlando, Florida) for his assistance in preparing this case.

out: Guests enter a darkened room, feeling their way around by hand-to-wall contact, and then suddenly the floor lights up to reveal they are standing on a clear Plexiglas floor. They are shocked to see, just inches below their feet, a screaming woman in a coffin flailing her arms and covered with 100 live crawling rats! Rick Hensler of USF promotions immediately dubbed her "The Rat Lady," and the group agreed this scare-element had terrific potential. Counsel wondered who was actually going to be the Rat Lady? She hadn't been selected yet, but it would be someone from the USF staff.

## The Strategy Develops

The challenge was to package the Rat Lady to create news, lots of it and early in the month, too. It was determined that a traditional news release—no matter how strong or cleverly written—just *wouldn't* meet the challenge. A totally different approach was necessary. It was decided to hire an "outside" Rat Lady to provide a "third-party" interview opportunity. To find the right candidate, the plan was to place a newspaper help-wanted ad to hire the yet-undetermined Rat Lady. The strategy was to treat the ad's wording as though it was a routine, everyday hiring situation, but with a full tongue-in-cheek approach. The USF human resources department agreed to provide an open Rat Lady staff position to which the public could apply.

The Rat Lady publicity strategy began to unfold. A special post office box was established for the applications to streamline the process and maintain timeliness. The help-wanted ad was placed in the highest-circulation daily newspaper in each of the major Florida cities and ran Friday through Sunday. The ad read:

**Rat Lady proved to be quite a treat for Universal**

*Source:* (Courtesy of Universal Studios Florida.)

**HELP WANTED:** Person to share small dark coffin with 100 live rats. Evening hours. No experience necessary, but must not have irrational fears of being buried alive, confinement, or all over body contact with crawling rodents. High-pitch scream desirable. Mail reply to: Universal Studios Florida, PO Box xxxxxx, Orlando, FL 32853. An equal opportunity employer.

The ad was to read "Woman to share," but newspapers would not run the ad if it was gender specific, because the work could be done by either a woman or a man.

## The Action Phase

The weekend ad timing was critical to the strategy of not having any USF comment (HR offices closed over the weekend), thereby letting the Rat Lady ad create some buzz on its own. By early morning on Saturday, radio stations were getting called by listeners who pointed out the Rat Lady ad, which fostered on-the-air patter and generated calls to USF to learn more—but USF offices were closed until Monday. The Rat Lady buzz continued to build, and by Monday morning the PO box was full of applications and the phones were ringing nonstop from news media asking questions on how many applied, who would dare apply, where these people were from, how much did the job pay, were they real rats, and so on.

Media frequently asked for a Rat Lady press kit and were coyly told this is an HR interview process and there was no press kit (a strategy to reinforce the publicity plan tactics). This response resulted in media taking "ownership" of "finding the story" and actually demanding that they be allowed to interview Rat Lady job applicants.

The huge and growing response (from both applicants and the media) immediately put a strain on USF staffing requirements and necessitated an increase in personnel dedicated to the project. This included additional PR and entertainment department staff to organize and conduct a Rat Lady "casting call" to provide media the information they were requesting.

The casting-call format was chosen to avoid any confidentiality issues of publicly disclosing employment applicant information. After USF determined a list of first-cut applicants, those agreeing to participate in the casting call were given new public information application forms that focused on basic data such as the applicant's name, city, and why they thought they were qualified to be chosen Rat Lady. Each Rat Lady applicant was required to do a "scream test," handle the rats, and then finally lie in the coffin and allow the rats to crawl all over her body. Media were allowed to tape the session, and they packed the casting-call soundstage and interviewed many applicants (some very strange and bizarre individuals), resulting in extensive story placement.

USF taped the casting-call events and up-linked a national VNR to build even more awareness. Media calls were made to outer markets that had hometown ties to applicants to provide a local angle and motivate pick-up.

Follow-up stories continued on the "working" Rat Lady during the regular HFN nights (media taping was allowed prior to and immediately after HFN public operational hours). Sidebar stories were created focused on "behind-the-scenes" of raising the rats:

- The rat litters were hand-raised by USF employees to be human-friendly.
- Peanut butter was smeared under the face makeup of Rat Lady to have the rats appear to be chewing on her face.
- The rats changed shifts many times a night to protect the rats and keep them active.
- Special costume alterations were developed that included Velcro ties at the Rat Lady's wrists, ankles, neck, and so on, to keep the rats from entering her garments.

- "I saw the Rat Lady" buttons were sold at HFN vendor booths to help hype the situation and create more awareness of the stunt (these sold out in the first few nights of HFN).
- Employees adopted the rats as pets following the HFN event, and demand for the rats exceeded the supply.

## Overwhelming Media Results

The media coverage was worldwide, being picked up and fed by virtually all major TV, radio, and print news networks and syndicates. Associated Press pick up resulted in placements in a majority of daily newspapers; radio pick up covered virtually all news services, including Paul Harvey doing two special reports. The Rat Lady story received widespread international coverage, including being translated for the media in Japan. Other media outlets included *Entertainment Tonight*, CNN, CNBC, *CBS This Morning*, the *Arsenio Hall* show, the Sci-Fi Channel, *New York Times* Syndicate, Associated Press, Knight-Ridder News Service, *Good Day New York* (FOX), and many other major shows and syndicates.

Rat Lady returned the next year in 1993 with a friend—Roach Man—who was covered with Madagascar hissing roaches; some that were three inches long!

The solid and continuing Florida media coverage resulted in a record sell-out crowd for the Second Annual Halloween Fright Nights and set the stage for the event to grow to the largest Halloween scare-celebration in the world. ■

-------------------------------------------------------------

## QUESTIONS FOR DISCUSSION

1. The goal of having a "Rat Lady" was to generate publicity for Universal Studios Florida. What is the value of publicity to a destination like this?
2. Assess the strategy of placing a classified ad? What other options might USF have considered?
3. Why was the "press kit" not distributed? Was this wise?
4. What would you say to PETA about the use of live animals in such a stunt?

## PROBLEM 7-A EMPLOYER INTERESTS AND MEDIA INTERESTS IN CONFLICT

Ted Square takes pride in his professional integrity. He has never deceived a news reporter, never offered a "pay off" for publicity, and never risked his own integrity for personal or employer gain.

Ted's boss is the owner of a multimillion dollar auto parts manufacturing firm whose foremost customer is a major auto maker. Ted's boss is a man of character. He has never pressed Ted for more publicity or more favorable press at whatever cost. He is a realist, taking and relishing whatever favorable publicity is generated by events, but not worrying about either the quantity, accuracy, or completeness of it. With his business strong and growing, the owner exhibits an attitude that is fully supportive of Ted.

One day, the owner is shocked when his vice president of operations confronts him and says it is time to make him a full partner. He claims that his efforts have made the business grow and prosper. The owner is in a quandary. He has been quietly preparing his son to run the business, figuring he could take over in about five years. Meantime, there is no denying that this vice president, acquired a few years ago from one of the Big Three automakers, is of huge importance to the parts firm.

The owner refuses to be pressured by the vice president. He does assure him that in time to come he will earn more and more income, and ultimately, he says, a limited partnership might be available.

The vice president at this point reveals that he has received an offer from a prime auto parts competitor, including a partnership, and the presidency of the competing firm. He presents his resignation to the owner on the spot.

In the hour following this shocking meeting, several events with public relations overtones take place:

1. The managers of the product design, engineering, manufacturing, and marketing departments turn in their resignations. They are moving to the competing company with the vice president of operations.
2. All these executives have been promised a "much better deal" by the vice president of operations.
3. Gossip is going around the office and shop that the business may have to be closed down and all employees terminated or furloughed without pay.

The owner is busy on the telephone, lining up successors for all the "defectors," and trying to reach the buyer at the large auto company customer to make sure the contract is intact and unaffected. His financial vice president is busy calling other customers, brokers, and others to reassure them that the business is not threatened. In the meantime, Ted's department is working on statements the owner wants to make to employees, automotive trade press editors, the local media, and wire service stringers.

Midway into these efforts, word is passed to Ted Square by his secretary that the local bureau chief of a financial newspaper, a long-time friend, is on the telephone. Ted has to take the call, and he hopes that it concerns some other subject. But it does not. The conversation goes this way.

"Ted, this is George. I'm up against our deadline in 15 minutes, but we have a rumor down here that your vice president of operations has resigned."

"Yeah, George. I've been working on a release about it. Do you want the name of the man who will succeed him?"

"Sure."

"It's Lem Jones. He has been the vice president's righthand man for several years. Consequently, the business will go right along."

"Thanks, I'll get this into the works. Let me have more details as fast as you know them."

That was it. George, despite being a trained newsman, failed to ask Ted where the vice president was going, or the full circumstances of his resignation. Ted, for his part, was aware of more than he told. He simply answered specific questions and minimized the importance of the events, even though he knew the story would get financial front-page coverage if he added more details.

As it developed later on that day, the financial newspaper was scooped by a local newspaper whose reporter had called the vice president of operations personally, had gotten the name of the company he was joining, had called them, and had obtained quotable details. The local bureau chief, Ted's friend, was embarrassed. His boss in New York had chewed him out. He blamed Ted for holding back information that was newsworthy, and said, "I'll never be able to trust you again."

"I'm sorry you feel that way," Ted told him. "I had no information from the operations vice president, or the other guys who were resigning, and no one gave me authority to speculate, or to speak for them. What I had officially from the president, I gave you. You didn't ask for anything else. If you had, I could have referred you to the operations VP."

"OK," the bureau chief said, "that's what you say now. But every time you call me, remember, I've got a long memory."

Obviously, this was something for Ted to think about. He reasoned that his obligation was first and last to his employer. He had to release information of news value for which he was the authoritative source. But he did not have to go beyond that, and particularly not if it might be harmful to his employer. The damaged relationship with the major financial newspaper was seriously worrisome.

Who was right: Ted? The bureau chief? Both? Neither? If you had been Ted, how would you have handled the situation so that your employer's interests and your good media relationship with George were both protected? What would you have done differently?

If your company was publicly owned, would you have acted differently when George called?

## PROBLEM 7-B DEALING WITH THE MEDIA IN A STICKY SITUATION

You are the public relations director of Alger Tiberius Software Inc., an up-and-coming software development company. Things have been exciting in the last few days since the introduction of a new software program, Manufacturing Efficiency Revolution (MER). When integrated into the computer controls of manufacturing equipment, it will increase the efficiency of that equipment and cut production time in half. This program will revolutionize the manufacturing industry. Magazine previews of the product have been complimentary, and it looks as if the company has an instant best seller on its hands.

But bad news hits one day when your morning coffee is accompanied by a newspaper clipping from the *Local Yokel Times*, quoting Don T. Figgle, your president and CEO, who is particularly proud of the new product and has taken every opportunity to brag about its merits in the press. In an off-hand comment he makes to a reporter at a local restaurant, Figgle is quoted as saying that "this product will virtually replace about 15 percent of the American manufacturing workforce. It cuts out about half of the unnecessary actions done in factory production."

Figgle's quote is followed by the reaction of the AFL-CIO in response to this new information about the product. Ned T. Green, official spokesman of the organization, is quoted as saying, "This new product was not presented with this information to the labor and computer industries. Efficiency gains in manufacturing were discussed but not the elimination of a sector of our workforce. AT Software in effect lied to the public about the impact this software program will have on the American workforce."

Needless to say, this turn of media coverage is unexpected and unwanted. Figgle was correct in saying that the software would revolutionize the computer and manufacturing industries but his statistics were incorrect. The product would eliminate 10 percent of jobs for the manufacturing workforce but would create jobs in a different area for other workers. Those who would lose their jobs could be retrained for other areas. You arrange another press conference for Figgle to disseminate the correct statistics available to the press, but whether the jobs are cut by 15 percent or 10 percent, loss of employment is the real story for the media. They are already printing a tidal wave of stories with headlines like "Computer Cover-Up Leaves Workers High and Dry" and "AT Software Sends Workers Packing."

By the following morning, negative media coverage has not abated. Although the news media now have the right statistics, emphasis is on the 10 percent of workers allegedly to be put out of work by the software. To top it off, a newly formed activist group, WACS (Workers Against Computer Software), is picketing outside of the main offices of AT Software with signs proclaiming "AT Software Trades in People for Programs." The local TV stations are all present to cover the protest and give up-to-the-minute reports.

In addition the media is out in full force and has gone to the local congressman Bill Zealot for reaction. His last election campaign was focused on creating jobs for America. Zealot, up for reelection in the fall, pledges his loyalty to the hard-working American public and vows to fight "big business pushing aside the little guy and trying to make him obsolete in the name of progress." It looks as if there may be legislative reaction against MER.

Later that afternoon you receive a call from the Computer Software Programmers Association (CSPA). Initially, they were behind this program, but with all the bad press they're getting a bit nervous. They don't want to endorse a program that will cause so much flak. Without the backing of CSPA, the future of this product is going to be difficult.

It is now 9:00 P.M. and things look a bit bleak for MER and AT Software. Clearly what should have been a great announcement has become garbled by the gatekeepers. You are wondering how to get the real message out to those audiences that matter. You ask yourself:

- Who are those groups that are garbling my message?
- What other groups are likely to become involved?
- What are the likely behaviors of each group?
- How can I minimize their messages and maximize mine to the publics
  I would like to reach?
- Can I reach those publics without utilizing usual venues, in order to avoid
  media, political, and activist gatekeepers?

1. With those questions in mind, how would you go about creating a plan to reach key publics with one-on-one communication in order to stay some of the immediate damage caused by the negative reactions of those groups who have been most vocal?
2. Could AT Software have avoided this negative uproar to MER? What actions should have been taken before presenting this product to the public through the media?

# CHAPTER

# 8

# Public Issue Campaigns and Debates

The backbone of Jeffersonian democracy is an intelligent, well-informed public and electorate.

The handling of public issues makes evident the link between public relations and the idea of democracy. For the people to be able to participate in decisions that affect their lives, those decisions must be put before them in a thorough, forceful manner. The ramifications, pro and con, of potential decisions need to be debated fully. *In the Court of Public Opinion, public relations practitioners are the attorneys.*

In this setting, an *issue* is a subject on which there are (1) two or more strongly opposing arguments, (2) emotional involvement of a large number of people, and (3) concern that the decision will have an impact on people's lives or the smooth functioning of society. Gun control, abortion, smoking policies, and the other topics in this chapter clearly meet these criteria.

When issues get out of hand—that is, cannot be settled before they become huge and threatening—they move to the category of *crisis*. A crisis is a public or organizational issue that has grown to such proportions that its ultimate resolution appears to mark a turning point. Depending on the decision, things may not be the same afterward. Chapter 9 presents several crisis cases.

Although businesses, schools, hospitals, and other established organizations with sophisticated public relations policies devote substantial effort to anticipating or avoiding issues that might have a negative effect, they will also raise issues when they believe that public discussion might be beneficial. In contrast, there are many special interest groups whose major activity is to raise issues—in the American democratic tradition in which the people ultimately decide. Because of the number of variables at play and the societal importance of public debate, dealing with issues is one of the most challenging segments of public relations.

## TYPES OF ISSUES

Issues can be assigned to four categories:

- **Latent.** Just being formulated by far-thinking scholars or social activists but with sufficient apparent validity that it could become an issue sooner or later.
- **Emerging.** Starting to be written about in scholarly journals or specialty media; perhaps a special interest organization adopts the idea or a new group forms around it; early adopter opinion leaders begin to be aware; it starts to spill over to wider publics, but no coherent action plan or broad support is yet evident.
- **Hot.** A full-blown issue in current debate.
- **Fallout.** Leftover remnants from the settlement of hot issues, which can come back onto the public agenda because they have already attained visibility.

Elements of all four categories are evident in many of the cases.

## TARGET AUDIENCES

Most of the time, practitioners work with specified target audiences such as employees, neighbors, stockholders, members, donors, and customers, who are perceived to have self-interest reasons to support the organization. These audiences make up the organization's constituency. Contacts with them seek to reinforce, broaden, or deepen the two-way commitment. (See Figure 8-1.)

## THEN THERE'S THE GENERAL PUBLIC

When the term *general public* is used, it usually describes the uncommitted, often uninterested bystanders whose support or opposition might ultimately have a bearing on the outcome of a situation or issue. Because they are unaware or uninterested, members of the general public do not feel much of a stake or depth of conviction.

If a matter eventually will be on the ballot, or voted on by a legislative body, or decided in the marketplace, where people "vote with their dollars," involvement of the general public can be vital. If social policy is being set, it is the general public that will decide what it will be—with or without laws to enforce it. At other times, interest in an issue will be so specialized that the general public will forgo its right to participate and leave the decision to the special interests who do care about the subject.

Therefore, the first problem faced by practitioners is to get people interested. Sometimes individuals or organizations will seek to do this by attempting to speak for the general public. When consumer advocates began questioning the quality and price of various products or services, they took on a task that most people had often done themselves—so people were happy to have this leadership. But when religious fundamentalists claimed to speak for average citizens in demanding the removal of certain books and magazines from libraries and newsstands, the public rejected them. In both cases, these spokespersons were not elected or otherwise appointed by those for whom they undertook to speak. They were accepted or rejected by public consent. This principle is key to understanding issue debate.

Persons or organizations that take stands on issues, pro or con, or neglect to do so, exercise a privilege and a prerogative in the democratic process. It is fundamental to effective public relations that this freedom of expression prevail. Without it, the

# STAKEHOLDERS

NCR

*We believe in building mutually beneficial and enduring relationships with all of our stakeholders, based on conducting business activities with integrity and respect.*

# SHAREHOLD

NCR

*We are dedicated to creating value for our shareholders and financial communities by performing in a manner that will enhance returns on investments.*

# EMPLOYEES

NCR

*We respect the individuality of each employee and foster an environment in which employees' creativity and productivity are encouraged, recognized, valued and rewarded.*

# COMMUNITI

NCR

*We are committed to being caring and supportive corporate citizens within the worldwide communities in which we operate.*

# CUSTOMERS

NCR

*We take customer satisfaction personally: we are committed to providing superior value in our products and services on a continuing basis.*

NCR's Mission: Create Value for Our Stakeho[l]

NCR's Mission: Create Value for Our Stakeholders

*Source:* (Courtesy of NCR Public Relations.)

individual or the organization is totally subject to the point of view of the state or of the noisy and the militant. Given freedom of expression as a basic underpinning of public relations practice, experience suggests that this concept is balanced and weighted by many adjustments. For example, the theoretical democratic process suggests that the majority rules. In reality, this does not always hold true. Quite often, a minority prevails. Less than half of eligible voters register to vote, and an even larger percentage of those who register do not vote. In almost all elections, it is a vocal, motivated, active minority who votes, and therefore rules. Within most organizations, to use another setting, there is almost always a relative few who hold the decision-making power for the whole body politic or membership.

Two cases in particular in this chapter illustrate the concept that a general public does exist, available to be influenced, but that the perceived will of that unorganized body is carried out through groups focusing on a particular issue or concern. One became an advocate for nonsmokers. Another wanted stores to be open on Sundays.

In a slightly different context, Planned Parenthood claims to speak for the rights of women, and across the aisle the Right to Life movement offers its position on moral issues as one that has precedence over personal choice.

The uncommitted general public provides an arena (via public relations campaigns, the news media, and sometimes the courts) in which the motivations of special interest groups can be challenged by those who openly represent viewpoints or programs claiming to deserve a higher priority or to embody a higher moral purpose.

The general public and its elected representatives hold the key in the continuing controversy between the business sector and government agencies over how much regulation there should be, what kind, by whom, and with what reporting requirements and penalties.

## PUBLIC SERVICE AS PREVENTIVE PUBLIC RELATIONS

Public service programs are expressions of an organization's concern for societal problems and needs. The public relations responsibility for organizations engaged in public service programs is normally that of creator and implementer. This role calls for the handling of:

- Strategy, planning, and research
- Program design
- Civic participation
- Government and educational liaison
- Meetings and events
- Media placement and relations
- Preparation of print, audio, and visual materials
- Interviews and news conferences

Some public service programs spring out of a crisis or an emergency, from criticism of an organization's doings, or from public clamor, as in the conservation of endangered species.

Increasingly, public service programs have not waited for problems to arise. They have been devised to head off the difficulties posed by protests, confrontations, or increased governmental regulations. Public service programs are seen as practical means of demonstrating socially responsible behavior, gaining trust for good deeds, building customer or clientele goodwill, or building working relationships with a constituency of public officials, investors, members, donors, or voters. For most successful enterprises and institutions, the attitude is that public service programs and expenditures are important to earn public approval. As a practical matter, management normally places two requisites on public service programs:

1. A program must fit logically into the mission, the objectives, the timetable, and the field of endeavor in which the organization has expertise.
2. There must be an identifiable, measurable benefit to the organization as well as to the public groups or noble purpose involved and affected.

Such strategic public service programs often call for cooperation between public relations or public affairs, human resources, marketing, and other departments.

## SPECIAL INTERESTS

Citizens in a democratic society tend to band together in polarized common interest groups such as labor unions or manufacturers' associations, meat eaters or vegetarians, hunters or conservationists. People feel that collectively, on a given issue, their voices and their votes can get the attention needed to favorably influence decisions.

The United States, more than any other free nation, has become the world's prime example of what happens, both good and bad, when the democratic process is carried to an extreme. The nation has become factionalized to a point where the decision process is hobbled by a host of single-issue champions, protesters, and crusaders. On many public issues, factionalization has generated such a severe confrontation that reconciliation becomes impossible.

The practice of public relations, historically and now, is deeply involved in helping factions to have their voices heard and their influences felt on behalf of their particular special interests.

In representing competing or opposing factions, practitioners face off against each other much as lawyers do in lawsuits or courts. The justification, if any is needed, is simply that each faction, in the eyes of its sponsors and its beneficiaries, holds that its view or needs do, in fact, serve the best interest of all. This freewheeling debate in the court of public opinion, or the marketplace of ideas, is exactly what Jefferson and the Founding Fathers had in mind when they created the United States as the first true democracy.

## IMPORTANCE OF COMPROMISE

Given factionalization and confrontation, it remains for elected government in a free society to assume the roles of *referee* among contestants and *interpreter* of the greater public good.

*When powerful and determined factions or special interests meet head on, the outcome is generally a reconciliation, with both sides compromising a bit.* For example, in the matter of environmental protection, the upper atmospheric layer, or ozone, high above the earth filters out some of the sun's ultraviolet rays, helping assure that humans can live above ground and expose themselves to the sun. Chlorofluorocarbons (as in spray deodorant, insecticide, and detergent cans) have been identified as damaging to the ozone layer. The government, acting in the public interest and spurred by environmentalists, considered a ban on certain chlorofluorocarbons. Makers of products using them said, in effect, "Give us some time to switch over without loss of the market." Granted time, manufacturers set about providing nonpressurized containers for their products and advertising and promoting the desirable features of roll-ons, pump-can devices, and wipe-ons.

There has been so much of this kind of compromise in areas of social concern, from integration to equal employment opportunity, from atmospheric pollution to metropolitan area blight and roadside litter, and even sexuality, that the phrase *an era of tradeoffs* has come into popular use.

## THE UNFORGIVING DECADE

However, there is a tendency today toward emphasizing those issues that have become so emotional, or are so deep-seated, as to evoke almost (or actual) religious fervor in their adherents. These divisive issues seem to tear at the social fabric and raise doubts about the future of the democratic process. Among them are abortion, assisted or legalized suicide, medical triage, sex education in schools, other items of educational curricula, gun control, smoking, gay marriage, and civil rights for animals.

Overzealous "believers" among activists have resorted to violence—the murder of physicians at feminine health clinics—and angry protest against organizations—picketing or boycotting companies that have, or don't have, medical coverage for homosexual "spouses." These zealots can swerve an organization far off course unless public relations practitioners are sufficiently knowledgeable and influential to prevent overreaction. Because a few zealots put you in the headlines is no reason to panic, or to pander to what are often their very undemocratic, minority-opinion demands.

One result of this social warfare is what public relations consultant Ann Barkelew terms "The Unforgiving Decade." She notes that no matter what actions you take or which policies you adopt, *someone* is going to be angry enough to denounce you—loudly and publicly.

Target Corporation discovered this principle when pickets ringed a company department store unexpectedly one day—protesting an activity the company had taken for granted. The "pro-life" picketers were angry that Target contributed (as it had for years) to Planned Parenthood, whom the picketers considered to be promoting abortion. (Planned Parenthood says this is not true; they counsel on abortion as well as all other choices available to pregnant women who seek their advice.)

Because the contributions had continued for years, a way out, thought one company official, seemed to be to discontinue them—with the rationale that under any circumstance contributions should shift among various causes. But when this "solution" was announced, an even *larger* number of pro-choice picketers surrounded the store.

No matter how the issue was to be resolved, the company was going to make enemies and probably lose some customers.

One resolution would be to count heads; which group has the most supporters, so could do the most damage? But what organization wants to be in such a losing situation? An alternative strategy is to work with the "side" that will be favored in order to gain pledges of extra business and support to make up for the lost customers. Neither is ideal, and both keep the organization on the hot seat of being identified with a divisive issue.

## ISSUE ANTICIPATION TEAMS*

Issue anticipation (IA) teams are working well for many organizations that wish to identify issues before they become a problem. In many organizations, setting up IA teams both meets the need *and* deals with the middle management "wall." Teams usually involve managers from all ranks and departments. To keep interest high, teams report every so often to a formal "issues board" composed of senior officers. Some organizations have one team that looks at the realm of issues. Others have several teams concentrating on specific areas of concern. At its simplest, the team answers two questions: (1) What's happening out there and in here? (2) Could it affect us or become an issue for us?

### BENEFITS OF TEAMS

- Serving on a team is an honor, which motivates the members.
- It forces them to read and observe things they previously didn't.
- Members interact with people they might not come in contact with otherwise.
- Consensus and teamwork are essential.
- Supervising managers start to think broadly about the implications of what the organization does and are sensitized to public relationships.
- Helps identify and train the rising stars.

*pr reporter, April 27, 1987.

## ISSUE ANTICIPATION

The way to avoid issues is to see them coming and to find ways to reach accommodation before they become public and "hot" (see box). Some say, indeed, that the real value of public relations is what *doesn't* happen! Jim Grunig's paradigm (see also Chapter 2) is a superb issue anticipation and planning tool:

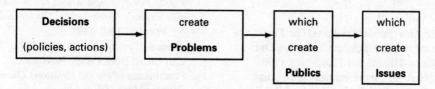

The most noticeable element of this paradigm is that publics are subsidiaries of stakeholder groups—not vice versa.

- Stakeholder groups are people who should care and be involved because the subject could or will affect them.
- Nevertheless they contain large contingents who don't get the message, can't be bothered, just plain don't care, or have such barriers that they won't do anything about the issue. *These segments together can be as high as 90 percent of the stakeholder group.*

The viable term for those who *do get excited* about the issue is therefore publics. He identifies three types who together are often limited to the 10 percent plus who will engage in the issue:

1. **Long haul**—those interested in the full ramifications of the topic
2. **Special interest**—those concerned only about certain elements of the topic
3. **Hot button**—those aroused only by emotionally debated elements

This is a useful way to manage issue anticipation by (1) focusing on which stakeholders are known to be skittish about which potential decisions, then (2) modeling how the three types of publics will fall out and what their response will likely be.

## SCENARIO TECHNIQUE

The way to find foresight is by creating multi-scenario possibilities,[1] advocates Kerry Tucker, CEO of the San Diego pr firm Nuffer, Smith, Tucker. This means "creating stories of equally plausible futures," then planning for them. Highlights of the advantages:

- Putting trends in some kind of logical story form creates a fresh sense of understanding.
- Scenarios are "what if" stories, taking the most pressing forces on your organization and putting them together in a narrative.
- Once you know the alternative futures, you can plan for them; otherwise strategic planning is "scratching at the surface."

As you review the cases in this chapter, observe whether there were early warnings that might have enabled public relations practitioners to help their organizations take action to steer around the public debate that ensued.

## REFERENCES AND ADDITIONAL READINGS

Alinsky, Saul. *Rules for Radicals: A Practical Primer for Realistic Radicals.* Vancouver, WA: Vintage Books, 1989.

Baskin, Otis. *Public Relations: The Profession and the Practice.* 4th ed. Columbus, OH: McGraw-Hill Higher Education, 1996.

Baus, Herbert. "Working with Influential Groups," in *Lesly's Handbook of Public Relations and Communications.* 5th ed. Chicago, IL: NTC Business Books, 1997, Ch. 32: 475–481.

Broide, Mace. "Having a Voice in Politics," in *Lesly's Handbook of Public Relations and Communications.* 5th ed. Chicago, IL: NTC Business Books, 1997. Chapter 7: 103–112.

Buchholz, Rogene. *Business Environment and Public Policy: Implications for Management and Strategy Formulation.* Upper Saddle River, NJ: Prentice Hall, 1989.

Coleman, Cynthia-Lou. "What Policy Makers Can Learn from Public Relations Practitioners." *Public Relations Quarterly* 34 (Winter 1989–90): 26–31.

*Corporate Public Issues and Their Management* offers a variety of information regarding public policy formation and issue management. For more information contact: Issue Action Publications, Inc., 207 Loudoun Street S.E., Leesburg, Virginia 22075, 703/777–8450, www.issuemanagement.org.

---

[1]Kerry Tucker, "Scenario Planning," *Association Management*, April 1999.

Cutlip, Scott, Allen Center, and Glen Broom. *Effective Public Relations,* 8th ed. Upper Saddle River, NJ: Prentice Hall, 1999.

Ewing, Raymond. *Managing the New Bottom Line; Issues Management for Senior Executives.* Homewood, IL: Business One Irwin, 1987.

Foundation for Public Affairs. *Public Interest Profiles 2001–2002.* Washington, DC: Congressional Quarterly, 2000.

Fox, J. F., "Communicating on Public Issues: A Changing Role for the CEO." *Public Relations Quarterly* 27 (Summer 1982).

Hammack, David. *Making the Nonprofit Sector in the United States: A Reader.* Bloomington, IN: Indiana University Press, 1998.

Heath, Robert. *Strategic Issues Management: Organizations and Public Policy Challenges.* Thousand Oaks, CA: Sage Publications, 1997.

Jones, Barrie, and Howard Chase. "Managing Public Policy Issues." *Public Relations Review,* Vol. 5, No. 2 (Summer 1979). A classic.

Kelley, Stanley, Jr. *Professional Public Relations and Public Power.* Baltimore, MD: Johns Hopkins University Press, 1966. Classic study of a perennial question.

Lesly, Philip. "Policy Issues, Crises, and Opportunities" in *Lesly's Handbook of Public Relations and Communications.* 5th ed. Chicago, IL: NTC Business Books, 1998. Chapter 2: 19–37.

Mathews, David. *Politics for the People: Finding a Responsible Public Voice.* 2nd ed. Champaign, IL: University of Illinois Press, 1999.

National Rifle Association. For pamphlets explaining the organization and its objectives and programs, 1600 Rhode Island Avenue, N.W., Washington, DC 20036, www.nra.org.

Newsom, Doug, Judy Van Slyke Turk, and Dean Kruckeberg. *This Is PR: The Realities of Public Relations.* 6th ed. Belmont, CA: Wadsworth Publishing Company, 1996. Chapter 9, "Laws Affecting PR Practice."

Olasky, Marvin, "Engineering Social Change: Triumphs of Abortion Public Relations from the Thirties through the Sixties." *Public Relations Quarterly* 33 (Winter 1988–89): 21.

*pr reporter,* Vol. 37 No. 14 (April 4, 1994). Lead article concerns the value of public relations in grassroots organizing and coalition building.

Public Relations Body of Knowledge. New York: PRSA. See abstracts dealing with "Ethics and Social Responsibility."

Scheel, Randall. *Maxims for the Issues Manager.* Stamford, CT: Issue Action Publications, 1991.

Sopow, Eli. *The Critical Issues Audit.* Leesburg, VA: Issue Action Publications, 1995.

Stoltz, V. "Conflict PR in the Formation of Public Opinion." *Public Relations Quarterly 28* (Spring 1983).

*The Futurist,* six times yearly magazine on significant trends and where those trends are leading, from the World Future Society, 7910 Woodmont Ave, Suite 450, Bethesda, MD 20814, www.wfs.org.

Public service programs are regularly reported in the following periodicals:

*pr reporter,* PR Publishing Co., P.O. Box 600, Exeter, NH 03833 or contact: ssmith@jjwpr.com.

*PR News,* 201 Seven Locks Road 300, Potomac, MD 20854.

*Public Relations Quarterly,* P.O. Box 311, Rhinebeck, NY 12572–0311.

------------------------------C A S E S------------------------------

# Case 8-1  Rights and Choices—for Whom?

*I have met thousands and thousands of pro-choice men and women. I have never met anyone who is pro-abortion. Being pro-choice is not being pro-abortion. Being pro-choice is trusting the individual to make the right decision for herself and her family, and not entrusting that decision to anyone wearing the authority of government in any regard.*

—HILLARY CLINTON

*The greatest destroyer of love and peace is abortion, which is war against the child. The mother doesn't learn to love, but kills to solve her own problems. Any country that accepts abortion is not teaching its people to love, but to use any violence to get what they want.*

—MOTHER TERESA

*The U. S. Supreme Court ruled in* Roe v. Wade *in 1973 that a Texas law criminalizing most abortions violated a woman's constitutional right of privacy, which the court said was implicit in the due-process clause of the 14th Amendment.*

*Jane Roe was an alias used to shield the identity of Norma McCorvey, who sued Dallas County District Attorney Henry Wade.*

*In the 7–2 decision, the court sought to balance a woman's right to privacy with a state's interest in regulating abortion . . .*

—USA TODAY, APRIL 17, 2006, P. 2A

The 1973 Supreme Court case of *Roe v. Wade* brought abortion to the forefront. The landmark case, legalizing abortion in the United States, came under fire in the early 1990s, and in the summer of 1992 the nine Supreme Court justices were faced with a decision that could have severely limited abortion rights or even have overturned *Roe v. Wade* altogether, again making abortion illegal. The justices ruled in favor of *Roe v. Wade,* however, allowing abortion to remain legal in the states.[1]

The beginning of the new millennium seemed to bring with it little hope for any kind of agreement on the abortion issue. New concerns surrounding the abortion debate emerged, and Congress was charged with developing new legislation. As in years past, right-to-life and pro-choice groups increased their efforts to sway public opinion.

Groups on both sides have continued to work different aspects to get the behaviors they prefer from society. The pro-lifers have worked hard to elect officials responsible for appointing Supreme Court justices who might limit or reverse *Roe v. Wade.* They have joined politically with other conservative causes to boost their power and influence on this subject. The pro-choice movement continues to focus on the precedent of the law and the majority opinion (for the moment) that abortion should be legal.

Although likelihood for a resolution of this issue is far from being reached, each side hopes to sway public opinion through the use of classic public relations strategies and tactics. Zealots, however, have

---

[1]*Planned Parenthood v. Casey.*

resorted to both illegal and immoral tactics—and this has influenced the debate as well.

## Where It All Started: Margaret Sanger's Crusade

Abortion as a political issue emerged nearly a century ago, in 1912, when Margaret Sanger launched a personal crusade in the form of two radical articles, titled "What Every Woman Should Know" and "What Every Girl Should Know," with the goal of emancipating women, via contraception, from sexual servitude. Sanger named her proposition "birth control," believing that *every child born should be wanted by parents who are prepared to care for that child.* Otherwise, conception should be prevented.

Her crusade continued with the establishment of the journal *The Woman Rebel*, in which she attacked the Comstock Law. *Her strategy was to test the law by breaking it. The Woman Rebel* was promptly banned from the mails, and Sanger was threatened with a prison term and a $5,000 fine. The magazine became a best seller overnight. This was the first planned event in this debate—breaking the law in order to get attention.[2]

Next Sanger published a pamphlet, *Family Limitation,* which she stored in a variety of cities *for release at a strategically right time.* When she was arraigned for *The Woman Rebel,* she fled to England, wiring her associates to release *Family Limitation* three days after she left.

Sanger returned from Europe to face charges for violating the Comstock Law after visiting the world's first birth control clinic in Amsterdam and conducting birth control research of her own in Europe.

Sanger found public attitude had shifted in her favor. The government was no longer pursuing the Comstock Law. It was then that she established the first birth control clinic in the United States.

Birth control leagues were started in several cities and joined together in what came to be known as the American Birth Control League (later becoming the Planned Parenthood Federation of America). The Clinical Research Bureau opened, as did scores of birth control clinics. Distinguished professionals and citizens alike began enthusiastically supporting the movement. Events from the 1930s to the present have strengthened the movement.

## Strategies and Tactics on Both Sides

Although the two sides have very different views on abortion, they present and communicate in a variety of ways—some that are similar (e.g., publications, rallies, general publicity) and others that are quite different (e.g., focusing on elected officials, controlling or not controlling zealots).

**Pro-life groups** have used techniques such as a special edition of the *National Right-to-Life News* reproducing a series of articles from the *Chicago Sun Times* on "Abortion Profiteers." One of their events has been an annual March for Life in Washington, D.C., that has been duplicated in several major cities. Another event is the annual National Right to Life convention. Other vehicles for pro-life views include counseling hotlines, speakers bureaus, informational videotapes, slide shows, and annual banquets. They also train volunteers, publish pamphlets and brochures,

---

[2]Comstock Law was enacted in 1873 banning the mailing of "obscene" literature. Contraception materials were among the materials deemed obscene.

provide information on the rhythm method of birth control, and organize protests at abortion clinics.

In the 1990s, the radical fringe of the pro-life movement undertook more violent actions. Radical groups bombed and burned abortion clinics. Radical groups such as Operations Rescue orchestrated violent protests outside abortion clinics. A pro-life zealot killed a Florida abortionist on his way into the clinic where he worked.

These extreme acts backfired in swaying public opinion and drowned out the more sensible voices of the pro-life movement for a time.

Pro-lifers currently find themselves "behind" on the issue. They have to create discontent with the status quo among voters, politicians, and Supreme Court justices in order to overturn *Roe v. Wade.* To do so, pro-lifers have continued to engage in shocking tactics, including traveling billboards

---

## RECENT LEGISLATION

Recent abortion laws at the federal level show the breadth of beliefs on this subject:

- **Freedom of Access to Clinic Entrances (FACE).** This federal statute provides criminal and civil sanctions for obstructing or interfering with a woman's access to abortion. (Pro-life oppose, pro-choice support.)

- **Child Custody Protection Act.** Would prohibit transport of minors across state lines in circumvention of laws requiring the involvement of parents in abortion decisions. (Pro-life support, pro-choice oppose.)

- **Informed Choice Act.** Would allow the Secretary of Health and Human Services to make grants to free, community-based pregnancy medical help clinics for the purchase of ultra-sound equipment, which would be used to provide free ultrasound examinations to pregnant women. Each grant recipient must, in return, (1) provide to each woman receiving services a visual image of the fetus from the ultrasound and a general anatomical and physiological description of the characteristics of the fetus and (2) provide information on abortion and alternatives to abortion, such as childbirth and adoption, and information concerning public and private agencies that will assist in those alternatives. (Pro-choice oppose, pro-life support.)

- **Partial-Birth Abortion Ban Act.** A bill designed to prohibit the performance of partial-birth, dilation and extraction, or intact dilation and evacuation late-term abortion procedures. This bill was vetoed. (Pro-life support, Pro-choice oppose.)

- **Abortion Non-Discrimination Act (ANDA).** This act is supposed to help clarify the 1996 Coats-Snowe Amendment, which was enacted to "protect the right of health care providers to decline to participate in the killing of unborn children." The National Right to Life Committee believes that some have read the 1996 law narrowly, protecting only residents and residency programs and only in the training context, and that the ANDA would clarify that the term *health care entity* includes the full range of participants involved in providing health care. (Pro-life support, pro-choice oppose.)

showing the graphic results of an abortion; displaying aborted fetuses; and convening emotional demonstrations adjacent to abortion clinics and Planned Parenthood offices.

**Pro-choice groups** such as Planned Parenthood and NARAL are well organized and have been in existence for decades. The pro-choice movement works from a different strategic perspective. Instead of trying to change a law, they are trying to protect it. Therefore, their strategies and tactics are slightly different.

Pro-choice groups work a great deal in the legal system and with Congress to defend the gains they have won, so they spend a lot of time in the public-policy arena. They defend against any and all attempts to limit access to abortion, whether it comes in the form of a legal challenge to *Roe v. Wade* or in conditions imposed on family planning funds in overseas programs.

With the 2001 election of a Republican Congress and president, they were busy rallying their own troops, primarily through mailings, rallies, and the Internet to voice support and contribute monetarily to their fight for the status quo. With the rising sophistication and influence of the pro-life movement, the pro-choice side has had to fight inroads at the local, state, and national levels simultaneously.

Increasingly, the sides and strategies have become more polarized while becoming more sophisticated. Pro-choice activists, so long as *Roe v. Wade* is in effect, have the advantage of being on the "winning side." With that advantage goes the so-called "moral high ground" of offering a "choice" to those affected by an unwanted pregnancy.

## Where Is the Debate Now?

Despite all the rhetoric and emotion, few minds are changed. It often seems that both sides are "preaching to the choir" in an effort to keep the troops mobilized and motivated. A 2005 Gallup Poll showed that 56 percent of Americans believe abortion should be legal under "certain circumstances," whereas 26 percent believe abortion should be legal under any and all circumstances. Only 16 percent believe it should be illegal in all circumstances.

In 2006, the national newspaper *USA Today* speculated that if *Roe v. Wade* were overturned and dominion over abortion was turned back to the states, 22 state legislatures would likely impose "significant new restrictions" on abortion. Sixteen states would likely maintain the existing status quo, whereas 12 states would be "in the middle."

Interestingly, a national poll taken at the same time showed that 60 percent of Americans oppose state laws to ban all abortions except those necessary to save the life of the mother.

So, the question remains, where do we go from here? Is there a "correct" answer? With all the controversy surrounding the issue, it is likely that there will never be a definitive answer. South Dakota has dropped the first shoe by making all abortions illegal with no exceptions for the mother's health. Whether, or when, the second shoe will drop is anyone's guess. The only thing we know for sure is that both sides will continue to work this issue for time to come. ■

## IMPORTANT EVENTS IN THE ABORTION CONTROVERSY

**1935** Radio censorship of birth control topics was ended by NBC.

**1936** The U.S. Circuit Court of Appeals ruled that physicians could distribute through the mails material "for the purpose of saving life or promoting the well-being of their patients."

**1937** The American Medical Association endorsed birth control.

**1942** The U.S. Public Health Service adopted a policy of giving requests from state health offices for financial support of birth control the same consideration and support given other state medical programs.

**1950** President Eisenhower became honorary chairman of Planned Parenthood and the first of many presidents, including John Kennedy, a Catholic, to endorse the aid program.

**1960** The first contraceptive pill was introduced. One of its three developers is a Catholic, Dr. John Roch, showing how far public and professional attitudes had moved.

**1966** The American Nurses Association recognized family planning education as part of the nurse's professional responsibility.

**1967** Social Security amendments created a family planning project grants program and mandated state welfare departments to service those with extremely low incomes.

**1967** The United Nations Fund for Population Activities was established in response to resolutions in the UN General Assembly and the Economic and Social Council.

**1970** Congress adopted the Family Planning Services and Population Research Act.

**1973** The Supreme Court ruled that abortion is a matter to be decided between a woman and her doctor in *Roe v. Wade*.

**1976** Congress enacted the Hyde Amendment, cutting off federal (Medicaid) funding for abortions for poor women.

**1981** President Reagan opposed abortion and asked that the 1973 ruling be overturned.

**1992** President Bush comes under fire during the election for his endorsement of the "gag rule," which prohibited staff and doctors in clinics receiving public funds from even discussing the abortion option. (Bill Clinton was elected president on a pro-choice platform, among other issues.)

**2005** President Bush appoints two "conservative" justices to the Supreme Court.

**2006** South Dakota governor Mike Rounds signs into law a bill banning abortion in that state.

## QUESTIONS FOR DISCUSSION

1. Breaking the law as a tactic to gain awareness and build public support has had a role in this debate, as well as others (e.g., Boston Tea Party, environmental movement). Should this tactic be part of a public relations strategy? If so, to what extent can it be used and be effective?

2. With *Roe v. Wade* in place, the "behaviors" needed by the pro-choice movement are significantly different from those needed by the pro-life movement. How do you feel the strategic decisions made by each side help or hurt in achieving these behaviors?

3. How might you see a resolution to this issue coming about? What public relations techniques might others, outside the core activists groups, take to help resolve the issue? What other issues now on the national agenda may become insurmountable in their resolution?

# Case 8-2    Take Your Choice—Tobacco or Health

## Introduction

The so-called "tobacco war" is just about over, and the health of Americans is the clear winner. The tobacco industry, buffeted by a relentless barrage of medical and legal setbacks, has abandoned its strategy of denial. In its place, industry leaders such as Philip Morris and R. J. Reynolds are trying to make peace with the American public while fighting over dwindling market share. Overseas markets and diversification into nontobacco ventures seem to be the future for a 400-year-old industry that once claimed some 50 percent of the American public as customers.

## History

Tobacco has been part of the American landscape and economy since there has been an America. Legend has it that when Columbus waded ashore in 1492 he discovered Native Americans smoking tobacco. The explorers took the habit back to Europe, and thus began the long intertwined history of tobacco and the American economy.

Two centuries later, the United States was exporting some 23 million pounds of tobacco to Europe, helping it to finance the Revolutionary War. Among the early tobacco producers were George Washington and Thomas Jefferson, both Virginia farmers when not busy creating and establishing "a new nation, conceived in liberty and dedicated to the proposition that all men are created equal."[1]

Tobacco remained at the forefront of American culture and deeply embedded in the economy until 1964 when the Surgeon General of the United States officially declared for the first time that smoking was hazardous to the health of the smoker. At that time more than half the male population of the United States regularly smoked, as did more than one-third of women. Estimates at the time placed regular and casual smokers at some 51 percent of the adult population.[2]

As of 2006, some 20 percent of Americans smoked, less than half of the number that smoked in 1964.[3] Although this represents approximately 45 million smokers, the number of cigarettes sold hit a 55-year low in 2005, the result of changing mores, tougher laws, and a landmark settlement with the tobacco industry that limits advertising of its products. Most important to the future of the issue, nearly 70 percent of young adults (aged 18–24) had never smoked cigarettes.[4]

Worldwide the picture isn't so clear. More than 1.1 billion people smoke, including some 622 million in Asia, where nearly 55 percent of the population smokes. Not surprisingly, the largest tobacco companies are in China.[5]

## The Situation

When Surgeon General Luther Terry issued his landmark announcement in 1964, he kicked off what would be a public relations

---

[1]Declaration of Independence, 1776.
[2]Smoking Prevalence Among US Adults. CDC, August 6, 2002.
[3]CDC report. http://www.cdc.gov/tobacco (accessed July 23, 2007).
[4]Smoking and Tobacco Use. CDC, November 2006.
[5]"Tobacco in China," *Far East Economic Review,* December 13, 1998.

## TOBACCO TIMELINE

**1492**  Columbus discovers America and Native Americans smoking tobacco.

**1703**  Tobacco exports to Europe exceed 23 million pounds.

**1881**  Cigarette-rolling machine invented, creating the modern tobacco industry.

**1920s**  American women socialized to smoke by public relations icons Edward L. Bernays and Ivy L. Lee.

**1964**  U.S. Surgeon General declares tobacco and cigarettes harmful to public health and linked to various types of cancer.

**1971**  Tobacco ads removed from U.S. television.

**1981**  Secondhand smoke declared to be a carcinogen by the Environmental Protection Agency.

**1984**  Stronger warnings mandated for U.S. tobacco packages by Congress.

**1989–1993**  RJR Nabisco introduces "Joe Camel" ad campaign, which increases youth market share by 50 percent.

**1997**  Liggett Group breaks ranks with the industry, admitting that cigarettes cause cancer, nicotine is addictive, and that the tobacco industry has historically targeted teens.

**1998**  Tobacco industry reaches landmark accord with U.S. attorneys general that requires reparations to 46 states and bans much traditional tobacco advertising.

**2003**  Lowe's (national hardware/building supplies retailer) bans smoking in stores or on premises. Ban applies to employees and customers alike.

**2005**  Weyco, Inc. (Michigan-based health-care administration company) bans its 200 employees from smoking on or off the job. Four employees lose jobs.

**2006**  Scott's (Ohio-based fertilizer company) follows suit, banning smoking by its 5,300 workers on or off the job. Employees are given 10 months to stop smoking or find another job. About one-third of employees are affected.

war of epic proportions. On one side was the tobacco industry with its deep pockets, lobbyists, public relations and advertising experts, and nearly half of the country regularly using its products. On the other side was a growing army of health professionals armed with an increasing array of facts and figures destined to become part of the national agenda. In between were media companies conflicted by the need to discuss vital public issues such as this one and the billions of advertising dollars annually offered up by the tobacco industry.

Although Terry's report was the first shot, it certainly was not fatal to tobacco. The industry fought back with the thinly disguised Tobacco Institute, firing facts about smokers' rights and tobacco's economic impact and denying that tobacco smoke was a major source of pollution. The Tobacco Institute also debated the legitimacy of the health issue and claimed that common courtesy should govern smoking, not state or federal law.

Health advocates, while lacking competitive budgets, were nonetheless active and effective. Study after study increasingly linked smoking to a variety of health woes, including lung cancer, heart disease, emphysema, breast cancer, and high blood pressure. Researchers isolated 69 cancer-causing chemicals in common cigarette smoke, 43 of which remain in secondhand smoke.

## The Facts

Tobacco is the leading cause of preventable death in the United States and probably the world. According to the 11th World Conference on Tobacco, more than 1.1 billion people smoke worldwide, 500 million of whom will die from tobacco-related causes. It is expected that tobacco smoking will soon result in more deaths than those from AIDS, murder, suicide, and auto accidents combined.

In the United States, about 20 percent of all deaths can be attributed to smoking and tobacco products. According to the CDC approximately 12 million Americans currently suffer with a tobacco-related disease, nearly half of whom continue to smoke. Tobacco-related fatalities in the United States number about 440,000 each year, with secondhand smoke estimated to cause some 50,000 deaths annually. "There is no such thing as a safe level of smoking," says Thomas Glynn of the American Cancer Society.

All the while, tobacco remains a legal product. Although the U.S. Department of Agriculture is phasing out tobacco subsidies, the economic impact of tobacco as an industry cannot be denied.

According to an industry publication "Tobacco. . . . Working for America," tobacco is America's seventh-largest cash crop behind wheat, hay, soybeans, corn, cotton and peanuts. On a revenue-per-acre basis, tobacco—at $4,000 yield per acre—is the most valuable of these crops. North Carolina and Kentucky account for two-thirds of U.S. tobacco production.

Tobacco wages contribute some $3.8 billion to the national economy. Seventy percent of finished tobacco products are sold via grocery and convenience stores, adding another $2.7 billion in impact. The entire tobacco process, including direct and indirect measures, contributes nearly $55 billion to the U.S. economy, according to "Tobacco . . . Working for America."

Taxes are a second high-dollar factor in tobacco's economic impact. The latest figures show that state and federal taxes from tobacco sales amount to more than $35 billion, according to the American Economics Group. Of these levies, more than $14 billion was collected by state governments in 2006, "Tobacco . . . Working for America" says.

A look at the industry leader Philip Morris USA (a division of Altria Group, Inc.) gives a clear picture of the economic realities of tobacco. In its annual report for 2005, tobacco sales topped $18 billion and profits from tobacco were more than $4.5 billion—43 percent of Altria's worldwide net profit. Altria is the 17th largest company headquartered in the United States and the ninth most profitable. Altria's other brands include Kraft Foods and Miller Beer.

## The Problem

For those trying to shut down smoking, the problem was twofold. First, most people who smoked were doing so because they enjoyed the smoking act or they were addicted. Second, the tobacco industry presented a well-financed and united front that conceded not one point in the discussion over health issues.

With the surgeon general's 1964 report, most casual smokers quickly dropped the practice, but that still left more than 40 percent of all Americans who regularly smoked. This was the group that became the target of health-care efforts. To win substantive behavioral change, however, is tough.

Smokers have to be convinced that their existing behavior (smoking) is wrong, and that quitting the habit is a suitable substitute. Benefits of not smoking and negative consequences of continuing to smoke must be obvious, and smokers must be able to see a brighter future before they will consider changing their behavior.

Further, communication alone usually isn't sufficient to get the desired behavioral change. Knowledge does not equal behavior, which means steps beyond communication need to be made to facilitate real behavioral change.

Sociologists have identified a three-step pattern leading to changes in societal behavior:

1. **Folkways** are feelings, perceptions, and actions common to a social group that when adopted by a wider audience become
2. **Mores** (MOR-rays), which are folkways that are conducive to the welfare of society and which become patterns that govern societal behavior. Sometimes these mores are codified into
3. **Laws**, either on the local, state, or national level.

It was this pattern that the health-care industry followed to effect a reduction in smoking. Communication was directed toward smokers and nonsmokers alike, pointing out the dangers to everyone—not just smokers. The goal was to make smoking socially unacceptable, creating an environment in which nonsmokers would be justified in protesting the actions of smokers.

Just as effective public relations tactics had made smoking acceptable to the masses in the 1920s, so would good public relations be used to reverse the trend. Shaping perceptions against smoking would be a strategy that was effective and affordable. The "truth" in the form of health-related facts would be the backbone of the campaign. The central message would be that smoking is harmful to your health, but it would be wrapped in a tongue-in-cheek message that smoking isn't "cool" either.

One well-known antismoking poster showed pictures of the posteriors of various animals—row after row of rear ends—concluding with an ashtray full of cigarette butts. The message? "Butts are Ugly." Another ad showed a similar ashtray with the notation, "Kissing a smoker is like licking an ashtray." No subtlety there.

Slowly, the tide of public opinion began to turn. Smoking in public became problematic. In one high-profile situation, television star Larry Hagman was spotted carrying a handheld fan. If someone lit up in his presence, he would activate the fan to blow the smoke back toward the smoker.

Research showing smokers to be at the lower end of various social scales further emphasized the bad choice that smoking presented. "Today . . . smokers are typically the least advantaged, low-income minorities in the nation's cities and low-income whites," says Dr. Cheryl Healton, president and CEO of American Legacy Foundation, a public health foundation devoted to tobacco issues. "Americans below the poverty level are 33 percent more likely to smoke than are those above the poverty line, and people without high school diplomas are also more likely to smoke."[6]

## Tobacco's Side

In 1967, New York Senator Robert Kennedy said when addressing the first World Conference on Smoking and Health, "The cigarette industry is peddling a deadly weapon," advising that it was up to Congress to regulate smoking and tobacco.

---

[6]"Adult Cigarette Smoking in the U.S." CDC report. http://www.cdc.gov/tobacco (accessed February 28, 2007).

The tobacco industry countered with a strategy initially designed to maintain the status quo. Included in the strategy is what the International Development Research Centre (a public corporation created by the Canadian government to monitor and address public issues) calls "The Nine Ds."[7]

**Deny** the health consequences of smoking.
**Deceive** consumers about the true nature of cigarettes through marketing and public relations.
**Damage** the credibility of industry opponents.
**Direct** advertising to women and youth, in addition to men.
**Defeat** attempts to regulate the industry or control smoking.
**Delay** legislation that can't be defeated.
**Destroy** legislation once it passes, either through legal challenges, exploiting loopholes, or simply ignoring the laws.
**Defend** lawsuits against the industry.
**Develop** new markets around the world.

At the forefront of this strategy was the use of front groups, such as the Tobacco Institute, to represent pro-tobacco arguments. While trying to maintain the appearance of grassroots organizations, most were in reality organized and financed to a large degree by pro-tobacco interests.

These groups focused their communication on a few key points:

1. Tobacco smoke is not a major source of air pollution.
2. People are not allergic to tobacco smoke.
3. Nonsmokers in a smoke-filled room don't inhale significant amounts of smoke.
4. Even though a surgeon general's report says that carbon monoxide in a smoke-filled room exceeds permissible levels, such conditions are only rarely found.
5. Antismoking efforts notwithstanding, hard evidence against smoking is not increasing.
6. Thorough review of the world's scientific literature indicates that smoke is not a significant health hazard to the nonsmoker.
7. Common courtesy, rather than laws, should determine nonsmokers rights.
8. Tobacco is a legal product, available to adults who chose to consume it.

## Evidence Mounts and Momentum Shifts

In 1981, the effect of secondhand smoke was magnified by research showing increased risk to nonsmokers exposed to it. The EPA was moved to declare that secondhand smoke causes cancer. Assistant Surgeon General John Duffy said, "There is no such thing as a nonsmoker in America today."

With these declarations, the tobacco lobby saw several key arguments slipping away.

In 1984, Congress passed legislation requiring stronger warnings on cigarette packs. With antismoking groups keeping up the pressure, Americans became more socialized against tobacco. Media events such as the Great American Smoke Out and Kick Butts Day drew continuing attention to the fact that smoking was no longer fashionable. Restraining laws would soon follow.

While this controversy rages on, some of the major tobacco companies have taken steps to protect their shareholders, and perhaps other stakeholders, by diversifying their product mix. As examples, Phillip Morris acquired General Foods, a $5.6 billion transaction. R.J. Reynolds put up $5 billion for

---

[7]http://www.irdc.ca.

## CARTOONS AND CIGARETTES: WHO'S THE AUDIENCE?

The controversy about using cartoon characters to sell a potentially harmful product such as cigarettes became a hotly debated issue in late 1991. The *Journal of the American Medical Association* devoted an issue to studies that researched the impact of smoking and its products on society. Of interest to many antismoking groups was one study that indicated that children as young as 3 or 4 years old could recognize the character Joe Camel, the cartoon logo for Camel cigarettes. In this study of brand recognition, the kids identified Joe Camel more than any other popular logo, such as those for NBC, Apple, and Cheerios.

From this study the researchers concluded that this type of advertising lures children to smoke by utilizing pleasing images to entice them and demanded the immediate discontinuation of the ad campaign. RJR Nabisco, the manufacturer of Camel cigarettes, countered this accusation by stating that brand recognition does not necessarily mean that the children will begin smoking and cited its own research statistics that indicate that the average age of a Camel smoker is 18 to 24. In addition, RJR Nabisco was effective in discrediting the study's main researcher, Dr. Joseph DiFranza. In court, RJR Nabisco produced evidence that indicated that DiFranza had decided he wanted to prove the detrimental effect cigarette advertising has on children *before* he conducted the study.

This controversy has further illuminated the issue of whether allowing cigarette companies to advertise their products is really a freedom of speech issue—or an opportunity to entice children to begin a harmful habit.

---

Nabisco. Then in 1988 RJR Nabisco was taken over for a whopping $25 billion by Kohlberg, Kravis, Roberts Co., corporate buyout specialists, proving, if nothing else, that there was still money to be made one way or another in tobacco.

Incongruously to some analysts of the tobacco industry, the tone of its promotional literature the past few years has been aggressive. However, many times it is seen working behind the scenes in promoting scientific research that casts doubt on the effects of smoking and championing individual rights causes to question the effectiveness of smoking laws. Then, on occasion, public statements by spokespersons have been moderate if not conciliatory. One observer of the industry has suggested that the moderated tone reflects the vulnerability of the industry in the liability suits being brought against it.

On the anti-smoking side, the Coalition on Smoking or Health (an alliance of the American Heart Association, American Lung Association, and the American Cancer Society) has increased its efforts, encouraged, no doubt, when Congress passed a law banning smoking on any domestic commercial airline flights. It didn't hurt matters for them, either, when the EPA issued its warning against secondhand smoke. They have taken this new evidence and used it to emphasize that smoking is not just an event that affects the smoker. Assistant Surgeon General John Duffy has stated that "there is no such thing as a nonsmoker in America today. As long as we have to live and work around smokers, we must accept some of the risks of smoking."[8]

---

[8]The Need for a Safe, Healthy, and Smoke Free Workplace, *World Smoking and Health,* American Cancer Society, Summer 1990, p. 3.

The prime source of programmed anti-smoking activity continues to be the American Cancer Society. It directs the annual Great American Smokeout, a national event in which smokers all quit on the same day (see Problem 8-A). The Society offers a promotion guide for that event. It also has available a news media handbook, *Smoke Signals,* with a variety of ideas and instructions for groups wanting to tell the story in news outlets (see Figure 8-2).

## TOBACCO DEBATE LEGAL HISTORY

In 1992 the Supreme Court ruled for Rose Cipollone's family (Ms. Cipollone died in 1984). (See Box, p. 229.) It has been an uphill battle for the tobacco industry since health issues, legal comments, and public opinion have all turned against the industry. The war is just about over, and the health forces are prevailing. Tobacco companies are left to fight over 22 percent of the American public still smoking while pushing diversification and overseas expansion. The following is a summary of the principal disputes faced by the major tobacco companies in recent years.

In the courts, there have been huge monetary judgments against the major tobacco companies. Additionally, they are facing a lawsuit filed against them in 1999 by the U.S. Department of Justice.

- In June 2001, a Los Angeles jury found the Philip Morris Company liable for the lung cancer killing the plaintiff (*Richard Boeken v. Philip Morris, Inc.*) in the case and ordered the company to pay $3 billion in punitive damages. As in most cases the industry loses, it will be appealed. According to the Tobacco Control Resource Center, Inc. and The Tobacco Products Liability Project of Northeastern University School of Law Web site (www.tobacco.neu.edu), this verdict was the seventh defeat for the tobacco industry over the last 23 jury verdicts on individual claims dating back to February 1999.

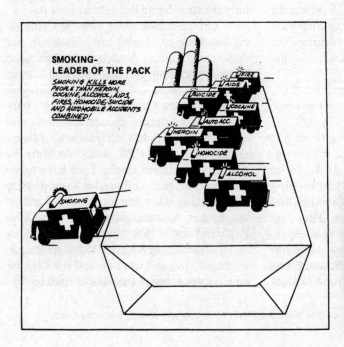

**SMOKING— LEADER OF THE PACK**

SMOKING KILLS MORE PEOPLE THAN HEROIN, COCAINE, ALCOHOL, AIDS, FIRES, HOMICIDE, SUICIDE AND AUTOMOBILE ACCIDENTS COMBINED!

**FIGURE 8-2**
Illustration in *Smoke Signals* booklet dramatizes smoking as the major killer among dreaded causes of death

*Source:* (Courtesy of the American Cancer Society.)

## CIPOLLONE V. LIGGETT

In one of the most famous liability suits, Rose Cipollone brought suit against three different cigarette companies, citing them as liable for her smoking-related illness. This suit paved the way for many more cigarette maker liability lawsuits when her case was brought before the Supreme Court in 1992. Their ruling stated that cigarette manufacturers may be sued if they have allegedly deceived the public about the dangers of smoking. The industry was claiming that the warning labels on the packages were enough to shield them against any personal injury suits.

The ruling, however, does not make it easy for a smoker to prove the liability of the cigarette manufacturer. The plaintiff must "convince juries that smokers were not primarily at fault for starting and continuing their habit because they relied on industry misrepresentations."[1] The depiction of healthy people in cigarette advertisements is not enough to prove that the industry has been deceptive.

[1]James H. Rubin, "Cigarette Makers Can be Sued," *Boston Globe,* June 25, 1992, pp. 1–4.

- In July 2000, in the first class action suit brought on behalf of smokers, the five major cigarette makers—Philip Morris, Lorillard, the Liggett Group, R.J. Reynolds Tobacco Company, and Brown & Williamson Tobacco Corporation—were ordered by a Florida jury to pay a record $145 billion in compensatory and punitive damages. This is known as the *Engle* case.
- The lawsuit filed by the Justice Department in 1999 "alleges that tobacco companies engaged in a 45-year pattern of false and misleading statements about the health effects of their products and tried to cover up information that contradicted their marketing."[9] The suit sought more than $100 billion in damages.

The Master Settlement Agreement (MSA), reached in November 1998 between the tobacco companies and the state attorneys general of 46 states, puts numerous restrictions on the tobacco industry. Some the regulations in the MSA include:

- Restrictions on outdoor advertising, including billboards
- Beginning in May 1999, there are restrictions on the types of cartoons that can be used in the marketing of tobacco; as a result, the use of the Joe Camel image was discontinued
- The tobacco industry is prohibited from directing its advertising at the youth market
- The dissolution of the Tobacco Institute and the Council on Tobacco Research

The apparent cooperation of the tobacco industry in the Master Settlement Agreement was actually part of a resolution to a lawsuit brought by the state of Minnesota against the cigarette producers. However, according to an article in *Advertising Age* magazine, the tobacco industry has already violated the Agreement by continuing to spend millions of dollars targeting the youth market.[10]

In July 1998, President Clinton issued an executive memorandum that the tobacco industry release documents that had historically been concealed from the public. There

[9]*Washington Post,* April 26, 2001, p. A2.
[10]*Advertising Age,* February 5, 2001, p. 18.

are now numerous Web sites providing tobacco industry documents. The increase of governmental intervention in the operations of tobacco companies is likely a result, in part, of the release of information about the industry's practices to the public.

One of the few places the tobacco companies can still present their explanation of the issues—outside of the courtroom—is on their corporate Web sites. Some of the points that are advocated on most of the company Web sites are:

- Smoking is a matter of choice.
- Cigarettes are a legal product.
- Through continued production and research, a safer cigarette may be created.
- Stopping the production of tobacco products would have a great economic impact on the industry's employees and their families and others in tobacco-related jobs.

The corporate Web sites also include tips for quitting smoking, descriptions of their youth smoking prevention programs, and information on their social responsibility programs. With continued governmental regulation, court-ordered damage payments, and general bad press, the tobacco companies are most likely grateful they have this one outlet for presenting their side of the story and their image as responsible corporate citizens.

Although the war is mostly over, skirmishes continue. One major battlefield is the college campus. Recognizing that some 90 percent of all smokers started smoking by their 19th birthday, tobacco companies have developed a sophisticated approach to college markets.

In a 1994 internal memo from Young & Rubicam, the advertising consultant to Philip Morris USA, released as part of the tobacco settlement describes college students as "an ideal market because of the stress they may feel in response to all the changes happening in their lives." Such students, away from the boundaries of home and high school, are likely to take up the habit or smoke more frequently.

To increase this likelihood, tobacco companies have aimed much of their marketing efforts toward the collective campus. The *Chronicle of Higher Education* detailed such efforts in a 2005 article entitled 'The Battle for Hearts and Lungs."[11] One study cited was from the *American Journal of Public Health* (2004), which showed that tobacco companies had sponsored at least one social event at 118 of 119 colleges surveyed. Such promotions seem to be working. A Harvard School of Public Health survey of 10,000 college students showed that nearly 33 percent had smoked during the last month.

Tobacco company representatives deny they are creating new smokers. "We're not soliciting new smokers," one Camel promoter is quoted in the *Chronicle* article. "We're just trying to get existing smokers to switch brands."

Smoking is banned in bars and clubs in California, and all tobacco company promotions—a number that exceeds 35,000 annually—must be registered with the attorney general. This gives California some of the most serious smoking regulations in the nation, yet at UCLA student smokers represent some 25 percent of the campus, compared with 17.8 percent of the general population aged 18 to 29. "We don't think it's a huge priority," says a UCLA health administrator, pointing out that students are far more likely to drop dead from alcohol abuse or eating disorders than lung cancer. "It's not a big health issue we need to address."

Such attitudes are music to the ears of the tobacco industry, which is spending

---

[11]*Chronicle of Higher Education*, March 18, 2005.

more than $15 billion on marketing cigarettes, a figure that has increased more than 120 percent since the industry settlement that included limits on advertising.

Included in those expenditures are some programs designed to win back some of the ground lost over the past decades. Philip Morris is the industry leader—both in sales and in communication designed to put smoking in context. A visit to the Philip Morris web site will find a consistent message that there is no safe cigarette and that the best way to avoid the dangers of smoking is to not smoke. In support of this position, Philip Morris has volunteered to not advertise in college newspapers.

R. J. Reynolds, Philip Morris' closest U.S. competitor, has a partnership with the Miss America pageant under which state title holders will visit schools to promote healthful choices. The Campaign for Tobacco-Free Kids (CBFK), among others, is not impressed.

Citing R. J. Reynolds' connection to Joe Camel, candy-flavored cigarettes, and other programs directed toward youth markets, CBFK president Matthew L. Myers called on Miss America organizers to eschew such a relationship: "Surely State Miss America Pageant winners do not want to represent that kind of irresponsible corporate behavior or take it into America's classrooms."

So, the battles continue. Anecdotal evidence indicates the tobacco industry is falling further behind:

- Leading companies such as Weyco, Inc. and Scott's (fertilizer) have banned employee smoking—at work or at home. Smokers will lose their jobs if they won't or can't quit.
- In Virginia, a smoker-mom was arrested for smoking around her two children.
- The American Legacy Foundation's "Truth" campaign reduced teen smoking by some 300,000 between 2000 and 2002.

- Nearly 700 localities restrict outdoor smoking, including the city of San Francisco.
- The Westin Group of hotels banned smoking from all of its 77 U.S., Canadian and Caribbean hotels. Nearly 75 percent of all hotel rooms in the United States are now smoke free.
- Sales of cigarettes in the United States reached a 55-year low in 2005.

Still, millions continue to smoke, making billions of dollars for domestic tobacco companies. Will it ever end?

A number of potential solutions loom on the horizon. Most likely is what sociologists call an "engineered solution." For tobacco users, this means a scientific approach to smoking. Today, patches and nicotine-laced gums are available to help curb the smoker's craving for nicotine.

Another proposed alternative to smoking would be a ceramic "cigarette" containing a nicotine element that releases small amounts of the narcotic to the "smoker." This addresses the problem of secondhand smoke while allowing the addicted smoker to satisfy the body's demand for nicotine.

Another solution would be for the Federal Drug Administration (FDA) to be given jurisdiction over nicotine. The FDA made an attempt in 2000 to declare nicotine a pharmaceutical, but failed. The Supreme Court, in *FDA v. Brown & Williamson,* ruled that nicotine had no medicinal properties. However, this might change with new studies showing that nicotine has a medicinal effect in the treatment of depression. If the FDA is successful in gaining control of nicotine, then it would be available only by prescription, lessening its availability to new users while permitting those currently using nicotine to get it as a prescribed drug.

Then, and only then, will the tobacco wars be over. ■

## QUESTIONS FOR DISCUSSION

1. On the basis of the information in this case, your personal knowledge, and a professional, objective mind-set, which, if any, of the following conclusions might be supported by maxims of persuasion or by the strategy and tactics used on either side?
   a. The antismoking coalition and the tobacco interests have been equally effective in their communication programs.
   b. One side (which one?) has focused more on influencing behavior than opinion.
   c. The aims and actions of both sides, one side, or neither, reflect a genuine concern for public opinion and behavior over the long haul.
   d. The tobacco interests give more evidence of "issue anticipation" than the antismoking coalition.
   e. The public relations thinking and actions on both sides can be decisive factors in attaining a reasonable solution.
2. On the smoking side of the debate, there is the personal freedom to make choices in life. On the antismoking side, there is personal health. Both are strong appeals to self-interest. Are there other appeals you find significant in the contest?
3. The chapter introduction talks about stakeholders. Among the tobacco interests, stakeholders would be vehicles that carry tobacco advertising. Can you think of any others? Among the no-smoking stakeholders would be insurance companies. Are there others? Does that leave anyone or any group in the middle, the neutral, or "don't care" category?
4. Are there moral and ethical considerations a practitioner should take into account before serving an employer or client involved in the tobacco, liquor, pornography, or handgun industries? Put another way, should the moral and ethical standards of a professional be essentially the same as those of his or her employer or client? Whether yes or no, can you think of a situation in which you would make an exception?
5. The issue of whether a company has the right to mandate what an employee can do in his or her spare time has been hotly debated in recent years. From the employer's viewpoint, what would be acceptable to make restrictions on and why? From the employee's viewpoint?

# Case 8-3   Guns—For Whom? For What?

An emotionally charged controversy has long swirled around the availability, ownership, and use of rifles and handguns. On one side are those who are shocked by crime rates and feel that violent behavior is encouraged by gun ownership. On the opposing side are the constitutional rights to keep arms and to be secure in one's home. There are legal provisions for game hunting and target shooting as sport, recreation, and employment. Somewhere in between are the wildlife conservationists, the millions who must walk dark streets at night, and the millions who, by nature, abhor violence and killing in any form.

## Fact Finding

The Second Amendment to the Constitution of the United States (Article 2 of the Bill of Rights) stipulates "a well-regulated militia, being necessary to the security of a free State, the right of the people to keep and bear arms shall not be infringed." The interpretation and the ongoing applicability of this amendment constitute the basis for the controversy involving the personal and private ownership of guns.

Key words in the constitutional amendment appear to be *militia* and *keep and bear arms*. One dictionary defines *militia* as "all able-bodied male citizens from eighteen to forty-five, not members of the regular military forces, and legally subject to call for military duty." That is clear enough as applied to Colonial times. But what is a "militia" in modern times when the United States has a trained standing army, large Reserve and National Guard units, a Pentagon brain center, and a worldwide intelligence network, all of which are backed by an enormous nuclear capability that could be unleashed by a word of command and the pressing of a few buttons?

As for the right to bear arms, did our nation's founders intend that one needed to be a *member* of the "militia," or might he be *any able-bodied man or woman*? And do "arms" apply only to flintlock weapons of 1776, or should they include the automatic pistols, AK-47s, and other weapons of today? Such questions of definition make up only one small part of a long and many-sided debate.

Meantime, since those pioneer days, the conversion of gun usage to criminal ends has unfortunately attained disturbing proportions. According to the Brady Campaign to Prevent Gun Violence Web site, in 2001 firearms were used to murder six people in New Zealand, 56 in Japan, 96 in Great Britain, 168 in Canada, and 331 in Germany. In comparison, firearms were used to murder 11,348 in the United States. The good news is that these statistics are declining in the United States. According to the FBI Uniform Crime Reports for 1999, there were 8,259 murders using firearms—65 percent of the total murders committed that year (12,658). Of the total, about 50 percent involved the use of a handgun, four percent a shotgun, and three percent a rifle. Firearm injuries are now the second leading cause of injury or death nationwide, surpassed only by those involving motor vehicles, according to the Centers for Disease Control and Prevention.

## The Legal Controls

The old cliché "There ought to be a law against it," seems appropriate. There have been four significant federal laws. The first one, the National Firearms Act of 1934, aimed at control of special weapons. This statute covers such firearms as sawed-off shotguns, but does not involve the pistols, revolvers, regular shotguns, and rifles commonly displayed in gun shops.

The second federal statute—The Federal Firearms Act—came four years later, in 1938. It prohibited the interstate shipment of all firearms to or by convicted felons, persons under criminal indictment, and fugitives from justice. In addition, it required manufacturers, dealers, and importers doing firearms business across state lines to have a federally issued license.

Twenty-five years later, in 1963, just a few months before President John F. Kennedy was assassinated, a third federal statute was introduced in the Senate (S.B. 1975). It was known as the Gun Control Act. Its purposes were to ban mail order and interstate shipment of firearms to individuals, to stop over-the-counter sales of guns to minors, to prohibit possession of guns by convicted criminals, and to bar the importation of concealable foreign handguns. This act, with some modifications from the form in which it was initially offered, was passed in 1968.

Then, after years of often acrimonious debate, the Brady Bill was enacted in 1993. The Brady Handgun Violence Prevention Act established a national system of background checks and waiting periods for people buying handguns from federally licensed firearms dealers. The Act is named after James Brady, a former press secretary who was wounded in the 1981 assassination attempt on President Ronald Reagan. The Supreme Court ruled in 1997 that it was unconstitutional for the federal government to require states to perform background checks as specified by the Brady Bill.

In 1998, Congress replaced the five-day-waiting-period clause in the Brady Bill with a "national instant felon ID system" that mandates gun dealers to perform background checks on all gun purchases. The FBI approves most gun purchases (72 percent) within 30 seconds after buyer information has been entered into the National Instant Criminal Background Check System (NCIS), a computer system designed to provide presale background screening for all types of firearms bought from federal firearms licensees. The remaining 28 percent of background checks have delayed responses. From a sample of delayed responses handled by an ad hoc selection of examiners, the FBI concluded that most of these responses (80 percent) were resolved within two hours or less and that the rest (20 percent) required several hours or days to resolve. In 2003, 126,000 permits (1.6%) were denied.

Local governments, meanwhile, have been free to establish certain controls of their own. All of the states and hundreds of cities and townships have done so. Localized restrictions are noted in a publication from the Bureau of Alcohol, Tobacco, and Firearms.[1]

This whole matter is complex and emotional. There are strong personal convictions and frequent flare-ups of public controversy. Hunters, hobbyists, competitive range shooters, law enforcement personnel, wildlife conservationists, gun and ammunition makers, and frightened nightshift workers, among others, hold strong convictions. The victims of armed robbery, rape at gunpoint, kidnapping, and hijacking, and the families and friends of those killed or maimed by gunshot, harbor deep emotional feelings. At times, a whole nation has been shocked with guilt.

---

[1] The particulars are available in *State Laws and Published Ordinances: Firearms,* from the Department of the Treasury Bureau of Alcohol. Tobacco and Firearms. Superintendent of Documents. N. Capitol and H Streets. Washington. D.C. 20401; or on the Web at www.atf.treas.gov/fieearms/statelaws/.

Numerous school shootings—from Virginia Tech to Bethel, Alaska, from Conyers, Georgia, to Johnston, Rhode Island to Jacksboro, Tennessee—have brought national focus on the horrors wrought by guns and emotional outcries for more gun control, longer waiting periods, mandated gun locks, stricter licensing, and restricted sales. On the flip side, NRA advocates point their fingers at people, not guns, and ask "how do you legislate sanity?" In the court of public opinion, both sides are strong participants.

## Representing Gun Owners

The National Rifle Association (NRA), founded in 1871, boasts more than 4.3 million members. It marshals and sustains resistance to restrictive firearms measures that its members feel might infringe on the Second Amendment. At the same time, it supports mandatory sentences for the misuse of a firearm in the commission of a crime (see Figure 8-3).

The objectives of the NRA extend to the use of firearms for pleasure and for protection by law-abiding citizens. The NRA describes itself as an independent, nonprofit organization. In its literature, the NRA asserts that law-abiding Americans are constitutionally entitled to the ownership and legal use of firearms. Some programs of the NRA, as it has described them, include:

- Guardianship of the Second Amendment right. Through its Institute for Legislative Action and Political Victory Fund, the NRA continually monitors, tracks, and systematically combats all threats to the right to keep and bear arms at the federal, state, and local level, and supports lawmakers who uphold that constitutional duty. For more information, visit www.NRA.org.
- Sponsorship of various shooting clubs and marksmanship programs. Initiation of civilian marksmanship programs more than 100 years ago and youth training more than 70 years ago.
- Participation on a national board to promote rifle practice and to operate national rifle and pistol matches.
- Assignment by the U.S. Olympic Committee as the national governing body for competitive shooting in the United States and membership in the International Shooting Union.
- Creation of a code of ethics for hunters and the nationwide "Sighting-In Day."
- Donation source for various trophy awards.
- Origination of safety training for hunters and safety courses for firearms in the home.
- Functioning as a certifying agency for instructors, counselors, and referees.
- Total financial support for all expenses of U.S. shooting teams in international competition.

A visit to the NRA web site gives a quick look at the many activities and member benefits it provides. A "featured story" leads the site, followed by other "top stories." "NRA in the Media" gives visitors a glimpse of news concerning the NRA, as does "NRA News and Information." Following these entries are 16 separate links to everything from "legislation and politics" to shooting range locations and services. Cover shots of six publications conclude the splash page.

### How the NRA Is Financed

The NRA has three affiliated organizations that qualify as 501(c)(3) tax-exempt, nonprofit charitable organizations, for which donations are tax deductible for Federal income tax purposes. These are (1) The NRA Special Contribution Fund (Whittington Center), (2) the Firearms Civil Rights Legal Defense Fund, and (3) The NRA Foundation. Through membership dues, contributions, and the sale of items related

**FIGURE 8-3    NRA poster urging greater jail sentences for crimes**

*Source:* (Courtesy of the National Rifle Association.)

to membership or gun ownership, the NRA has an annual budget of about $220 million.

The NRA publishes *American Rifleman, American Hunter,* and *America's First* *Freedom* magazines for members. *Shooting Sports USA* is available to members and nonmembers by subscription only. Advertising in these publications is another source of income. The NRA also has a publication called *InSights* for its junior members, publishes range plans and instructions, handbooks, instruction manuals, and a wide variety of pamphlets (see Figure 8-4).

Ancillary sources of revenue include the sale of jewelry, books, brochures, clothing, collector coins, competition aids, decals, pins, patches, glassware, handbooks, hats, videos, targets, charts, and many other items.

## An Active Constituency

Despite a strong public support among Americans for federal gun legislation, the NRA claimed, as far back as the 1960s, the ability to produce "within seventy-two hours more than half a million letters, postcards and telegrams to members of Congress on any gun bill issue."[2] Its target constituency includes owners of some 192 million firearms, comprising 39 percent of American households; veterans of all wars; licensed hunters; gun club members; gun collectors; gun dealers; and manufacturers of equipment for hunting and target shooting.

## The NRA Strategy and Tactics at Points of Controversy

When shocking incidents such as assassinations, school shootings, and gang-related violence seize the front page, public opinion swings suddenly and widely. The public often sympathizes with the families and friends of the victims, deploring the senselessness of violence and demanding the apprehension of the perpetrator, swift and stern justice, and stricter controls of firearm ownership. Concerned citizens write letters to editors. Law enforcement officials speak up for gun registration, regulation, and other controls.

- In the immediate aftermath of tragic episodes and public outrage, the NRA has not often taken a stance of overt rebuttal. Its strategy seems to be to lie low, knowing that the pendulum of opinion will in time return to positions held before the shocking event.

In its dealings at the political or legislative level, however, the NRA has not wavered or gone silent. Its lobbying strategy for many years has emphasized that "Guns don't kill people: people kill people," implying that people rather than guns require more control—sterner penalties for criminal use of a gun are what is really needed. Its lobbying tactics, with an amazing track record of successful opposition to restrictive legislation, have been assertive, not defensive. Its opposition to the Brady Bill, first proposed in 1985, helped to delay the passage of this bill for seven years.

In its public information and education, the NRA has emphasized these points:

1. Firearms legislation would disarm the law-abiding citizen without affecting the criminal, who would ignore the legislation.
2. If firearms were not available, some other weapon would be used by the criminal.
3. Most weapons found in criminal hands have been stolen.
4. Registration of arms might leave law-abiding citizens at the mercy of criminals, of a subversive power if it infiltrated, or of the nation's enemies if they occupied the country.

The NRA is active whenever the rights of gun owners are in question. For example, in the wake of Hurricane Katrina's devastation, police were quick to confiscate guns in the area of destruction. The NRA's 2006

---

[2]Richard Harris, "Annals of Legislation: If You Love Your Guns," *New Yorker,* April 20, 1968.

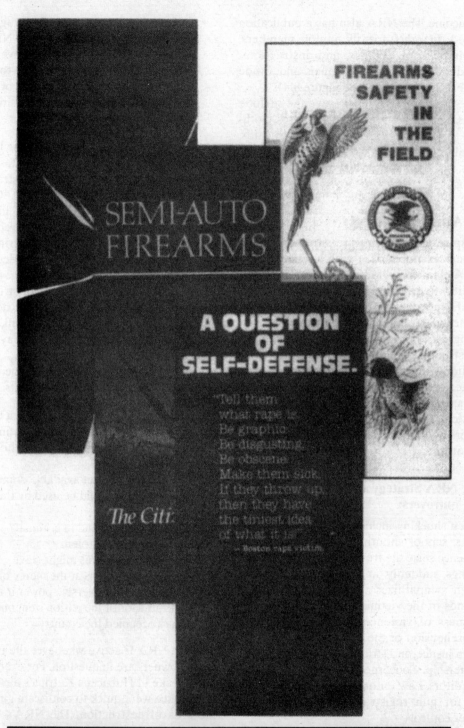

FIGURE 8-4   **Example of the many brochures and manuals available from the NRA**

*Source:* (Courtesy of National Rife Association.)

agenda was topped by efforts to prevent this from happening in the future. The goal: a federal law making it a felony for local officials to confiscate legal weapons.

## The Role of Public Relations

Within the structure of NRA, its Institute for Legislative Action includes governmental affairs, field services, information services, member services, and fiscal services. This is the organization's area of expertise. Since 1997, NRA has been steadily ascending *Fortune* magazine's "Power 25"—the magazine's listing of the most influential lobbying groups in America. In 1997, NRA ranked sixth. In 1998, it moved to fourth. In 1999, it made second place. *Fortune* did not do the rankings in 2000. In 2001, NRA reached the number one spot, displacing AARP, which held the spot for years.[3] Although *Fortune* no longer rates lobbying firms, the NRA retired on top.

Since 1981, public relations and advertising have been handled by the Mercury Group, the Washington affiliate of advertising giant Ackerman-McQueen. Ginny Simone, an ex-local newscaster, is a public face for the NRA. Visit the "live news" section of the NRA's Web site and you'll see her presenting "news" gun lovers can use. Until 2003, actor Charlton Heston was president of NRA, until the spread of Alzheimer's disease caused him to step down. The office is now held by Sandra Froman.

## On the Other Side of the Issue

The persuasive power of the NRA has given the impression in the past that those on the other side, the gun control advocates, are invisible and silent, perhaps overwhelmed or intimidated. To many neutrals or fence sitters, it might seem that the success of the NRA reflects popular public sentiment. Neither impression is complete or valid.

Polls of the general public have shown that a majority of people of all ages, both men and women, in all geographic regions of the United States, favor federal legislation for control of guns, and particularly handguns—the "Saturday night specials"—called junk guns because they are small, cheap, and flimsily made.

Gun control advocates have made these points:

1. There are as many firearms in the United States as there are people.
2. In most states, no license is required to purchase a handgun.
3. The United States is the only civilized nation in the world that does not regulate the ownership of firearms.
4. In 2002, 30,242 people in the United States died from firearm-related incidents. Of these, 39 percent (11,829) were murders; 57 percent (17,108) were suicides, and three percent were accidents (762). In 2003, there were 163 "justifiable homicides" in the United States.
5. Guns should be treated like cars—they should be registered, and the people who use them should be licensed.

Statistical information backing up the gun control advocates is impressive. The U.S. General Accounting Office (GAO), in a survey of crime for one full year, found that 63.8 percent of all murders, 24.6 percent of all aggravated assaults, and 42.7 percent of all robberies were committed by persons using guns. The GAO asked Congress to consider specifically the denial of a gun to a person with a criminal record and the regulation of transfers of guns from one person to another.

In the past, attempts at federal legislation have failed repeatedly. Out of frustration, many states and communities have exercised

---

[3]"The NRA Goes Global" by Jason Vest in *Salon Politics 2000*, April 3, 2000.

local options. California, as one example among hundreds, enacted a "use a gun, go to jail" mandatory prison sentence for crimes involving use of a gun—as well as mandating a 15-day waiting period to purchase a handgun. The city of Oakland, California, has passed a local ban on junk guns, and Illinois has passed a state ban on junk guns. In 1989, a law banning semiautomatic assault weapons was passed by the California legislature. And in the wake of brutal shooting sprees, many state legislatures have banned the use of semiautomatic guns.

Not all local efforts at control gained popular support. In Massachusetts, voters had the opportunity of deciding whether to restrict handguns. On one side were police officials and citizens. On the other were state and national organizations and the arms industry, including a Massachusetts manufacturer of handguns. People versus Handguns got 31 percent of the vote. They had to settle for raising the level of public consciousness.

### There Are Grassroots Citizens' Groups

In recent years, the most vocal national citizens' lobby has been Handgun Control Inc. James and Sarah Brady joined this group, as well as its sister organization, The Center to Prevent Handgun Violence (CPHV), after the attack on President Ronald Reagan where James Brady was wounded. Sarah Brady became the chair of CPHV in 1991. In 2001, Handgun Control was renamed the Brady Campaign To Prevent Gun Violence and CPHV became the Brady Center to Prevent Handgun Violence. Later that same year, these sister organizations merged with the Million Mom March—another gun control group with 230 chapters across the country. The three combined are the largest national, nonpartisan, grassroots organization leading the fight to prevent gun violence.

"This alliance sends a clear message that the gun control movement is uniting and targeted. For many years, we have been successful in passing effective legislation, while increasing public awareness of the scourge of gun violence. Today's announcement is an exciting next step in further raising an army of supporters that will enable us to continue to effect change in Congress and in state Legislatures," reads the Brady Campaign's announcement of the merger.

This merged organization seeks to attract enough contributing members to face off with the NRA in lobbying Congress for legislation, to alert its constituents to those candidates up for election who favor gun controls, to report the voting records of congresswomen and men on gun issues and the amount of financial support each gets from the NRA, and otherwise to provide a continuous rallying point.

### Bringing Things Up-to-Date

In legislative confrontations, the NRA is a single-issue organization. Its strategy is to take an inflexible posture. Officials are convinced that to make one concession would establish a precedent and invite a nibbling away at the Second Amendment right. One advertising approach was quite dramatic (see Figure 8-5).

However, this ironclad stance received many blows in the 1990s because of the turning tide of public opinion and the lobbying efforts of the Brady Campaign and other gun control advocates, including police organizations. Specifically:

- *1994:* President Clinton signed into law the Violent Crime and Control Act, which includes the first-ever federal Assault Weapons Ban, banning the future manufacture and importation of military-style assault weapons.
- *1995:* In the wake of the Oklahoma City bombing, the NRA faced intense public scrutiny and widespread criticism for its views. NRA membership dropped and President George Bush resigned his life membership after it was revealed that

the NRA called Bureau of Alcohol, Tobacco and Firearms agents "jack-booted thugs" in a fund-raising letter.

- *1996:* Congress passed legislation to prohibit anyone convicted of a misdemeanor domestic violence offense from buying or owning a gun.

- *1997:* Supreme Court struck down the background check requirement of the Brady Law. Still the waiting period and other provisions of Brady survived an NRA-financed challenge. Law enforcement continued to conduct background checks

**FIGURE 8-5   Bold NRA ads make the point that crime is rampant**

*Source:* (Courtesy of the National Rifle Association.)

voluntarily until the National Instant Check System went into effect in 1998.

- *1998:* New Orleans became the first public entity to sue the gun industry.
- *1999:* In the wake of Columbine High School shooting, the U.S. Senate passed legislation to close the gun show loophole, which allows unregulated private sales. Similar legislation in the House was defeated and the Senate bill stalled in conference committee.
- *1999: Merrill v. Navegar* achieved the first appeals court ruling that a gun maker can be held liable for negligence leading to the criminal use of a gun.
- *2000:* District of Columbia became the 30th jurisdiction to sue the gun industry.
- *2000:* Smith & Wesson became the first gun manufacturer to settle with cities and counties suing the gun industry, agreeing to make sweeping changes to its manufacturing and distribution practices.
- *2000:* After two years of court battles, the Attorney General of Massachusetts became the first in the nation to use consumer protection powers to regulate guns.
- *2002:* The United States Supreme Court refused to interpret the Second Amendment phrase "right to bear arms," thereby leaving unanswered the question of a modern-day militia.
- *2005:* Congress passes the Protection of Lawful Commerce in Arms Act, which protects gun manufacturers from civil law suits related to "criminal or unlawful misuse of a firearm."

As a societal issue and as a legislative issue, gun control is a subject that is not going to go away. An online search of "gun-control legislation" yields 723,656 mentions. During the final years the George W. Bush administration, two conservative judges were added to the Supreme Court, to the complete delight of the NRA. Among the NRA's top legislative goals was a law to permit employees to bring guns to work so long as they were left in personal vehicles. This proposal was met with round opposition.

Meanwhile, the gun-control lobby is gaining strength and some focus. In a 2000 Gallup Poll, 76 percent of Americans favored the registration of handguns and 69 percent favored federal licensing of gun owners. However, no major gun control legislation has been passed since the Brady Bill in 1994. Many of its provisions expired in 2004. Further, major bills favorable to the gun industry and its lobby have been passed.

President Bill Clinton said after the 2000 elections that the NRA had likely defeated Al Gore in key states such as Tennessee (Gore's home state) and Arkansas (Clinton's home state). Gore also lost West Virginia, a state that hadn't voted Republican in years. Clearly, the NRA isn't losing traction. Since the election of George W. Bush in 2000, the NRA has been, for all intents and purposed, silent to the general public. There has been no need to be visible to the opposition while its supporters are in control. ■

## QUESTIONS FOR DISCUSSION

1. The strategy of the NRA has been to oppose any legal measures that might tighten controls. The grounds are that any of these would be a foot in the door leading to demands for more such laws. As an objective communications professional, how do you feel about this "no exceptions," "no compromise," "not one inch" attitude? Has your attitude changed at all by your studies of the ultimate purpose of public relations? If so, how and why?

2. For those who hold to a hard line on the gun issue (on either side) and those who hold to a hard line on abortion (either way), what similarities and differences do you find in the basis of their convictions? In their strategies and tactics?

3. Using the definitions of a public issue and a crisis given in the introduction to this chapter, which of the following would you consider issues, which crises, and which are neither?
   a. Abortion rights
   b. Gun control
   c. Integrity in public office
   d. Insurance rates
   e. Crime rates
   f. Drug usage

4. Can you think of a strategy that the NRA could take in order to influence the public along its line of thinking? What strategies are they using that soften their position? That strengthen it?

5. Was this case presented in a biased manner? Give evidence for your position. This type of analysis is a regular task of public relations practitioners preparing plans and strategies.

6. How can a group with only 10 to 15 percent of the public supporting its views—which has historically been the case with the NRA—be so powerful? Why would officeholders listen to its views? What strategies do you feel enable such a minority view to prevail for so long? What must the Brady Campaign and others opposed to unregulated gun ownership do to successfully make their case?

# Case 8-4 United Way and the Boy Scouts of America: A Question of Funding

Neither the United Way nor the Boy Scouts of America wanted the social and political standoff that materialized after numerous local United Way chapters instituted and enforced a "nondiscrimination" policy that excluded from United Way funding any organization that excluded anyone because of sexual orientation, including the Boys Scouts of America. This case examines the fallout from the dilemma and how both organizations met the inherent public relations challenges.

In June 2000, the U.S. Supreme Court ruled that the Boy Scouts of America (BSA), as a private organization, has the right to establish its own membership and leadership standards and that this right is protected under the Constitution's First Amendment right of expressive association. This protection allows the BSA to exclude homosexuals, whom the BSA believes are not appropriate role models, from serving as Boy Scout troop leaders. Although the BSA has adopted a policy of "don't ask don't tell," some troop leaders whose sexual orientation has become known are now being terminated from their leadership responsibilities.[1]

The laws of the land, it seems, were in conflict, and so were the Boy Scouts and the United Way.

United Way of America (UW) is a national service organization that provides training, resources, and technical assistance to 1,350 member (local) United Ways, down from more than 1,400 in 2000. Together they raised $3.8 billion in their latest campaigns, supporting over 45,000 agencies in delivering programs and services for millions of people from all walks of life. Of this, some $61 million (2005) helped fund 305 Local Councils of the Boy Scouts of America, comprising 9.2 percent of the BSA's $662 million budget.

The Boy Scouts of America, founded in 1910, currently comprises more than 2.9 million scouts, 1.6 million young adults in a program called "Learning for Life," and 1.2 million adult volunteers serving through the 305 Local Councils and some 122,000 packs and troops. Membership has been falling, across the board, a condition veteran scouting officials say is more related to America's busy family agenda than any knock on scouting. "We have conducted focus groups," says Gregg Shields, spokesperson for BSA, "and parents tell us they are 'just too busy' to participate. Americans are just not joining organizations the way they used to."

United Way organizations have a long history of funding Boy Scouts Councils across the country. However, because each of the 1,350 United Way agencies is autonomous, local offices can individually decide how they will handle the funding of regional Boy Scout Councils with regards to the recent Supreme Court ruling. A variety of methods have been developed by the independent United Way chapters, which include:

- Funding only those organizations that are willing to sign a member agency agreement that contains a nondiscrimination clause.

---

[1] *Boy Scouts of America v. Dale.*

- Giving donors the opportunity to designate which organizations will receive their contribution, including earmarking donations for the BSA.
- Abiding by the BSA membership policies and continuing funding.

Because each United Way chapter is unique, an individual office might use one of these methods, a combination of them, or create its own policy.

Numerous local United Way offices chose to withdraw their funding of the BSA, and *USA Today* reported "In September 2000 alone, 'the Scouts lost nearly $530,000 in public money and charitable aid as one local government after another voted to end relations with the group because it excludes gay people.' "[2]

BSA representatives are quick to point out that funds from United Way have been declining for more than 20 years. "As a percent of overall funding for BSA, money from the various United Way chapters has been declining for the last 20 years or so," says Shields. "However, more than 90 percent of these United Way chapters are still funding Boy Scout Councils in their communities."

Unfortunately for the BSA, that money now has to be made up via other fundraising activities or compensated for in loss of services. Neither is a desirable option. In 2006, BSA president Rick Cronk told *USA Today* that his goal for the organization was to double the size of the population served, not cut back in any way.[3]

Specifically, BSA is looking to nontraditional audiences—urban, ethnic, and underrepresented in scouting. Three Cub Scout manuals are currently printed in Spanish, Shields says, and other materials are offered in nearly 15 languages besides English. One program, aimed specifically at Hispanic youth, is called "Soccer in Scouting," playing on the popularity of the sport for Hispanic kids. In African-American communities, BSA is sponsoring college-aged leaders to organize and promote scouting among populations currently underrepresented.

Such activities seem to be working. Shields says research shows external audiences have "overwhelmingly" positive perceptions of scouting—"similar to the Girl Scouts." Meanwhile, internal behavior, as measured by participation and activities, is on an upward trend. Eagle Scout awards during 2005–2006 were at an all-time high, while everything from merit badges earned to days in camp show positive trends, even in the face of declining numbers.

Unfortunately for the United Way, no matter which policy a local chapter uses in connection with the BSA, it is sure to offend people on one side of the issue or the other, which can result in a substantial drop in funding. If donations are withheld because of a chapter's funding policies, the loss of donations also affects all the other programs that a chapter supports in its community. Both the United Way and BSA appear to be faced with a no-win situation on this issue.

In 1992, then United Way President William J. Aramony was accused of misusing funds, and was fired. The United Way of America took a nationwide and very proactive approach in responding to the news of its president's illegal dealings. The actions taken were aimed at regaining credibility with both the public and the local chapters. Some local chapters, however, used this situation to distance themselves from the national United Way by emphasizing the distinction between the national office and the autonomous local chapters.

In the case of the BSA and the Supreme Court ruling of June 2000, the national United

---

[2]Laura Parker, *USA Today*, October 10, 2000, p. 1-A.
[3]*USA Today*, May 23, 2006.

Way office has employed the "distance" strategy used by the local offices previously. Because the United Way of America does not dictate policy or funding decisions to the local offices, and the issue of funding the BSA rests solely with the local chapters, this was an opportunity for the national office to recuse itself from the controversy. *(Editor's note: Spokespersons for the national United Way declined any opportunity to contribute to this case presentation.)*

When the issue first arose, the United Way of America Web site (national.united-way.org) had a section entitled *United Way Funding Boy Scouts* in which it emphasized in a variety of ways that the national office does not dictate policy to the local chapters and that each local chapter is a separately incorporated, independent organization that sets its own funding policies. At the time (2000), about 30 local United Way chapters decided to implement the nondiscrimination policy, according to Brian Quail, then-executive director of the Heart of Florida United Way in Orlando, Florida, itself one of the 30. Later that number would grow to more than 50. However, in 2005–2006, at least two high-profile chapters–in Atlanta, Georgia, and Fox River, Wisconsin—decided to reinstate funding to BSA.

That the United Way of America does not take a firm stand on such issues seems to be a plus, because any stand could potentially jeopardize future donations for an array of local organizations. The uncommitted stance taken by the national office may help to retain the public's trust and therefore also protect the interest of the local offices. In addition, the United Way has no problem funding BSA with contributions specifically earmarked for the organization.

## The Orlando Situation

The standoff was particularly heated in Central Florida where the Heart of Florida United Way (HOFUW) funds 180 programs and 74 organizations with more than $20 million collected (2000) through some 750 contributing businesses.

Among the largest contributors are Orlando's large theme parks and the tourism industry—the backbone of the Central Florida economy. Other major players are regional banks, the service industry, and the *Orlando Sentinel*, which is owned by Tribune Media Services. Many of these companies have "strong diversity policies," according to Quail, and an initial contact by one large organization started Heart of Florida United Way on the road to its nondiscrimination policy. At the time, the agency was funding programs with 75 organizations, and 74 of them quickly signed the policy agreement. The lone holdout was the Central Florida Council BSA, some of whose programs have been funded by Heart of Florida United Way.

"We are not being politically correct or setting a moral standard," Quail said. "What we said is, we won't dictate who (recipients of funding) hire. But, all must be served. The Boy Scouts will take the opportunity to dismiss a scout if he is a homosexual."

To Tico Perez, then-head of the Central Florida Council BSA, the issue is not one of strictly sexual orientation. "Our bylaws say we can't accept atheists," he says. "We think that you have to have a God."

Although a reluctant participant in the turmoil between BSA and United Way, Perez likes his position. "This is Central Florida," he explains, "When the *Orlando Sentinel* did a poll on this, it was 92–8 (percent) in favor of our position."

The Central Florida Council comprises seven counties around Orlando, with 52,000 Boy Scouts active in 2001. In addition to paid administration, the CFC/BSA enjoys the support of some 11,000 volunteer (adult) leaders. Among its signature programs are "scouting scholarships," which bring many urban boys into scouting for the first time. Another high-profile program is the annual food collection in which Boy Scouts distribute bags in which residents place canned goods for donation. The Scouts pick up the bags and deliver the food to local food banks that distribute it to needy families at Thanksgiving. "We just want to be partners with the community," Perez says.

When the line was drawn in the sand early in 2001, the situation immediately became tense. The chairman of the HOF United Way resigned, citing a conflict of interest because of his homosexual son. Radio talk show hosts fanned the flames daily. Quail received death threats against him and his family. Feelings were running high, and both sides looked for a possible resolution.

"Our board was just trying to be fair," Quail explained, "to meet community needs and to serve all people. I am proud of our board. These people tackled a tough issue and provided leadership," citing a new diversity policy at the *Orlando Sentinel* that "goes farther than ours."

Quail equated the new policy to the early days of the civil rights movement. It, too, was unpopular with several audiences, but now it is not only the law of the land, but accepted widely as the right thing to do. "Sexual orientation is not a protected class under federal law (and most state law)," he points out, "but as a private, non-profit organization, we have to look at our mission. We have to be open to all."

The impasse finally led to the Central Florida Council being designated a "contract agency" of the United Way, which meant that only gifts specially earmarked to the Boy Scouts by the donor would fund that organization. Perez said that his funding improved by some 10 percent in 2001, as compared to its traditional $300,000 request.

## Public Relations Implications

Although the problem can be addressed in the near term via one of the options described earlier, there are long-term consequences that have to be considered. Public relations must take the long-term perspective, looking at the big picture before making plans, offering advice, or deciding on a course of action.

What are the social trends? What does an environmental scan show? Perez is quick to point out that the vast majority of local United Way chapters have decided not to implement a nondiscrimination policy that includes sexual orientation. Quail, however, draws the comparison with the civil rights movement, which started as a difficult decision, got ugly, but is today the accepted law of the land. So, which way is the pendulum swinging?

More important, should public opinion or social mores determine what an organization should do? Is there an ultimate "right" posture? Is there even an ultimate correct social moral law? Is it possible that the answer differs from situation to situation?

Nowhere is the news good. For whatever reason, membership in BSA is down— 6.6 percent from 2004 to 2005. For United Way chapters across the country, there is another cloud on the horizon. Competitive agencies are springing up, promising "open giving" for all donors. If this becomes established, the obvious loss of funding organizations to the United Way would curtail its ability to meet its mission. Charitable organizations have to be cognizant of future funding.

The 2001 fall campaign in Orlando brought this issue into clear focus. With a goal of $20.6 million, the Heart of Florida campaign came up $2.6 million short—only the second time in recent years the campaign failed to make its goal. An obvious reason for the shortfall was the September 11 tragedy, of course, which diverted more than $1 billion to the victims of the terrorist attacks. The resultant economic tailspin only exacerbated the problems for all charitable organizations. But these problems were not the only ones facing HOFUW.

Competitive fundraisers are eating into what had been a corporate monopoly for United Way. For example, City of Orlando employees pledged $332,000 to local charities in 2001, about 30 percent more than in 2000. But HOFUW received less than half of that amount. The other half went to the competing charities. In terms of net dollars, HOFUW received all of the City's pledges of $247,000 in 2000. In 2001, pledges to the United Way dropped to $121,735. Similar scenarios were played out with Universal (Studios) Orlando and Seminole County employees.

The *Orlando Sentinel*, in an editorial following the fall campaign, said:

United Way agencies face an additional challenge that is likely here to stay: increased competition. More workplace donors have options now about where to direct their donations. Other organizations, such as America's Charities, are aggressively pushing into the workplace.

United Way organizations must be prepared to compete in that new marketplace.

That's especially urgent for Heart of Florida United Way, which fell $2.6 million short of its $20.6 million goal in its recent campaign. In addition to the factors listed above, the local organization also fell short because of its antidiscrimination policy, which banned discrimination against all groups, including gays. After the Boy Scouts refused to endorse that policy, United Way compromised, upsetting people on both sides of the issue.[4]

The editorial continued to say that the HOFUW should maintain its antidiscrimination stance, first because it is the right thing to do, but also because to alter this stance "might prompt an even larger number of people who support the policy to withhold their donations."

Donations to HOFUW continued to drop for four years. Finally, in 2006 the Orlando-based agency was able to halt the slide, raising $16.75 million, an increase of $1.45 million over 2005, but still far below the $21 million level from before the BSA problem emerged.

With a fragmented marketplace, a divided giving public, and difficult economic times, HOFUW, BSA, and all those trying to help create a healthy community have a daunting challenge—building (and rebuilding) positive relationships that lead to positive behavior. Shields believes the solution is to continue to work together. "It is not an 'us-versus-them' situation," he says. "In most communities, often it is the same people working with both organizations, or at least people closely connected. Close personal friends who don't want either side to suffer."

It is in these tight situations that a legitimate public relations counselor can make a major difference. Wise counsel can help establish how the organization wants to be perceived by its stakeholders and can suggest programs and decisions to bring those perceptions to reality. ■

---

## THE SCOUT OATH

On my honor, I will do my best to do my duty to God and my Country, and to obey the Scout Law; to help other people at all times; to keep myself physically strong, mentally awake and morally straight.

---

[4]"Less United," *Orlando Sentinel*, December 10, 2001, p. A-14.

## QUESTIONS FOR DISCUSSION

1. When laws conflict with mores, how can one decide what is right?
2. Are the positions of the Boy Scouts of America and the United Way really mutually exclusive?
3. Discuss the strategy of United Way America pushing decisions down to the local-chapter level.
4. If you were public relations counsel to the Boy Scouts of America, what advice would you offer?
5. If you were public relations counsel to United Way, what advice would you offer?

# Case 8-5 A Classic: Free the Texas Shopper!

Some behavioral scientists say that the "silent majority" can be riled up only once a decade, after prolonged and careful focus on the subject of controversy. However, this tenet may be altered when it comes to issues that hit the general public close to home. For example, shopping.

## Background

Before 1985, the state of Texas had legislation on its books called "blue laws." These blue laws were based in the Christian ideal that everyone goes to church on Sunday—or ought to—and were responsible for keeping most retail stores closed that day. Most states once had such laws, but nearly all had been repealed. Not in the Bible Belt state of Texas, however.

A coalition was formed of like-minded retailers, including Target Stores, Kmart, and Zales, who believed it was time to do away with the blue laws. Organizations against repeal of the law were nonchain retailers, large department stores, car dealers, and especially churches.

The coalition was caught in a bind, because they knew Sunday shopping would mean greater sales but were concerned they would lose customers angered by the campaign. There was a long-standing assumption that fundamentalists, other church groups, and people living in rural areas would be against repeal, but no one knew for sure.

## Time for Research

The coalition decided to arm itself with data in order to know where the people of Texas really stood. A massive survey uncovered data that told them that:

- Two out of three Texans wanted the law repealed.

- Support for repeal was broad, including substantial support in rural areas and among fundamentalist groups.

Research was specific enough to determine *how each legislative district felt*. These data were subsequently made available to the legislators, who had to vote on repeal. Coalition representatives felt this was a very important part of their effort. When a legislator opposed the bill, evidence of support by his or her constituents was available.

## Campaign Philosophy

The coalition decided to run a straightforward, honest, open, objective campaign so nobody could criticize them on those grounds. Retailers stressed their solid reputations in the communities, their support of local nonprofit agencies, their substantial business operations (representing a large share of total retail business in the state), and the large number of people employed.

Members of the coalition were accused by the opposition of being out-of-state companies, trying to change the Texas lifestyle and overturn local values.

But Target Stores' programs of social responsibility and community participation paid off. "After 16 years," they said, "we feel as much a part of the state as others do."

## Moving Thousands to Action

After gathering the research and deciding on a campaign philosophy, the coalition's next task was to convert expressed support to active support. This is how it was done:

1. Newspaper ads were run that strongly advocated action (see Figure 8-6). The bold copy and strong illustration generated

FIGURE 8-6   **Ads run by coalition that echoed in media and word-of-mouth**

*Source:* (Courtesy of Target Corp.)

substantial media coverage and word-of-mouth publicity.

2. The same ad was used as a bag stuffer in coalition members' stores.

3. An 800 number was set up for people to call to obtain information. Operators gathered personal information from callers, especially their shopping habits and location. They also read a prepared statement and requested permission to send it to each caller's legislator over that person's name. The 800 number was prominently carried in the newspaper ads and bag stuffers.

This strategy gathered 80,000 names in the coalition's databank. When the vote was being taken, if a legislator wavered, the coalition called these registered supporters and suggested they contact the legislator.

### Defusing the Opposition

The Texas Automobile Dealers Association—effective lobbyists with a long track record of political support for candidates—was a powerful force to be up against. They did not want to open their showrooms on Sunday. The coalition needed to devise a strategy that would remove them from the equation. The bill, as it was finally adopted, excluded them. They would remain closed on Sundays. They were then standing on the sidelines, no longer in the battle.

### Final Decision

The Texas Senate required a two-thirds majority to have the matter put on the docket for vote. Once on the docket, it needed only a simple majority to pass.

Documented research and personal contacts from people in their districts spoke loudly to legislators. The coalition expected the bill to take at least two legislative sessions to pass—but it took only one.

### Testimonial to Research and Planning

The campaign lasted six months and showed how effectively public relations can influence public policy. It also showed how important public relations is to the bottom financial line; retail sales subsequently increased because of Sunday shopping. The key was fact finding, discovering that the people of Texas support Sunday openings. This knowledge put the coalition in the position of representing the will of the people. Without the research, or with different findings, an entirely different approach would have been required—with, very possibly, a different result.

### Blue Laws Update

In recent years, blue laws have faded as an issue of public concern. However, they are still debated in some states. Beer and liquor sales are limited in Massachusetts, but not in the competing neighbor states of New Hampshire and Vermont, which is a controversial issue for some merchants and customers. Counties and municipalities in Bible Belt states are often "dry" by local ordinance even though state statutes allow the sale of liquor. On the opposite side, in 1991, Kansas car dealers proposed a new blue law to prohibit automobile sales on Sundays. This proposal caused great conflict and debate, and the bill did not pass. ■

## BLUE LAWS ADDRESS MORE THAN JUST SHOPPING

In addition to blue laws that keep stores closed on Sundays, there are other blue laws on the books. Some states still have anti-adultery laws, for instance. Though ignored as archaic by law enforcement agencies, these laws have been used by some people to keep spouses in control, especially in divorce proceedings, and some people have attempted to have their spouses arrested if caught in the act of adultery.

Questions of violations of rights to privacy have arisen. But this is a relatively new "right," formulated by Supreme Court Justice Brandeis in the early years of the twentieth century. To many, the repeal of blue laws is imperative. Others would welcome more laws regulating personal conduct according to what they believe is "proper" conduct. When any specific action is taken by specific groups in either direction, emotional debate usually ensues—and you can be sure public relations counsel will be in the thick of it, ideally representing both sides so each gets its point across and the public can make an informed decision.

## QUESTIONS FOR DISCUSSION

1. Suppose research showed that about half of the key Texas population opposed Sunday sales, while half supported them. What counsel would you have given the retail group? How would you have dealt with opposing groups?

2. If you were counsel to the opposing group, what would you have suggested they do to defeat the repeal proposal?

3. Assume that your employer is moving into a new state and wants to build the type of consumer support that Target and its allies created. What types of activities would you pursue? Draw up a plan.

4. In light of Chapter 2, what are some of the considerations that go into strategic thinking leading to a plan and a program? What are some of the elements beyond media and messages? Is your response to this question reflected in your response to questions 1, 2, and 3?

# Case 8-6   Mothers Against Drunk Driving— MADD

In response to tragedy, people often reach out to others for support. Many find comfort in doing what they can to right a terrible wrong or prevent others from going through what they have gone through. Often these support groups can become a powerful and compelling voice for social change. One of the most successful and accomplished of these coalitions is Mothers Against Drunk Driving (MADD). MADD's mission is twofold: (1) to provide support for those who have experienced the tragedy of a drunk driving accident and (2) to advocate, both socially and legislatively, against the act of operating a vehicle under the influence of drugs and alcohol.

MADD was established by Candy Lightner in 1980 in response to the loss of her daughter in a drunk driving accident. The organization currently has over 400 chapters across the United States. Between 1984 and 1989, MADD increased its membership of supporters and volunteers by over 500 percent. That trend continues today as drunk driving increasingly is recognized as a debilitating social illness. Funding raised and spent in support of education, public awareness, victims' assistance, and other programs has increased four times over (see Figure 8-7). Donations to MADD total nearly $43 million annually.

Although the incidence of fatalities in alcohol-related accidents decreased by 21 percent in the period between 1982 and 2004, the numbers are still staggering. In 2004, 16,694 people were killed in alcohol-related vehicle accidents.[1] Despite MADD's positive influence, there is still much to be done to change people's behavior relative to drinking and driving.

## The Publics

MADD targets several audiences, all on different sides of a drunk driving accident.

- Along with its sister organization, Students Against Drunk Driving (SADD), MADD educates *teens* (a group with a high incidence of alcohol-related accidents) against the dangers of drunk driving.
- Another focus is the *adult driver* who may become impaired after a social night out (see Figure 8-8).
- The *repeat and reckless drunk driver*—the cause of many alcohol-related deaths—is targeted in MADD's legislative efforts for harsher penalties.
- MADD also supports *public service professionals*, such as police, paramedics,

# CAMPAIGN TO ELIMINATE DRUNK DRIVING

**FIGURE 8-7   CEDD logo**

The centerpiece of MADD's modern program is the Campaign to Eliminate Drunk Driving

*Source:* (Courtesy of MADD.)

---

[1]*Fatal Accident Reporting System,* U.S. Department of Transportation, National Highway Traffic Safety Administration, 2006.

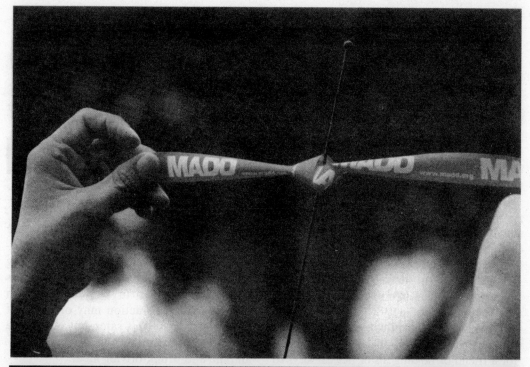

**FIGURE 8-8** One of MADD's most successful programs has been Project Red Ribbon to remind that reminded drivers against drinking and driving

*Source:* (Courtesy of MADD.)

and physicians, who must deal with the daily consequences of one person's carelessness.

- Finally, MADD maintains programs aiding family and friends who have experienced the trauma of a drunk driving accident.

## Goals and Objectives

MADD works at the grassroots level to end the senseless deaths and crippling physical and emotional injuries caused by drunk drivers. MADD supports programs that:

1. Achieve *voluntary* liquor and beer industry support to curb alcohol advertising when television or live audiences have large percentages of those under age 21. One goal is to find alternate advertisers.

2. Encourage sponsors of sporting events to limit alcohol sales too late in the event, thereby increasing the probability that fans will arrive home safely.

3. Convince Congress to add a victim's rights amendment to the U.S. Constitution—similar to the Victim's Bill of Rights in the Michigan, Florida, and Rhode Island state constitutions.

## Activities and Tactics

*Project Red Ribbon* has become one of MADD's most successful campaigns. During

**MADD**

Activism | Victim Services | Education®

FIGURE 8-9   MADD's new logo represents its new goals of activism, victim services, and education

*Source:* (Courtesy of MADD.)

the holiday season, red ribbons are distributed to drivers to be tied on car antennas and mirrors (see Figure 8-9).[2] The ribbon acts as a *reminder* not to drive if they become impaired, and as a *sign of solidarity* against drunk driving. The act of tying the ribbon also reminds the individuals of other preventive behaviors as well, such as calling a cab for a friend or holding his or her car keys to prevent drunk driving. The program is successful because it links a specific behavior (tying the ribbon) to a commitment against drunk driving *before* the first toast is raised, and it does this at the *point of behavior.*

- Alcohol-related deaths decreased from 76 per day in 1980 to 64 in 1989.
- According to the National Parents Resource Institute for Drug Education, beer, which is the number one drug of choice for teens, is most often consumed in vehicles.
- An independent research group found that television programs with a large percentage of under-21 viewers feature a high incidence of alcohol advertisements.

More than 30 million red ribbons are distributed each year by volunteers, MADD chapters, and supporting organizations, such as 7-Eleven stores, across the country (see Figure 8-10). In addition to grassroots support, several companies have tied marketing efforts to the program. Welch's promoted its nonalcoholic cider in conjunction with the program. This action may or may not have boosted Welch's sales, but it did give more exposure to the MADD program— and the anti-drunk-driving ideal.

MADD's ultimate goal is to get year-long commitment against drunk driving, not just during the holidays. There is evidence that Project Red Ribbon helps reach this goal—

Since 1990, Consolidated Freightways Motorfreight, a national trucking company based in California, has been a sponsor for MADD's Project Red Ribbon. From November to January, the company ties red ribbons to its fleet of 12,000 trucks. In addition, several Project Red Ribbon kick-off events are organized by Consolidated Freightways Motorfreight employees and held at their terminals. Some companies have found that supporting a social cause boosts employee morale by adding meaning to job performance, as well as creating public goodwill.

---

[2]Originally, they were tied on door handles to keep drunks from getting into their cars—but most present-day handles have no place to attach them.

**FIGURE 8-10 An example of the box of ribbons that MADD offered to organizations to promote Project Red Ribbon**

*Source:* (Courtesy of MADD.)

---

## ONE-WAY AND TWO-WAY COMMUNICATION TOOLS THAT HELP MADD CARRY OUT ITS MISSION

1. *Support for the MADD message in television programming.* In 1988–1989, millions of Americans tuned in to their favorite television show and got a clear warning about drinking and driving— "The two don't mix." A portion of the credit goes to the Harvard School of Medicine Alcohol Project campaign, which encourages producers and writers to promote responsible drinking and designated-driver programs. MADD's national office served as script advisers.

2. *National poster contest.* More than 45,000 young people participated in the Annual Nationwide Poster/Essay contest aimed at preventing drunk-driving. Cultural barriers were breached by including Spanish-language entries.

3. *Toll-free Victim's Assistance Crisis hotline* was established by MADD to provide support to those affected by a drunk driver's actions.

4. *Formation of Victim Impact Panels.* One hundred Victim Impact Panels were formed to serve as a forum for voicing grief, pain, and frustration associated with drunk driving accidents. These can send a powerful *emotion-laden* message to the public. Convicted drunk drivers are occasionally required to attend one of these panels as part of their sentence.

5. *Candlelight Vigils* are held to honor drunk driving victims and serve as a reminder.

6. *Crisis Response Teams* have been formed to assist families and friends of victims.

7. MADD is a strong *lobbyist for legislation for stiffer penalties* to keep the drunk driver off the road and to curb underage drinking.

8. MADD publishes *MADDvocate*, a magazine for victims and advocates.

---

MADD receives requests throughout the year for replacements for worn-out ribbons.

### The Outcome

Coalition efforts are paying off. In addition to the 7.7 percent decrease in fatalities over 10 years, the Omnibus Anti-Drug Act was passed in 1988. It is a significant victory in federal anti-DWI legislation. The enactment of the federally sponsored national minimum drinking age of 21 is another significant gain.

### Legislation: Another Form of Persuasion

Years of scholarly research of public relations programming have combined to establish a four-point method for effecting mass behavior change—which is MADD's goal, of course (See Box, page 260). Step 2 is enforcement, and

this is where restrictive and punitive laws play their part. Thus, MADD"s program must include enforcement (including punishment) to preserve the whole agenda of behavior change.

MADD deserves much of the credit for one of the most remarkable behavior change efforts in recent times. Only a decade ago it was still acceptable to talk about the "drunken party" you went to over the weekend. Today, in most circles, anyone who mentioned such behavior would be scolded and possibly shunned. In large measure, this change can be traced to the catalytic leadership of Mothers Against Drunk Driving. Here are some of the laws that MADD— along with a host of coalition partners, often brought together by MADD—has been successful in having enacted.

1. *Drunk Driving Prevention Act of 1988.* States were offered incentives

in the form of highway safety fund grants for passing legislation aimed at reducing alcohol-related offenses and deaths, including a minimum 21 drinking age—up from 18 in most states. The act was controversial, but eventually most states adopted the age to avoid losing federal funds.

2. *Victim's Crime Act of 1984.* This act provides compensation rights and grants for the survivors of drunk driving accidents.

3. *Alcoholic Beverage Labeling Act of 1988.* This act states that all alcoholic beverage containers bear a warning about the dangers of driving after drinking.

The laws that have been passed are a good example of using "enforcement" to change behaviors. Lately, car companies incorporating Breathalyzer systems right into the ignition. "Social reinforcement" will continue with the red ribbons and public service ads. (See Box, page 260). ■

| TABLE 8-1 | Alcohol-Related Deaths in the United States, 1982–2004 | | |
|---|---|---|---|
| | *Total Fatalities* | *Alcohol-Related Fatalities* | |
| *Year* | *Number* | *Number* | *Percent* |
| 1982 | 43,945 | 26,173 | 60 |
| 1983 | 42,589 | 24,635 | 58 |
| 1984 | 44,257 | 24,762 | 56 |
| 1985 | 43,825 | 23,167 | 53 |
| 1986 | 46,087 | 25,017 | 54 |
| 1987 | 46,390 | 24,094 | 52 |
| 1988 | 47,087 | 23,833 | 51 |
| 1989 | 45,582 | 22,424 | 49 |
| 1990 | 44,599 | 22,587 | 51 |
| 1991 | 41,508 | 20,159 | 49 |
| 1992 | 39,250 | 18,290 | 47 |
| 1993 | 40,150 | 17,908 | 45 |
| 1994 | 40,716 | 17,308 | 43 |
| 1995 | 41,817 | 17,732 | 42 |
| 1996 | 42,065 | 17,749 | 42 |
| 1997 | 42,013 | 16,711 | 40 |
| 1998 | 41,501 | 16,673 | 40 |
| 1999 | 41,717 | 16,572 | 40 |
| 2000 | 41,945 | 17,380 | 41 |
| 2001 | 42,196 | 17,400 | 41 |
| 2002 | 43,005 | 17,524 | 41 |
| 2003 | 42,643 | 17,013 | 40 |
| 2004 | 42,518 | 16,694 | 39 |

*Source:* (Fatal Accident Reporting System, U.S. Department of Transportation, NHTSA, 2006.)

## FOUR STEPS TO PUBLIC BEHAVIOR CHANGE
## THROUGH PR CAMPAIGNS

The work of Jim Grunig, Harold Mendelsohn, Brenda Darvin, Maxwell McCombs, and many others suggests this approach.

1. **Coalition campaign,** so that the target audience gets the feeling that everyone who counts is trying to persuade them, that it is obviously the thing to do socially. Appeals in such a campaign must follow three phases:
   - *Problem (or opportunity) recognition.* Gaining widespread understanding that the issue is an opportunity or a problem.

   - *Problem (or opportunity) personalization.* Making target audience realize it involves them, they could be affected.
   - *Constraint removal.* Letting them know they can do something about it.

2. **Enforcement.** Establishing rules and laws mandating or outlawing the behavior.

3. **Engineering.** Enacting a structural change to work around the situation, for example, raising the drinking age to reduce drunk driving accidents by young drivers.

4. **Social reinforcement.** When the behavior becomes the societally accepted norm and social rewards and punishments take over the job of enforcing it.

---

## QUESTIONS FOR DISCUSSION

1. MADD was an organization established by one who had suffered a great tragedy because of the carelessness of a drunk driver. Today the organization has been extremely successful in exacting changes in societal attitudes against drunk driving. What does their success indicate about relationships formed when people who have suffered the same tragedy band together?

2. Can you think of another organization that was formed because of an emotion-laden circumstance? Has it been as successful as MADD? Explain your answer.

3. What other communication vehicles could MADD utilize to spread its message?

## PROBLEM 8-A SMOKEOUT CAN BE A HOT POTATO

You are a first-year employee at W. L. Fixit Associates, a public relations firm in Piedmont, North Carolina, a city of 40,000 people that has long thrived on tobacco growing and manufacturing. Mr. Fixit started the agency 10 years earlier after handling communications for the local Chamber of Commerce. He is well known and knows everybody important in the region.

You're doing well. You've just been advanced to Associate Account Executive and assigned the Piedmont General Hospital as your very own client. Among other clients of the agency are a nearby college, a large resort hotel, a new downtown shopping mall, and the United Way.

At the hospital, you're helping them deal with complaints about the high costs of health care, as well as promoting greater use of a new day-care adjunct, annual fund-raising campaign, and employee morale.

One day in August, the Fixit senior account executive comes into your office and says, "You're about to get your first sticky wicket to handle." He tells you that the United Way has committed to implement the "Great American Smokeout" annual event of the American Cancer Society and has asked the Fixit agency to implement it with all their clients. Mr. Fixit feels that the agency could duck out by pleading a conflict of interest, but with a public health issue like this that would do the agency more harm than coming up with a plan that has a chance of keeping everybody happy.

Your supervisor tells you: "It will be your job to come up with a catchy, contagious 1-day event at Piedmont General." He hands you a packet that explains the Smokeout concept of affecting smokers' behavior, suggests ways to get the cooperation of various organizations, tie in local public health officials and other community leaders, attract the media, instruct those in the facilities how to prepare, make it a fun event, recognize and reward those who abstain for a day, and measure the success. The packet includes examples such as the organization that gave out survival kits including chewing gum and candy, another that put baskets of apples all around, another that set up smokeaters in designated smoke areas, another that removed cigarette vending machines on Smokeout Day, and another that sent a congratulatory letter from the president to each smoker employee who reported successfully abstaining on Smokeout Day. Then the account supervisor threw the curve.

"This is no piece of cake," he said. "Your hospital's largest contributor is the tobacco company over in Winston. There's a wing named for their founder, Colonel Piedmont. Also, have you noticed that the Piedmont's administrator is a chain smoker? That's why all the major committee meetings are held out on the penthouse roof in good weather. You've got to come up with an event that makes us look good enough to nonsmokers and the United Way without doing damage to our relationship with the hospital administration. Maybe you can persuade them there is a tradeoff for them. As for smokers and the tobacco industry around here, don't do anything that could cause permanent alienation. Mr. Fixit wouldn't mind landing a tobacco account someday, and tobacco companies are branching out more and more into food products."

He added, "Mull it over. If you can't involve both sides working with each other, at least figure out a project in which neither's ox is gored so badly they have to fight back. Put your ideas down on paper with a reasonable objective; keep in mind that United Way isn't a big-spending account; list what's new and newsworthy about your event, and explain what you have built into the plan to protect against seriously riling the tobacco people, including Colonel Piedmont's family, who made their millions on tobacco. Give me a call in 10 days and we'll take a look together at what you've come up with."

As you start thinking about a solution to this situation, you remember that the basis of a successful message strategy

- Emphasizes the benefit statement
- Avoids stiffening the resistance
- Asks for a willing suspension of disbelief

With this in mind, what further background research will you do before you start defining the objectives and activities of your program? Who will you talk to, what concerns do you anticipate, and how will you deal with them?

Using the feedback from this research, define the objectives of your program and describe and explain how the proposed activities will support your communications strategy; include some means of measuring the success in obtaining your objectives.

Do you see any ethical issues that might arise in handling this situation? If you do, how would you deal with them?

## PROBLEM 8-B REFEREEING A NEW KIND OF GAME

After earning three letters for sports at Louisiana State University, you were sidelined by a knee injury that kept you out of the professional draft. Fortunately, your journalism/public relations major helped you land a good job with Dorino, Marion public relations agency. The firm does some work for professional sports teams and suppliers and has good connections in the state capital. They also have a reputation for public service assistance to nonprofit organizations. You like it at Dorino, Marion. They like you.

The main account you personally handle is the subcommittee of the Mardi Gras, which brings in celebrities for the annual event. Your work tends to be seasonal except for periodic planning meetings, some out-of-town contacts, and some correspondence. Thus you have considerable spare time.

That situation changed suddenly one day, when the agency was approached to take on the public relations problems arising from the actions of Brother Omans, the charismatic, activist minister of the local Bible-for-Everybody Church. It seems that Omans, with the active support of a doctor who wrote an antiabortion book, has challenged the activities of the local Birth Control Institute Inc., an affiliate of Planned Parenthood International. They are known to perform and arrange abortions.

Brother Omans has notified the institute by mail that they are "committing murders" and that they risk "harsh judgment" in which "proper penalties can be imposed." He has led a picketing group, some of whose members went beyond passing out pamphlets to shouting at clients heading into the institute.

Mrs. Safeway, head of the institute, has gone to the police for protection. The police say that the pickets do not trespass as long as they stay on the sidewalk, that they have rights of assembly, and freedom of speech. If and when Brother Omans or his constituents break any law, they will be apprehended.

   Mrs. Safeway is concerned that this reactive attitude may allow further escalation of potential violence. She therefore approaches Dorino, Marion to ask for advice in seeking a more proactive approach to the situation.

   You are assigned the task of analyzing the situation and coming up with a pro-active approach as a public service of your agency. You know that Louisiana favors restricting abortion rights and probably would, if it were legal, forbid any abortions except in very narrow circumstances.

   To get your facts straight, even before you go to see Mrs. Safeway, you talk to a member of the local media with whom you went to school. He tells you that Brother Omans set up shop locally about eight years ago. A profile the newspaper did on him shows that he has had quite a career. At one time he was a circus barker hailing origi-nally from San Antonio, Texas, traveled through the southern Bible Belt, became a minister, and then moved to New Orleans. If he had anything in his background of moral turpitude, or arrests, there is nothing about it in the newspaper morgue.

   From other sources, you find that in the past eight years, Brother Omans, from the pulpit, has taken on or opposed witches, homosexuals, pornography, X-rated movies, the "mercy death" of a 93-year old comatose man, Mormon missionaries in general, and any woman who goes into politics specifically.

   Armed with this information, you go to see Mrs. Safeway at the Birth Control Institute. She's scared. There have been so many instances of bombing or arson at Planned Parenthood clinics, she can envision some of Brother Omans' constituents mak-ing her place a target. She has notified the Planned Parenthood national office. She has read their Clinic Defense Manual and notified the appropriate offices in New Orleans of her concern. She hopes you can do something to calm the situation down, not antagonize Brother Omans, his doctor supporter, or his followers. She appreciates that your agency has agreed to take on this project as a public service. You respect her professionalism but recognize that some of her actions have themselves been adversarial.

## Time to Fish or Cut Bait

Back at your office, you talk it over with your boss. You agree that there are such strong feelings on both sides that it would be tough to marshal enough neutral public opinion to induce a reconciliation without at the same time rousing special interests with strong bias toward a confrontation or worse.

   "This looks like one of those situations calling for a brainstorming session at the agency, bringing together representatives of groups with a stake in peaceful coexis-tence, and no ax to grind, on abortion," your boss says. "Maybe we can get a strategic plan out of the session. If not, it will put Brother Omans on notice that some important people are watching him, and it may reassure Mrs. Safeway she isn't about to be bombed."

   Your boss instructs you to make up an invitation list of about 15 organizations, starting with city hall, the police department, and the county medical society; a brief statement of the meeting's purpose; and a tentative agenda for the meeting. "When you get those done, let me have a look," your boss says.

   **1.** Before you start on this project, what issues affecting other members of the firm and the firm's reputation in the community might you want to discuss with your supervisor? How would you suggest dealing with them?

2. Do you agree with the suggestion that the invitations list should include city hall and the police department? If so, why? If not, on what basis would you suggest omitting them?

3. Would you include Mrs. Safeway or Brother Omans or both in this initial meeting? What could be the positive and negative results of having them there?

4. What would be your list, the statement to invitees, and the agenda?

5. What would be your recommendation in alerting or not alerting the media and dealing with the possibility of a premature leak?

## PROBLEM 8-C ANTICIPATING EMERGING ISSUES

You are in a one-person public relations department for a large public school in the Midwest. You've done everything from writing newsletters to campaigning to passing a referendum for a school addition. The school is doing well, no big problems to contend with, just the day-to-day communications. But your antenna is always up, listening to your publics—students, teachers, administrators, community members, parent-teacher organization, elected officials, etc.

Last week you had a call from a parent complaining about the name of the school's mascot—The Braves. You also noticed an article in the local paper about a group called Find Another Name dealing with this issue of using American Indian names and mascots. An emerging issue? Or just a coincidence? A staff meeting with the principal is coming up on Friday. You decide to look into the issue and make a recommendation.

There currently is no issue anticipation team within the school and it crosses your mind that it would be beneficial for the school to have one, but everyone is so over-worked you wonder how it could happen. Even so, you decide to recommend an issue anticipation team be formed and the subject of the school's mascot be considered.

For the upcoming meeting, put together a report regarding the school's mascot and make a recommendation for the school. Consider the ramifications of changing and of not changing the name. Also make recommendations for forming an issue anticipation team, where members would come from (school, parents, community, etc.), how often they would meet, what work they need to do between meetings, and how this would help the school and the community.

# CHAPTER

# 9

# Crisis Management

Because a true crisis is a turning point, after which things may change drastically, an organization not prepared to deal with crisis is constantly at risk. Even sudden emergencies of crisis proportion can be anticipated—if not avoided—so risk management, issue anticipation, and crisis communication programs have become an important part of public relations technology.

Despite this sophistication in the work, the term *crisis management* does not imply that an organization or its public relations staff can *manage* external influences. What can—and must—be managed is the *response*. This depends on the practitioner's thorough understanding of three things:

1. The **public and political environment** in which the crisis is occurring.
2. The **culture and inner workings of the organization** facing the crisis.
3. **Human nature**—how will the persons and groups involved most likely react to the crisis itself, to attempts to alleviate it, and to various communications, events, or activities?

## UNDERSTAND HOW PEOPLE TYPICALLY RESPOND TO ISSUES

Philip Lesly, a veteran public relations counselor and philosopher/critic of the field, developed the following model. On any given issue dividing public opinion, people will fall into these groups:

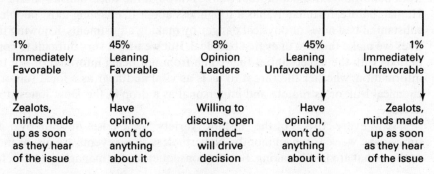

| 1%<br>Immediately<br>Favorable | 45%<br>Leaning<br>Favorable | 8%<br>Opinion<br>Leaders | 45%<br>Leaning<br>Unfavorable | 1%<br>Immediately<br>Unfavorable |
|---|---|---|---|---|
| Zealots,<br>minds made<br>up as soon<br>as they hear<br>of the issue | Have<br>opinion,<br>won't do<br>anything<br>about it | Willing to<br>discuss, open<br>minded–<br>will drive<br>decision | Have<br>opinion,<br>won't do<br>anything<br>about it | Zealots,<br>minds made<br>up as soon<br>as they hear<br>of the issue |

Zealots will be the first to take firm stands on the issue—for and against. The majority, however, will watch to see which way the opinion leaders go before they are firm enough in their views to speak or act.

Public relations efforts must focus on the opinion leaders—the 8 percent who can influence the 90 percent. Resist the temptation to capitalize on the zealots who support your view. They anger people on both sides of the issue, including those inclined to agree with them.

Keep in mind that opinion leaders are rarely the visible leaders (elected officials or organization officers). Look for them at all levels and in all segments of society. The opinion leaders are not necessarily the educated and articulate, but are always the familiar and trustworthy. Most of us are inclined to seek reinforcement for our choices from people who are in the same situation we are, not from people who are "different."

## HUMAN NATURE

When people are subjected to great emotional stress, their normally self-controlled behavior tends to become irrational and unpredictable. Their reactions turn down the steps of Maslow's hierarchy of human needs. At the bottom, of course, are a person's physical needs. One step above are a person's safety needs. When people feel that physical needs and safety needs are threatened, they are prone to panic. In panic, people's baser instincts for survival take command. This "survival" might be physical, financial, social, or some other component vital to a person's life, but you can count on self-interest or self-preservation to take command of a person's emotions and actions.

These phenomena become immediately apparent in such catastrophic circumstances as fires, floods, explosions, and tornadoes (see Case 9-1). The same pattern emerges, with less severity, in noncatastrophic situations such as a scarcity of gasoline or coffee, a spate of crime in a community, or even a standing-room-only crowd at a public event. The symptoms of potential panic and the concern for self are there. Similarly, sensations approaching panic may invade us when it appears that we may miss a departing airflight, lose a dear friend, find ourselves unexpectedly deprived of light in our home at night, or walk a dark street to our parked car.

## THE ROLE OF COMMUNICATIONS

People tend to get reassurance concerning their physical well-being and safety largely from believable information that pierces through the uncertainty, rumors, and gossip. Human nature, fortunately, has a toughness about it, enabling most people to handle substantial bad news or physical danger by making adjustments. Knowing the alternatives, we make the best of even a bad deal. But we find it very difficult to cope for long periods with the uncertainties that come from not being informed or not trusting the information, whether the threat to us is as vital and near as a local rumor of a toxic chemical leak or as remote and impersonal as a drop in the Dow Jones stock market average.

Not every crisis is of the "instant" variety. Some crises develop over a period of time—days, weeks, or even months. Nevertheless, these events are just as much a crisis as those that are fast-breaking. But the consequences for managing a crisis, for keeping credible communication flowing, are intensified when the situation drags out. In any case, the public expects the leaders of trusted organizations to act with total honesty and sensitivity during and after a crisis.

## TYPES OF CRISES

Institute for Crisis Management (ICM) defines a crisis as "a significant business disruption that stimulates extensive news media coverage. The resulting public scrutiny will affect the organization's normal operations and also could have a political, legal, financial, and governmental impact on its business." ICM identifies four basic *causes* of a crisis:

1. **Acts of God** (storms, earthquakes, volcanic action, etc.)
2. **Mechanical problems** (ruptured pipes, metal fatigue, etc.)
3. **Human error** (the wrong valve was opened, miscommunication about what to do, etc.)
4. **Management decisions, actions, or inaction** (the problem is not serious, nobody will find out)

Most fall in the last category and are the result of management not taking action when they were informed about a problem that eventually would grow into a crisis.

There are two basic types of crises, depending on the amount of warning time: (1) a **sudden crisis**, which comes without warning (employee injury, death of a key executive, oil spills, product tampering, etc.) and (2) a **smoldering crisis**, which is generally not known internally or externally until it goes public and generates negative news coverage. These problems are operational or organizational weaknesses, bad practices, and other discoverable or predictable bombs waiting to explode. Issue anticipation teams (see Chapter 8) can expose and eliminate these crises. ICM's analysis of business crises since 1990 indicates that the sudden crises are the minority. The majority are smoldering crises.

## NEWS MEDIA INFLUENCE

The interpretation of public events affecting our lives falls heavily on the news media. News prerogatives and privileges are legally assured by the First Amendment to the U.S. Constitution. Abuses of these rights surface most often when fierce competition among the media makes a competitive advantage more important or urgent than simple truth and accuracy in protecting the public interest.

In recent years, few would argue that news media have been responsible carriers of information needed by citizens; most would say they have concentrated on scandals and titillating trivialities that provided public entertainment. This perception must be taken clearly into account when planning crisis strategy.

Similarly, the obligation of public relations toward the public interest is sometimes submerged or subverted by the desire to attain the special competitive interests of employers or clients.

A classic example of news media importance in alleviating uncertainty and preventing panic, or fostering the causes of panic, was the Three Mile Island nuclear plant accident in 1979. The onslaught of newspeople from literally all over the world was a new experience for the few thousand residents of the area. They were accustomed to the presence of the nuclear plant but not to the swarm of reporters and photographers seeking to outdo each other in shock-inducing coverage under the pressure of news deadlines. Some news media, in spite of the temptations, did not yield to the competitive advantage that might have come from purveying rumors and gossip of dire predictions. Others clearly did.

For the power company and the Nuclear Regulatory Commission, this was an experience for which there were no precise precedential guidelines, no rules. Their early silence was lamentable. However, an admission that they did not know what was happening might have been even worse.[1]

Under the circumstances, local panic was averted more by what President Carter's visit communicated *symbolically* than by any *information* issued by the company or nuclear authorities or by any suggestions, analyses, or complaints on the part of news media.

After the problem had been brought under control and an evaluation was conducted in an unemotional environment, testimony brought out that it was the lack of information that distressed neighbors and local officials most of all. Lacking trustworthy information, humans tend to assume the worst. Trust must precede information.

The ability to communicate trustworthy information, whether directly or via news media, is a measure of a practitioner's effectiveness or ineffectiveness. In unexpected situations of disaster, crisis, or emergency, the news media and the practice of public relations have had their finest examples of public service and their most severe episodes of failure and ineptitude. The cases in this chapter illustrate this point.

## FUNDAMENTAL GUIDELINES

There are some guidelines that continue to help organizations handle crisis communication situations. Among them are:

1. **Anticipate the unexpected.** There are few events that cannot be anticipated. You might not know when they will happen, but an organization can anticipate a fire, a flood, a strike, a fatal accident on the job, a robbery, and many other unexpected events. Unfortunately, *the greatest single obstacle to effective crisis preparation is management denial that one will occur*, notes ICM.
2. **Institute and practice a crisis communications plan** for those events that may happen to your organization.
3. **Train employees** in what to do in these circumstances.
4. Have **one spokesperson** communicating to the public and media during the crisis.

---

[1] Rear Admiral David M. Cooney, former Chief of Information, Department of the Navy, makes the point that "in the early stages of a crisis situation, you don't tell people things you don't know or aren't sure of. . . . You never involve yourself in conjecture . . . because the chances are that you are going to be wrong. A crisis situation breaks down to certain questions. What happened? Why did it happen? What are you going to do to keep it from happening again? What is the overall impact on the people who are involved and their dependents?" He recommends, "Be organized always to handle a crisis in the next 15 minutes."

5. If it is a crisis affecting the public, rather than just the organization, **another spokesperson** or persons will also be required to keep elected officials and opinion leaders directly advised.
6. **Do not speculate** on the cause, the cost, or anything else. Provide information about only what is known.

## REFERENCES AND ADDITIONAL READINGS

Armbruster, Timothy. "Crisis in Cleveland." *Public Relations Journal* (August 1968). Classic community crisis.

Barton, Laurence. *Crisis in Organizations II.* Cincinnati, OH: South-Western Publishing Company, 2000.

Fink, Steven. *Crisis Management: Planning for the Inevitable.* London, England: Kogan Page Ltd., 2000.

Gorski, Thomas. "A Blueprint for Crisis Management." *Association Management* 50, 1 (January 1998): 78–79.

Hudson, Howard Penn. "Crisis Communications." *Public Relations Quarterly* 42, 3 (Fall 1997).

Institute for Crisis Management, P.O. Box 219, Louisville, KY 40201-0219, 812/284-8351, www.crisisexperts.com (has a crisis bibliography online).

Irvine, Robert. *When You Are the Headline.* Louisville, KY: ICM, 1987.

Jackson, Debbie. "Bayer Mobilizes Resources to Counter Crisis at Home." *Chemical Week* 152 (April 21, 1993): 24–31.

Johnson, Daniel. "Crisis Management: Forewarned Is Forearmed." *Journal of Business Strategy* 14 (March/April 1993): 58–64.

Lerbinger, Otto. *The Crisis Manager: Facing Risk and Responsibility.* Mahwah, NJ: Lawrence Erlbaum Assocs., 1996.

Lerbinger, Otto. *Managing Corporate Crises.* Boston: Barrington Press, 1986.

Lerbinger, Otto. "Beyond Crisis Management— Issues Raised by Three Mile Island." *purview* (supplement of *pr reporter*, September 10, 1979). Discusses three articles in *Public Opinion* (June/July 1979).

Lerbinger, Otto, and Nathaniel Sperber. *Managers Public Relations Handbook.* Reading, MA: Addison-Wesley, 1982. See chapters 1 and 2.

Lesly, Philip. *Overcoming Opposition.* Upper Saddle River, NJ: Prentice Hall, 1984.

Lukaszewski, James. *Crisis Communication Planning Strategies: A Crisis Communication Management Workbook.* White Plains, NY: Lukaszewski Group, 2000.

Maggart, Lisa. "Bowater Incorporated—A Lesson in Crisis Communication." *Public Relations Quarterly* 39, 3 (Fall 1994): 29–31.

Marra, Francis. "Crisis Communication Plans: Poor Predictors of Excellent Public Relations." *Public Relations Review* 24, 4 (Winter 1998): 461–474.

Mindszenthy, Bart, T. A. G. Watson, and William Koch. *No Surprises: The Crisis Management System.* Toronto: Bedford House Communication, 1988.

Nagelschmidt, Joseph, ed. The *Public Affairs Handbook.* New York: Amacom, 1982. Several leading public relations practitioners and corporate executives share their experiences on all aspects of issues and crises.

*pr reporter* Vol. 43 No. 33 (August 21, 2000). "Lessons from Firestone—and Ford—in Massive Recall. First Rule Violated: Always Begin by Saying You're Sorry."

*pr reporter* Vol. 36 No. 19 (May 10, 1993). "United Way Case: Answer to Crisis Is Prior Work on Basics."

*pr reporter* Vol. 31 No. 26 (June 27, 1988). Lead article emphasizes challenge to influence behavior and induce action by supertargeting, focused appeals, rather than broadsides to shape attitude or opinion.

*pr reporter* Vol. 22 No. 38 (October 8, 1979). "Investigative Reporter Says Candor and Immediate Answers Not Always Necessary, Even in Crisis Communications." Cites views of Les Whitten, senior reporter on Jack Anderson's staff.

*Public Relations Body of Knowledge.* New York: PRSA. See abstracts dealing with "Media Relations, Including Crisis Management."

Rosnow, Ralph. "Rumor as Communication: A Contextualist Approach." *Journal of Communication* 38 (Winter 1988): 12–28.

Schoeny, Heather. "Koala Springs International's Product Recall." *Public Relations Quarterly* 36 (Winter 1991–92): 25–26.

Shell, Adam, ed., "Communicating Foreign Crises; Panel Debates Best Approach," *Public Relations Journal* 50 (February, 1994): 4.

Shell, Adam. "At City Hall, Every Day's a Crisis." *Public Relations Journal* 48 (February 1992): 7.

Snyder, Leonard. "An Anniversary Review and Critique: The Tylenol Crisis." *Public Relations Review* 9 (Fall 1983): 24–34.

Tiller, Michael. "Is Your Disaster Plan Effective?" *Management Review* 83 (April 1994): 57.

Wylie, Frank. "Anticipation: Key to Crisis Management." *Communication World* 14, 7 (July 1997): 34–35.

Four classic programs worthy of investigation:

1. The handling of employee news when a company president and four employees were killed in an air crash, Southern Company Services, P.O. Box 720071, Atlanta, GA 30346.

2. A disaster plan by Johns-Manville, in *pr reporter*, June 18, 1979.

3. Closing an oil refinery in a small town, Amoco Company, P.O. Box 5077, Atlanta, GA 30302, ask for PR manual *Communications During an Emergency.*

4. Oil spill off Santa Barbara, California, in "Effects of the Santa Barbara Blowout," *US News and World Report,* February 8, 1971.

-------------------------------C A S E S-----------------------------------

# Case 9-1   Hurricane Katrina: A Disaster from Beginning to End*

> *One of the most shocking disclosures after Katrina and Rita was how little prepared the local and state governments were not only in handling the hurricanes but also their aftermath.*
>
> —JONATHAN TURLEY, PROFESSOR OF PUBLIC INTEREST LAW AT GEORGE WASHINGTON UNIVERSITY

## The Situation

The morning of August 29, 2005, Hurricane Katrina first struck the lower Louisiana coast and then the Mississippi Gulf coast with a 20-to-30 foot storm surge and winds in excess of 165 miles per hour. By late morning, the levees protecting New Orleans at the Industrial Canal and 17th Street Canal were breached, allowing 8 to 13 feet of water to rush into New Orleans. In the meantime, Katrina's power swept away 74 miles of Mississippi coastline.

In its wake, Katrina left thousands stranded and homeless. The devastation looked like a flooded war zone. Now the recovery began. However, in Louisiana, the gumbo pot would face many obstacles before help arrived.

## Political/Turmoil and Communication Breakdowns

Perception and fact merge in the toxic sludge of Louisiana. From the beginning, Louisiana Governor Kathleen Blanco, a

Democrat, clashed with President George W. Bush, a Republican, over whether to federalize the Louisiana National Guard. Thousands of Louisianans were suffering in New Orleans while all three levels of support—city, state, and federal—crumbled.

Former White House Press Secretary Mike McCurry sends a memo to Bob Mann, Blanco's communications director, saying, "By the weekend (September 2–4) the Bush Administration will have a full blown PR disaster/scandal on their hands because of the late response to needs in New Orleans." The Louisiana blame game had begun, and the Blanco officials were becoming concerned who would get the blame for the slow response, them or the president's team.

Like most states dealing with a disaster, after Hurricane Katrina state officials first looked to National Guard units under the control of the governor and then drew additional guardsmen from other states to assist under the same command. The president also provided federal ground troops under his command. During the week after the storm, tensions rose between Gov. Blanco and the White House over when President Bush would deploy his troops and whether Bush would "federalize" the National Guard forces, which would have moved them from Blanco's to Bush's control.

## The Facts

The facts about Hurricane Katrina are well known: hundreds of thousands of people displaced; hundreds of lives lost; property

---

*Appreciation to Joseph V. Trahan, III, APR, Fellow PRSA, for his assistance in the preparation of this case.

damage in the billions of dollars; confusion, consternation, and complacency coming together to leave a landmark American city in shambles.

The devastation in New Orleans was real. Only the famous French Quarter escaped destruction. The rest of the city and outlying parishes were flooded and destroyed, along with the lives of those who lived there. People had nowhere to go. Many fled the city. Others tried for makeshift shelters. Many perished.

There was no plan in place for dealing with the 165-mile-per-hour winds, the storm surges, the breached levies, and the thousands of gallons of seawater pouring throughout the city. No one was ready; not the people of New Orleans, not the Federal Emergency Management Agency (FEMA), not the State of Louisiana, nor the City of New Orleans. All seemed equally surprised at the developments that brought a once-proud city to its knees.

No one was ready for the hurricane. No one was ready for its aftermath of displaced citizens, lost services, disease, death, and destruction. Many people failed to evacuate, despite more than 48 hours of advanced warnings. No shelters were in place for those who stayed. No transportation was established for those who wanted to leave. No destinations were established for those who had transportation.

One telling image from the aftermath of Hurricane Katrina is that of Interstate 10 out of New Orleans crammed with cars—all lanes backed up,—with completely empty lanes coming into the city. No one thought to open the in-bound lanes to out-bound traffic.

One problem, possibly, was that many affected people were unable to prepare for or respond to a disaster of this magnitude. Most didn't fully understand the potential danger of a Category 5 hurricane. Considering that nearly two-thirds of those involved were living below the poverty line at the time, many had no other options than to wait it out and hope for the best.

Perhaps most telling, however, was the fact that no one was prepared to communicate through the crisis. One axiom of crisis communication is that how one communicates through the crisis fixes in most people's minds how the crisis was addressed. The general public, for the most part, isn't able to fully evaluate how well a crisis is handled. These people know what they hear and see, and this communication helps form opinions as to the handling of the crisis.

Tylenol, for example, communicated well through its well-known crisis, and even though no one has ever been arrested and no one knows why or how the tampering occurred, Tylenol and Johnson & Johnson generally get high marks for handling the crisis.

No one in New Orleans approached the problem in a Tylenol-like way. There seemed to be no one setting a realistic agenda—telling people what was going on. There was no attempt to set expectations—how long and how bad or how soon before it gets better. Those who knew what to do either were not heard or were ignored. Politics seemed more important than the people.

## Perceptions

In most crisis events, facts and perceptions are seldom congruent. Things are seldom as they seem. In the aftermath of Katrina, however, the perceptions seemed pretty much in line with reality.

The vast majority of Americans watching this horrible story unfold were of the opinion that no one knew what to do. That there was no plan in place was obvious. No one seemed to be in charge. Avoiding responsibility and affixing blame on someone of another political party seemed the top priority.

In reality, that was fact as well as perception. Veteran public relations practitioner Art Stevens once defined public relations as "the shaping of perceptions through communication . . ." By Stevens' definition, no one was practicing public relations in New Orleans that fateful August.[1]

One perception that lingers is that the recovery might have been more expeditious if those affected had been attractive, affluent people of Anglo-Saxon ancestry. Most of the misery was vested in the minority communities, and the images of people in the Superdome, wading down streets in water up to their waists, and in the Wal-Marts pushing carts of "reclaimed" goods reinforced this fact. The mayor's "Chocolate City" comment only added to this perception, but it did help him get re-elected.

Regardless, perception is reality, facts notwithstanding. And the perception around the globe was that Katrina was awful, but those in charge of cleaning up the mess were worse.

## The Problem

The problem in New Orleans was a bifurcated one—half operations and half communication. On the operational side, the cleanup suffered from:

- Poor planning
- Poor anticipation

*Source:* (Copyright 2005, 'KAL' Cartoonists and Writers Syndicate and Cartoon Arts International.)

[1]"PR All-Stars," *Reputation Management*, Fall 1992.

- Poor execution

On the communication side, the story was similar. Communication efforts suffered from:

- Poor planning
- Poor anticipation
- Poor execution
- Lack of anything to communicate

No one knew what needed to be done or said. There was little compassion from FEMA or state or city officials. The people of New Orleans were suffering from the hurricane, but they were also suffering from neglect. No one was able or willing to meet the needs of those most affected by Katrina.

Elected and appointed leaders had nothing to tell their publics. There was little good news. There was no rainbow, let alone any pot of gold. With no operational plans in place, no one could accurately predict what relief might appear or when it would arrive. Communicators were left with little or nothing to communicate.

One great truth of public relations is that "communication must follow performance." In New Orleans, performance didn't happen. Little was getting done. There was no performance for communication to follow.

That left public officials pointing fingers at each other, posturing for votes and decrying the lack of others' contributions. Said former FEMA Director Michael Brown, "If I had an opportunity to re-do what happened after Katrina, I'd communicate more often." But what could he have said? Unless the facts could have been different, nothing he could have said would have made much difference. People were still homeless and helpless. Without performance, communication is hollow, and even disingenuous.

## The Public Relations Impact

There was no consideration prior to, during, or after how a coordinated public relations plan would help the Katrina aftermath. There was no One Clear Voice. No one was able to set a positive agenda. No reasonable expectations were established. No one seemed to have "expected the unexpected" and made any preparations. If there were competent public relations counsel available, it was difficult to see amid the confusion that was New Orleans in August 2005.

Decision makers were equally impaired. The mayor, the governor, the director of FEMA, no one was able to make sense of what was going on. Rumors thrive in the vacuum of no information, and rumors ran rampant after Katrina. It is likely that the finest public relations counsel would not have made much difference, but, then again, it might have.

Planning and preparation are invaluable. When disaster strikes, it's too late to write a crisis plan or develop a legacy of trust with key publics. What might some good public relations planning and preparation have added to the situation in New Orleans?

First, **One Clear Voice could have been established**. In a disaster of this magnitude, having one spokesperson is not practical, but speaking with One Clear Voice is. Establishment of a chain of command, having a coordinated communication effort, and making trained communicators available might have helped shape perceptions away from the ego-driven images that America saw.

**Regular news alerts could have been scheduled** to report on what is known at the time. All the media need from those in public relations is access and accuracy. This can be provided, even under the most difficult of circumstances. Believable communicators speaking through trusted channels of communication will drive out rumors every time.

With a **good crisis communication plan in place** perhaps there would have been more to communicate. Such a plan would have an operational component, of course, and the implementation of that component would give the communicators something to say. Even if the news wasn't "good" it would at least be news—accurate information of interest to those affected by, and those attracted, to the story.

Good public relations **could have anticipated the conditions**, at least to a certain extent. An environmental scan of pre–Katrina New Orleans would have told a wise counselor that some of these people won't get the message and many won't be able to respond. That information, alone, would have helped New Orleans prepare for what was to come.

In addition, **opinion leaders trusted by disenfranchised publics could be lined up**, providing effective intervening publics to those who might not hear or believe mainstream media.

**Messages could be pretested** to be sure what is being said is being heard and understood by those to whom it is being said. The traditional communication model actually does work. Governmental jargon is deadly enough without the chaos of rising water and diminishing hope. Pretested messages can smooth the path to better understanding.

Good public relations planning could, and should, spill over to operational departments as well. In lining up dependable communication tools, the public relations counselors would have **anticipated traditional media being out of operation**. Phone lines, cell towers, and broadcast media won't survive 165-mile-an-hour winds. So the savvy practitioner will look for short-wave/ham operators, satellite communication, and other ways to keep in touch with key audiences. This type of planning would have served FEMA and the others well.

None of this is meant to imply that good public relations planning is the answer to a Class 5 hurricane. It's not. However, in the mess that was Katrina, any planning and preparation would have lessened the hardships that followed. Michael Brown was partly right when he said he should have communicated more. What he also should have said was to communicate better. ■

---

## HURRICANE KATRINA STRIKES LOUISIANA

**Day 1:** The majority of Louisiana National Guardsmen are in Iraq, but 5,671 members are deployed in the storm-impact areas in Louisiana. The U.S. Coast Guard is positioned to respond. Support from the U.S. Navy, Air Force, and Army is put into action, including medical, supply, and rescue missions, but no federal ground troops are deployed.

Joint Task Force Katrina Commander Lt. Gen. Russell Honore, in charge of federal forces responding in the Gulf region, sets up headquarters in Mississippi. State officials oversee the response from the Office of Emergency Preparedness center in Baton Rouge, Louisiana.

Gov. Blanco calls President Bush and says, "We need everything you've got." The White House later says it heard no request on August 29 for federal troops.

**Day 2:** 6,124 National Guard members are deployed, with numbers increasing as Guardsmen arrive from other states. Blanco visits New Orleans and the Superdome, a shelter for thousands with short supplies, twice during the day. Evacuation is a priority.

(*continued*)

*(continued)*

That evening, responding to a request by Blanco, Adjutant General for the Louisiana National Guard Major Gen. Bennett Landreneau asks Honore for federal troops, whose main mission would be to help with the evacuation.

**Day 3:** 6,137 National Guard members deployed.

In a comment recorded off air while awaiting a television interview, Blanco whispers to an aide that she should have requested troops earlier. The incident is cited as evidence that she was tardy calling for federal military relief, but Blanco discounts that.

Blanco visits the Superdome again and sees increased suffering. Only Louisiana National Guard members are on duty. Thousands take refuge at the city's Convention Center, but it has few supplies because it is not an official shelter. Blanco places calls to the White House to ask when the federal forces are coming, but her question does not reach a top official until later in the day, according to the governor's timeline.

Later, Honore arrives at state emergency office and greets Blanco, who asks why he has not shown up with federal troops.

Talking with Blanco chief counsel Terry Ryder at the state emergency center, Sen. David Vitter says he spoke with Bush strategist Karl Rove who said the White House wants to federalize the storm response operation.

Blanco officials and the military discuss proposal for federalization.

Still later, learning of Vitter's conversation, Blanco calls Bush to say she wants U.S. troops but does not want to federalize them, according to administration notes of that conversation. She pushes for federal troop mobilization "today" and asks to be informed when they will arrive. Blanco asks for 40,000 additional troops, but does not specify what kind.

**Day 4:** 7,403 National Guard members deployed.

National media focuses heavily on slow relief and evacuation efforts and the suffering at the Superdome and Convention Center.

The White House, Pentagon, and U.S. Department of Justice discuss legal options for sending in federal active-duty troops, including resorting to the Insurrection Act, which would give federal authorities extraordinary powers for the response effort. Blanco people later say the Insurrection Act was never discussed with them.

At the state emergency center, U.S. District Attorney Jim Letten, on the phone with the U.S. attorney general's office, ask a Blanco aide for specifics about what troop deployments the governor wants. Blanco officials interpret this as further evidence the White House wants to federalize the operation.

Later, Blanco communications director Bob Mann, attributing an observation to former President Clinton press secretary Mike McCurry, writes a memo saying, "By the weekend, the Bush administration will have a full-blown PR disaster/scandal on their hands because of the late response to needs in New Orleans." It is one of several memos among Blanco officials indicating their concern about who will get the blame—the White House or Baton Rouge.

That evening, Rear Admiral Robert Duncan, commander of the 8th Coast Guard District in New Orleans, returning from a day of rescue operations, tells Ryder that law and order must be restored and recommends federalization of troops.

Speaking with the governor at the state emergency center, Lt. Gen. H. Steven Blum, chief of the National Guard Bureau, says that if the state agrees to federalize it will lose control of response operation and not gain any additional troops. He says National Guard units from around the nation are flowing in fast and he will get more military police to assist.

Late that night, Michael Fleming, an assistant adjutant general for the Florida Army National guard who is in Louisiana assisting the state's response effort, gives similar advice as Blum's not to federalize.

**Day 5:** 8,417 National Guard members deployed.

Bush and Blanco meet on Air Force One in New Orleans, and the president offers to put Honore in charge of combined state and federal operation. The president, his chief of staff, and the governor talk privately for about half an hour.

Later that morning, Blanco sends a letter to Bush repeating her request for 40,000 additional troops and other military and relief support and requests the "expeditious return" of the Louisiana-based 256th Brigade Combat Team from Iraq to help with the storm relief effort.

By end of day, the Superdome evacuation is complete and the Convention Center is secured. But many people are still being evacuated from the overpass departure point.

Late that night, a fax from the Bush administration arrives at the state emergency center with a draft letter for Blanco to sign and a memorandum of understanding that would put Honore in charge of all guard and federal troops and relief operations. Blanco is awakened by a call informing her of Bush's memo, which Blanco officials say was unexpected. They work through the night forming a response to Bush memo.

**Day 6:** 9,328 National Guard members deployed.

Before dawn, Landreneau relates his phone conversation with Blum, who had flown to Washington for a meeting at the White House and now recommends that Blanco sign the memo putting Honore in charge. Landreneau advises the governor to reject the offer.

Blanco Chief of Staff Andy Kopplin sends memos to fellow staff indicating he thinks the memo is a maneuver by Rove to gain the upper hand, and comments, "Rove is on the prowl."

Mid-morning, Blanco talks on phone with White House Chief of Staff Andy Card, who says the president is about to make a Rose Garden announcement that he will send U.S. troops. He will not federalize the National Guard or require a change in the governor's role. About this time, Blanco faxes letter to Bush saying its OK with her if Honore takes charge of all federal forces in the Gulf region, but not inviting him to take over the National Guard.

Bush announces he will sign the troop deployment order.

That evening the Convention Center evacuation is mostly complete.

**Day 7:** 11,145 National Guard members deployed.

An advance team of federal Army and Marine forces arrives in New Orleans.

*(continued)*

(*continued*)

On CNN and on later TV appearances, New Orleans Mayor Ray Nagin, who was with Blanco and Bush on Friday, says Blanco dropped the ball by delaying a decision for 24 hours on Bush's federal troops offer. "It didn't happen, and more people died," he said.

**Day 8:** 19,708 National Guard members deployed.

Thousands of federal active-duty soldiers and hundreds of vehicles with the 82nd Airborne and 1st Cavalry divisions begin arriving at Belle Chasse Naval Air Station and Hammond. During another Louisiana visit with Blanco and a Congressional delegation, Bush says he is satisfied with the command structure.

**Day 9:** 27,065 National Guard members are now deployed in Louisiana. In total, more than 18,000 federal active duty personnel and 42,990 Army and Air Force National Guard members are at work supporting relief operations in the Gulf area.

---

## QUESTIONS FOR DISCUSSION

1. If you were responsible for your community's crisis plan, what three areas would you focus on primarily and why?
2. What do you believe was unique about the New Orleans culture that should have been taken into consideration by practitioners?
3. What might local public relations professionals have done on behalf of the city to assist in the days following? Do you believe the political stranglehold was too strong to make a difference?

# Case 9-2  A Classic: Bhopal—A Nightmare for Union Carbide

In effective handling of a crisis, preparation and anticipation are key considerations. Managing issues means intercepting the ninety percent that are self-inflicted. Crises may be created in any of the following manners:

- Maintaining irresponsible policies
- Failing to monitor internal activities
- Not applying sound response strategies when faced with criticism
- Failing to allocate adequate resources and priority to anticipating issues

And, of course, sometimes crises will occur even when all possible preparations have been made.

When an issue escalates, it may become a crisis. A crisis is defined as a highly stressful struggle or conflict within an adversarial environment. It is marked by a potentially damaging turning point that could result in financial or mortal disaster—after which things will never be the same.

Effective communication is an essential part of trying to control any crisis situation. It is the responsibility of the company or organization to provide information about what is happening, the effects it will have on numerous publics, and what the company plans to do to resolve the situation. The questions most asked by the publics involved are:

1. What exactly has happened?
2. Why was information about the crisis not released sooner?
3. What could have been done to prevent it from happening?

When a crisis hits, its effects are felt throughout an organization. The atmosphere is emotionally unstable and forces those involved to react quickly and sometimes without thinking of long-term ramifications, even if there is some sort of anticipatory plan in place.

The focus of this case (as well as Case 9-3) is the analysis of a major industrial corporation and how it anticipated and managed its crisis—or, you be the judge, how it failed to do so.

## History

In December of 1984, Union Carbide Corporation (UCC), a chemical manufacturer, was the 37th-largest industrial organization in the United States.[1] The chain of events that occurred on December 2 and 3 in Bhopal at Union Carbide India, Ltd. (UCIL), dramatically affected UCC.

UCC had incorporated UCIL in 1934 to manufacture UCC's products in India. After India gained its independence from Britain in 1947, the government began to push for greater ownership in the country's businesses.

According to J. J. Kenney, the director of federal government affairs (now retired), construction of the Bhopal plant in 1977 was controlled by the regulations of the Indian government. After UCC gave the preliminary designs to the Government of India (GOI) and the GOI approved them, UCIL took over the final design and construction of the plant. The GOI approved the

---

[1]Our thanks to Union Carbide for providing us with a wealth of information for this case.

plant design when the facility was built and monitored construction.[2]

The government wanted the plant to be as labor-intensive as possible—in order to provide needed employment—so UCIL had not installed the computer systems in use at UCC plants in the United States to monitor operations.

By the time of the Bhopal tragedy, UCC had reduced its share of ownership to 50.9 percent, while the Indian government and private citizens owned the other 49.1 percent. Plant operations were managed solely by Indians.

## The Crisis Hits

At about 11:30 P.M. on December 2, a leak in one of the valves was discovered by employees at the plant. The leak was detected after a report that the eyes of some employees were tearing from irritation. At approximately 12:15 A.M. a control room operator reported an increase in tank pressure. The tank contained liquefied methyl isocyanate (MIC), a lethal pesticide. A safety valve ruptured and released excess liquid into an adjacent tank, where a caustic soda solution should have neutralized the chemical. This neutralization did not occur.

In the case of an emergency, the safety system was supposed to flash (instantaneously light and burn) any escaping gas to prevent it from entering the outside atmosphere. This system was not operating, and 40 tons of deadly gas poured into the neighboring community.

Theories as to how the leak had occurred were many and widespread. One popular theory reported extensively in the newspapers was that an employee had failed to follow correct procedures and

thus started the reaction that released the MIC gas: It wasn't until $1\frac{1}{2}$ years later that investigators found that an employee had sabotaged the tanks by deliberately connecting a water hose to the MIC tanks (see Figure 9-1).

## Death in the Community

Many residents in the area thought UCIL manufactured *kheti ki dawai*, a harmless medicine for the crops. In reality, the chemical-turned-gas was lethal to humans because it formed liquid in the lungs of its victims. While some died in their sleep, others drowned from the liquid in their lungs while running through the streets looking for help.

Official estimates stated that 1,700 residents were killed. In addition, 3,500 were hospitalized and 75,000 were treated for injuries sustained from exposure to the gas. Death figures range from anywhere between 1,700 to 4,000. It was also estimated that 60,000 people will require long-term respiratory care. These figures earned it the designation as "the worst industrial disaster ever."[3]

Many of those killed were living in shantytowns constructed illegally near the plant. UCIL had repeatedly requested that these be moved from the area. Instead of requiring the people in these illegal shantytowns to move, the Indian government changed the law to make it legal for them to be so close to the plant.

## UCC Policies Broken

The magnitude of disaster at the Bhopal facility was partly attributed to the many breakdowns in its safety equipment (see Figure 9-2). The plant would poorly repair or

---

[2]Lee W. Baker, *The Credibility Factor,* Homewood, IL: Business One Irwin, 1993, p. 48.
[3]Ibid., p. 45.

# Union Carbide and Bhopal

*Setting the Record Straight on Employee Sabotage and Efforts to Provide Relief*

**WHAT REALLY HAPPENED AT BHOPAL?** Since the tragedy in December 1984, Union Carbide Corporation's primary concern has been with providing relief and assistance to the victims, and determining how the incident happened. Generally, initial details and subsequent news reports and books have contained a great deal of erroneous information. New information uncovered during an on-going investigation has led UCC to the conclusion that the tragedy was caused by employee sabotage and that there was a cover-up afterwards by certain operators on duty that night.

**FIGURE 9-1**   Union Carbide published a brochure that illustrated its hypothesis as to how the tragedy in Bhopal happened. Shown here is "Setting the Record Straight on Employee Sabotage and Efforts to Provide Relief"

*Source:* (Courtesy of Union Carbide.)

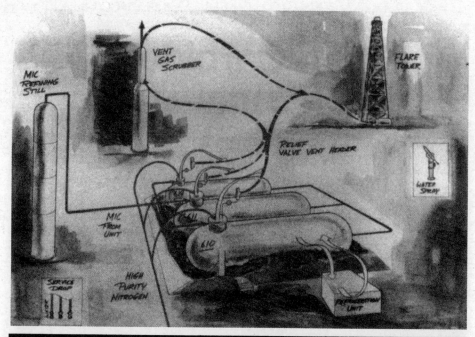

**FIGURE 9-2   A diagram of the system setup at the UCIL plant in Bhopal**

*Source:* (Courtesy of Union Carbide.)

simply shut off malfunctioning equipment. Both of these actions are serious violations of UCC policy. The following inconsistencies contributed to the conditions during the emerging crisis:

- A cooling unit was shut down months before the incident. Policy stated that this unit must remain functioning to prevent overheating.
- A flare tower, designed to flash escaping gases, had been out of service for six days.
- A scrubber (an apparatus used for removing impurities from gases), which was to be continuously running, had been down for two months.
- The warning system was inadequate for the tasks that the plant was performing. There were no alarms, no employee drills, no public education, and so on.

## Communications Difficulties

From the beginning, UCC encountered problems in addressing public concerns because of the physical communication difficulties it encountered:

- *In an international incident such as Bhopal, communication difficulties can be caused not only by physical boundaries but also by cultural ones.* UCC communicators in the United States from the beginning tried to be open and candid. However, UCIL officials in India were advised by legal counsel not to communicate.
- *Bhopal, a city of 750,000, had only two international telephone lines serving the city. This situation hampered any communications that were necessary.* Because of this obstacle, UCC was receiving the bulk of its information from media reports.

- *The company's communication specialists who were put on this case found it extremely difficult to obtain reliable information from India.*
- *The Bhopal facility failed to educate the community.* Death could have been avoided if the citizens had been instructed to place a wet cloth over the face. Most of the deaths that occurred were the old and the young because their lungs could not withstand the poison.
- *Communications management for UCC in the United States was among the last to know about the incident.* Hours after the incident, Edward Van Den Ameele, former UCC press relations manager and officer on duty, received a call at 4:30 A.M. at his home from a reporter from CBS radio. The reporter was calling for a reaction to the pesticide leak. This was the first that Van Den Ameele had heard of it.
- *The plant manager of the Indian subsidiary had no background in communication, let alone crisis management.* He told a local official that "this will probably have no ill effect."

## UCC Accepts Moral Responsibility

UCC did have a domestic crisis plan, but what happened in Bhopal was unimaginable for all. The initial reactions of UCC executives in the United States were humanitarian ones. Within hours of hearing the news of the chemical leak and what limited information was available, CEO Warren Anderson declared he was traveling to India to serve as the immediate supervisor of the situation and offer any assistance that the company could contribute. UCC also announced it would cease producing MIC until the cause of the explosion was known. Anderson

announced that UCC would be open with the public and the media.

Unfortunately, communication was poor *in* Bhopal as well. While the Indian government had assured Anderson that he could travel safely there, when he arrived he was placed under "house" arrest for charges of "culpable homicide." In addition, he was faced with the challenge of conducting communications in an area that displayed an emotionally gripping scene.

UCC declared that it accepted moral responsibility for the tragedy. One week later, UCC offered $1 million to the Prime Minister's Relief Fund, which was accepted. Four months later it offered another $5 million in humanitarian aid to the Indian government. In this instance it was refused. UCC then offered the money to the Red Cross to disburse to those who needed it in India—and that was turned down for more than a year.

## The Aftermath of Bhopal

After the Bhopal incident and the intense scrutiny and criticisms UCC received from the public and the media, UCC also faced a hostile takeover attempt by GAF Corporation. UCC defeated this attempt by selling off its consumer products businesses and paying a special distribution to shareholders. This sale began UCC's efforts to focus on its core chemicals and plastics businesses and the subsequent sale of other non-core businesses. By the early-to-mid 1990's, Union Carbide had regained a positive image on Wall Street.

UCC poured money into its safety systems and supervisory procedures, some analysts said too much, according to *The Wall Street Journal*.[4] Maintenance practices that should have taken 30 minutes began to take three or four hours to complete. Even CEO Robert D. Kennedy (replacing Anderson in 1986) conceded that the same

---

[4]"Wounded Giant: Union Carbide Offers Some Sober Lessons in Crisis Management," *The Wall Street Journal*, January 28, 1992.

---

### LESSONS LEARNED FROM BHOPAL

According to Union Carbide's Public Affairs Department, UCC learned four very important lessons from the Bhopal incident.[*]

1. It is important to be *open and candid* in every message prepared to deal with a situation. Attempts to shield information are immediately picked up by the public.

2. In the event of a huge crisis, *make immediate use of existing programs that are*

*identified with the organization* and accentuate their strengths.

3. Don't forget secondary stakeholders. In addition to employees and the media, you must consider shareholders, federal, state and local government officials, customers and retirees.

4. Don't underestimate cultural differences that may exist in a crisis that involves multinational operations.

5. Each crisis is different—*there is no formula for dealing with them.*

[*]*pr reporter*, April 23, 1990.

---

safety levels were achieved at some of his rivals' plants, while spending a fraction of the cost incurred by UCC.

As for the legal outcome of the Bhopal tragedy, UCC settled Indian civil suits in 1989 for $470 million. The Indian courts recommended and the GOI did seek extradition of former UCC CEO Anderson to India to face charges for culpable homicide. However, in September 2004, the U.S. Justice Department refused to extradite Mr. Anderson to India. ■

---

### QUESTIONS FOR DISCUSSION

1. As indicated from the Bhopal disaster, Union Carbide India, Ltd., did nothing to prepare the community for any potential hazard that could have and did occur. What are some proactive actions or programs that UCIL could have implemented in order to avoid the fatal tragedy that occurred? What is the public relations role in them, if any?

2. Compare Bhopal with the Responsible Care program (Case 4-1). What part do you think the differing cultures and governments in the United States and India played in the Bhopal tragedy?

3. From all appearances, it seems that UCC was innocent of any direct causes of the Bhopal tragedy. Yet the company was all but destroyed by it. Did public opinion actually cause this near destruction? Might it have been caused by company overreaction or feelings of guilt? If not these, then what were the causes?

# Case 9-3   A Classic: When Positive Actions Don't Result in Positive Perceptions

On March 24, 1989, the *Exxon Valdez* struck Bligh Reef in Prince William Sound,[1] releasing 11 million gallons of crude oil (one-fifth of its cargo) into the sea.[2] This incident created a crisis of epic proportions for Exxon. The mission was to clean 1,300 miles of shoreline, approximately 15 percent of the area's 9,000 miles of shoreline, and restore the area to its original condition. In 1992, after the completion of successful and extensive cleanup efforts, a federal on-scene coordinator (the U.S. Coast Guard) declared the cleanup complete saying, "Further shoreline treatment would provide no net benefit to the environment." The State of Alaska confirmed these findings. However, the damage for Exxon did not end with the termination of cleanup efforts. What was the real problem?

## Perceptions, Not Facts; Actions, Not Words

Although it was only the 34th largest oil spill at that time, it goes on record as one that people will remember the most. In one study, the *Exxon Valdez* remains one of the most remembered corporate crises.[3] Environmentalists have perceived it as limitless in damage even though there are few remaining signs of the spill. Many have characterized the accident as civilization once again trouncing on nature in order to reap the benefits of its limited resources and associate it with the deaths of many birds, otters, and other aquatic life.

In reality, the Alaskan food chain has survived (see Figure 9-3). Pink salmon harvests set records in 1990 and 1991.

---

### FACTORS TO CONSIDER WHEN DEVELOPING A CRISIS COMMUNICATION PLAN

- Develop a crisis communication plan in advance to handle any situation; determine exactly how and what key publics will be instructed to do in case of an emergency.
- Conduct research to discover information that is not readily available.

- Insist that all company operations be monitored regularly. A crisis that results because of operational failure without these preparations will surely cause the company to lose credibility.

---

[1]This case was developed from a case study authored by two University of Central Florida students, Fred Forlano and Greg Lorenz, under the direction of Frank Stansberry, who retired from UCF in 2006.
[2]Lee W. Baker, *The Credibility Factor*, Homewood, IL: Business One Irwin, 1993, p. 38.
[3]*pr reporter,* July 12, 1993.

**FIGURE 9-3**   **Exxon published a series of reports about the aftermath of the *Valdez* oil spill and its effect on Prince William Sound and the Gulf of Alaska. Shown here is a report entitled "Three Years After" from October 1992**

*Source:* (Courtesy of Exxon Company, U.S.A.)

Tourism has rebounded strongly and so have Exxon's profits. It appears that the only thing severely damaged was the company's reputation. Those who remember it perceive it as a disaster that was poorly handled by Exxon.

## How Did These Perceptions Develop?

Today, the spill has been cleaned up and Exxon is thriving as it was previously, but the residual effects of the ordeal linger.

From the beginning, Exxon concentrated on emphasizing cleanup efforts rather than addressing the public perception that it

didn't do enough, soon enough (see Figure 9-4). This emphasis was apparent from the moment that CEO Lawrence G. Rawl entered the picture. Unfavorable media comparisons were made of Rawl with the positive images of James Burke of Johnson & Johnson and his handling of the Tylenol incident (see Case 6-3). He was characterized as opposed to serving as a spokesperson, or even publicly showing interest, because he remained in New York until two days after the spill. When he finally entered the scene, he presented himself as rigid and aggressive, not bowing to the groups that opposed him or to the media. His inflexibility may have cost him

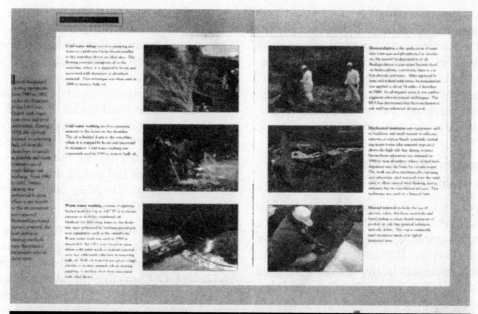

**FIGURE 9-4    Exxon used many techniques in order to clean up the shoreline along Prince William Sound in Alaska**

*Source:* (Courtesy of Exxon Company, U.S.A.)

opportunities to seek positive relationships with the various publics.[4]

When Exxon designated a location for a crisis center, the company created another situation that conflicted with its goals. It staffed the media center in Port of Valdez. Information was often slow in coming, and communication lines to Port of Valdez became jammed with information inquiries from media. It was also hard for management in New York to get information.

Another problem hampering Exxon's credibility was that it did not address how the public was perceiving the spill and its effects. It focused primarily on the *facts* concerning cleanup efforts and let *impressions* about long-term effects on the region form on their own. These facts consisted of dollar amounts, size of work force, and stories about the confusion they had to overcome to begin the process. The public, knee deep in "green issues," found no reassurance that Alaska's vast natural regions would recover.

For legal reasons, it was difficult for Exxon to show remorse or even admit to the environmental ramifications of the crisis. It did not realize the significance of visual images and the emotional response they evoked. Media images of animals in distress were displayed often and increased negative perceptions of the company. Exxon's credibility and reputation were being strongly questioned at this time.

Exxon's full-page apology ads on April 3, 1989, were badly timed and plagued with conflicting messages. They claimed that,

---

[4]When Rawl was asked later why he did not become more of a force in the crisis communications, Rawl replied that "his first instinct was to head to Alaska . . . but he was swayed by his colleagues' arguments that he would 'just get in the way.'" From Lee Baker, *The Credibility Factor,* Homewood, IL: Business One Irwin, 1992, p. 41.

"Exxon has moved swiftly and competently to minimize" the damage. In the *same* papers, front pages reported how slowly the company had been in starting the cleanup, with a specific list of unflattering reasons why. The actual "we're sorry statement" appeared in the last paragraph, vastly minimizing readership in today's sound-bite world.[5]

## Communications Is the Hub of a Crisis Situation

Exxon became the scapegoat for all environmental causes. CEO Rawl served as a prime example of stereotypical negative perceptions of the corporate executive. Topics discussed in the media portrayed Exxon as being money-focused and inhuman. How could a company so vast have such poor crisis communication planning? Hadn't they learned by other companies' examples what they should do and how they should act during a crisis? Remembering that hindsight is 20/20, here are some basic communication principles that Exxon should have kept in mind before and after the *Valdez* ran aground.

- Develop a plan that will construct a positive image. Or at least try not to create a situation that will put you two steps back.
- Exxon could have spent more time emphasizing the personal commitment being made, rather than the processes involved and the $2.5 billion spent on cleanup.
- Conduct media research to discover the realities of opinions conveyed to the public. Are the messages strong, or do they have gaps that you can fill with your own information? Whose side is the media on? What are they saying to whom? Where are they getting their information, and is it accurate?

In addition, conducting gap research (gap research measures the gap between reality and expectations of an audience) with publics would have been fruitful.

- Attempt to establish credibility by being honest and personable with the public. If Rawl was not an effective spokesperson, he could have been replaced with someone who had the training and experience. The faces and images the public saw on television were the ones that are associated with Exxon.

Much like UCC in the Bhopal case (Case 9-2), Exxon needed to make certain that all information was accurate, consistent, and complete. Cases like this illustrate why candor is the best policy. Reveal what is being done and why. Convey what is known and when it became known. Don't let the media find out for themselves. Exxon did not follow these basic guidelines when cleanup efforts halted for the winter in September of 1989. Rather than telling the public that because of weather limitations, cleanup would prove fruitless, Exxon simply discontinued efforts for the season. Cleanup continued until the federal on-scene coordinator and state declared it complete in 1992, but the public did not completely understand the cleanup process. They needed someone to explain it to them, and *it could have been Exxon.*

When it comes to the source of communication, make certain that the spokesperson is qualified, with proper crisis communication training. Shooting from the hip should be avoided, and a clear message should be sent at all times. Providing the image of sympathy and remorse, complemented with sincerity, may have saved Exxon's reputation and, in turn, made the future seem brighter for all the parties involved.

A plan that defines all necessary contacts and a proposed sequence of events could have

---

[5]*pr reporter*, April 17, 1989.

been developed. A spill of any variety would involve the media, state and local governments, environmental groups, and internal and external publics. The support of employees is crucial. At a time when it is difficult to reach the spokesperson, the media often will create their own in a security guard or a technician.

The cleanup effort was not effectively coordinated with the efforts of all groups involved. No one knew what each group should do or when. Observers felt that both of these aspects should have been considered and put into the crisis plan as well. Even if a plan was not in place, as soon as the smoke cleared Exxon could have been initiating the coordination of communications and development of a strategy and plan with all pertinent groups.

A better understanding of how the media works in relation to delivering a prescribed message to different publics would also have been beneficial. As mentioned earlier, the public can and will sympathize with helpless animals. A good portion of media attention was given to oil-covered birds vividly depicted on television and in magazines. Even journalists said at the time that it would have been more sensible for Exxon to divert this attention by devising *proactive* programs the media could focus on. Because hard news sells, a program of hard-hitting environmental programs and principles could have been implemented. This strategy could have made the media a channel for communicating to the public

that Exxon was aware of and cares about the environment and its inhabitants.

## Lessons Learned

**Issue anticipation is the key to averting many crises.** Some top management advisers insist that positive leadership is the only way to develop positive relationships. They believe that to think negatively would not be consistent with their goals or beneficial to the company. Exxon learned that even a very large company has a malleable reputation that can change in an instant.

Exxon was forced to realize that perceptions control reputation. In relation to other oil companies, Exxon's cleanup and spill control plan was reportedly top-of-the-line. However, by communicating specifics about the cleanup process, rather than the effects the spill would have on the environment, the company was not addressing the issues of concern. Displaying emotion and remorse for the outcome could have created a positive image of Exxon in the public's eye.

The hard lesson learned is that *anticipation*, while it may not prevent a crisis, certainly makes the road a little less bumpy. Ignoring possible situations that may occur, be they positive or negative, can lead to reputation and relationship disruptions that continue for years. An organization must be forward-thinking in order to survive in our volatile world. ■

---

## QUESTIONS FOR DISCUSSION

1. As evidenced by the Exxon case, perceptions speak louder than the actual facts. Can you think of anything more that Exxon could have done to avoid this public relations disaster and salvage its soiled reputation? Can you think of any proactive measures Exxon should take now to repair battered relationships with publics still disgruntled with the company?

2. Exxon received a blow to its reputation from the *Valdez* oil spill, but its profits really weren't hurt. Does its financial muscle and lack of real competition in the oil market move it beyond control of the court of public opinion? Why do you think this?

# Case 9-4  Holden Heights Hostage Crisis

## The Situation Leading Up to the Hostage Crisis

During the early morning hours of December 9, 1997, a man broke into a home in the Orlando suburb of Winter Park, Florida. Inside the house, he shot and killed a man and seriously wounded a woman. Then, he slipped into the pre-dawn darkness and disappeared.[1]

The Winter Park police suspected John Armstrong was the one responsible for this crime. Armstrong was a convicted felon and violent criminal offender, with crimes ranging from grand theft to attempted murder. He had served time in prison, but was released early.

Police spotted Armstrong, accompanied by his young daughter, driving on the freeway toward Orlando. Armstrong crashed his car into another vehicle and, leaving his daughter alone in the car, fled on foot into Holden Heights, a low-income neighborhood. Ignoring orders from the police to stop, he leaped through the front window of a nearby home occupied by Iris Vickson and Adrienne Phillips. At home with their two small children, two-year-old Tedi and four-year-old Malcolm, the women were surprised and frightened. Armstrong, with a gun in his hand, ordered the mothers out of the house and took the children as hostages, thus beginning a 3-day siege. The crisis participants were:

- **John E. Armstrong**—convicted felon and violent criminal released early from prison, and a suspect in a homicide in a suburb of Orlando

- **Tedi Priest**—two-year-old girl taken hostage in her Holden Heights home
- **Iris Vickson**—mother of Tedi Priest and resident of Holden Heights
- **Malcolm Phillips**—four-year-old boy taken hostage in his Holden Heights home
- **Adrienne Phillips**—mother of Malcolm Phillips and resident of Holden Heights

## Hostage Crisis

Armstrong's actions created a crisis on two levels. The first crisis was a situation in which people's lives were in danger. The second was a public relations nightmare. Alone with the two young children, Armstrong started threatening to kill the children and making demands. The demands ranged from a get-away car to pizza.

The Orlando Police Department called a professional hostage negotiator to the scene. Inside the house, Armstrong was listening to the television news reports of the events at the scene while talking on the telephone with the police. At one point, police got a listening device and were monitoring Armstrong's actions. The key resolution participants were:

- **Mayor Glenda Hood**—mayor of the City of Orlando
- **Jim DeSimone**—Communication Director, City of Orlando
- **Chief Bill Kennedy**—Orlando Chief of Police
- **Captain Frank Fink**—SWAT team commander

---

[1]This case was prepared by Jamie Karpinski, a senior at the University of Central Florida under the direction of instructor, Frank R. Stansberry, APR, Fellow PRSA, now retired.

- **Lieutenant Bill Mulloy**—Public Information Officer for the City of Orlando
- **Captain Jerry Demings**—Commander of the Crisis Negotiations Team and Orlando Deputy Police Chief

After days of negotiating, Captain Jerry Demings and Chief Bill Kennedy decided the time was finally right to act. Armstrong had been awake for much of the 68-hour siege, taking only a few catnaps. The negotiations had ground to a halt. Armstrong kept promising to release the children but never did. He was a desperate man with nothing to lose.

Armstrong had finally fallen asleep. He was lying on a bed in the back bedroom with a gun at his side. The children were asleep inches away. The Orlando SWAT Team entered the house with orders by team commander Captain Frank Fink to keep the children safe at all costs. Once in the back bedroom, SWAT Officer Scott Perkins jumped onto Armstrong and shielded the children. Perkins' hand was shot during the rescue and Armstrong was killed. The children were returned safely to their frantic mothers.

## Public Relations Crisis

One of the first things a public relations professional should know is that planning and preparation are invaluable. When disaster strikes, it is too late to prepare a crisis plan or build a legacy of trust. In this respect, the City of Orlando was right on target. Although city officials could not foresee this specific event, they were prepared for a crisis. The City of Orlando's mission statement calls for "Serving Orlando with innovation, responsiveness, knowledge, courtesy, and professionalism." This mission is the cornerstone of Orlando's legacy of trust with the community. The mission is held in high regard and followed by all city agencies. Because of the commitment to this mission, city officials began preparing a crisis plan in

case of emergency. This plan was a large factor in the successful handling of the hostage crisis. For example, the Public Information Office (PIO) of the Orlando Police Department is usually run by one person— Lieutenant Bill Mulloy. However, as a part of the crisis plan, 12 new PIO officers were trained. This training had been completed a few months before the hostage crisis began. (All 12 officers were called to duty by the time the crisis ended.)

The media covered the story from the beginning. However, when Armstrong took the small children hostage, the media attention intensified. Not only were local media present, but national and international media in town on other business also covered the story. This international media presence made the handling of the information even more critical because Orlando and Central Florida are international tourist destinations. As a result, area leaders must continually emphasize the security and wholesomeness of the area to those whose travel plans might be influenced by any negative news reports.

However, because extra Public Information Officers were recently trained for crisis situations, the PIOs were able to satisfy all media requests for special interviews and give out timely information to meet news deadlines and the Orlando Police Department (OPD) became the source of most of the information the media reported.

From the beginning, Orlando's media strategy was to meet the needs of the media without compromising the efforts to resolve the crisis. Included in this plan was the knowledge that the media can sometimes help with crisis resolution. For example, city and OPD officials made an early decision to let the electricity, phone, cable, and other external communication devices remain "on" inside the hostage site so negotiators could talk to Armstrong. This communication worked to the city's advantage in two ways.

First, without trustworthy information, people assume the worst. Rumors thrive in the vacuum of no information. Since the city was controlling the information flow, it kept control of the situation and what information was released. Second, if you have to say something, the truth is always best. The PIOs were honest with the media and told them of new developments as soon as they happened. This created a cooperative, positive atmosphere with the media. This cooperative atmosphere allowed hostage negotiators to communicate with Armstrong through the media—primarily television—throughout the ordeal.

Two messages were constant: appeal to the hostage-taker to release the children and surrender and compliment Armstrong in an effort to keep him from harming the hostages. Complimenting Armstrong at first confused some of the media who knew the "outside" story—that OPD, given the opportunity, would use any means necessary to stop Armstrong. Background briefings cleared up this confusion and reinforced the policy of honesty with the media.

At the same time, the other target audiences were being addressed. This proves the wisdom of the strategy of speaking to niche audiences (as well as mass audiences) through the media. City residents, city officials, and employees, and the population of Central Florida looked to the media for current information on the situation, but those viewing around the world were also important audiences.

Throughout dealings with the media, five basic message points were repeated. The media helped convey these messages to the public. These points were:

1. John Armstrong was responsible for his fate.
2. The children's safety came first.
3. The Orlando Police Department and its law enforcement partners did an excellent job.
4. This could have been prevented.
5. Expert testimony supports this view.

## Conclusion

This crisis had both a successful hostage resolution and a successful public relations outcome. This can be attributed to several factors.

First, public relations must be involved from the beginning to have maximum impact. The cameras had been rolling ever since Armstrong was fleeing down the interstate. However, the City of Orlando was in control of the situation and helped the media get the information they needed and successfully solved the hostage crisis.

Next, public relations needs to always play its position and let other departments play theirs. It is highly unlikely that the PIOs would have been as successful at saving Tedi and Malcolm from their captor without the SWAT Team. It is also unlikely that the SWAT Team would have been successful at handling the media. The five key message points of the city were reinforced in every communication. This allowed a unified and constant message to reach the public.

Throughout the ordeal, Mayor Glenda Hood and the city's public relations officer, Jim DeSimone, remained in constant contact with the SWAT team and the PIOs. The mayor knew that every aspect of the situation was being handled by experts and always knew the status of the rescue operation. However, the mayor's focus was to convey her whole-hearted support and encouragement for city employees. She also spent a lot of time behind the scenes visiting and encouraging the mothers of the hostages. The rescue was successful in part because Mayor Hood supported the plan.

The five message points the city used were addressed and accepted by both the media and the community. This crisis was successfully resolved because the city believed in its mission and the OPD had already established a legacy of trust with the citizens.

The Mayor was behind the crisis plan. Departments worked together but managed their own specialties. The result was a coordinated effort that kept the various publics informed and satisfied throughout the three-day ordeal. Armstrong was the only casualty. Good police work and good communication kept the situation under control. ∎

---

## QUESTIONS FOR DISCUSSION

1. Was this situation handled well from a public relations standpoint? Why or why not?
2. Five primary publics were identified by the OPD. List them and tell how successfully each was addressed.
3. Who was setting the agenda for the media coverage—the media or the city? How?
4. Why was it important that Mayor Hood supported the operation?
5. Did the city use One Clear Voice when addressing the media? How?
6. What could be done to improve the handling of the public relations aspect of this situation?
7. What was the outcome of each of the city's five message points at the end of the hostage crisis? Was the city successful in getting the message points out through the media?

# Case 9-5   Trouble in the Pews: The Catholic Church and Child Molestation

The sexual abuse of minors by some priests in the Roman Catholic Church looms as one of the saddest situations in recent history and gave way to one of the most aggressively covered stories in recent history. One diocese learned that the "traditional wisdom" on handling crises did not always work. The challenge became one of keeping an eye on the final destination while changing course, taking different tacks, and a combination of sailing under full sail and trimming back to navigate some rocky sections.

At the onset, it must be clear that the abuse of minors by priests—or by anyone—is wrong and deplorable. The harm done to those who were abused has lasted for decades and will continue to have a profound affect on their lives. No one in the Church ever excused this terrible behavior. The Church people involved in this situation wanted to first help those who had been harmed and then to be sure they did everything in their power to prevent future occurrences. At the same time, the leaders in the diocese needed to manage a crisis of unprecedented scope and intensity.

## Crisis Didn't Break—It Erupted

On January 6, 2002, the *Boston Globe* published the first of two parts of a *Globe* Spotlight Team story on the Rev. John J. Geoghan, who was about to stand trial for the criminal abuse of minors. The story raised questions about the Catholic Church's policies and practices regarding the assignment of priests who had allegations of abuse made against them.

If this article was the first rumble, then the following two and a half years were full-force eruptions for the Roman Catholic Church in Boston and other dioceses around the country. The neighboring Diocese of Manchester in New Hampshire was the first to feel the effects of the explosion in Boston.

The Diocese of Manchester encompasses the state of New Hampshire. The Manchester bishop served in the cabinet of Cardinal Bernard F. Law in Boston for 10 years. His final two years included responsibilities as the Cardinal's Delegate for Sexual Misconduct. His name began to be mentioned in context of the Archdiocese's is practices regarding sexual abuse of minors by priests.

As the *Globe* stories continued, more individuals came forward stating that they had also been abused by priests, and not just Geoghan. The story grew in force, and its effects were now spreading quickly to other dioceses.

## If All Politics Is Local, Then All News Has a Local Angle

The southern part of New Hampshire—the part where the bulk of the population lives—is influenced by Boston media. As the *Globe's* coverage of the sexual abuse story increased, so, too, did the *Boston Herald's* and that of the network and independent television stations. The effect was that New Hampshire was abuzz with the details coming from Boston. Soon, the New Hampshire media were devoting space and time to this story.

Lay people, clergy, and the state's top law enforcement officer all asked the same question: "Is there a similar problem here?"

The bishop and diocesan officials reviewed the records of priests who were in the ministry, retired, or on leave. They developed a list of priests who had allegations of sexual abuse of a minor made against them. Only one priest was still in ministry, and he was immediately removed.

The media and the state's attorney general were asking the diocese for information. After considering the right of the public to know what the situation was—as well as considering the rights of priests who had never been charged or tried—the bishop decided to send the attorney general a letter describing what the diocese's policy was for removing priests and to append a list of 14 priests who had allegations and what their current status was. Simultaneously, the bishop opted to hold a news conference and release the names to the public. The diocese knew that the names would eventually be made public and wanted to demonstrate that it was not trying to hide anything.

Following the tried-and-tested crisis management technique of getting bad news out quickly and completely, the diocese released this information barely a month after the first story appeared in the *Globe*. The diocese hoped that this painful revelation would mark the end of the problem in the New Hampshire. It soon found out that was wishful thinking.

## Issue Consolidation

After the release of the names of priests with allegations of abuse against them, the diocese hoped it could concentrate on moving forward. A number of related—but distinct—issues, however, soon made that hope impossible:

- The attorney general decided he wanted to conduct an investigation into the past practices of the diocese and to determine if any laws were broken and if there were sufficient safeguards in place to prevent any priest from being in the active ministry if he had abused a minor.
- Many—eventually hundreds—of individuals came forward to state that they had been abused in the past. Many of the priests named in these

allegations had no previous allegations against them. Those who were still alive were placed on what most would recognize as administrative leave. This meant they could not be in the ministry, they could not present themselves publicly as priest, and they could not wear clerical garb.
- Activist groups quickly became vocal in their condemnation of the Church and their calls for action. The groups became convenient sources of comment for the media as the story became solidly framed.
- The attorney general in Massachusetts announced he would begin an investigation of the archdiocese and would be calling the bishop of Manchester to testify.
- Numerous civil lawsuits were initiated, with wide media attention.

## Media Sets the Agenda and Frames the Story

To be certain, the media did not create the situation, but they certainly gave it shape and propelled it to the forefront of the nation's consciousness. This is not an attempt to "blame" the media. However, in order to learn some lessons on how to manage crises in the future, one must understand how the media behaved in this situation.

The horrible and salacious nature of sexual abuse makes it an issue the media love. Like every good story, however, there needs to be a framework, good guys and bad guys, and a simple resolution. The media are not equipped to handle numerous subplots, subtle distinctions, and multiple shades and nuances regarding actions taken and decisions made.

Most crisis communication lectures will recommend setting a positive agenda and creating reasonable expectations. In this case, however, the media reports made this nearly impossible. For example:

- First, the *time frame for the story was seriously condensed.* The reports of sexual abuse of minors the diocese received covered a span of years beginning in the 1940s and ending in the late 1980s. This was 2002, but the media reported each new allegation as if it were happening now. Many readers and viewers felt like these allegations were recent, when in fact most of them were 20 years old or more.
- Next, the *story condensed to a simple story line.* A priest abused a minor, the Church covered it up, reassigned the priest, and ignored the victim. Terms such as "shuttling" priests from parish to parish were regularly used. Although no one today would ever condone placing a priest back in the ministry if he had sexually abused a minor, the media did not try to place the Church's actions in any sort of historical context. The Church did remove priests, it did send priests for extensive treatment and evaluation, and it often did place restrictions on their ministry if they did return. Again, none of this applies today, but 20, 30, and 40 years ago, this was an acceptable way of handling these situations. This past approach does not excuse poor judgment, but it also is not consistent with the media's interpretation that priests were simply assigned to a new parish after an incident of abuse.
- The media needed to find an *easy-to-understand analogy* for the Church's organization. The Roman Catholic Church is over 2,000 years old, and its traditions have developed over centuries. Although it is hierarchical, it does not easily fit into secular organizational molds. The media needed to find a model, and it chose a corporate model. The bishop was a CEO, and the priests were employees. If an employee (priest) misbehaved, the CEO (bishop) should fire him. If the problem continued, then the CEO (bishop) should resign. After all isn't that what happened in major corporate scandals?

Although the bishop is the shepherd and leader of the diocese, the Church is not a corporation. A Church is organized with a goal of enabling its members to lead a holy life on earth in order to be united in eternity with God. So, a bishop acts out of concern for all—saints and sinners. When a priest commits a crime, the bishop has an obligation to try to help that person repent. This concept of forgiveness of the sinner—while detesting the sin—was difficult for the media to grasp. Actions of a bishop that seemed to give any consideration to an accused priest were viewed as a cover-up or, at the least, a condoning of sinful and illegal behavior. No one denies that bishops and others made errors, trusted too much in evaluations that indicated priests who abused could be trusted not to abuse in the future, and tried to handle a sensitive matter in a confidential manner. The problem was that the media in interpreting all these actions placed them in context of situations such as failed corporations and drew analogies between the Church and businesses. So the media soon settled in on a convenient telling of the story in black and white, omitting many shades and complexities. It also pointed to a simple resolution. The bishop should resign.

Another factor that influenced this situation was the highly competitive nature of the media. This is not unusual. What made it different was the extended time that the media competed on this story. If a newspaper had a story in the morning papers, all the electronic media had to have something that same day. In some cases, individual reporters

*Reinvented History* has become a way of describing the behavior of our society when judging past actions based on today's values. **Stakeholders look at the actions the Church took 50 years ago in response to the sexual molestation and, with today's views and opinions, find it appallingly lacking.** In those days, that is how things were typically handled. This has occurred for other organizations as well. For instance, environmental dumping was perfectly legal and acceptable back 20 years, but not today. Consider Love Canal, asbestos, Dow Corning, even tobacco.

It is the practitioner's responsibility to look at its organization's actions and reactions not only through the eyes of stakeholder today, but how stakeholders will view those actions in the future as well.

made this situation their main focus and spent extraordinary amounts of time on it. Finally, for a small diocese in New Hampshire the focus of national media was a tremendous pressure.

On a regular basis, sometimes daily, the *New York Times* and *Washington Post* called the diocese for information and interviews. The national news shows and news magazines all expressed interest in the story. On a particularly active day, there could be as many as 25 to 35 media calls from local, regional, and national media. It was not unusual to have two or three television microwave broadcast vans outside the diocese with reporters doing stand-ups.

## Setting Goals, Managing Expectations

After the initial disclosure of names did not establish a point where the diocese could begin to separate the past from the present and move forward, it was clear that a more sophisticated crisis management strategy was needed. The diocese realized that it was not going to be successful in communicating to its critical publics through the media. The media had framed the story in such a way that everything the diocese said appeared to be defensive.

The diocese developed a crisis management plan with clear goals and identified its core constituencies. The diocese also developed a crisis management team. The bishop delegated management of the crisis to a priest in his cabinet. The team included communications, legal, and support members. From time to time, the team called on the expertise of canon (in-house) lawyers, accountants, ministry personnel, and others.

The goals of the diocese's plan were:

- To respond pastorally to those who had been harmed
- To concentrate on Catholics to help them retain their faith in the Church
- To act with as much transparency as possible to help restore public confidence in the Church

The diocese's main audiences were:

- Those who brought forth claims of abuse by a priest
- The "people in the pews"
- Clergy
- Employees and volunteers in the diocese and parishes

## Strategies and Tactics

In order to respond to those who brought allegations of abuse to the diocese, the bishop formed a legal team that included the person responsible for insurance coverage in the diocese and lawyers from three firms. His instruction was clear that this legal team was to *first be sensitive to the pastoral needs of the individuals.* By this he meant he wanted to help them, not engage in hostile legal tactics. The team built a working relationship with the attorneys representing the victims. They established a system of how to work toward settlement of claims that would not make those who were abused go through a public trial or disclosure of the abuse. In the end, the diocese was able to settle all claims out of court.

The main strategy the diocese employed was to *go direct.* It wanted to find ways to communicate to its key constituencies without the filter of the media. From past research, the diocese knew that the most trusted source of information for Catholics was their own parish priest. Catholics preferred to receive information in Church through the bulletins and handouts. Using this knowledge, the diocese developed some key action steps:

- **E-mail to priests.** The crisis team decided that no information should go out to the media before it was available to the priests. The diocese set up an e-mail distribution system, supplemented by a fax system for those priests without e-mail. Every time a news release or announcement was being made public, the priests received a copy first.
- **A live TV address.** The crisis team was able to convince the only network affiliate television station in the area to dedicate a half hour of programming to the bishop. Taped live and shown later in the day, the bishop was able to make a 15-minute statement that covered his regret over the past, that offered an assurance that there was no priest in ministry with a credible allegation of sexual abuse of a minor, and that described what the diocese was doing to prevent any further abuse. The remainder of the program was devoted to questions to the bishop from two reporters. Because this was taped live, there was no filtering of the message.

- **Taking it to the people.** The team knew that the pastors and parish leaders needed to hear directly from the bishop. In February 2003, one year after the initial release of the names, the bishop invited the pastor and two to five lay leaders from every parish in the state to Concord for a meeting. At the meeting, held in a parish church, the bishop laid out a clear and direct plan for how the Church was going to move forward. He recognized his own failings in the past and reaffirmed that he was not planning to resign, but planned to continue to dedicate his ministry to making the Church safe for all. The media was invited to attend and cover this event.
- **Regular bulletin announcements and information.** The diocese used parish bulletins to inform the faithful about programs to protect children and to describe other steps it was taking.

In order to be transparent, the diocese established several practices:

- **Return all media calls.** The spokesperson for the diocese returned every media call on the day it was received—if possible. The spokesperson would try to respond to all inquires and provide information, although some information was not made available due to its confidential nature. The diocese determined that local media had preference over regional and national media. In most cases, requests from the national news and entertainment programs were politely declined. The diocese kept its focus on its local audience who followed local media.
- **Announcements of priest's removal.** When a new complaint was received about a priest still in the ministry, the diocese would conduct an immediate review to ascertain that the complaint was at least probable. After that, the bishop would remove the priest from

active ministry pending a complete investigation of the claim. The bishop, auxiliary bishop, or the delegate for ministerial conduct would go to the parish where the priest was serving and announce the allegation, the fact that the priest would be on leave, and that there would be a priest appointed to serve as administrator of the parish. The bishop would also meet with parishioners after each Mass.

- **Public notice of priests on leave.** After notifying the parishes and the other priests, the diocese would make public via news releases that the priest was on leave because of a credible allegation of sexual abuse of a minor.

- **Meeting with activist groups.** The bishop met with the members of a protest group who appeared at the Cathedral. After Mass, the bishop invited the 20 or more individuals to the church hall and listened to their issues. He also met with leaders of other groups and established a liaison from the diocese to the Voice of the Faithful group in New Hampshire.

- **Financial disclosure.** In 2004, the diocese published the results of the first-ever outside audit of the central administration. Although in the works for a couple years, this audit was seen as a response for calls for more transparency. The diocese disclosed the total dollars in settlements reached with victims of past abuse.

- **Parish visits.** The bishop decided that his time was best served meeting directly with parishioners. He was in a parish almost every weekend that he did not have another commitment. He would say Mass, meet with parish leadership, and go to the church hall to meet with any parishioner who wanted to speak with him. He found that while many had questions, most parishioners were focused on moving forward and making sure that no such scandal would ever reoccur.

## Managing an Extended Crisis

Most crises deal with an incident and the aftermath of the incident. It has a flash point, a high point, and a resolution.

The sexual abuse crisis in the Church kept unfolding, taking new turns, and extending over time because of lawsuits and government investigations. It lasted in an active crisis mode for two-and-a-half years. Managing such an extended crisis requires flexibility on the part of the team and an ability to keep focused while new distractions flare up.

In the diocese, the team kept its message on target: that it was acting forcefully with new allegations; trying to assist victims; and instituting policies and procedures to prevent future abuse.

The bishop did not resign, but rather followed the tradition of the Church that he was sent by the Pope to serve the people. As a shepherd, the bishop saw his responsibility as one of dedication to solving a problem, not walking away from it. This view of a bishop as someone who stays to serve as opposed to a CEO who resigns was the most difficult aspect of the situation to communicate. Many felt that the bishop should resign, but they could not say how this would make the Church safer or how it would improve what the Church was doing.

The Church eventually was able to move out of crisis mode and begin to rebuild trust with members. This process will take a long time, but the majority of people in a recent statewide survey indicate that they trust there is no one in ministry known to have abused or been credibly accused of abusing a minor. With that acknowledgment as foundation, the Church can begin to leave the crisis behind. ■

## QUESTIONS FOR DISCUSSION

1. Some critics of the Catholic Church won't accept the church's position that crimes that occurred years ago should be judged by the standards of the day. What can/should the church say to those people?

2. Most crisis communication strategies recommend gaining or setting the "agenda" and establishing reasonable expectations. In this case, the media and the critics seem to have jumped on both the agenda and expectations. What can the church do to get control of the issue?

3. This case focuses on New Hampshire and the Boston area, but the problem is much more widespread than New England. Shouldn't there be some national or international effort on behalf of the Church?

4. Is public relations strategies really what the Catholic Church needs now?

# Case 9-6   The West Virginia Mine Disaster: An Emotional Roller Coaster and Public Relations Train Wreck

In the wee hours of a cold January morning, an underground explosion in the Sago mine in West Virginia left the fate of 13 miners in serious jeopardy. Although rescue efforts began immediately, it was 22 hours later before a fresh-air tunnel could be drilled into the mine shaft and workers could make their way to the trapped miners. There were no signs of life, even though the miners were veterans and each had been issued survival equipment. Monday, January 2, 2006, was a long day for family and friends.

Late the next day, rescue workers were able to penetrate deeply enough into the mine to reach an area near where the trapped miners were thought to be. Initial reports were that one miner's body was found, then, around midnight, reports that the other 12 miners were alive began circulating among friends and family gathered at the site. Joyous pandemonium erupted. Families hugged and danced. The governor of West Virginia, Joe Manchin, made an "official announcement" of the good news.

All across America, morning newspapers went to press carrying the banner headline "They're Alive!"

But, they weren't.

## Miscommunication Causes Second Catastrophe

Through some dreadful miscommunication, the message was reversed. One miner, Randal McCloy, Jr., was alive. The other 12 were dead. It was West Virginia's worst mining accident in 28 years.

So early Wednesday morning, Ben Hatfield, president and CEO of International Coal Group (ICG), which operated the mine, told the families that the news—now about three hours old—was wrong and that their loved ones were not coming out alive. About 45 minutes later Hatfield made a general announcement that the initial reports were wrong and that the news was bad, not good.

Many Americans awoke on Wednesday to read the "good news" in their morning papers. Like the families, they later learned the truth. The broadcast media and online news services, of course, were able to more easily correct the misinformation. But nearly everyone was asking: How could this have happened? Why was everyone misinformed?

The answer is probably never going to be known for sure, but among the contributing factors would be:

- Rescue workers were wearing full-face oxygen masks, making clear communication difficult.
- The rescue crews were exhausted.
- Communication was taking place in code.
- Poor connections and conditions made static-free transmissions impossible.
- The command center lines were "open," which meant that anyone standing near could hear (misunderstand?) the communication between rescue workers and those at the base.

It is important to note that Hatfield and ICG didn't make an official announcement about the miners' safety. Governor Manchin

**FIGURE 9-5    West Virginia Gov. Joe Manchin addresses the media**

*Source:* (Courtesy of Steven Wayne Rotsch.)

was apparently repeating what he heard at the scene, and even ICG officials were deceived for a while by the unconfirmed reports. Of course, everyone wanted to believe.

The misinformation likely came from well-intentioned bystanders who thought they heard good news. Cell phones were prominent among those present, making it easy to spread what was thought to be good news.

### The Company Takes Extreme Criticism for Poor Communication

With the truth came a firestorm of emotional criticism, much of it directed to Hatfield and ICG. Family members believed the initial reports came from ICG. "He strictly told us they was alive," said one relative. "Three hours later, he comes back and said they was dead." Others promised to sue. Just who and on what grounds wasn't clear, but the emotions were raw. Police stood by to restore order if necessary.

Once the truth was known, Hatfield and ICG followed textbook procedures in communicating the hard facts. "We prayed for miracles," he said. "Despite our grief and despair at the loss of our 12 co-workers, we want to celebrate the one miracle that was delivered." People in the crowd screamed, "He lied to us."

Hatfield would later say that he deeply regretted "allowing the jubilation to go on longer than it should have." He understood the people, even those who were critical of him. "They certainly have some basis for their frustration, having been put through this emotional roller coaster. I wouldn't wish that on anyone. I regret that it happened. I would do anything if it had not happened."

Those thoughts were small consolation to a nation seeking answers. One online poll taken on Wednesday, January 4, showed 61 percent of the respondents felt ICG had done a poor job of communicating. Another 20 percent thought the company was right in withholding any news until all the facts were in, and 19 percent just didn't know.

As might be expected, law firms in Charleston, Morgantown, Bluefield, and other West Virginia cities cranked up the advertising, one claiming to be specialists in "West Virginia Coal Mine Accident" lawsuits.

## Seeking to Lay Blame, All Became a Target

In the aftermath, one Democratic blog suggested President George W. Bush was to blame for the accident because "he didn't do anything to prevent the accident" (MyDD.com). The AFL-CIO accused Congress of doing too little, too late to improve mine safety. There was plenty of blame to go around.

Mine officials and politicians were not the only ones on the hot seat. Media critics were quick to point out that reporters, editors, and correspondents passed along the unfounded information, often without attribution. Others could see how the problem evolved. Alex Jones of the Harvard University's Shorenstein Center on the Press, Politics, and Public Policy speaking the day after on PBS observed:

This is a huge public interest story, the kind of story that grips a country like ours. Everybody was watching it. The news media were there; of course the families were gathered there.

And a miscommunication happens when someone overheard or misoverheard a statement that they had found the miners, interpreted that to mean that they were alive, and started cell phone calls to family members, giving them the idea that their loved ones had been saved.

The bells started ringing, the governor spoke; everyone was clamoring. And it was very, very clear that something wonderful had happened, except it didn't happen to be true.

This was not, of course, an official piece of information. But it's very hard for me fault the press in reporting that the families were saying they had gotten word that this had happened because that was literally the truth.

Rachel Smolkin, managing editor of the *American Journalism Review*, offers other considerations:

Well, a lot of it is deadline-driven. And this is a story that happened right on deadline for many papers, particularly papers on the East Coast. Then you have your deadline looming, you're hearing news that appears to be wonderful news, certainly news you want to get out to your readers; this is a miraculous ending to what seemed like it could be a very sad story, that these miners had been found.

I think the problem, if there is one, what the media maybe can be faulted for to some degree is not being a little more careful with their qualifiers. You have to be very careful about attributing information.

Dave Byron, APR, Volusia County, Florida, Community Information Director, puts the controversy into perspective for public relations practitioners:

The coal mine tragedy in West Virginia brings to light some immediate public information lessons that we need to remember:

- It is absolutely essential only factual, confirmed information be released. This especially is true when it comes to injuries and fatalities and the numbers of them.
- We must always remember the impact information has (good or bad) on family members and others close to a situation.
- We again learn the lesson that affected family members want to be given straightforward, unfiltered information as quickly as possible, again either good or bad news. They do not want their emotions to be toyed with.
- We learn that a Governor's Office may or may not have all the straight information. Local public information officers (or corporate spokespersons) must take control and rise and fall with their own abilities. We cannot rely on outside agencies.
- We learn . . . that being defensive about a bad situation only creates the perception of there's something to hide.

- We again confirm the fact that speaking with one voice during a tragedy is essential.
- We also learn that if we are an agency with inspection/oversight responsibility, we will be held accountable if we do not follow through with corrective action before a tragedy occurs. Burying the head in the sand hardly ever brings good.
- We also learn that once a tragedy occurs, we cannot knee jerk react from emotion. Investigation will take months. It's important to allow the authorities/agencies the time it takes to get to the bottom of the cause/solution, etc.

In the beginning, everyone feared the worst. Mine accidents, many times, have no happy endings.

In the end, everyone's fears were realized. That one escaped was a miracle.

The victims even understood their plight. Some used their dying moments to pen letters to their families.

It is the middle that is troublesome. There should have never been a middle. The concept of "One Clear Voice" has never been more important.

Better communication systems, better communication techniques, better control of the communication command base would have eliminated the false hope that miscommunication brought. This is a lesson for all practitioners. Be prepared. Once disaster strikes, it's too late to write a crisis plan or develop a legacy of trust. ■

------------------------------------------------

## QUESTIONS FOR DISCUSSION

1. What preparations might ICG have made to (a) anticipate the incident at the Sago mine and (b) avert the communication fiasco? Is it possible to "expect the unexpected"?

2. Did you detect a public relations presence during this case? Explain.
3. What role did the governor's pronouncement play in the scenario? Was this a good idea? Why or why not?

## PROBLEM 9-A WHEN ASSOCIATES DISAGREE IN HANDLING AN EMERGENCY

Three months ago, you were hired to start a public relations department at Reliable Steel Products Company. This is a young company with big ambitions. It is located in a medium-sized city in an area where industrial and residential building are predicted to boom. Reliable manufactures pipes, beams, rods, and other heavy parts for just about any kind of building.

After 3 months, your "department" consists of you and a secretary. Your outlook is bright, however. You report directly to the president, and she wants to be publicly known and highly regarded in the community and in the industry. To be of maximum help, you have done your homework by checking on the reputation of Reliable around town and in the industry. In the home community, Reliable and its president are not universally known, but employees, neighbors, and the people at the Chamber of Commerce feel that Reliable is well-managed, makes good products, and is a civic-minded neighbor. A few people did say that there have been a few accidents involving employees; it seems a rather dangerous place to work.

One morning, when the president is on her way to the state capital, you get a call from a reporter at the local daily newspaper. He says that an ambulance driver told him a Reliable employee had been killed a few minutes earlier, when some pipes rolled off a pile while a truck was being loaded in the shipping yard. The reporter asks for details.

You tell him you will check it out at once and get back to him. You call the safety supervisor. He blows up and insists that no details be released to any outsider until all the facts can be determined, the employee's family notified, the insurance company alerted, and the company lawyers informed. He says for you to hold off until the president returns the next morning. You agree on the priority of the employee's family, but explain that you cannot prevent the newspaper from publishing anything they have gotten elsewhere, whether it is accurate or not.

The safety supervisor says to take it up with the personnel director. You call her. She says they have someone out at the employee's home now, but she agrees with the safety supervisor that situations like this have all sorts of possible problems, with a chance of backlash. She thinks an unplanned response without the president's knowledge would be dangerous. She wants no part in it.

There are a number of alternatives open to you, but not much time to choose among them. What would be the best course to follow now? Everything considered, what immediate initiatives—if any—would you take?

What further issues can be anticipated as a result of the crisis? How would you recommend dealing with them?

## PROBLEM 9-B WHAT TO DO WHEN AN EMPLOYEE'S PROBLEMS AFFECT THE COMPANY

You have been called in to offer public relations advice to an appliance service company involved in a crisis. ABC Appliance Repair, a local company with 10 employees, has become enmeshed in an employee's legal problems. One of the employees was accused of raping a young woman on the local college campus. The owner of ABC Appliance Repair is a boss who treats his employees like family. He didn't think twice about putting up bail to get his employee out of jail. Unfortunately the media got wind of the circumstances and it made the front page of the next morning's newspaper: "ABC Appliance Repair Pays to Free Alleged Rapist Employee."

The owner calls you, angry at the way the newspaper presented the case and afraid he will lose customers. He doesn't know what to do: Should he call the media and fight back? Take out an ad and plead his case? He believes in his employee and would pay the bail again if he had to. Maybe, though, he wouldn't have talked so freely with the reporter.

The case will be going to court in about a month. The employee, in the meantime, is coming to work. Already, however, the company is receiving calls from irate members of the community complaining about his actions. He's afraid of what this might do to his business. Two scheduled clients have called to cancel. It may get worse when his employee goes to court—especially if the media continues to follow the story.

To whom does he need to communicate? Prioritize his publics and identify how to reach each one. Then put together a plan (strategy and tactics) that will deal with the current crisis ABC Appliance Repair is facing.

What would you recommend the owner do about the media? Should he respond? If he does, what might happen? If he doesn't, how else can he communicate his message?

# CHAPTER

# 10

# Standards, Ethics, and Values

Regulation of human conduct by standards rather than brute force or basic biological drive is the definition of civilization. Social conduct is regulated by five factors:

- **Tradition.** How has the situation been viewed or handled in the past?
- **Public opinion.** What is currently acceptable behavior to the majority of one's peers?
- **Law.** What is permissible and what is prohibited by legislation?
- **Morality.** Generally connotes a spiritual or religious prohibition; immorality is a charge usually leveled in issues on which religious teachings have concentrated.
- **Ethics.** Standards set by a profession, an organization, or oneself, based on conscience—what is right or fair to others as well as to oneself? (See Box, page 307.)

Admittedly, these factors, as described, are attempts at pragmatic definitions. It would not be hard to get into an argument over the differences or the details. The point is that, however we use the words, there are forces that keep society functioning despite the strong pull of self-interest, ego, competitiveness, antisocial behavior, criminality, and other ills that could destroy it.

## THE ROLE OF CONSCIENCE

Corporations and other formal organizations exist only on paper, and therefore have no conscience. Those who manage and decide for organizations may be guided by codes of ethics, but are also influenced by their personal ethics.

The difficulty in trying to pin down ethics in terms of standards or principles of conduct is that there is so little uniformity. Short of what is legal or illegal, determination of what kinds of conduct are acceptable, in various kinds of circumstances, comes down to the individual or the group conscience. And among individuals or groups having differing functional roles, the threshold of conscience can be high or low, near or far.

Consider the range of conscience or early warning sensations in a clergyman, prostitute, used-car dealer, illiterate, doctor of medicine, judge, or addicted derelict, to name but a few. Also, there are wide variations within each functional role, based on the personal makeup of the individual. The range varies from the person who feels

## ETHICS PROGRAMS ARE BIG BUSINESS

As evidenced by the cases you are about to read in this section, organizations today are finding it imperative to establish codes of ethics—and then to educate their members about them: two jobs for public relations.

Ethics training and education have become hot topics as centers such as the Josephson Institute of Ethics in California, the Ethics Resource Center in Washington D.C., and the Center for Business Ethics at Bentley College in Massachusetts, among many others, offer assistance to organizations to create ethics programs.

In 1991, the Center for Business Ethics established the Ethics Officer Association. An ethics officer is in charge of creating and maintaining an organization's ethics program. Currently the Association has 250 individual members representing more than 200 companies. Today 35 to 40 percent of major U.S. companies have an ethics officer, up from 15 to 20 percent 10 years ago.

The 2000 National Business Ethics Survey conducted by the Ethics Resource Center shows that companies today are doing more in terms of their ethics programs, compared to 1994. More companies have written ethics standards, ethics training programs, and means for employees to get ethics advice. A majority of employees are positive about ethics in their organizations. As a result, employees say they are more satisfied with their organizations overall. Concern for ethics is an important reason, they say, for continuing to work there.

What does this new emphasis on ethics mean for the practice of public relations? What many esteemed practitioners have been saying all along—without ethical behavior there is no credibility. And without credibility there is no business.

An already distrustful public is wary of the motives of business, government, and even nonprofit agencies, as scandal after scandal surfaces about improprieties and mismanagement. A solid commitment to an ethics program by management and employees can help to gain, regain, or hold public trust and credibility, both internally and externally.

Transparency and accountability are going to be matters of rising public concern around the world in the years ahead, according to Frank Vogl, a senior ethics advisor with Ethics Resource Center and a communication professional.

that "anything in my own interest is right as long as I don't go to jail," to "anything that pricks my conscience is wrong, no matter what anyone else says or does."

Then, too, most people tend to prescribe for others ethical standards of conduct that they do not practice themselves.

Customs and changing times are significantly involved in ethics and standards. Gifts and favors of various kinds are accepted in many countries as part of the cost of doing, or expediting, business. U.S. businesses that are international in scope claim they must comply to compete. In this country, public attitude in general frowns on gifts and favors as thinly disguised forms of bribery or payoff.

As another example, the dogma and ways of groups committed to strict standards and stern discipline come under assault. Consider the pressure on the Amish people as they see the luxuries and laxity of their neighbors. Or the differing practices of orthodox and reform

Jews. Or the Catholic dogma, or the "Protestant work ethic" opposing a wave of permissive-ness, liberation of the young, and psychiatric forgiveness for lapses in self-discipline.

## APPLICATION TO THE PRACTICE OF PUBLIC RELATIONS

Any effort to bring these considerations down to the practical world of public relations finds generalizations fraught with exceptions. The practice of public relations has been codified for the 20,000 members of the Public Relations Society of American since 1950. In 2000, PRSA adopted a member code of ethics (see Figures 10-1 and 10-2). But there

### FIGURE 10-1   PRSA Member Statement of Professional Values

This statement presents the core values of PRSA members and, more broadly, of the public relations profession. These values provide the foundation for the Member Code of Ethics and set the industry standard for the professional practice of public relations. These values are the fundamental beliefs that guide our behaviors and decision-making process. We believe our professional values are vital to the integrity of the profession as a whole.

**ADVOCACY**

- We serve the public interest by acting as responsible advocates for those we represent.
- We provide a voice in the marketplace of ideas, facts, and viewpoints to aid informed public debate.

**HONESTY**

- We adhere to the highest standards of accuracy and truth in advancing the interests of those we represent and in communicating with the public.

**EXPERTISE**

- We acquire and responsibly use specialized knowledge and experience.
- We advance the profession through continued professional development, research, and education.
- We build mutual understanding, credibility, and relationships among a wide array of institutions and audiences.

**INDEPENDENCE**

- We provide objective counsel to those we represent.
- We are accountable for our actions.

**LOYALTY**

- We are faithful to those we represent, while honoring our obligation to serve the public interest.

**FAIRNESS**

- We deal fairly with clients, employers, competitors, peers, vendors, the media, and the general public.
- We respect all opinions and support the right of free expression.

*Source:* (The PRSA Member Code of Ethics is reprinted with permission from the Public Relations Society of America, www.prsa.org.)

**FIGURE 10-2   PRSA Code Provisions**

## FREE FLOW OF INFORMATION

### Core Principle

Protecting and advancing the free flow of accurate and truthful information is essential to serving the public interest and contributing to informed decision making in a democratic society.

### Intent

- To maintain the integrity of relationships with the media, government officials, and the public.
- To aid informed decision-making.

### Guidelines

A member shall:

- Preserve the integrity of the process of communication.
- Be honest and accurate in all communications.
- Act promptly to correct erroneous communications for which the practitioner is responsible.
- Preserve the free flow of unprejudiced information when giving or receiving gifts by ensuring that gifts are nominal, legal, and infrequent.

### Examples of Improper Conduct Under This Provision:

- A member representing a ski manufacturer gives a pair of expensive racing skis to a sports magazine columnist, to influence the columnist to write favorable articles about the product.
- A member entertains a government official beyond legal limits and/or in violation of government reporting requirements.

## COMPETITION

### Core Principle

Promoting healthy and fair competition among professionals preserves an ethical climate while fostering a robust business environment.

### Intent

- To promote respect and fair competition among public relations professionals.
- To serve the public interest by providing the widest choice of practitioner options.

### Guidelines

A member shall:

- Follow ethical hiring practices designed to respect free and open competition without deliberately undermining a competitor.
- Preserve intellectual property rights in the marketplace.

*(continued)*

(*continued*)

### Examples of Improper Conduct Under This Provision:

- A member employed by a "client organization" shares helpful information with a counseling firm that is competing with others for the organization's business.
- A member spreads malicious and unfounded rumors about a competitor in order to alienate the competitor's clients and employees in a ploy to recruit people and business.

## DISCLOSURE OF INFORMATION

### Core Principle
Open communication fosters informed decision making in a democratic society.

### Intent

- To build trust with the public by revealing all information needed for responsible decision making.

### Guidelines
A member shall:

- Be honest and accurate in all communications.
- Act promptly to correct erroneous communications for which the member is responsible.
- Investigate the truthfulness and accuracy of information released on behalf of those represented.
- Reveal the sponsors for causes and interests represented.
- Disclose financial interest (such as stock ownership) in a client's organization.
- Avoid deceptive practices.

### Examples of Improper Conduct Under This Provision:

- Front groups: A member implements "grass roots" campaigns or letter-writing campaigns to legislators on behalf of undisclosed interest groups.
- Lying by omission: A practitioner for a corporation knowingly fails to release financial information, giving a misleading impression of the corporation's performance.
- A member discovers inaccurate information disseminated via a Web site or media kit and does not correct the information.
- A member deceives the public by employing people to pose as volunteers to speak at public hearings and participate in "grass roots" campaigns.

## SAFEGUARDING CONFIDENCES

### Core Principle
Client trust requires appropriate protection of confidential and private information.

### Intent

- To protect the privacy rights of clients, organizations, and individuals by safeguarding confidential information.

## Guidelines

A member shall:

- Safeguard the confidences and privacy rights of present, former, and prospective clients and employees.
- Protect privileged, confidential, or insider information gained from a client or organization.
- Immediately advise an appropriate authority if a member discovers that confidential information is being divulged by an employee of a client company or organization.

## Examples of Improper Conduct Under This Provision:

- A member changes jobs, takes confidential information, and uses that information in the new position to the detriment of the former employer.
- A member intentionally leaks proprietary information to the detriment of some other party.

# CONFLICTS OF INTEREST

## Core Principle

Avoiding real, potential or perceived conflicts of interest builds the trust of clients, employers, and the publics.

## Intent

- To earn trust and mutual respect with clients or employers.
- To build trust with the public by avoiding or ending situations that put one's personal or professional interests in conflict with society's interests.

## Guidelines

A member shall:

- Act in the best interests of the client or employer, even subordinating the member's personal interests.
- Avoid actions and circumstances that may appear to compromise good business judgment or create a conflict between personal and professional interests.
- Disclose promptly any existing or potential conflict of interest to affected clients or organizations.
- Encourage clients and customers to determine if a conflict exists after notifying all affected parties.

## Examples of Improper Conduct Under This Provision

- The member fails to disclose that he or she has a strong financial interest in a client's chief competitor.
- The member represents a "competitor company" or a "conflicting interest" without informing a prospective client.

*(continued)*

(*continued*)

## ENHANCING THE PROFESSION

### Core Principle

Public relations professionals work constantly to strengthen the public's trust in the profession.

### Intent

- To build respect and credibility with the public for the profession of public relations.
- To improve, adapt and expand professional practices.

### Guidelines

A member shall:

- Acknowledge that there is an obligation to protect and enhance the profession.
- Keep informed and educated about practices in the profession to ensure ethical conduct.
- Actively pursue personal professional development.
- Decline representation of clients or organizations that urge or require actions contrary to this Code.
- Accurately define what public relations activities can accomplish.
- Counsel subordinates in proper ethical decision making.
- Require that subordinates adhere to the ethical requirements of the Code.
- Report ethical violations, whether committed by PRSA members or not, to the appropriate authority.

### Examples of Improper Conduct Under This Provision:

- A PRSA member declares publicly that a product the client sells is safe, without disclosing evidence to the contrary.
- A member initially assigns some questionable client work to a non-member practitioner to avoid the ethical obligation of PRSA membership.

## RESOURCE

### Rules and Guidelines

The following PRSA documents, available on line at PRSA.org. Provide detailed rules and guidelines to help guide your professional behavior:

- PRSA Bylaws
- PRSA Administrative Rules
- Member Code of Ethics

If, after reviewing them, you still have a question or issue, contact PRSA Headquarters as noted below.

## QUESTIONS

The PRSA is here to help. Whether you have a serious concern or simply need clarification, contact Judy Voss at judy.voss@prsa.org.

*Source:* (The PRSA Member Code of Ethics is reprinted with permission from the Public Relations Society of America, www.prsa.org.)

are more than 200,000 persons engaged in activities identifiable as public relations, most without equivalent standards or discipline.

That the public relations calling has been able to outgrow such labels as "flackery" and to rise above recurrent instances of news manipulation, cover-up, sugar coating, and some cases of deliberate deceit testifies eloquently to the potential power and promise of two-way communications and positive relationship building when the skills are turned to noble purposes.

For most practitioners, the Golden Rule is seen as an ethical guide—even as a definition of public relations. *If we do unto others as we would have them do unto us, harmonious public relationships will result.*

## THE ASPIRATIONS AND CONCEPT ARE PURE

Consider the following concept. If people would communicate more—and better—in a spirit of compromise and reconciliation, most problems in human relations would be solved. There would be understanding and peace. Lifestyle would include self-discipline and acceptance of responsibility, affluence with charity, possession without greed or avarice, and personal integrity under rules of law and mutual respect.

It is in this area that the public relations function has sought to fulfill its aspirations by exerting an ethical and moral force as well as technical skill and, by doing so, developing an identity and a professional discipline of its own.

It has been a long road to travel, but the destination is getting closer: The body of knowledge has been codified; there is an accepted academic curriculum leading to a distinct, recognized public relations doctorate. Today, approximately 70 schools offer master's degrees or a graduate emphasis in public relation. Four universities offer doctoral programs specifically in public relations. There is still no *licensing* of practitioners, but there is a Universal Accreditation Program formed in January 1998 by the Public Relations Society of America and nine other public relations organizations. Members with at least five years of full-time paid professional pr experience must pass a written and oral exam to be accredited APR.

In the past, practitioners have functioned generally as skilled communicators and persuaders on behalf of the organizations that employ them. Ethical standards have tended to be the reflections of the employers and clients served. Putting it another way, the public relations voice has generally emerged publicly more as an echo of an employer's standards and interests than that of a professional discipline applied to the employer's problems.

The practitioner still may come on as narrowly organizational rather than broadly professional, but this situation is changing as both employers and the profession embrace a new wave of ethics. Today, public relations continues its struggle for broad recognition as advocates of understanding and public interest, qualified by academic discipline and professional accreditation.

## WHAT IS ACCEPTABLE ETHICALLY?

- Is it acceptable for food companies, in the name of nutrition and education, to provide elementary schools with educational kits prominently featuring their labels, product photographs, slogans, and product recipes?
- Is it acceptable for a county agency supported by taxpayers to spend money for a public relations firm to put out its news and promote its work?

- Is it acceptable for a utility to include in the rates to customers the cost of donations it makes to charity, for which it gets credit as being generous?
- Is it acceptable for soft drink, cereal, and other product manufacturers to shower television and movie prop people with free merchandise so that their products appear to be "standard" on television and in motion pictures?
- Is it acceptable for big businesses to preach that their growth creates jobs, when many of them have doubled in sales over a 10-year period yet their employment total remains what it was 10 years ago?
- Is it acceptable for a corporation to hand out a news release at the outset of its annual meeting saying that its presentation was accorded a standing ovation?
- Is it acceptable for television networks to tie in a tire-company blimp with their newscasts at sports events, giving the blimp owner free publicity?
- Is it acceptable for a public relations counselor to send a client a flattering clipping with a note, "I knew you'd like to see this as soon as we got it," as if the counselor had something to do with generating the publicity, though actually he or she had not?
- Is it acceptable for an incumbent member of Congress to use perks of office such as staff paid by taxpayers, free mailings, pork barrel (including $25 million for grasshopper control back home), and PAC money to clobber any opposition and perpetuate himself or herself in office?
- Is it acceptable for a public relations director to tell the public a lie on a matter of no real significance if the intent is to protect the privacy or reputation of his or her boss?
- Is it acceptable to use fear in advertising to raise funds for poor people flooded out of their homes? To help cut down on the sale of tobacco? To sell a fire detection device? Insurance?
- Is it acceptable for a congressperson to accept a box of oranges from a grateful fruit grower in his district? An envelope with $20 in it? Season tickets to the Washington Redskins games? A television set? A new automobile?
- Is it acceptable to announce publicly that an official has resigned "for personal reasons" when in fact he or she was fired for the good of the organization, or at the whim of a more powerful, jealous individual?

"So what" is often the reaction after reading these ethical situations. This comment comes from two different concepts: (1) I'd never do any of those, or (2) I'd have to wait until I saw what else was involved before I decided what I would do.[1]

With regard to the first concept, it would be the exceptional person who has a high standard and never goes against it. Lives are a mixture of doing exactly what we think should be done and being "flexible" where the area is more gray than black or white.

The second concept suggests situation ethics, where a person not only waits to make a decision but may make different decisions involving the same situation at different times. Ethics are often gray, but there are situations in which a person should be able to be counted on to do or not to do. Certainly your peers and employers want to believe this. The Public Relations Code of Ethics sets standards we are expected to follow.

---

[1]For an interesting classroom exercise in professional ethics, see Lynne Masel-Walters, "Playing the Game: Ethics Situations for Public Relations Courses," *Public Relations Research and Education Journal* 1, Winter, 1984, pp. 47–54.

## REFERENCES AND ADDITIONAL READINGS

Baker, Lee. *The Credibility Factor.* Homewood, IL: Business One Irwin, 1992.

Bernays, Edward L., et al. *tips & tactics* (supplement of *pr reporter,* October 21, November 18, and December 2, 1985). Bernays and others express divergent views on the proposal that practitioners be licensed, like doctors and lawyers, in a three-part *tips & tactics* series.

Bovet, Susan Fry. "The Burning Question of Ethics: The Profession Fights for Better Business Practices." *Public Relations Journal* 49 (November 1993): 24–25, 29.

Brain, John. "Openness or Irrationality." *Public Relations Journal* 44 (December 1988). Editorial dealing with ethical questions in openness; cites cases involving Nestlé, Gerber, and Johnson & Johnson.

Center, Allen. "What About the State of the Art?" *Public Relations Journal* 32 (January 1976). A timeless discussion piece.

Center for Business Ethics at Bentley College, 175 Forest Street, Waltham, MA 02452–4705, 781/891–2981, http://ecampus.bentley.edu/dept/cbe. Established the Ethics Officer Association.

Cutlip, Scott, Allen Center, and Glen Broom. "Ethics and Professionalism." Chapter 5 in *Effective Public Relations.* 8th ed. Upper Saddle River, NJ: Prentice Hall, 1999.

Ethics Resource Center, 1747 Pennsylvania Ave. NW, Suite 400, Washington DC 20006, 202/737–2258, www.ethics.org. Conducts National Business Ethics Survey.

*Ethikos* (a bimonthly publication, which joined forces with Rutgers University's *Corporate Conduct Quarterly* in 1998) takes a case study approach to corporate ethics and compliance programs. For sample articles go to www.singerpubs.com/ethikos.

Grunig, James, and Todd Hunt. *Managing Public Relations.* New York: Holt, Rinehart and Winston, 1984. See Chapters 3 and 4.

Hoffman, W. Michael. *The Corporation, Ethics & the Environment.* Westport, CT: Greenwood Publishing Group, 1990.

Jackson, Patrick, and John Paluszek. "Demonstrating Professionalism." *Public Relations Journal* 44 (October 1988). Discusses the options available for practitioners to demonstrate their value to society.

The Joseph & Edna Josephson Institute for Ethics provides a variety of materials and training tools to prepare business for ethical issues and scenarios. For more information contact, Joseph and Edna Josephson Institute of Ethics, 4640 Admiralty Way, Suite 1001, Marina del Rey, CA 90292–6610, 310/827–1864, www.josephsoninstitute.org.

Lesly, Phillip. *The People Factor: Managing the Human Climate.* Homewood, IL: Dow Jones Irwin, 1974.

McElreath, Mark. *Managing Systematic and Ethical Public Relations Campaigns.* New York: McGraw-Hill Higher Education, 1996.

Nevins, Allan, et al. *Public Relations Review* 4 (Fall 1978). A series of six scholarly lectures on the relationship of public relations to eras in U.S. history.

Newsom, Doug, Alan Scott, and Judy Van Slyke Turk. "PR Ethics and Social Responsibilities." Chapter 8 in *This Is PR: The Realities of Public Relations.* 6th ed. Belmont, CA: Wadsworth, 1996.

Olasky, Marvin. "The Aborted Debate Within Public Relations: An Approach Through Kuhn's Paradigm." Chapter 4 in *Public Relations Research Annual.* Volume 1. New York: Lawrence Erlbaum, 1989.

Pearson, Ron. "Beyond Ethical Relativism in Public Relations: Co-orientation, Rules and the Idea of Communication Symmetry." Chapter 3 in *Public Relations Research Annual.* Volume 1. New York: Lawrence Erlbaum, 1989.

Pearson, Ron. "Albert J. Sullivan's Theory of Public Relations Ethics." *Public Relations Review* 15 (Summer 1989): 52–61.

*pr reporter* Vol. 43 No. 11 (March 13, 2000). "Ethical Behavior Seen by Utility CEO as Essential Tool in New Competitive Electric Market—A Sample Program."

*pr reporter* Vol. 41 No. 35 (September 7, 1998). "Does Professionalism Translate to Ethical Practice?"

*pr reporter* Vol. 37 No. 19 (May 9, 1994). "False Fronts, Trying to Buy Relationships Demean Profession."

*pr reporter* Vol. 34 No. 43 (November 4, 1991). "Ethics Seen As (1) Competitive Advantage, (2) Way to Earn Trust, (3) Heart of Environmental & Social Responsibility Policies."

*The Public Relations Body of Knowledge.* New York: PRSA. See abstracts dealing with Ethical Issues.

*tips & tactics*—a supplement of *pr reporter*— Vol. 39 No. 5 (May 7, 2001). "Corporate Integrity & Globalization: The Dawning of a New Era of Accountability & Transparency" by Frank Vogl.

*tips & tactics*—a supplement of *pr reporter*— Vol. 38 No. 14 (October 30, 2000). "PRSA Changes Its Landmark Code of Ethics, Drops Enforcement Provision to Focus on Educating."

Walsh, Frank. *Public Relations and the Law.* Institute for Public Relations, University of Florida, P.O. Box 118400, Gainesville, FL 32611–8400, 1991. Summarizes laws and regulations that form the basis for the right of representation in the "court of public opinion" by all who seek to influence public and private decisions.

Walsh, Frank, and Philip Lesly. "Considerations of Law in Public Relations." Chapter 48 in *Lesly's Handbook of Public Relations and Communications.* 5th ed. Chicago, IL: NTC Business Books, 1998.

Ward, Gary. *Developing and Enforcing a Code of Business Ethics.* Babylon, New York: Pilot, 1989.

Wilcox, Dennis, Philip Ault, and Warren Agee. "Ethics and Professionalism." Chapter 3 in *Public Relations Strategies and Tactics.* 6th ed. New York: Longman, 2000.

-----------------------------------C A S E S---------------------------------

# Case 10-1 Corporate Ethics—Armstrong Williams

The beginning of the twenty-first century brought with it a focus on ethics, especially corporate ethics. To be sure, there were ethical concerns across the board, but America's gaze seemed locked onto what was going on in the corporate boardrooms, and with good reason.

The list of executives and companies involved in scandals of their own doing seemed endless:

- Martha Stewart and her personal portfolio
- Ken Lay and Jeffrey Skilling of Enron
- Richard Scrushy and HealthSouth
- Bernie Ebbers and WorldCom
- The John Rigas family and Adelphia
- Dennis Kozlowski and Tyco

While the players in the ethics game all had their day in court, a disturbing trend was emerging: There is a lot of questionable behavior going on. It is no wonder that public trust in business leaders overall fell from 36 percent in 2002 to only 28 percent in 2006, and only 39 percent of investors were confident of the ethical practices of CEOs in January 2006, down from 47 percent a year earlier.[1]

In one February 2006 edition of the national newspaper *USA Today,* were stories detailing the following:

- A plea bargain for the chief executive officer and the chief financial officer of the Federal National Mortgage Association involving some $11 billion in fraud

- Testimony by the investor relations vice president of Enron that Lay and Skilling had lied to investors, employees, and analysts (both were later convicted)
- HealthSouth settling fraud lawsuits for some $445 million
- A biomedical company being accused of stealing body parts in a scheme with funeral homes

Meanwhile, the public relations profession was not immune from its own controversies. Governmental entities seemed particularly disposed to bend the rules. The U.S. military was found to be paying media in Iraq to print favorable stories about U.S. involvement in that country, for example. But it was a contract involving the U.S. Department of Education; a leading public relations firm, Ketchum; and a Washington-based communicator named Armstrong Williams that brought the most attention to public relations ethics—or lack thereof.

## Armstrong Williams: A Question of Principles

In the early days of 2005, Armstrong Williams was an influential African American with his fingers in several pies. He was partner with Stedman Graham (Oprah's boyfriend) in the Graham Williams Group, a Washington-based advertising and public relations firm. In addition, he had a syndicated television show and was a conservative columnist for several

---

[1]Charles H. Green, "Who Should You Trust on Trust in Business?" www.trustedadvisor.com, May 29, 2007.

newspapers. His conservative tone and minority credentials made him popular with the Bush administration.

Two years earlier, in 2003, Williams had been the recipient of a $240,000 contract to promote the No Child Left Behind (NCLB) initiative of the Bush Administration and the U.S. Department of Education (DOE). The contract called on Williams to "comment regularly" on NCLB and to provide media time for Department of Education secretary Rod Paige.

When *USA Today*, acting on information obtained via the Freedom of Information Act, broke the story, Democrats immediately called for an investigation, saying the deal smacked of illegally manipulating public opinion.

Questions were raised about whether Williams was a member of the media or if he was a public relations consultant. He called the contract "advertising" and said that he was paid to advertise the NCLB initiative. To others, it seemed to be paid editorial, something that violates the "contamination of the channels of communication" provisions of most public relations codes of conduct.

Equally troubling was the involvement in a high-profile public relations firm, Ketchum & Associates. Ketchum had a contract with the DOE to promote NCLB. At worst, Ketchum initiated the contract with Williams. At best, Ketchum failed to stop it. Regardless, the public relations profession quickly found itself linked with Enron, WorldCom, and the others as ethics took center stage.

Much of the public relations industry reacted quickly. Judith Phair, president of the Public Relations Society of America at the time, said, "This does not describe the true practice of public relations."

Daniel Edelman, whose Chicago-based Edelman & Co. is the largest independent public relations firm in the country, was critical of Ketchum's ethics. Elliott Sloane of Sloane & Company resigned from the Council of PR

Firms because the Council's response to the affair was "tepid." Practitioners across the country posted comments on bulletin boards and blogs decrying Ketchum's role in the controversy.

Interestingly, some industry insiders didn't see the ethical dilemma. Kathy Cripps of the Council of PR Firms pinned the responsibility on Williams and said that Ketchum didn't violate the Council's Code of Ethics.

Ketchum, in a *PR Week* op-ed piece, passed the ball to Williams and called for a "clarification of the rules . . . for everyone." Some Web postings likened the situation to "bribing an editor with lunch" or merely providing access to information—public relations' traditional role.

## Ketchum Takes Responsibility . . . Finally

Two weeks later, however, Ketchum apologized for its part in the Williams affair, saying "We should have recognized the potential issues in working with a communications firm operated by a commentator. This work did not comply with the guidelines of our agency and our industry. Under those guidelines, it is clear that we should have encouraged greater disclosure. There was a lapse of judgment in this situation. We regret that this has occurred."

If Williams was more "media" than "public relations," then he had plenty of company during his ordeal. Dan Rather was forced off the air after reporting unverified charges about President George W. Bush's military experience. The conservative broadcaster Rush Limbaugh was having problems with prescription drugs, and the *New York Times* was changing managing editors after a series of stories fabricated by one reporter. And in Alabama, a writer for a small weekly newspaper said HealthSouth CEO Scrushy paid her—through his public relations firm—to write favorable stories about him through his trial. (Scrushy was acquitted on 36 counts of fraud.)

What this one episode means to the industry is that the profession of public relations needs to get its collective house in order. These practitioners broke faith with the public, the media, and the government. Ethical codes and guidelines should promote adherence and respect rather than ignorance or disdain. ∎

------------------------------------------------------------

## QUESTIONS FOR DISCUSSION

1. How does the Armstrong Williams affair compare in severity with such scandals as Enron and WorldCom?
2. How did Williams' various enterprises contribute to his problems?
3. Assess Ketchum's role in this situation. What caused the change in Ketchum's response? How does a "lapse in judgment" differ from weak ethics?
4. Discuss the responses of the public relations industry. Was this reaction strong enough for the situation?
5. Compare/contrast the response from the Public Relations Society of America and that of the Council of PR Firms. Why the difference?

# Case 10-2  A Classic: Baby Formula Raises Questions

In capitalist theory, the law of supply and demand and the human virtues of honesty and fairness are determinants regulating competition in the marketplace. If and when these get out of kilter, appropriate restraints or regulations can be imposed by governmental authority.

However, laxity in self-imposed standards back in the 1960s led to a number of consumer protection laws and to the growing intervention of the consumer's advocate. The advocate came in the form of either a person or an organization, acting as investigator or quality control manager, on behalf of the consuming public. Over time, nongovernmental consumer protection and advocacy have come to involve the Better Business Bureaus, *Consumer Research* and *Consumer Reports* magazines, telephone hotlines, television programs, newspaper and magazine features, newsletters, and dozens of special interest groups with their networks for investigation and communication.

## Competition Is the Culprit

Product producers who are in business for the long haul don't set out to deliver an unsafe, fragile, or overpriced product. Occurrences when consumers are harmed or abused by gutter-level tactics and ethics are the exceptions. More often, breaches of the buyer-seller relationship stem from competitive pressures resulting in use of substandard materials; inadequate research, testing, or quality control; improper packaging; overstated claims of product benefits or capabilities; or faulty instructions. When consumer complaints pile up and a protectionist group moves in or litigation threatens, product makers go on the *defensive*, sometimes to stonewall, and other times to recall, to replace, or to refund.

## Mothers, Babies, and Nutrition

To exemplify a breached buyer–seller relationship and a consumer group moving in, we have chosen powdered infant formula as the product, and two giant producers, Nestlé, the world food colossus based in Switzerland, and Bristol-Myers, a multi-billion dollar U.S. company diversified in pharmaceuticals, household products, cosmetics, and may other products.

The problem arose when powdered infant formula was distributed by these two competitors in underdeveloped areas of the world. Medical studies conducted by world health organizations found that when the product was administered it was a contributing factor in malnutrition and the cause of diarrhea and a higher mortality rate in babies in underdeveloped countries (see Figure 10-3).

At the core of the problem was the reality that most infant formulas sold in underdeveloped countries come in powdered form, and these milk solids must be mixed with water before they are usable. According to the reports, babies frequently received contaminated milk because in many areas there is a general ignorance of hygiene, unclean water, or limited fuel for sterilizing bottles. These conditions prevented mothers from following formula preparations correctly.

## High Cost of Powdered Formula

Moreover, according to the reports, the powdered formula was so expensive that mothers often diluted it to make it last longer. It was

FIGURE 10-3   Emotion-packed photo carried by *Mother Jones* magazine dramatically shows the impact of the use of powdered formula sold in underdeveloped nations

estimated that in Nigeria, where American-made formula was widely used, the cost of feeding a three-month-old infant with formula was approximately 30 percent of the minimum urban wage. Making matters worse, there was a sweeping shift away from breastfeeding throughout developing countries. The shift was associated with the rapid urbanization of these countries.

Critics admitted that the infant formula manufacturers were not responsible for the trend away from breastfeeding. However, faced with stagnant or declining birthrates in the developed world, the critics maintained that these companies encouraged the abandonment of breastfeeding by stepping up their sales effort in the baby-booming areas of Latin America, the Far East, Africa, and the Middle East.

Profits from baby formula sales reached new highs for some of the companies. In 1975, Bristol-Myers enjoyed a one-year record in profits largely because of formula sales. For another company, baby formula sales increased by more than 30 percent for two years in a row.[1]

## Ethical Misconduct, Clever Marketing, or Social Irresponsibility?

Most of the criticism of the companies focused on how they achieved their sales. In underdeveloped countries, they relied heavily on "milk nurses" or "mother craft workers" who went into hospitals, clinics, and private homes to instruct new mothers on child care and on the advantages of using the company's formula. The "nurses" wore traditional nurses' uniforms, which, the critics charged, lent a spurious air of authority to their sales appeal, and in some cases they

[1]*New York Times,* September 11, 1975.

were paid on a commission or bonus basis, adding a conflict-of-interest charge to the matter of morality.[2]

As public awareness of the controversy grew, better-known organizations became involved. The Protein Calorie Group of the United Nations issued a statement that emphasized "the critical importance of breast-feeding under the sociocultural and economic conditions that prevailed in many developing countries." Later, the Twenty-Seventh World Health Assembly passed resolutions strongly recommending the encouragement of breast-feeding as the "ideal feeding in order to promote harmonious physical and mental development of children." The resolutions called for countries to "review sales and promotional activities on baby foods and to introduce appropriate remedial measures, including advertisement codes and legislation where necessary."[3]

## Publicity Continues for Years

The controversy continued at the publicity level four years before organizations within the United States adopted the role of consumer advocate. Perhaps the most influential advocate was the Interfaith Center on Corporate Responsibility (ICCR), a division of the National Council of Churches. The group represents 14 major Protestant denominations and more than 150 Catholic groups. In an annual report, ICCR stated that it "exists to assist its member boards, agencies and instrumentalities to express

social responsibility with their investments. Members of ICCR agree that as investors in businesses, they are also part owners and therefore have the right and obligation to monitor the social responsibilities of corporations and act where necessary to help prevent or correct corporate policy that produces social injury."[4]

## Consumer Interest Strategy

As an initial step, ICCR members filed shareholder resolutions with U.S. baby formula manufacturers, including Bristol-Myers. Management met with ICCR members and disclaimed any responsibility for formula misuse. Despite this disclaimer, other organizations supported the resolutions. The Ford Foundation joined the other shareholders in support of the resolution—calling for a report on sales and promotional activities. The president of the Rockefeller Foundation wrote to the chairman of Bristol-Myers requesting the "publication of all relevant information to the outer limits permitted by competitive considerations."

## Tactics and Debate

A short time later, Bristol-Myers published a 19-page report entitled *The Infant Formula Marketing Practices of Bristol-Myers Company in Countries Outside the United States.* ICCR called the report "an attempt to obfuscate the issue" and sought responses by experts in infant nutrition. Dr. Derrick

---

[2]Ibid.

[3]Other studies and reports were made both in the United States and in foreign countries. They told the same stories using different examples from different places in the world. While most of these reports went unchallenged by the producers of baby formula, one exception should be noted. An organization called Third World Action Group reprinted a report entitled *The Baby Killers.* The booklet was aimed at Nestlé and reported on infant malnutrition and the promotion of artificial feeding practices in the Third World. When the booklet was released in Switzerland, Nestlé sued for defamation. The suit made news throughout the world for two years before it was settled. In the end, Nestlé dropped three of the four defamation charges. On the fourth charge regarding the new title, *Nestlé Kills Babies,* the judge said that since it could not be shown that Nestlé directly kills infants—the mothers who prepare the formula are third-party intermediaries—the title must be defamatory. However, the judge imposed only minimal fines and asked Nestlé to "fundamentally rethink" its advertising policies.

[4]ICCR 1977 Annual Report.

Jelliffe, one of the early expert critics in the baby formula controversy, condemned the report as "inadequate and evasive." Within a couple of months, more than 20 ICCR members, joined by staff members of the Rockefeller and Ford foundations, met with Bristol-Myers management. The meetings changed little, and ICCR members filed another shareholder resolution with Bristol-Myers, requesting the correction of the company's report.

Four months after the ICCR resolution requesting a correction, Bristol-Myers issued a proxy statement stating that the company had been "totally responsive to the concerns [of ICCR members]" in the stockholders' resolutions. Feeling sure the proxy was inaccurate, the Sisters of the Precious Blood and ICCR members filed a lawsuit against Bristol-Myers. The suit charged Bristol-Myers with making a "misstatement" in its proxy and called for "a resolicitation of proxy votes, free from the taint of fraud." The Sisters of the Precious Blood submitted massive evidence in support of their claim, but the U.S. district judge dismissed the suit. The judge declined to rule on the accuracy of the proxy statement, saying the Sisters were not caused "irreparable harm" by the statement. The text of the decision implied that since a shareholder resolution is "precatory," or not binding on management, it is not relevant whether a company fails to tell the truth in responding to a shareholder proposal. Sometimes even the courts seem to condone or encourage ethical lapses.

## SEC Supports Sisters

The Sisters of the Precious Blood announced plans to appeal the dismissal on the grounds that the ruling "did not address the merits of the charge and makes a mockery of Securities and Exchange Commission laws requiring truth in corporate proxy statements." The Securities and Exchange Commission added pressure to Bristol-Myers when it indicated a plan to file a brief in court in favor of the Sisters if the appeal went forward. In the end, the appeal did not have to be filed because Bristol-Myers agreed to send a report to stockholders that included evidence from Third World countries, details of sales of Bristol-Myers in poverty areas, and a description of the medical problems caused by these practices. Bristol-Myers also agreed to halt the use of all consumer-oriented advertising and to withdraw milk nurses.

About the same time as the Sisters of the Precious Blood filed their lawsuit against Bristol-Myers, members of Congress began to act on the controversy. The first step was a resolution co-sponsored by 29 members of Congress calling for an investigation of U.S. formula companies. A year later, an amendment to the International Development and Food Assistance Act urged the president to develop a strategy for programs of nutrition and health improvements for mothers and children, including breastfeeding. The report accompanying the House version of the amendment stated that "businesses involved in the manufacture, marketing, or sale of infant formula have a responsibility to conduct their overseas activities in ways which do not have adverse effects on the nutritional health of people of developing nations."

Legislative involvement continued the following year as the U.S. Senate subcommittee on Health and Scientific Research heard testimony on the infant formula controversy. Dr. James Post of Boston University stated that "for eight years, the industry's critics have borne the burden of proving that commercial marketing practices were actually contributing to infant malnutrition and morbidity. . . . From this time forward, the sellers of infant formula must bear the burden of proving that their products . . . actually serve a public purpose in the developing world." While no legislation came from the U.S. Senate, Senator Edward Kennedy did request that the World Health Organization sponsor a conference on infant formula promotion, marketing, and use.

Group action then fastened on Nestlé. However, when competition is international, what the U.S. Congress thinks or does is not always binding on foreign-based businesses. A responsive set of tactics came into play.

## Nestlé Forms Council

To disarm critics and defuse the issue, Nestlé led a number of large baby formula companies to form the International Council on Infant Food Industries (ICIFI). One of the major undertakings of ICIFI was the publication of a "Code of Ethics" for formula promotion. While the "Code" appeared to strengthen the position of baby formula manufacturers, it was criticized as being vague and meaningless. It was further weakened by the fact that two of the largest formula marketers, including Bristol-Myers, refused to join ICIFI.

While stockholder resolutions continued to put pressure on American companies, a new citizens' action group formed to bring pressure on Nestlé. INFACT (Infant Formula Action Coalition) began a national campaign. The Minnesota chapter initiated a boycott of Nestlé's products. The boycott became necessary, according to INFACT, because Nestlé did not change its policies on infant formula marketing techniques. INFACT made these demands of Nestlé:

1. Immediately stop all promotion of Nestlé artificial formula.
2. Stop mass media advertising of formula.
3. Stop distribution of free samples to hospitals, clinics, and homes of newborns.
4. Discontinue use of Nestlé milk nurses.
5. Stop promotion through the medical profession.

6. Prevent artificial formula from getting into the hands of people who do not have the means or facilities to use it safely.

Nestlé representatives made themselves available to groups across the United States. They met with representatives of various health advocate groups, medical professionals, and others. Nestlé's basic position stemmed from a history of manufacturing and selling formula in developing countries for more than 60 years. The root causes of infant malnutrition and mortality in the Third World, according to Nestlé, were poverty, lack of food, ignorance, and poor sanitation. Nestlé advocated breastfeeding, but stated that most Third World infants needed a supplement to mother's milk to sustain normal physical and mental growth for a period of months.

The national INFACT conference reacted to the meetings with Nestlé officials by deciding to continue the boycott. Boycott endorsements came from the Democratic Farmer-Labor Party of Minnesota and Ralph Nader. Nestlé representatives again met with action group representatives. Nothing was resolved, and the groups indicated that they would continue the boycott until Nestlé made substantial policy changes.

## Spicing up the Boycott to Build a Bigger Constituency

To bring more attention to the boycott, action groups sponsored "Infant Formula Action Day" across the United States. The activities included a Boston Nestea[5] Party, demonstrations, leafleting, letter writing, fasts, and other public events. Later the same year, INFACT sponsored a program called "Spook Nestlé." The program urged Halloweeners not to buy or accept Nestlé

---

[5]Nestlé's brand of instant tea.

---

## TIMELINE TO CONTROVERSY

**1867**   Henri Nestlé develops the first breastmilk substitute, noting that "during the first months, the mother's milk will always be the most natural nutriment."

**1965**   The Protein Advisory Group (PAG) is formed as a coalition of representatives (United Nations, doctors, manufacturers, etc.) concerned with infant nutrition.

**1966**   A PAG consultant, Derrick Jelliffe, writes "Child Nutrition in Developing Countries," published by the U.S. government as a warning against improperly used infant formula.

**1971**   The infant formula controversy is joined as Jelliffe presents his conclusions to a UN meeting in Colombia, drawing response from others who contend formula is needed to reduce infant mortality and morbidity.

**1972**   PAG emphasis shifts from formula to marketing practices around the product. Nestlé responds that its only change should be an emphasis on the importance of breastfeeding in its advertising material.

**1973**   An article, "The Baby Food Tragedy" is published in the magazine the *New Internationalist.* Later, an editorial, "Milk and Murder" is printed. Nestlé responds by inviting interested journalists to Switzerland to "get the complete story."

**1974**   After interviewing Nestlé officials, a British journalist representing the ad hoc group "War on Wants"

issues a pamphlet, "The Baby Killer," which is then published by a German group, the Third World Action Group (TWAG). They title the pamphlet "Nestlé Kills Babies." Nestle sues for libel, citing:

- The title
- A statement that Nestlé's actions are "unethical and immoral"
- The allegation that Nestlé is responsible for deaths of babies
- An allegation that Nestlé employed "milk nurses" or sales people dressed in nurses' uniforms

Nestlé later drops all but the first charge, and the case goes to trial.

**1975**   TWAG sets the public discussion agenda on "the activities of a Swiss multinational in developing countries." The World Council of Churches takes in interest in the issue. Eight major manufacturers form the International Council of Infant Food Industries (ICIFI), which adopts a code of ethics for formula sales. Bristol-Myers and Ross Labs decline to join. Nestlé breaks its silence with a press conference to address the issue and the looming trial.

**1976**   TWAG is found guilty of libeling Nestlé and is ordered to pay fines of 300 Swiss francs (about $150 US). The judge advises Nestle to change its advertising and market-ing practices.

**1977**   The U.S.–based pressure group Infant Formula Action Coalition, or INFACT, calls for a boycott of

*(continued)*

(*continued*)

Nestlé products as well as an end to infant formula promotional activities.

**1978**   U.S. Senate holds hearings led by Sen. Edward Kennedy, who asks the World Health Organization (WHO) to hold hearings on infant health and nutrition.

**1979**   WHO and UNICEF recommend international codes for marketing formula.

**1980**   Many U.S. church groups join the boycott, but not the United Methodist Church, which studies the issue and declines to join.

**1981**   WHO adopts the international code of infant marketing. Nestlé establishes its Nestlé Coordination Centre of Nutrition (NCCN).

**1982**   Nestlé agrees to follow the code. The Nestlé Infant Formula Audit Committee, also known as the Muskie Committee for its leader, Edmund Muskie, is formed.

**1984**   The boycott is ended. The Infant Food Manufacturers group is formed to replace ICIFI.

**1988**   Activists re-institute the boycott, claiming Nestlé reneged on its 1984 agreement.

**1991**   Muskie Committee disbands, saying its work is finished.

**1992**   Church of England Synod announces its boycott of Nestlé.

**1994**   The report "Breaking the Rules" is issued, claiming to show which manufacturers have violated the WHO agreement. Nestlé says charges against it are unfounded or represent old actions that have long been corrected. Church of England Synod suspends its boycott.

**1997**   Yet another publication, "Cracking the Code," accuses manufacturers of violating the WHO code. UNICEF praises the report.

**1998**   WHO proposes roundtable discussion with industry, governmental, and nongovernmental (pressure groups) representation. Nongovernmental groups decline.

**2004**   International Baby Food Action Network (IBFAN) publishes "Breaking the Rules, Stretching the Rules," which purports to document WHO code violations in 69 developing countries. According to the report, Nestlé is the leading violator.

**2006**   Twenty countries (not including the United States) continue boycott against Nestlé.

candies. Leafleting at grocery stores and film showings were also part of the program (see Figure 10-4).

The list of those endorsing the boycott continued to grow. At the top of the list was the governing board of the National Council of Churches, which had facilitated earlier meetings.

The stalemate continued for more than five years. Nestlé published a list of 19 excerpts from letters indicating support of Nestlé activities in Third World countries, but this action did not swing public opinion in its favor and end the boycott. The boycott cost Nestlé millions of dollars, yet these costs did little to actually hurt the giant

## WHAT YOU CAN DO ABOUT THE BOTTLE BABY SCANDAL

**1. Boycott Nestlé.** Nestlé is the largest infant-formula distributor in the Third World. A boycott of the company's products has been under way for some time in Western Europe; one in the U.S. began on July 4, 1977. Don't buy Taster's Choice/Nescafé/Nestlé Quik/Nestlé Crunch/Nestea Libby, McNeill & Libby products (Libby's tomato juice, canned vegetables, etc.)

**2. Join the campaign.** As we go to press, active groups in more than a dozen American cities are working to spread the Nestlé boycott, distributing articles and a documentary film called *Bottle Babies*, speaking about the problem in churches and on talk shows, and so on. To find out how to link up with the campaign where you live, write or call:

| | | |
|---|---|---|
| Interfaith Center on Corporate Responsibility 475 Riverside Drive New York, NY 10027 (212) 870-2294 | Third World Institute of the Newman Center 1701 University Ave. Minneapolis, MN 55414 (612) 331-3437 | Earthwork 1499 Potrero Ave San Francisco, CA 94110 |

**3. Sound Off.** Clip or copy the coupon below and send it to:

Name of Your Representative
U.S. House of Representatives
Washington, DC 20515

Name of Your Senator
U.S. Senate Office Building
Washington, DC 20510

Send a copy of your letter to:

Bristol-Myers
345 Park Ave.
New York, NY 10022

Nestlé Co., Inc.
100 Bloomingdale Road
White Plains, NY 10605

Add a note to Nestlé saying that you are boycotting its products until it stops all promotion, advertising and free-sample distribution of infant formula in the Third World, and all distribution of formula anywhere where people do not have the money or the facilities to use it safely.

------------------------------------------------

Dear_____ :

*The attached article details the growing problem of death and disease that results from aggressive infant-formula sales in the Third World. I am outraged by this practice. We need legislation that will bring it to a halt. Please inform me what you intend to do about this.*

Sincerely,

------------------------------------------------

**FIGURE 10-4  Boycott Nestlé was promoted in a variety of ways, including advertisements such as this one appearing in *Mother Jones***

corporation, which had profits in the billions during these years. What Nestlé wanted to get rid of was "the public relations nightmare." Church groups, labor unions, feminists, and other activists accused Nestlé of killing babies.

## A Code of Ethics in Practical Form

In the 1980s, the World Health Organization (WHO) tackled the problem by establishing the International Code of Marketing of Breastmilk Substitutes. The membership of WHO voted 118 to 1 to adopt the nonbinding code. The United States cast the one dissenting vote, claiming that the code's restrictions violated the constitutional guarantees of free speech and freedom of information.

The code restricted the promotion of infant formula and prohibited the widespread practice of free formula samples to new mothers and the use of "mothercraft" nurses, a long criticized marketing aspect. Advertisements and other promotions to the general public were forbidden, as were gifts to mothers given to promote the use of breastmilk substitutes. The code also required that manufacturers discontinue use of product labels that idealized the use of infant formula. All products were to be labeled explaining the health hazards of bottle feeding.

After the passage of the code in 1981 by individual governments, Nestlé changed several of its marketing practices, even in countries where the code had not formally been adopted. Despite these advances, the

---

### OF ALL THE PARTICIPANTS, WHO WON WHAT?

The news coverage of the accord between Nestlé and the health advocate organizations indicated that the health advocate organizations had won the long battle. For example, an article in *Newsweek* included a photo of a Nestlé ad with the subhead: "A Boycott That Hurt." The headline on the article stated, "Nestlé's Costly Accord." The lead in the story set the tone and clearly put the health advocate organizations in the winning position:

For the past 7 years, scores of religious, women's health and public-interest groups have waged a very rough and costly boycott against the Swiss-based Nestlé company. . . . Last week, after spending tens of millions of dollars resisting the boycott, Nestlé finally reached the accord with the protesters.

Nestlé agreed to change four of its business practices as the basis of the accord.

1. Put information on labels.
2. Update and provide all information in literature.
3. Stop giving gifts to health officials.
4. Stop distributing samples and supplies.

---

ICCR and the National Council of Churches found a long list of violations by Nestlé.

On its own, Nestlé released a revised set of policies designed to follow the code. The boycott continued, however, with focus on Nestlé's Tasters' Choice brand product. Several groups gathered and dumped 112,000 signatures onto the front steps of the company's headquarters in Switzerland.

## A Resolution of Sorts

Just as it seemed as though the standoff would go on forever, Nestlé reached an accord with the protest groups in 1984. Bristol-Myers, Ross division of Abbot Laboratories, and Wyeth Laboratories, a unit of American Home Products, major baby formula manufacturers in the United States, also reached accords with the protestors.

## An Update

In 1988, the International Baby Food Action Network (IBFAN) released a detailed and illustrated report on the international marketing practices of the infant food and feeding bottle industry prepared initially for the World Health Assembly. The report was titled "Still Breaking the Rules" and IBFAN continues to update this report (see Figure 10-5).[6]

The report indicated that the infant foods industry, in pushing its products around the world, continued to employ methods that "endanger infant health and undermine the efforts of national policy makers, primary health-care workers, consumer protection organizations and international agencies which have worked for more than a decade to encourage mothers to implement inexpensive and simple measures, including breastfeeding, to protect their babies' health and lives."

In naming offenders, the report went beyond Nestlé and Bristol-Myers. The list was far-reaching, demonstrating that the international infant food market has attracted entries from many countries, making control or discipline extremely difficult. Success in competition comes first in business whether local or worldwide.

---

[6]For a copy of the report, write to IBFAN USA, c/o ACTION, 129 Church Street, New Haven, CT 06510.

FIGURE 10-5   The report "Still Breaking the Rules" examines all baby food makers and their compliance to the international marketing practices

*Source:* (Courtesy of IBFAN and Action for Corporate Accountability.)

Also in 1988, *Action News*, a publication issued by an IBFAN member named "Action For Corporate Accountability," reported that despite the code, Nestlé continued to "dump supplies of formula on hospitals" and thus gave the impression of medical endorsement for artificial baby feeding. If Nestlé persisted, the planned responsive action would be a renewal of the boycott in the United States starting on October 4, 1988, the fourth anniversary of the date the first boycott was ended.

As promised, the boycott was initiated again that year and is still ongoing. Action for Corporate Accountability spearheaded the effort against Nestlé in the United States and has focused attention on another company in this most recent boycott, American Home Products. AHP and Nestlé control about 65 percent of the global infant formula market and refused to succumb to ACTION's demands to end the practice of supplying their formulas free to hospitals. It began circulating a petition and collected over 50,000 names that it has presented to Nestlé to pressure it with grassroots support. To emphasize its point, ACTION sent out frequent newsletters and fact sheets to update the violations Nestlé and AHP have recently

committed in marketing and selling their baby formula worldwide. To follow up the U.S. effort, boycotts were initiated against AHP, Nestlé, and local formula companies in 12 other countries from 1988 to 1990.

In 1992, the "Baby-Friendly" Hospital Initiative was issued by UNICEF and WHO. It is a global campaign to foster support for breastfeeding and an effort to end the supply of free and low-cost formula to maternity institutions. Both AHP and Nestlé agreed to the initiative and to stop supplying hospitals with free samples of their formulas. However, ACTION remained unconvinced of the formula manufacturers commitment to the initiative, citing the company's behavior of "business as usual" as an indicator of how seriously the companies are taking the proposal. Enforcing the Baby-Friendly Hospital Initiative also may be sticky, considering that "UNICEF and WHO have no power to implement this initiative globally," says ACTION's Executive Director, Dr. Idrian N. Resnick. "Only an intense campaign of consumer and media pressure will force these corporations to quit stalling and do what's right."[7]

And where is Nestlé in all this? Nestlé continued its efforts with the International

---

[7]Taken from a press release issued by Action for Corporate Accountability on March 11, 1992.

Association of Infant Food Manufacturers (IFM) to prove its commitment to work with "international agencies, governments, non-governmental organizations, and all others concerned, to end all supplies of infant formula in developing countries except for the limited number of infants who need it." This statement, taken from a Nestlé policy update in December of 1990, suggests its continued commitment to ending free baby food supplies to hospitals of Third World countries.

The battle continues and can be followed on the Internet. In 1999, Nestlé released a publication titled "Nestlé Implementation of the WHO Code" in defense of its marketing practices. IBFAN declared it "a public relations offensive on the baby milk issue."

But once a company or organization behaves irresponsibly, it takes more than words to regain trust. Many are therefore undoubtedly asking, "Does Nestlé mean it this time?"

## The Saga Continues

By 2006, the impasse was still on. According to Baby Milk Action, "Nestlé is the target of a boycott in 20 countries because it aggressively markets baby foods, breaking World Health Assembly marketing requirements and contributing to the death and suffering of infants around the world."

According to UNICEF: "Marketing practices that undermine breastfeeding are potentially hazardous wherever they are pursued: in the developing world, WHO estimates that some 1.5 million children die each year because they are not adequately breastfed. These facts are not in dispute."

Nestlé does dispute the facts. Its efforts, however, are widely decried as "bogus arguments," by IBFAN and Baby Milk Action. "In a global Internet vote for the world's most irresponsible company, coinciding with the World Economic Forum in 2005, Nestlé received 29 percent of the vote, more than double the second-placed company," the organizations' newsletter gloats.

As the world's largest food company (annual sales of more than $67 billion), Nestlé is chastised by IBFAN as being "the largest single source of violations of the WHO/UNICEF International Code of Marketing of Breast-milk Substitutes." And, the boycott continues.

The boycott is now coordinated by the International Nestlé Boycott Committee, the secretariat for which is the UK group Baby Milk Action. Company practices are monitored by IBFAN, which comprises more than 200 groups in over 100 countries.

In November 2000, the European Parliament invited IBFAN, UNICEF, and Nestlé to present evidence to a public hearing before the Development and Cooperation Committee. Evidence was presented by the IBFAN group from Pakistan and UNICEF's legal officer commented on Nestlé's failure to bring its policies into line with the World Health Assembly Resolutions. Nestlé declined an invitation to attend, though it sent a representative of the auditing company it had commissioned to produce a report on its Pakistan operation.

In parallel with the boycott, campaigners work for implementation of the Code and Resolutions in legislation and claim that 60 countries have now introduced laws implementing most or all of the provisions.

Many hundreds of European universities, colleges, and schools, including over 200 in the United Kingdom, have banned the sale of Nestlé products from their shops and vending machines. ■

## QUESTIONS FOR DISCUSSION

1. As between the open system and the closed system, which label fit the posture of Nestlé and of IBFAN, expressed in their policies and actions? How about proactive versus reactive?

2. To change peoples' opinions, there are several options in strategy and tactics, such as persuasion, coercion, compensation, and compulsion. Which ones among these, or others, do you see employed by various opposing groups in this case study?

3. In 1988, when IBFAN announced a plan to renew the boycott of Nestlé products, would that clearly constitute a more effective or less effective threat as stated in a Chapter 1 maxim? Might the factor of mildness or harshness depend on Nestlé management's reaction based on its marketing strategy and practices? Whether it would or not,

what does that say to you about the practical application of maxims?

4. If you feel this was a matter on which the opponents could work out a reasonable resolution in the public interest, and both sides had professional counsel morally committed to reconciliation, what could have been done better or differently so that the matter wouldn't drag on for years? After you figure out your answer to this, try coming up with a resolution for the abortion issue. Are the intervening forces and stubborn issues the same?

5. Is it possible for Nestlé (and other baby formula manufacturers) to come to a definitive accord with these activist groups? What is the issue each is fighting for or against? Compare the underlying value systems of the two sides.

# Case 10-3 Corporate Social Responsibility and Ethics: Nike's Labor Practices Under Scrutiny

Corporations are no longer accountable to only their investors, nor can they base their success solely on high sales figures. A legacy of the social movements of the 1960s and a demand for political correctness now compels organizations to have practices in place that demonstrate their commitment to social responsibility.[1] Corporate social responsibility can include embracing the issues of environmentalism, animal testing, human rights, or other social or political concerns affected or perceived to be affected by an organization's policies. Corporations are now finding that stakeholders expect them to have an ethical, and not necessarily financial, interest in their policies and how those policies affect the rest of the world.

It has become important to organizations to cultivate their socially responsible image. Socially responsible corporate practices and ethical standards are a reflection of each organization. Corporations have learned that being socially responsible is good for business; that their beneficence also benefits the company.

Although some companies are following through on their commitments, others only project the appearance of being socially responsible. This discrepancy between a company's environmental image and actions has been referred to as *greenwashing*. This term has earned an entry in the 10th edition of the *Concise Oxford English Dictionary* and is defined as "disinformation disseminated by an organization so as to present an environmentally responsible public image." Mark Twain must have experienced early versions of greenwashing in his time when he said, "The secret of success is honesty and fair dealing—if you can fake these, you've got it made."

If an organization is accused of social irresponsibility or demonstrating unethical practices, it may not necessarily be doing anything illegal. Violating an Environmental Protection Agency regulation or discriminating against an employee are illegal acts. Selling fur products or making a corporate donation to Planned Parenthood are not illegal but some may see these acts as unethical. Many companies have experienced boycotts based on their actions that are legal but perceived to be unethical by groups that disagree with specific actions.

The German philosopher Immanuel Kant (1724–1804), in his works on ethics, wrote, "Act only on that maxim through which you can at the same time will that it should become a universal law." Before a company advances a policy or produces a new product, it may want to address the issue of business ethics by asking the following questions:

- Will anyone be damaged or compromised by our actions?
- Will anyone gain an unfair advantage?
- Is there anything inherently wrong with these actions?
- If these practices reach the media, will we look bad?

---

[1]Betsy Reed, "The Business of Social Responsibility," May 1998; Jon Entube, "Corporate Ethics and Accountability." Corporate Governance Web site (www.corpgov.net).

- Are we able to feel good about utilizing these practices? Would we be happy applying the practices or policies to ourselves?

In other words, should the Golden Rule also apply to business practices? Does there have to be a tradeoff between corporate social responsibility and making a profit?

## Nike's Problems Foreshadowed— Nike Forewarned

Nike, Inc. is the world's number-one shoe company and controls more than 20 percent of the U.S. shoe market. Nike employs some 26,000 people worldwide. In addition, about 650,000 work in Nike-contracted factories around the world, more than 550,000 of which are in the Asia-Pacific region, where Nike contracts with nearly 500 factories. Revenues worldwide in 2006 exceeded $14 billion. Nike established its own Code of Conduct in 1992 to ensure that specific guidelines on wages and working conditions are followed at all of its facilities, including those under the supervision of subcontractors overseas.

Nike began to receive negative coverage concerning its labor practices in the early 1990s. In 1992, Jeff Ballinger, who had spent four years in Indonesia helping workers to organize unions, returned to the United States with information on abusive labor practices in Nike factories in Indonesia. In 1993, CBS flew Ballinger back to Indonesia to narrate a story on the workers' struggle for a living wage in those facilities.

After the CBS report, Nike received a flurry of negative media coverage from the press in both the United States and United Kingdom over the next two years. During this time, the company issued various press releases and statements asserting its commitment to the welfare of its workers and to improving factory conditions. Nike seemed to successfully endure the reactions to the bad press. After its stock price fell slightly at the end of 1993, it began a steady upswing starting in 1995. Between 1996 and 2006, Nike stock rose from about $55 to $80 per share, reaching more than $90 at one point. Nike shares gained 17 percent from 2005 to 2006.

## Someone Blows the Whistle on Nike

In November 1997, a disgruntled Nike employee leaked a secret, internal report to The Transnational Resource and Action Center (TRAC), a San Francisco-based organization now known as Corporate Watch. Nike had hired the Ernst & Young accounting firm to audit the working conditions at one of its shoe manufacturing plants in Vietnam. The inspection report stated that workers were exposed to harmful levels of carcinogens because of poor air ventilation in the plant and that 77 percent of the employees had respiratory problems. The report also detailed that employees were forced to work 65 hours a week yet did not receive a living wage. This information seemed to contradict Nike's earlier statements of commitment to the welfare of its workers.

The Ernst & Young report was supplied to the *New York Times,* which then printed a story on it on November 8, 1997. Nike responded by pointing out that, soon after they had received the report, the problems were addressed and steps had been taken to improve the working conditions.

However, this time, with the release of the Ernst & Young report, the damage was done. The problem of Nike's apparent exploitation of its overseas employees, based on long hours and low pay, was now compounded by the issue of the unhealthy environmental condition of the factories. Six months later, Nike was presented with another hurdle.

In April 1998, a lawsuit was filed against Nike in a California Superior Court alleging that Nike's statements of protection of its workers amounted to false advertising under California's consumer-protection laws.[2] Under California's broad consumer-protection laws, a plaintiff is not required to prove he or she has suffered personal injury—only that there was a likelihood of deception.

The main question of the lawsuit is whether Nike's public statements are considered advertising for the company and therefore subject to truth-in-advertising laws, or if they are simply public statements that are protected by the First Amendment.

The California Court of Appeal agreed with Nike that the information in question was "corporate speech" and therefore protected by the First Amendment, saying, in effect, that Kasky could not proceed with a lawsuit on the merits of the case. The California Supreme Court, however, sided with Kasky, ruling that the intent of Nike's speech was to advance its commercial interests and therefore was not protected by the First Amendment. Under this ruling, Kasky was permitted to proceed with his legal actions.

Nike appealed to the U.S. Supreme Court, which initially agreed to hear the case. However, in June 2003, the court decided to dismiss the "writ of certiorari, thereby refusing to decide the questions presented, at least for now" (*Nike v. Kasky*, U.S. Supreme Court). In September 2003, Nike and Kasky buried the legal hatchet. Nike agreed to donate $1.5 million to the Fair Labor Association, settling the legal battle without ever having the facts of the case go to trial (see box "*Nike v. Kasky:* More at Stake Than Labor Issues).

## Nike Puts Its Best Foot Forward

Nike was now experiencing some financial repercussions—drops in stock prices and sales—from the coverage of their labor practices that were viewed by many as exploitive and unethical. Nike was finally facing the fact that its policies *did* make it look bad in the press, were inherently wrong, and engendered a feeling of ill will. This time, the company took a more proactive approach.

In May 1998, at the National Press Club in Washington, D.C., Chairman and CEO Philip Knight announced Nike's New Labor Initiatives aimed at improving factory working conditions worldwide. The main elements of the Initiatives are:

- Increase the minimum age of new employees in the shoe factories to 18 years of age
- Improve the air quality by using the standards enforced by OSHA
- A commitment to a policy of open communications on corporate responsibility issues
- A pledge to allow independent monitoring of its factories by nongovernmental organizations (NGOs)

However, the Initiatives do not address the issues of forced overtime and increasing earnings to a living wage. (*Editor's Note: Just what constitutes a "living wage" is at the heart of the debate over Nike's business practices. Many U.S.–based manufacturing operations are moving jobs to countries such as China, Indonesia, Singapore, and so on, because the workers earn much less than those in similar jobs in the United States. Such countries often have nothing like the EPA, OSHA and similar workplace watchdogs that can add to manufacturing*

---

[2]Josh Richman, "Greenwashing on Trial," MoJo Wire (*Mother Jones Magazine* online), February 23, 2001.

*costs. Union representation is much less likely in off-shore factories as well. Although wages paid in these countries might be "normal" for the area, they frequently pale in comparison to wages in the United States.)* In his speech, Philip Knight said, "These moves do more than just set industry standards. They reflect who we are as a company."

## Both Sides Utilize the Internet

As the Internet has become an everyday resource for more and more people, companies of all sizes now use it as a worldwide marketing and public relations tool. If a company wants to let people know what it has to offer by promoting itself globally, the Internet provides that outlet.

The Internet is also an outlet for activism against corporations.[3] The online attacks can take place on specific Web sites, in chat rooms, or on Web bulletin boards. Negative postings on the Internet are considered a serious public relations problem by companies because millions of people could potentially see those messages. Controversial information about a company, whether factual or not, can result in a public relations nightmare that could take years to resolve.

Personal journals or Weblogs (blogs) also are of increasing concern to companies. A Technorati.com search of "Nike" yielded 413,964 blogs with some reference to the company or its namesake brand.

Nike's website (www.nikebiz.com) became operational in 1996. The site contains a great range of information on the company, including a section entitled "Responsibility." Within that section, Nike addresses the issues of global community, the environment, and diversity. In the section on labor,

the company provides information on factory monitoring results and updates on working conditions at various factory locations.

However, Nike also has to contend with "anti-Nike" websites such as Boycott Nike, Just Stop It, or Nikewages.org. These sites continue to provide information about the status of Nike's pledge to improve conditions for its workers. Judging by the names of these Web sites, it is clear that the operators of these sites do not think that Nike has fulfilled that pledge. (See Figure 10-6.)

## 2001—The Three-Year Anniversary of Nike's Labor Initiatives

In May 2001, Nike, Inc., on the three-year anniversary of the new labor initiatives, issued a press release that reviewed the successes and challenges of its corporate responsibility. It noted that Nike is "working collaboratively alongside human rights groups and various NGOs" and that it had "increased wages more than 100 percent over the past several years for entry-level Indonesian footwear factory workers." Despite these and other successes, the release also stated that "there is still progress to be made." As Dusty Kidd, Vice President of Corporate Responsibility put it, "As in every area of Nike's business, there is no finish line, and improving the lives and working conditions of the workers who make Nike products is no exception."

Within 24 hours of the release of Nike's statement, the *Wall Street Journal* reported on May 16, 2001, that Global Exchange, a human-rights organization, had accused Nike of failing to follow through on many of its 1998 initiatives. In addition to other

---

[3]Jamie Carrington, "Answering to the Internet," *The World Paper,* October 2000.

criticisms, Global Exchange says that the living wage issue has still not been fully addressed and that Nike's factory monitoring resources are not truly independent of the company.

Nike suspended releasing its "Corporate Responsibility Report" for three years, reintroducing it again in 2005.

In recent years, Nike has continued to be a target of boycotts, media investigations, and international protest. A frequent complaint is that the company treats the labor problems as a public relations issue and not as a human rights issue in that it *presents* itself as a socially responsible corporation. Most any company would want to be viewed as doing the right thing but how much should good intentions alone be rewarded? Nike contends it is improving conditions in its many plants, but acknowledges "there is no finish line" when it comes to human rights and humane working conditions. So the question remains: Who determines if the socially responsible steps a corporation has taken are enough? ■

## NIKE v. KASKY: MORE AT STAKE THAN LABOR ISSUES

When Nike decided to settle the *Nike v. Kasky* lawsuit by donating $1.5 million to the Fair Labor Association (a labor-conditions watchdog group), it was the official end to a case that had (and has) immense ramifications for the public relations industry.

Still unsettled, however, are the issues that brought the case to the U.S. Supreme Court in the first place: Can a company defend itself in the court of public opinion and have that speech fall under the Freedom-of-Speech clause of the First Amendment? The companion question is: Can anything (and everything) said by a profit-making company be construed as commercial speech (and unprotected), because of the assumption that everything a profit-making organization does is focused on a commercial purpose?

In the *Nike v. Kasky* suit, the Supreme Court first decided to hear the case and determine if Nike was under the protection of the First Amendment when it mailed news releases; letters to the editors of papers, including the *New York Times*; brochures to retail customers; and letters to key colleges and others who had a stake in Nike's business. After accepting briefs and hearing oral arguments, the Court "took the highly unusual step of deciding that the appeal had come to them prematurely and sent the case back to California" (Ken Paulson, executive director, First Amendment Center, September 28, 2003). That left the California Supreme Court decision intact, but did nothing to address the larger question that Paulson said "could have forever altered the free-speech rights of corporations. . . . "

Nike's mailings—standard public relations tools—were based, in part, on a study of working conditions in Third World nations completed by Dr. Andrew Young in 1997. Dr. Young, a close associate of Dr. Martin Luther King during the 1960s civil rights movement, later served as U.S. Ambassador to the United Nations under President Jimmy Carter and was elected to two terms as mayor of Atlanta. It was this pedigree that made his report so credible— and worthy of broad distribution by Nike. Essentially, he found Nike's contract shops to be at least up to standards in their countries and, in many cases, above standard. The report didn't address wages, but rather focused on working conditions.

Kasky's 1998 suit was based on these actions and similar efforts by Nike to offer the public a different look at the so-called "sweatshop" issue. Nike, naturally, wanted a rosier view of its practices, but Kasky, a veteran activist with environmental and community-service groups, protested that Nike's statements were misleading and, therefore, constituted false advertising. The California court agreed, and the U.S. Supreme Court did not disagree.

"The clear winner here was Kasky, and workers' rights organizations," said Paulson. "The list of losers is not limited to Nike. Every corporation doing business in California now has to think long and hard about any public statements concerning its company."

This is a major hurdle for the public relations profession, for perhaps the primary function of public relations is advocacy. We are supposed to be strong, ethical advocates for our employers and clients. If robbed of that function, then public relations, as a profession, loses one of its major strengths. Nike's defense was bolstered by more than 40 briefs filed by such strange bedfellows as media corporations, chambers of commerce, and the American Civil Liberties Union. None wanted corporate speech to lose its First Amendment protection.

The good news surrounding *Nike v. Kasky* is that the decision now in effect in that case applies only to California. California is well known for its interesting legal and political climate. At the time of the *Kasky* suit, the State of California permitted a private citizen to act as a *de*

*facto* attorney general suing on behalf of people with whom no relationship was established and on matters in which the citizen had no personal standing. Those were the conditions of Kasky's suit against Nike. He needed to show no personal loss or damage to bring action against Nike.

Since that time, that avenue has been closed in California, but the state is still known for liberal interpretation of laws, especially those related to advertising and commercial speech. For example, the book the *Beardstown Ladies Common Sense Investment Guide* claimed on a cover blurb that the amateur-investor ladies had realized investment gains exceeding 23 percent over a 10-year period. However, some independent math put the gains at less than 10 percent. In 1988, a class-action lawsuit was filed on behalf of all book buyers (some 800,000), but a New York court decided the cover-blurb copy was a summary of information contained in the book—and therefore protected by the First Amendment.

A similar suit was filed in California, where the court decided the blurb constituted "commercial speech" and was therefore "false advertising." The publisher settled the suit by offering a free book to those affected, but it spent more than $1 million in its defense.[1]

This *Beardstown* example illustrates the different legal climates between states. This is why a California decision applies only to California. That is also why there is a U.S. Supreme Court. Laws of the land that apply generally need to be consistent. The same suit shouldn't get polar opposite rulings in two states.

The real danger of allowing *Nike v. Kasky* to stand lies in the "chilling effect"

*(continued)*

*(continued)*

of such a lawsuit. Paulson quotes Quentin Riegel, vice president of litigation for the National Association of Manufacturers, saying "companies will be pressured into cutting back their participation and dialogues on important issues."

So-called "corporate speech" (also known as "political speech") has been around since landmark cases such as *First National Bank of Boston v. Bellotti* (1978) and *Bolger v. Young's Drug Products* (1983). In these cases, the Supreme Court ruled that corporations have First Amendment rights to free speech on issues of importance to society. The content of the speech, not the nature of the "speaker," was determined to be paramount.

Nike was looking to the courts to declare its defense part of that public debate on important issues. For now, that's not happening. With the financial settlement, no determination as to the accuracy or validity of Nike's statements will be made. Constitutional issues and financial expediency took that determination off the table.

[1]Available at writ.news.findlaw.com/ramasastry/20060202.html.

---

## QUESTIONS FOR DISCUSSION

1. Does Nike have a responsibility to monitor working conditions in plants owned and operated by contractors? Why?
2. Is a "low wage that is better than no wage" a sound public relations strategy for Nike? Why?
3. What role did falling stock prices and dwindling sales play in Nike's strategy and actions?
4. Is the working environment in a contract shoe plant an operational or a public relations problem?

# Case 10-4 Dow Corning and Breast Implants: Dealing with the Perception of Deception

One of the biggest headaches for manufacturers these days is the proliferation of product liability suits. Some companies are taking products off the market because of the risk of these suits, yet a number of the cases are filed with reason. What would be the responsible and ethical thing to do if a product has been implicated as defective or harmful, even if research may indicate the opposite? What can be done to make it up to those who may have been harmed or to allay the fears of those who *perceive* the product as harmful?

In the early 1990s, Dow Corning was faced with a great number of angry women when silicone-gel breast implants (manufactured by Dow Corning and several others) were indicated as a possible cause of health problems the women were experiencing. This case examines how public *perception* of Dow Corning's behavior evolved into a question of credibility for the organization.

The company *did* have an ethics policy in place since 1976 that was guiding decision making, but the public perceived that it was making business and legal decisions without addressing the ethical issues around the continued use of its breast implants.

## History

The history of breast implantation in the United States is a long one. Since 1962, women have been paying to have doctors surgically enhance their breast size, for various reasons, through the use of silicone-gel or saline solution implants encased in silicone envelopes. Many do it for self-esteem reasons (about 80 percent), and others want reconstructive surgery after having a mastectomy due to breast cancer (about 20 percent). Almost 2 million women have had breast implants to date.

Silicone-gel was the choice for many women because it seemed more "lifelike" after implantation. Saline solution implants (made of salt and water) are considered less risky for the body, but women chose them less often because they did not feel as natural and sometimes made "sloshing sounds."

Until 1991, the highest perceived risk from breast implantation was in the surgical procedure itself. (Like any device implanted into the body, it may have adverse effects in a small number of patients.) However, silicone's effects on the human body's autoimmune system were not known. An enormous amount of breast implant testing had been done beginning in the 1950s, but when the issue arose in the 1990s there was a perception that there was little, if any, product testing completed. Despite the amount of research that had been done, breast implants were alleged to be the possible cause of serious medical problems, including immunological disorders, arthritis, infections, reduced mammogram effectiveness, and cancer.

The possible risks of breast implants fall into two basic categories: those related directly to the breast (easy to observe) and those that may involve distant parts of the body (much harder to observe and difficult to measure).

Some of the possible breast-related risks are:

- Difficulty in detecting abnormalities in the breast when mammographic X-rays are taken
- Breast may harden—as a result of fibrous tissue growing around the implant—possibly causing discomfort and pain
- Breakage of the envelope, causing the gel filling to be released

Other risks are:

- Migration of the gel filling throughout the body (with possible unpleasant cosmetic effects)
- The perception that breast implants may cause autoimmune diseases

## Dow Corning's Role

Dow Corning Corporation, jointly owned by The Dow Chemical Company and Corning, Incorporated, has been one of the most visible manufacturers of silicone-gel breast implants, although implants represented less than one percent of the company's sales. Dow Corning came under fire in 1991 when Marianne Hopkins, who had received silicone-gel breast implants in 1976, brought suit—claiming the product was responsible for damage to her immune system. The alleged cause was silicone leakage. With this case, many questions began to surface about implants.

One contributing factor to the uproar is that all medical devices were unregulated until 1976, 14 years after the procedure of breast implantation had begun. There was no standard of testing and regulation to follow. Devices in use before the regulations were considered "grandfathered," which meant the manufacturers of those products were not required to provide the Food and Drug Administration (FDA) with scientific evidence of safety and effectiveness. That stipulation in the law is based on the premise that more is known about the safety of a device that has been in use for some time than about one that is newly developed. However, if questions arise over time that cast any doubt about a grandfathered device's safety, the law gives the FDA the authority to go back and require that its manufacturer provide evidence to demonstrate it is safe and effective.[1]

In the 1980s, the FDA Devices Division did not have the budget or personnel to regulate adequately and had adopted a lax attitude in testing and regulating new medical devices put on the market. Finally, in April 1991, with intensified publicity and court cases, implant manufacturers were ordered to prove that their silicone implants were safe. This regulatory action had been recommended by an FDA advisory panel a decade earlier, although it had not been enforced—a damaging fact in forming public perceptions.

## Credibility Problems

In June 1991, Dow Corning documents surfaced in a *Business Week* article that implied that the implant might have been rushed to market without proper medical testing. Top management was reassuring the general public of the relative safety of this product, but internal memos (created by those not aware of research taking place or past research that had been conducted) were being passed around that alleged there was awareness of animal studies that linked the implants to cancer and other illnesses. In addition, investigative reports dating back 25 years were brought to light indicating

---

[1]From "Background Information on the Possible Health Risks of Silicone Breast Implants," released by the FDA December 1990 and revised February 1991.

that implants could break or leak into patient's bodies. (Those reports had been a matter of public record, but now received attention with this new public scrutiny.) The company *appeared* as if it had been covering up the reports and hiding the true facts.

At first, Dow Corning attacked investigators. This action was interpreted as a lack of concern for the public interest and prompted many to criticize the company as lacking any code of corporate ethics, concerned only with covering itself legally. The irony behind this was that the company did have a code of ethics in place.[2] Some of the initial communications actions that it implemented to allay public misconceptions were:

- Developed a packet of information that physicians could share with their patients that was user-friendly and explained the research conducted by Dow Corning and others about the implants. It outlined the risks that could be possible with silicone breast implants. (See Figure 10-6.)
- Company physicians and scientists scheduled technical presentations at medical meetings to discuss the scientific implications of implants.
- Made public all proprietary information available to competitors in publicly releasing all the scientific studies used to support its Pre-Market Approval Application for the implant.
- Met directly with breast cancer support groups and representatives of other consumer groups, both for and against breast implants.

## Company Is Dealt Painful Legal Blow

Judgment in the Marianne Hopkins case was handed down in December 1991. She was awarded $7.3 million in compensatory and punitive damages, and Dow Corning was found to have committed fraud and malice by failing to disclose evidence from its research about the implants. With this damaging judgment, public scrutiny intensified and many questions were brought up in the media about the implants and what other information Dow Corning may have withheld.

The company was taking the hard line in dealing with this issue in the media. Dow Corning was finding it difficult to appear sympathetic to the women who did have problems without undermining its legal strategy and admitting fault. It appeared to be a classic case of legal versus public relations. And it was not helped by CEO Lawrence A. Reed, who unfortunately was not adept in media situations. This deficiency reduced his ability to take command of this crisis or to stay ahead of the critics. Reed's invisibility as a spokesperson confirmed the prevalent perception in the court of public opinion that the company was not concerned with the welfare of those who had received the implants.[3]

The task of presenting the Dow Corning "voice" to the public was passed around to many people until it rested on the shoulders of the vice president in charge of health care, Robert T. Rylee, and others on his staff. There was no One Clear Voice responding to the public.

Reed's failure as a leader in the public eye was compared in the news media

---

[2]Lee W. Baker, *The Credibility Factor*, Homewood, IL: Business One Irwin, 1992, p. 35. An informative book emphasizing the importance of ethics in the practice of public relations by examining the mistakes and successes of organizations in varying ethical situations.

[3]Kevin McCauley, "Dow Corning Fumbles PR in Breast Implant Crisis," *O'Dwyer's PR Services Report* 6 (March 1992), p. 1.

*Implant Information Center*

Supplemental Information
To
Most Frequent Questions

**DOW CORNING**
**WRIGHT**
P.O. Box 994   Midland, MI 48686
1-800-442-5442   In Canada 1-800-255-2155

**FIGURE 10-6** This Packet if information was distributed by Dow Corning to outline all the risks that could be possible with silicone breast implants

to the fumbling responses and lack of reaction from Exxon CEO Lawrence Rawl in handling the *Valdez* oil spill in 1989 (see Case 9-3). At Dow Corning, spokespeople were taking a reactive stance and focusing on the fact that there was little or no *scientific* evidence proving that the implants caused these health problems—ignoring the fact that women had gotten the implants for *emotional and cosmetic* reasons and would predictably respond on an emotional plane.

To deal with the barrage of questions from the public, Dow Corning set up an "Implant Information Hotline" in July 1991. By the end of the year that, too, was receiving criticism from the FDA and high-profile

news media coverage. Callers to the hotline were being reassured by the operators about the safety of the implants, and Dow Corning was accused of overselling their safety. The company then agreed to send only printed information to callers. However, the operators of the hotlines were ultimately retrained to offer only factual information in order to allay any public misconceptions. More than 50,000 women called the hotline to obtain information.

## The FDA Takes Action

On January 6, 1992, as public scrutiny intensified, FDA Commissioner David Kessler proposed a voluntary moratorium on the sale and use of silicone implants pending further investigation. Most all silicone-gel implant manufacturers complied.

Dow Corning complied with the request, still claiming that the implants did not have a damaging effect on the body. However, public and media scrutiny did not abate; instead it intensified. The *Wall Street Journal* and the *New York Times* ran articles giving Dow Corning failing marks for its handling of the crisis. The rising tide of lawsuits was threatening the corporation and further thinning its already waning credibility.

The *New York Times* stated that Dow Corning failed in the court of public opinion because it was ignoring how consumers respond to health threats:

1. Even a small number of people who feel they have been mistreated by a company or received a poor product can rally enough friends and allies to have a great impact against the company involved.
2. The number of defective or dangerous products often turns out to be higher than the company that manufactures them originally projects. With the publicity that the implants were receiving, many more complaints, both valid and invalid, were bound to surface.
3. Consumers who feel they have been deceived often become extremely upset. The information that leaked out over the years of litigation about the implants suggested that Dow Corning was trying to cover up information that may be damaging to its product without concern for the consumer.[4]

## Media Coverage Intensifies Problem

As the issue unfolded, Dow Corning began to track the media coverage of the controversy. While the news media were widely reporting the issue as it ensued, most of the coverage was incomplete and unbalanced (see Figure 10-7). Women were clamoring for information because of the intense media scrutiny. In order to respond to the

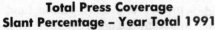

**Total Press Coverage**
**Slant Percentage – Year Total 1991**

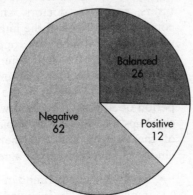

Balanced 26

Negative 62

Positive 12

**FIGURE 10-7   This graph illustrates the media tracking that showed an imbalance of coverage**

*Source:* (Courtesy of Dow Corning.)

---

[4]Barnaby J. Feder, "Dow Corning's Failure in Public Opinion Test," *New York Times*, January 29, 1992, pp. D1 & D2.

need for information, Dow Corning took communications actions to reach out to those concerned:

- Became more responsive to the news media by distributing an 800-page book compiling memos, scientific studies, and related issues.
- Gave a grant to the American Society for Plastic and Reconstructive Surgical Nurses to distribute educational materials to patients.
- Proposed a national communications registry; a collaborative effort between the FDA, consumers, health professionals, and current and former breast-implant manufacturers to provide periodic newsletters to breast-implant recipients.[5]

## Dow Corning Responds

On February 10, 1992, Dow Corning began to take steps to repair its battered reputation. Lawrence Reed was replaced by Keith McKennon, a former Dow Chemical executive well known for his conciliatory abilities. McKennon had helped Dow steer itself out of potentially damaging public relations situations that involved the Agent Orange defoliant used in Vietnam. McKennon's attitude was much more take-charge and less defensive, and from the start of his appointment he was the company voice concerning the issue. In the spirit of this new openness, McKennon gave almost 100 interviews on the issue.

In keeping with this new attitude, Dow Corning announced in March 1992 its plans to get out of the breast-implant-manufacturing business. In addition, it promised to spend $10 million on research into the safety of the implants and would contribute up to $1,200 per patient (depending on financial need) to remove the silicone-gel implants. While Dow Corning still maintained that the implants were safe, it was finally taking conciliatory actions that recognized the need for further research to satisfy the concerns of the FDA and those women possibly at risk.

Dow Corning succeeded in removing some of the damaging attention from the information that had suddenly been brought into public view. Now the company focused on the *positive* actions it would take in order to make restitution to those women who felt they had been wronged.

## Rebuilding Its Credibility

Dow Corning has succeeded in making small gains to win back public opinion. It is funding 30 laboratory and clinical safety tests and epidemiological studies on a global basis to establish the risks of the implants in the human body. Some women have been allowed to have the silicone implants if they agree to become part of a long-term study on the implants' effects. Also, a national registry of those with implants has been proposed to help monitor their health.

In September 1993, the company announced that a global settlement had been proposed, a $4.75 billion fund for breast-implant recipients, funded by the manufacturers, suppliers, doctors, and insurance companies involved in the implant issue. It would give women the opportunity to recover money for their injuries over the course of 30 years. Dow Corning would contribute up to $2 billion to the fund over a period of 30 years. The fund would pay for checkups for women with implants, removal of the devices, and treatment of varied illnesses. Other terms of the agreement were:

- Recipients of any brand of breast implant would be included.

---

[5]Ralph C. Cook, Myron C. Harrison, and Robert R. LeVier, "The Breast Implant Controversy," *Arthritis and Rheumatism* 37, February 1994, pp.1–14. A thoughtful article examining the medical issues and communication problems of the breast implant controversy, written by three Dow Corning scientists (available from the company, Midland, Michigan).

- Claimants would not be required to prove that their breast implants caused their injuries.
- Those who claimed the breast implants had caused damage to their health would be able to exclude themselves from the general settlement and then sue individually.
- A recipient of breast implants who had sued a financially unstable company would be able to submit a claim to the fund.[6]

## Continued Controversy

In the wake of this financial settlement, the effects of silicone implants continue to be greatly disputed. The FDA has engaged in heated debates with the American Medical Association (AMA) about the level of risk posed by silicone breast implants. To date, the AMA has supported allowing all women the right to have breast implants once they have been informed of the risks. Former FDA Commissioner Kessler disagreed because he felt physicians were not being responsible about informing women of risks, in spite of the fact the FDA panel that looked at the breast implant studies recommended the implants be kept on the market. He faulted physicians for using implants for 30 years without adequately discussing the risk.[7]

One irony is that, as the multibillion-dollar settlement was established by the other implant manufacturers, and Dow Corning filed for Chapter 11 to avoid the onslaught of more than 19,000 lawsuits, new evidence has emerged that shows no causal link between the implants and the autoimmune diseases allegedly caused by them. Since there is no link between the implants and the diseases they have been accused of causing, should Dow Corning still have to pay close to $5 billion to emerge from Chapter 11? Should women still be allowed to file lawsuits against Dow Corning? What would be the ethical thing for Dow Corning to do in the future? These questions pose some interesting public relations problems. ■

---

In November 2006, the FDA removed its 14-year ban on silicone breast implants. Dow Corning is no longer in that business, but two companies—Mentor and Allergan—are expected to enter the market. The hometown paper of Dow Corning, the *Midland Daily News*, wrote the following on the day the announcement was made.

### OUR VIEW: WHO'S SORRY NOW?

Something was missing in Friday's announcement by the Food and Drug Administration that it was lifting a 14-year ban on silicone-gel breast implants: an apology to Midland's Dow Corning Corp.

That's the least the agency could do, since it was the FDA's ban on the implants in 1992 that sparked an onslaught of lawsuits—19,000 of them—and forced Dow Corning into Chapter 11 bankruptcy to keep the company afloat.

Billions of dollars later, Dow Corning emerged from bankruptcy. Perhaps along with an apology, the FDA should have offered some help in paying those billions the company had to shell out to settle its legal claims. Isn't that the least the FDA could do, since it played such a huge role in

*(continued)*

---

[6]"Dow Corning Nears Implant Settlement," Associated Press story, as it appeared in *Bangor Daily News*, September 10, 1993.
[7]Christopher Connell, "Doctors Protest Curb on Breast Implants," Associated Press story as it appeared in *Bangor Daily News*, December 1, 1993.

*(continued)*

casting doubt about the silicone-gel implants the agency now is saying are safe?

Dow Corning officials, in their response to the FDA announcement, took the high road, simply pointing out that this case shows "the critical need for science literacy and its importance in making informed decisions, as individuals, as government agencies and as a society."

We'll take it one step further. This case shows the problems that occur when a government agency becomes a pawn for a class-action-eager civil lawsuit system willing to take down an innocent company for the sake of the almighty buck.

The FDA's announcement Friday was welcome, but it was more than a decade overdue.

*Source:* "FDA," *Midland Daily News*, Midland, MI, November 21, 2006.

## QUESTIONS FOR DISCUSSION

1. Dow Corning fumbled this crisis because it found it difficult to initially show concern for the recipients of breast implants while still maintaining a legal stance that endorsed the safety of the product. What could the company have done differently to keep this issue from rising to the epic proportions it did in the public arena? Could the entire issue have been avoided through appropriate communications?

2. Can a company act unethically and maintain credibility? Why or why not? Can you think of examples one way or the other? Is it unethical to withdraw a product from the public when there is no proof of a problem, thus denying the public access to the product?

3. Several companies manufacture implants. It is surgeons who suggest them to women and perform the operation. Yet only Dow Corning drew unfavorable public reaction. Why?

4. Whose responsibility is it to inform women who are interested in having breast implants of the risks of the procedure? Why do you believe this?

5. What are the ethical implications now that it has been found by scientific study that there is no known health effect of the implants? What are the implications for Dow Corning?

6. Does the ultimate vindication of Dow Corning and silicone implants change your perspective on this case?

## PROBLEM 10-A WHETHER TO BLOW THE WHISTLE

You are nearing the end of your second year of employment as editor of the main publication for employees in one of the three largest nonprofit hospitals in the county. You have a good deal. Your boss, the director of public relations, a woman of about 35, listens to your ideas about the publication. You have converted it from a tabloid appearing once a month to a weekly illustrated newsletter. An audit shows that readers, including staff doctors and donors as well as employees, find it more dynamic. They like it. The only intervention you have had from your boss was near the end of your first year. At that time, she told you to follow the hospital's policy of getting three competitive printing bids annually and then to award the contract for the next year to a particular one of the three. You noted that this bid was not the lowest. Your boss explained that she preferred the quality of their work and added that the printing firm had made generous financial contributions to the hospital. At that time you followed the directions of your boss.

The future looks bright to you. And why not? You are aware that your boss has her eyes on the next job up, as director of development, a position now occupied by a woman scheduled to retire in a few years. You can see yourself succeeding your boss at that time.

Looking back, you consider your first two years to have been a period of learning the ropes and how the game goes in the hospital. During this period, the owner of the printing firm doing the newsletter has established a social relationship with you and your spouse, including taking you to dinner at their country club.

You have also noticed that the printer has a close personal relationship with your boss and the hospital's director of development. You know that they receive entertainment and gifts. When the director of development decided to buy a new car, the printer sent her to a dealer where she got a fantastic discount. As for the public relations director, your boss, she was sponsored for membership in the printer's "Executives Only" tennis club.

Here you are, finishing up your second year. A few days ago, quite by coincidence, you overheard some disconcerting comments during a cocktail party. The comments indicated that your boss's husband is the brother of the printer's wife—this you didn't know. Also, your boss apparently has had some sort of financial interest in the printing firm. Your director of development's daughter, you heard, has worked at the printing firm as a typist-receptionist. Someone at the party said that she earned more than other clerical employees, including those with greater skills and experience.

Naturally, this information is upsetting to you, and, to make matters worse, this is the week the three competitive printing bids for next year's contract have come in. You have looked at them. The present printer, whom you have again been told to favor, has submitted a bid 20 percent higher than the lowest of the three.

You have every right to be upset and in a quandary. If you grant the business for the coming year, amounting to $60,000, to the highest bidder, and someone in the treasurer's office questions it, you could be in big trouble. If you tell the present printer he has to submit a second bid at a figure 50 percent lower, you will be unethical in conduct and in contravention of the hospital's stated policy. Beyond that, what if one of the other bidders found out and turned in a complaint to the consumer advocate in the state's attorney general's office? If you take the matter to your boss, you may have to confront her with what you have heard about an apparent conflict of interest on her part.

Of course, an alternative would be to go over the boss's head to the director of development. She, too, has accepted favors from the printer on a social basis. Maybe she would just as soon not get involved. On the other hand, perhaps she has been involved in helping the printer get work from other departments in the hospital. If so, where would that leave you?

Then there is the hospital administrator. If you bypass both of your superiors in the structure, you will almost surely wind up with an unhappy working situation—or be out looking for a new position.

Finally, if you do nothing, are you committed to a standard of honesty or business ethics that you cannot live with?

Everything considered, what are you going to do—specifically, in what sequence, with what goals, and what personal strategy and tactics?

## PROBLEM 10-B WRITE THE TRUTH OR "MAKE US LOOK GOOD"?

You've just been hired by a prestigious philanthropic organization that donates a lot of money to help the poor and the undereducated. You are joining a well-oiled pr department where you report to the vice president. You are excited by the chance to "serve," to do something "meaningful" with your expertise.

At the first all-departments meeting you notice some derogatory comments being made about the people the organization serves. You overlook it as just people being people. But then as discussion comes up about where to focus the organization's money you notice the direction isn't where it's most needed but where the organization can get the most "bang for the buck" in terms of building its image.

You're beginning to have a dilemma. The organization does good deeds by giving out its money and helping others. But inside the culture stinks in the way it talks about its clients and where its goals are for the use of its money. No one else there seems to share your view—or at least no one acknowledges that they do.

Now your boss is asking you to write the news release announcing the organization's newest funding project and wants you to "make us look good. The folks getting the money won't mind if you make some of it up." You want to just write the truth and let that speak for itself, but you're afraid your boss might question your ability. You don't want to get fired. What will you do?

# INDEX